Moving to the Cloud

Moving to the Cloud
Developing Apps in the New World of Cloud Computing

Dinkar Sitaram

Geetha Manjunath

Technical Editor
David R. Deily

AMSTERDAM • BOSTON • HEIDELBERG • LONDON
NEW YORK • OXFORD • PARIS • SAN DIEGO
SAN FRANCISCO • SINGAPORE • SYDNEY • TOKYO

Syngress is an imprint of Elsevier

ELSEVIER

Acquiring Editor: Chris Katsaropoulos
Development Editor: Heather Scherer
Project Manager: A. B. McGee
Designer: Alisa Andreola

Syngress is an imprint of Elsevier
225 Wyman Street, Waltham, MA 02451, USA

Notices

Knowledge and best practice in this field are constantly changing. As new research and experience broaden
our understanding, changes in research methods or professional practices, may become necessary.

Practitioners and researchers must always rely on their own experience and knowledge in evaluating and using
any information or methods described herein. In using such information or methods they should be mindful of
their own safety and the safety of others, including parties for whom they have a professional responsibility.

To the fullest extent of the law, neither the Publisher nor the authors, contributors, or editors, assume any liability
for any injury and/or damage to persons or property as a matter of products liability, negligence or otherwise, or
from any use or operation of any methods, products, instructions, or ideas contained in the material herein.

Library of Congress Cataloging-in-Publication Data
Sitaram, Dinkar.
  Moving to the cloud: developing apps in the new world of cloud computing / Dinkar Sitaram and
Geetha Manjunath; David R. Deily, technical editor.
    p. cm.
  Includes bibliographical references.
  ISBN 978-1-59749-725-1 (pbk.)
1. Cloud computing. 2. Internet programming. 3. Application programs–Development. I. Manjunath, Geetha.
II. Title.
  QA76.585.S58 2011
  004.6782–dc23

                                        2011042034

British Library Cataloguing-in-Publication Data
A catalogue record for this book is available from the British Library.

For information on all Syngress publications
visit our website at *www.syngress.com*

Typeset by: diacriTech, Chennai, India

Printed in the United States of America
11 12 13 14 15   10 9 8 7 6 5 4 3 2 1

Dedication

*To Swarna, Tejas, and Tanvi for their encouragement
and support.*
—Dinkar

*To my dear husband Manjunath, wonderful kids Abhiram
and Anagha and my loving parents.*
—Geetha

Contents

About the Authors

 **Dr. Dinkar Sitaram** is a Chief Technologist at Hewlett Packard, Systems Technology and Software Division, in Bangalore, India. He is one of the key individuals responsible for driving file systems and storage strategy, including cloud storage. Dr. Sitaram is also responsible for University Relations, and Innovation activities at HP. His R&D efforts have resulted in over a dozen granted US patents. He is co-author of *Multimedia Servers: Applications, Environments and Design*. Morgan Kaufmann, 2000. Dr. Sitaram received his Ph. D from the University of Wisconsin-Madison and his B. Tech from IIT Kharagpur. He joined as a research staff member in IBM's Research Division at the IBM T. J. Watson Research Center. At IBM, Dr. Sitaram received an IBM Outstanding Innovation Award (an IBM Corporate Award) as well as IBM Research Division Award and several IBM Invention Achievement Awards for his patents and research. He also received outstanding paper awards for his work, and served on the editorial board of the Journal of High-Speed Networking.

Subsequently, he returned to India as Director of the Technology Group at Novell Corp. Bangalore. The group developed many innovative products in addition to filing for many patents and standards proposals. Dr. Sitaram received Novell's Employee of the Year award. Before joining HP, Dr. Sitaram was CTO at Andiamo Systems India (a storage networking startup later acquired by Cisco), responsible for architecture and technical direction of an advanced storage management solution.

 **Geetha Manjunath** is a Senior Research Scientist and Master Technologist at Hewlett Packard Research Labs in India. She has been with HP since 1997 working on research issues in multiple systems technologies. During these years, she has developed many innovative solutions and published many papers in the area of Embedded Systems, Java Virtual Machine, Mobility, Grid Computing, Storage Virtualization and Semantic Web. She is currently leading a research project on cloud services for simplifying web access for emerging markets. As a part of this research, she conceptualized the notion of Tasklets and lead the development of a cloud-based solution called SiteOnMobile that enables consumers to access web tasks on low-end phones via SMS and Voice. The solution was awarded the NASCOM Innovation Award 2009 and has been given a status of "HP Legend". It was also the winner of Technology Review India's 2010 Grand Challenges for Technologists (2010 TRGC) in the healthcare category.

Before joining HP, she was a senior technical member at Centre for Development of Advanced Computing (C-DAC), Bangalore for 7 years – where was a core member of PARAS system software team for a PARAM supercomputer and she lead a research team to develop parallel compilers for distributed memory machines.

She is a gold medalist from Indian Institute of Science where she did her Masters in Computer Science in 1991 and pursuing Ph. D at the time of this writing. She was awarded the TR Shammanna Best Student award from Bangalore University in the Bachelors degree for topping across all branches of Engineering. She holds four US patents with many more pending grant.

About the Technical Editor

David R. Deily (CISSP, MCSE, SIX SIGMA) has more than 13 years of experience in the management and IT consulting industry. He has designed and implemented innovative approaches to solving complex business problems with the alignment of both performance management and technology for increased IT effectiveness.

He currently provides IT consulting and management services to both midsize and Fortune 500 companies. His core competencies include delivering advanced infrastructure consulting services centered on application/network performance, security, infrastructure roadmap designs, virtualization / cloud, and support solutions that drive efficiency, competitiveness, and business continuity. David consults with clients in industries that include travel/leisure, banking/finance, retail, law and state and local governments.

Mr. Deily has held leadership roles within corporate IT and management consulting services organizations. He is currently a Senior Consultant at DATACORP in Miami, FL. He would like to thank his wife Evora and daughter Drissa for their continued support.

Contributors

Badrinath Ramamurthy is a senior technologist at Hewlett Packard, Bangalore. India. He has been with HP since 2003 and has worked in the areas of High Performance Computing, Semantic Web and Infrastructure Management. He currently works on HP's Cloud Services.

During 1994–2003 he served on the faculty of the CSE Department at the Indian Institute of Technology, Kharagpur. He spent the year 2002–2003 as a visiting researcher at IRISA, France.

Badrinath obtained a Ph.D. in computer science from Rensselaer Polytechnic Institute, NY, in 1994. He has over 30 refereed published research works in his areas of interest. He has served as the General Co-Chair for the International Conference on High-Performance Computing (HiPC) for the years 2006, 2007 and 2008.

In this book, Dr. Badrinath has contributed the section titled "Cells as a Service" in Chapter 2.

Dejan Milojicic is a senior researcher and director of Open Cirrus Cloud Computing testbed at Hewlett Packard Labs. He has worked in the areas of operating systems and distributed systems for more than 25 years. Dr. Milojicic has published over 100 papers. He is an ACM distinguished engineer, IEEE Fellow and member of USENIX. He received B.Sc. and M.Sc. degrees from University of Belgrade and a Ph.D. from University of Kaiserslautern. Prior to HP Labs, he worked at Institute "Mihajlo Pupin", and at OSF Research Institute.

In this book, Dr. Dejan has contributed the section titled "OpenCirrus" in Chapter 10.

Devaraj Das is a co-founder of Hortonworks Inc, USA. Devaraj is an Apache Hadoop committer and member of the Apache Hadoop Project Management Committee. Prior to co-founding Hortonworks, Devaraj was critical in making Apache Hadoop a success at Yahoo! by designing, implementing, leading and managing large and complex core Apache Hadoop and Hadoop-related projects on Yahoo!'s production clusters. Devaraj also worked as an engineer at HP in Bangalore earlier in his career. He has a Master's degree from the Indian Institute of Science in Bangalore, India, and a B.E. degree from Birla Institute of Technology and Science in Pilani, India.

In this book, Devaraj has shared his knowledge on advanced topics in Apache Hadoop, specially in section titled "Multi-tenancy and security" of Chapter 6 and "Data Flow in MapReduce" in Chapter 3.

Dibyendu Das is currently a Principal Member of Technical Staff in AMD India working on Open64 optimizing compilers. In previous avatars he has worked extensively on optimizing compilers for PA-RISC and IA-64 processors while at HP, performance/power analyses for Power-7 multi-cores at IBM and VLIW compilers for Motorola. Dibyendu is an acknowledged expert in the areas of optimizing compilers, parallel languages, parallel and distributed processing and computer architecture.

Dibyendu has a Ph.D. in computer science from IIT Kharagpur and an M.E. and B.E. in computer science from IISc and Jadavpur University, respectively. He is an active quizzer and quiz enthusiast and is involved with the Karnataka Quiz Association.

In this book, Dr. Dibyendu has contributed the section titled "IBM Smart-Cloud: pureXML" in Chapter 3.

Gopal R Srinivasa is a Sr. Research SDE with Microsoft Research India. Before joining Microsoft, he worked for Hewlett-Packard, Nokia Siemens Networks, and Cyber-Guard Corporation. Along with cloud computing, his interests include software analytics and building large software systems. Gopal has a Masters' degree in computer science from North Carolina State University.

In this book, Gopal has shared his expert knowledge on Microsoft Azure in Chapter 3 as well as the section titled "Managing PaaS" in Chapter 8.

Nigel Cook is an HP distinguished technologist and technical director for the HP CloudSystem program. He has worked in areas of data center automation and distributed management systems for over 20 years, spanning environments as diverse as embedded systems for power utility control, telecom systems, and enterprise data center environments. At HP he created the BladeSystem Matrix Operating environment, and prior to that he served as chief architect on the Adaptive Enterprise and Utility Data

Center programs. Prior to HP, he established and ran the US engineering operations of a software R+D development company specializing in telecom distributed systems. He received a BEng from University of Queensland, and is currently pursuing an MSc degree from University of Colorado, Boulder in the area of cloud computing based bioinformatics.

In this book, Nigel has contributed the section "HP CloudSystem Matrix" in Chapter 2, as well as to the Chapter 8 on "Managing the Cloud".

Prakash S Raghavendra has been a faculty member at the IT Department of NITK, Surathkal from February 2009. He received his doctorate from the Computer Science and Automation Department (IISc, Bangalore) in 1998, after graduating from IIT Madras in 1994.

Earlier, Dr. Prakash worked in the Kernel, Java and Compilers Lab in Hewlett-Packard ISO in Bangalore from 1998 to 2007. Dr. Prakash has also worked for Adobe Systems, Bangalore from 2007 to 2009 in the area of flex profilers.

Dr. Prakash's current research interests include programming for heterogeneous computing, Web usage mining and rich Internet apps. Dr. Prakash has been honored with the 'Intel Parallelism Content Award' in 2011 and the 'IBM Faculty Award' for the year 2010.

In this book, Dr. Prakash has contributed about Adobe RIA in the section titled "Rich Internet Applications" in Chapter 5.

Praphul Chandra is a Research Scientist at HP Labs India. He works on the simplifying web access and interaction project. His primary area of interest is complex networks in the context of social networks and information networks like the Web. At HP Labs, he also works on exploring new embedded systems architecture for emerging markets.

He is the author of two books – *Bulletproof Wireless Security* and *Wi-Fi Telephony: Challenges and Solutions for Voice over WLANs*. He joined HP Labs in April 2006. Prior to joining HP he was a senior design engineer at Texas Instruments (USA) where he worked on Voice over IP with specific focus on wireless local area networks. He holds an M.S. in electrical engineering from Columbia University, NY, a PG Diploma in public policy from University of London and a B.Tech. in electronics and communication engineering from Institute of Technology, BHU. His other interest areas are evolution and economics.

In this book, Praphul has shared his expert knowledge on Social networking in the section titled "Social Computing Services" in Chapter 4.

 **Vanish Talwar** is a principal research scientist at HP Labs, Palo Alto, researching management systems for next generation data centers. His research interests include distributed systems, operating systems, and computer networks, with a focus on management technologies. He received his Ph.D. degree in computer science from the University of Illinois at Urbana-Champaign (UIUC). Dr. Talwar is a recipient of the David J Kuck Best Masters Thesis award from the Dept. of Computer Science, UIUC, and has numerous patents and papers, including a book on utility computing.

In this book, Dr. Vanish has contributed to the Chapter 8 titled "Managing the Cloud" and sections on "DMTF" and "OpenCirrus" in Chapter 10.

Foreword

Information is the most valuable resource in the 21st century. Whether for a consumer looking for a restaurant in San Francisco, a small business woman checking textile prices in Bangalore, or a financial services executive in London studying stock market trends, information *at the moment of decision* is key in providing the insights that afford the best outcome.

We now are sitting at a critical juncture of two of the most significant trends in the information technology industry – the convergence of cloud computing and mobile personal information devices into the Mobility/Cloud Ecosystem that delivers next-generation personalized experiences using a scalable and secure information infrastructure. This ecosystem will be able to store, process, and analyze massive amounts of information around structured, unstructured and semi-structured data. All this data will be accessed and analyzed at the speed of business.

In the past few years, the information technology industry began describing a future where everything is delivered as a service via the cloud, from computing resources to personal interactions. The future mobile internet will be 10 times the size of the desktop internet, connecting more than 10 billion "devices" from smartphones to wireless home appliances. Information access will then be as ubiquitous as electricity. Research advancements that the IT industry is making today will allow us to drive economies of scale into this next phase of computing to create a world where increasing numbers of people will be able to participate in and benefit from the information economy.

This book provides an excellent overview of all the transformations that are taking place in the IT industry around Cloud computing, and that, in turn, are transforming society. The book provides an overview of the key concepts of cloud computing, analyzes how cloud computing is different from traditional computing and how it enables new applications while providing highly scalable versions of traditional applications. It also describes the forces driving cloud computing, describes a well-known taxonomy of cloud architectures, and discusses at a high level the technological challenges inherent in cloud computing.

The book covers key areas of the different models of cloud computing: infrastructure as a service, platform as a service and software as a service. It then talks about paradigms for developing cloud applications. It finally talks about cloud-related technologies such as security, cloud management and virtualization.

HP Labs as the central research organization for Hewlett Packard has carried out research in many aspects of cloud computing in the past decade. The authors of the book are researchers in HP Labs India, and have contributed to many years of research on these topics. They have been able to provide their own personal research insight into the contents of the book and their vision of where this technology is headed.

I wish the readers of the book the best of luck in their journey to cloud computing!

Prith Banerjee
Senior Vice President of Research and
Director of HP Labs
Hewlett-Packard Company

Preface

First of all, thanks very much for choosing this book. We hope that you will like reading it and learn something new during the process. We believe the depth and breadth of the topics covered in the book will cater to a vast technical audience. Technologists who have a very strong technical background in distributed computing will probably like the real-life case studies of cloud platforms that enable them to get a quick overview of current platforms without actually registering for trials and experimenting with the examples. Developers who are very good in programming traditional systems will probably like the simple and complex examples of multiple cloud platforms that enable them to get started on programming to the cloud. It will also give them a good overview of the fundamental concepts needed to program a distributed system such as the cloud and learn new techniques to enable them to write efficient, scalable cloud services. We believe even research students will find the book useful to identify some open problems that are yet to be solved and help the evolution of cloud technologies to address all the current gaps.

Having worked on different aspects of systems technology particularly related to distributed computing for a number of years, we both were often discussing the benefits of cloud computing and what realignment in technology and mindset that the cloud required. In one such discussion, it dawned on us that a book based on real case studies of cloud platforms can be very valuable to technologists and developers, especially if we can cover the underlying technologies and concepts. We felt that many of the books available on cloud computing seemed to have a one-dimensional view of cloud computing. Some books equate cloud computing to just a specific cloud platform, say Amazon or Azure. Other books discuss cloud computing as if it is simply a new way of managing traditional data centers in a more cost-effective manner. There is also no dearth of books that hype the benefits of cloud computing in the ideal world.

In fact, the different perspectives about cloud computing that exist today remind us of the well-known story of the six blind men and the elephant. The blind man who caught hold of the elephant's tail insisted that the elephant is like a rope, while another who touched the elephant's tusks said that the elephant is like a spear, and so on. It definitely seemed to us that there is a need for a book that ties together the different aspects of cloud computing, both at the depth as well as breadth. However, we knew that covering all topics related to cloud in a single book, or even covering all popular cloud platforms as case studies, was not really feasible. We decided to cover at least three to four diverse case studies in each aspect of cloud computing and get into the technical depth in each of those case studies.

The second motivation for writing this book is to provide sufficiently deep knowledge to programmers and developers who will create the next generation of cloud applications. Many existing books focus entirely upon writing programs, without analyzing the key concepts or alternative implementations. It is our belief that in order to efficiently design programs it is necessary to have a good understanding of the technology involved, so that intelligent trade-offs can be made. It is also important to design appropriate algorithms and choose the right cloud platform so that the solution to the given problem is scalable and efficient to execute on the cloud. For example, many cloud platforms today offer automatic scaling. However, in order to use this feature effectively, a high-level understanding of how the platform handles scaling is required. It is also important to select the right algorithm for special cloud platforms so that the solution to the given problem can be solved in the most efficient way for the use case and cloud platform (such as Hadoop MapReduce).

The challenge for us has been how to cover all the facets of cloud computing (provide a holistic view of the elephant) without writing a book that itself is as large as an elephant. To achieve this, we have adopted the following strategy. First, for each cloud platform, we provide a broad overview of the platform. This is followed by detailed discussion of some specific aspect of the platform. This high-level overview, together with a detailed study of a particular aspect of the platform, will give readers a deep insight into the basic concepts and features underlying the platform. For example, in the section on Salesforce.com, we start with a high-level overview of the features, followed by detailed discussion of using the call center features, programming under Salesforce.com, and important performance trade-offs for writing programs. Further sections cover the platform architecture that enables Salesforce.com, and some of the important underlying implementation details. The technology topics are also discussed in depth. For example, MapReduce is first introduced in **Chapter 3** with an overview of the concept and usage from a programming perspective. In later sections, a detailed look at the new programming paradigm that MapReduce enables along with fundamentals of functional programming, data parallelism and even theoretical formulation of the MapReduce problem are introduced. Many examples of how one can redesign an algorithm to suit the MapReduce platform are given. Finally, the internal architecture of the MapReduce platform, with details of how the performance, security and other challenges of cloud computing are handled in the platform, is described.

In summary, this book provides an in-depth introduction to the various cloud platforms and technologies today. In addition to describing the developer tools, platforms and APIs for cloud applications, it emphasizes and compares the concepts and technologies behind the platforms, and provides complex examples of their usage as invited content from experts in cloud platforms. This book prepares developers and IT professionals to become experts in cloud technologies, move their computing solutions to the cloud and also explore potential future research topics. It may be kindly noted that the APIs and functionality described in this book are as per the versions available at the time of the writing of this book. Readers are requested to refer to the latest product documentation for accurate information. Finally, since this area is evolving rapidly, we plan to continuously review the latest cloud computing technologies and platforms on our companion website *http://www.movingtocloudbook.com*.

STRUCTURE OF THE BOOK

Chapter 1 of the book is the introduction and provides a high-level overview of cloud computing. We start with the evolution of cloud computing from Web 1.0 to Web 2.0, and discuss its evolution in the future. Next, we discuss various cloud computing models (IaaS, PaaS, and SaaS) and the cloud deployment models (public, private, community and hybrid) together with the pros and cons of each model. Finally, the economics of cloud computing and possible cost savings are described.

Chapters 2–4 describe the three cloud service models (Iaas, PaaS, and SaaS) in detail – from a developer and technologist stand point. The platform models are explained using popular cloud platforms as case studies (for example, Amazon for IaaS and Windows Azure for PaaS) through sample programs, as well as an overview of the underlying technology. While describing program development, the book tries to follow a standard pattern. First, a simple *Hello World* program that allows users to get started is described. This is followed by a more complex example that illustrates commonly used features of the major APIs of the platform. The complex example also introduces the concepts underlying the platform (for example, MapReduce in Hadoop). These chapters will provide programmers interested in developing cloud applications a good understanding of the features and differences between the various existing cloud platforms. In addition, professionals who are interested in the technology behind cloud computing will understand key platform features that are needed to motivate a discussion of the technology and evaluate the suitability of a platform for their specific use case.

Chapter 2 describes three important IaaS platforms – Amazon, HP CloudSystem Matrix, and a research prototype called Cells-as-a-Service. The first section of the chapter describes the Amazon storage services – S3, SimpleDB, and Relational Database Service with GUI and programming examples. The chapter also describes how to upload large files and multi-part uploads. The next section describes Amazon's EC2 cloud service. This contains descriptions of how to administer and use these services through the Web GUI, and also a code example of how to set up a document portal in EC2 using a running example called Pustak Portal (details of which are described towards the end of this Preface). Methods are presented for automatically scaling up and down the service using both Amazon Beanstalk as well as custom code (when Beanstalk is not suitable). The next sections of the chapter describe HP CloudSystem Matrix, and Cells-as-a-Service, a research prototype developed by HP Labs. Here again, after describing the basic features of the offering, the section describes how to set up the document portal in our running example (Pustak Portal). Methods for autoscaling up or autoscaling down the portal are described.

Chapter 3 describes some important PaaS cloud platforms – Windows Azure, Google AppEngine, Apache Hadoop, IBM PureXML, and mashups. The Windows Azure section first describes a simple "Hello World" program that illustrates the basic concepts of Web and Worker roles, and shows how to test and deploy programs under Azure. Subsequently, the architecture of the Azure platform, together with its programming model, storage services such as SQL Azure, as well as other services such as security are described. These are illustrated with the running example of implementing Pustak Portal. In the Google App Engine section, the process of developing and deploying programs is described, together with use of the Google App Engine storage services and memory caching. Next IBM PureXML, which is a cloud service that exposes both a relational as well as XML database interface, is discussed. Examples of how to store data for a portal such as Pustak Portal are described. The next section describes Apache Hadoop, including examples of MapReduce programs, and how Hadoop Distributed File System can be used to provide scalable storage. The final section describes mashups, a technology which allows easy development of applications that merge information from multiple web sites. Yahoo! Pipes in particular is described with an example that includes the use of Yahoo! Query Language, an SQL-like language for mashups.

Chapter 4 describes Salesforce.com, social computing, and Google Docs. These are example services under the Software-as-a-Service (SaaS) model. As can be seen, SaaS embraces a very wide diversity of applications, and the three popular applications selected above are intended to be representative. Salesforce.com is an example of an enterprise SaaS application. As described previously, the Salesforce.com section contains a detailed description of functionality for support representatives. Subsequently the section presents a high-level architecture and functionality of Force.com, the platform upon which Salesforce.com is built. The architecture is illustrated by describing how to write programs to extend the Salesforce.com functionality for the requirements of sales and marketing employees of a publisher like Pustak Portal. The next section describes Social Computing, a development that we argue is central to cloud computing. After defining social computing, and social networks, the section describes the features of Facebook. The description includes how enterprises are using Facebook for marketing. It also describes the various social computing APIs that Facebook provides, such as the Open Graph API, that allow developers to develop enterprise applications that leverage the social networking information in Facebook. Equivalent functions in Picasa, Twitter, and the Open Social Platform, are also described, together with privacy and security issues. The last section is on Google Docs, a typical consumer application that also has programming APIs. Subsequently, an example of how to develop a portal like Pustak Portal that uses Google Docs as a backend for storage of books is described.

Chapter 5 is meant to specifically aid application developers. It describes the novel design and programming paradigms that an application developer should be aware of in order to create new cloud components/applications. The first section on scaling storage describes database sharding and other partitioning techniques, as well as NoSQL stores such as HBase, Cassandra, and MongoDB. The second section takes a deeper look at the novel MapReduce paradigm, including some theoretical background and solutions to most common sub-problems. The final section discusses client-side aspects of the cloud applications, which are complementary to server-side techniques, and which also allow creation of compelling rich client applications.

Chapters 6–9 provide an in-depth description of the technology behind cloud computing and ways to address the key technical challenges. Chapter 6 describes the overall technology behind cloud computing platforms, detailing multiple alternative approaches to provide compute and storage scalability, availability and multi-tenancy. It aims at enabling developers and professionals to understand the technology behind the different platform features and enable effective use of the APIs. The compute scalability section describes how this is achieved in platforms such as OpenNebula and Eucalyptus. In the storage scalability section, the CAP theorem and weak consistency in distributed systems, together with how these are overcome in HBase, Cassandra and MongoDB, are discussed. The section on multi-tenancy describes the general technology and describes the implementation of Salesforce.com. Chapter 7 of the book focuses on security, which, as has been noted earlier, is one of the key concerns for the deployment of cloud computing. This is an abridged version of *Securing the Cloud* published by Syngress. Chapter 8 describes manageability issues unique to the cloud because of the scale and degree of automation found in clouds. Chapter 9 focuses on data center technologies important in cloud computing, such as virtualization.

Cloud computing is an evolution of several related technologies aiming at large scale computing. Chapter 9 of the book is aimed at providing a good understanding of such technologies, e.g., virtualization, MapReduce architecture, etc. The chapter gives an overview of those technologies, particularly relating cloud computing to distributed computing and grid computing. It also describes some common techniques used for data center optimization in general.

Finally, **Chapter 10** describes the future outlook of cloud computing, detailing important standardization efforts and available benchmarks. First, emerging cloud standards from DMTF, NIST, IEEE, OGF and other standards bodies are discussed, followed by a look at some popular cloud benchmarks such as Cloud-Stone, YCSB, CloudCMP and so on. The second part of this chapter lays out some future trends and opportunities. Being a developer centric book, the future outlook cloud applications being developed by end users without any programming is narrated with a research project from HP Labs around the concept of Tasklets. Another research project from HP Labs, OpenCirrus, which addresses the energy and sustainability aspects of Cloud Computing and also provides a research testbed for any future research to be done, is elaborated. Finally, the chapter lists some of the open research issues that are yet to be addressed in cloud computing, hoping to motivate researchers to further move the state of the art of cloud technologies.

A Running Example: Pustak Portal

Pustak Portal is actually a **common running example** that is used by many sections of the book. We believe use of such a running example will enable the reader to compare and contrast the functionality provided by different platforms and assess their suitability. The functionality of Pustak Portal has been chosen so that it can be used to highlight different APIs, and simple as well as advanced features of a cloud platform. **Pustak Portal** is somewhat like a combination of Google Docs, Flickr and Snapfish labs. Consumers can use the document services hosted by this portal to store and restore their selected documents, perform various image-processing functions provided by the portal (like document cleanup, image conversion, template extraction, and so on). The portal provider (owner of Pustak), on the other hand, uses the IaaS and PaaS features of the cloud platforms to scale to the huge number of users manipulating their documents on the cloud. The document manipulation services are compute and storage hungry. The portal provider is also interested in monitoring the usage of the portal and ensuring maximum availability and scalability of the portal. Different client views of the document services portal will be provided using client-side technologies.

Acknowledgments

This book would not have been possible without the help of a large number of people. We would like to thank the developmental book editor Heather Scherer, project manager Anne McGee and the technical editor David Deily, for their many helpful comments and suggestions which greatly improved the quality of the book. We are grateful to editor, Denise Penrose, for her immense help on structuring the book.

Many sections of this book have been contributed by experts in their respective fields. Thanks to our friends, Badrinath Ramamurthy, Dejan Milojicic, Devaraj Das, Dibyendu Das, Gopal R. Srinivasa, Nigel Cook, Prakash S. Raghavendra, Praphul Chandra and Vanish Talwar for their expert contribution which has made the book more authentic and useful to a larger audience. We would like to thank Hitesh Bosamiya and Thara S for their code examples on Google Docs, Google AppEngine and Salesforce.com. We are thankful to Sharat Visweswara from Amazon Inc. for his insights into Amazon Web Services and Satish Kumar Mopur for his inputs on storage virtualization. We are grateful to M. Chelliah from Yahoo!, M. Kishore Kumar, and Mohan Parthasarathy from HP for their valuable inputs to the content of the book. We are indebted to Dan Osecky, Suresh Shyamsundar, Sunil Subbakrishna, and Shylaja Suresh for their help in reviewing various sections of the book. We thank our HP management Prith Banerjee, Sudhir Dixit, and Subramanya Mudigere for their encouragement and support in enabling us to complete this endeavor. Finally, our heartfelt thanks to our families for their patience and support for enduring our long nights out and time away from them.

Introduction

INFORMATION IN THIS CHAPTER

- Where Are We Today?
- The Future Evolution
- What Is Cloud Computing?
- Cloud Deployment Models
- Business Drivers for Cloud Computing
- Introduction to Cloud Technologies

INTRODUCTION

Cloud Computing is one of the major technologies predicted to revolutionize the future of computing. The model of delivering IT as a service has several advantages. It enables current businesses to dynamically adapt their computing infrastructure to meet the rapidly changing requirements of the environment. Perhaps more importantly, it greatly reduces the complexities of IT management, enabling more pervasive use of IT. Further, it is an attractive option for small and medium enterprises to reduce upfront investments, enabling them to use sophisticated business intelligence applications that only large enterprises could previously afford. Cloud-hosted services also offer interesting reuse opportunities and design challenges for application developers and platform providers. Cloud computing has, therefore, created considerable excitement among technologists in general.

This chapter provides a general overview of Cloud Computing, and the technological and business factors that have given rise to its evolution. It takes a bird's-eye view of the sweeping changes that cloud computing is bringing about. Is cloud computing merely a cost-saving measure for enterprise IT? Are sites like Facebook the tip of the iceberg in terms of a fundamental change in the way of doing business? If so, does enterprise IT have to respond to this change, or take the risk of being left behind? By surveying the cloud computing landscape at a high level, it will be easy to see how the various components of cloud technology fit together. It will also be possible to put the technology in the context of the business drivers of cloud computing.

WHERE ARE WE TODAY?

Computing today is poised at a major point of inflection, similar to those in earlier technological revolutions. A classic example of an earlier inflection is the anecdote that is described in *The Big Switch: Rewiring the World, from Edison to Google* [1]. In a small town in New York called Troy, an entrepreneur named Henry Burden set up a factory to manufacture horseshoes. Troy was strategically located at the junction of the Hudson River and the Erie Canal. Due to its location, horseshoes manufactured at Troy could be shipped all over the United States. By making horseshoes in a factory near water, Mr. Burden was able to transform an industry that was dominated by local craftsmen across the US. However, the key technology that allowed him to carry out this transformation had nothing to do with horses. It was the waterwheel he built in order to generate electricity. Sixty feet tall, and weighing 250 tons, it generated the electricity needed to power his horseshoe factory.

Burden stood at the mid-point of a transformation that has been called the Second Industrial Revolution, made possible by the invention of electric power. The origins of this revolution can be traced to the invention of the first battery by the Italian physicist Alessandro Volta in 1800 at the University of Pavia. The revolution continued through 1882 with the operation of the first steam-powered electric power station at Holborn Viaduct in London and eventually to the first half of the twentieth century, when electricity became ubiquitous and available through a socket in the wall. Henry Burden was one of the many figures who drove this transformation by his usage of electric power, creating demand for electricity that eventually led to electricity being transformed from an obscure scientific curiosity to something that is omnipresent and taken for granted in modern life. Perhaps Mr. Burden could not have grasped the magnitude of changes that plentiful electric power would bring about.

By analogy, we may be poised at the midpoint of another transformation – now around computing power – at the point where computing power has freed itself from the confines of industrial enterprises and research institutions, but just before cheap and massive computing resources are ubiquitous. In order to grasp the opportunities offered by cloud computing, it is important to ask which direction are we moving in, and what a future in which massive computing resources are as freely available as electricity may look like.

> *AWAKE! for Morning in the Bowl of Night*
> *Has flung the Stone that puts the Stars to Flight:*
> *…*
> *The Bird of Time has but a little way*
> *To fly – and Lo! the Bird is on the Wing.*

The Rubaiyat of Omar Khayyam,
Translated into English in 1859, by Edward FitzGerald

Evolution of the Web

To see the evolution of computing in the future, it is useful to look at the history. The first wave of Internet-based computing, sometimes called Web 1.0, arrived in the 1990s. In the typical interaction between a user and a web site, the web site would display some information, and the user could click on the hyperlinks to get additional information. Information flow was thus strictly one-way, from institutions that maintained web sites to users. Therefore, the model of Web 1.0 was that of a gigantic library, with Google and other search engines being the library catalog. However, even with this modest change, enterprises (and enterprise IT) had to respond by putting up their own web sites and publishing content that projected the image of the enterprise effectively on the Web (Figure 1.1). Not doing so would have been analogous to not advertising when competitors were advertising heavily.

Web 2.0 and Social Networking

The second wave of Internet computing developed in the early 2000s, when applications that allowed users to upload information to the Web became popular.

FIGURE 1.1

Web 1.0: Information access.

This seemingly small change has been sufficient to bring about a new class of applications due to the rapid growth of user-generated content, social networking and other associated algorithms that exploited crowd knowledge. This new generation Internet usage is called the Web 2.0 [2] and is depicted in Figure 1.2. If Web 1.0 looked like a massive library, Web 2.0, with social networking, is more like a virtual world which in many ways looks like a replica of the physical world (Figure 1.2). Here users are not just login ids, but virtual identities (or personas) with not only a lot of information about themselves (photographs, interest profile, the items they search for on the Web), but also their friends and other users they are linked to as in a social world. Furthermore, the Web is now not read-only; users are able to write back to the Web with their reviews, tags, ratings, annotations and even create their own blogs. Again, businesses and business IT have to respond to this new environment not only by leveraging the new technology for cost-effectiveness but also by using the new features it makes possible.

As of this writing, Facebook has a membership of 750 million people, and that makes 10% of the people in the world [3]! Apart from the ability to keep in touch with friends, Facebook has been a catalyst for the formation of virtual communities.

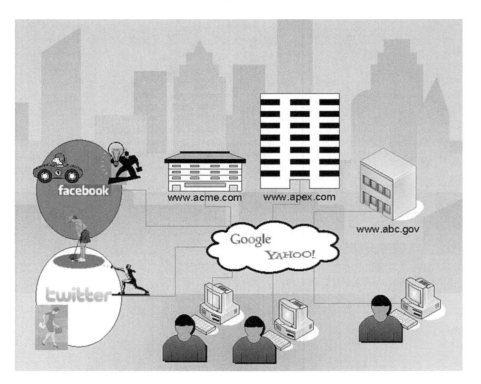

FIGURE 1.2

Web 2.0: Digital reality: social networking.

A very visible example of this was the role Facebook played in catalyzing the 2011 Egyptian revolution. A key moment in the revolution was the January 25th protest in Cairo's Tahrir Square, which was organized using Facebook. This led to the leader of the revolution publicly thanking Facebook [4, 5] for the role it played in enabling the revolution. Another effective example of the use of social networking was the election campaign of US president Obama, who built a network of 2 million supporters on MySpace, 6.5 million supporters on Facebook, and 1.7 million supporters on Twitter [6].

Social networking technology has the potential to make major changes in the way businesses relate to customers. A simple example is the *"Like"* button that Facebook introduced on web pages. By pressing this button for a product, a Facebook member can indicate their preference for the advertised product. This fact is immediately made known to the friends of the member, and put up on the Facebook page of the user as well as his friends. This has a tremendous impact on the buying behavior, as it is a recommendation of a product by a trusted friend! Also, by visiting *"facebook/insights"*, it is possible to analyze the demographics of the Facebook members who clicked the button. This can directly show the profile of the users using the said product! Essentially, since user identities and relationships are online, they can now be leveraged in various ways by businesses as well.

Information Explosion

Giving users the ability to upload content to the Web has led to an explosion of information. Studies have consistently shown that the amount of digital information in the world is doubling every 18 months [7]. Much information that would earlier have been stored in physical form (e.g., photographs) is uploaded to the Web for instantaneous sharing. In fact, in many cases, the first reports of important news are video clips taken by bystanders with mobile phones and uploaded to the Web. The importance of this information has led to growing attempts at Internet censorship by governments that fear that unrestricted access to information could spark civil unrest and lead to the overthrow of the governments [8, 9]. Business can mine this subjective information, for example, by sentiment analysis, to throw some insights into the overall opinion of the public towards a specific topic.

Further, entirely new kinds of applications may be possible through combining the information on the Web. Text mining of public information was used by Unilever to analyze patents filed by a competitor and deduce that the competitor was attempting to discover a pesticide for use against a pest found only in Brazil [10]. IBM was similarly able to analyze news abstracts and detect that a competitor was showing strong interest in the outsourcing business [10].

Another example is the food safety recall process implemented by HP together with GS1 Canada, a supply chain organization [11]. By tracing the lifecycle of a food product from its manufacture to its purchase, the food safety recall process is able to advise individual consumers that the product they have purchased is not safe, and that stores will refund the amount spent on purchase. This is an example of how businesses can reach out to individual consumers whom they do not interact with directly.

Mobile Web

Another major change the world has seen recently is the rapid growth in the number of mobile devices. Reports say that mobile broadband users have already surpassed fixed broadband users [12]. Due to mobile Internet access, information on the Web is accessible from anywhere, anytime, and on any device, making the Web a part of daily life. For example, many users routinely use Google maps to find directions when in an unknown location. Such content on the Web also enables one to develop location-based services, and augmented-reality applications. For example, for a traveler, a mobile application that senses the direction the user is facing, and displays information about the monument in front of him, is very compelling. Current mobile devices are computationally powerful and provide rich user experiences using touch, accelerometer, and other sensors available on the device as well. Use of a cloud-hosted app store is becoming almost a defacto feature of every mobile device or platform. Google Android Market, Nokia Ovi Store, Blackberry App World, Apple App Store are examples of the same. Mobile vendors are also providing cloud services (such as iCloud and SkyDrive) to host app data by which application developers can enable a seamless application experience on multiple personal devices of the user.

THE FUTURE EVOLUTION

Extrapolation of the trends mentioned previously could lead to ideas about the possible future evolution of the Web, aka the Cloud. The Cloud will continue to be a huge information source, with the amount of information growing ever more comprehensive. There is also going to be greater storage of personal data and profiles, together with more immersive interactions that bring the digital world closer to the real world. Mobility that makes the Web available everywhere is only going to intensify. Cloud platforms have already made it possible to harness large amounts of computing power to analyze large amounts of data. Therefore, the world is going to see more and more sophisticated applications that can analyze the data stored in the cloud in smarter ways. These new applications will be accessible on multiple heterogeneous devices, including mobile devices. The simple universal client application, the web browser, will also become more intelligent and provide a rich interactive user experience despite network latencies.

A new wave of applications that provide value to consumer and businesses alike are already evolving. Analytics and business intelligence are becoming more widespread to enable businesses to better understand their customers and personalize their interactions. A recent report states that by use of face recognition software to analyze photos, one can discover the name, birthday, and other personal information about people from Facebook [13]. This technology can be used, for example by grocery stores, to make special birthday offers to people. A study by the Cheshire Constabulary estimated that a typical Londoner is photographed by CCTV cameras on the average of 68 times per day [14]. There are huge amounts of customer data that can be analyzed to derive great insights into the buying behavior, buying pattern and even methods to counteract competitors. Businesses can use the location of people, together with personal information, to better serve customers, as certain mobile devices keep detailed logs of the location of their users [15]. Due to all these reasons and more, the next generation Web, Web 3.0, has been humorously called *Cyberspace looks at You*, as illustrated in Figure 1.3.

The previous discussion shows that privacy issues will become important to address going forward. Steve Rambam has described how, using just the email address and name of a volunteer, he was able to track 500 pages of data about the volunteer in 4 hours [16]. The data collected included the places the volunteer had lived, the cars he had driven, and he even was able to discover that somebody had been illegally using the volunteer's Social Security number for the last twenty years! In *Google CEO Schmidt: No Anonymity Is the Future of Web* [17], a senior executive at Google predicted that governments were opposed to anonymity, and therefore Web privacy is impossible. However, there are also some who believe privacy concerns are exaggerated [18], and the benefits from making personal information available far outweigh the risks.

FIGURE 1.3

Web 3.0: Cyberspace looks at You.

An additional way businesses can leverage cloud computing is through the **wisdom of crowds** for better decision making. Researchers [19] have shown that by aggregating the beliefs of individual members, crowds could make better decisions than any individual member. The Hollywood Stock Exchange (HSX) is an online game that is a good example of crowd wisdom. HSX participants are allowed to spend up to 2 million dollars buying and selling stock in upcoming movies [20]. The final value in the Hollywood Stock Exchange is a very good predictor of the opening revenue of the movie, and the change in value of its stock a good indication of the revenue in subsequent weeks.

Finally, as noted earlier, the digital universe today is a replica of the physical universe. In the future, more realistic and immersive 3-D user interfaces could lead to a complete change in the way users interact with computers and with each other.

All these applications suggest that computing needs to be looked at as a much higher level abstraction. Application developers should not be burdened by the mundane tasks of ensuring that a specific server is up and running. They should not be bothered about whether the disk currently allotted to them is going to overflow. They should not be worrying about which operating system (OS) their application should support or how to actually package and distribute the application to their consumer. The focus should be on solving the much bigger problems. The compute infrastructure, platform, libraries and application deployment should all be automated and abstracted. This is where Cloud Computing plays a major role.

WHAT IS CLOUD COMPUTING?

Cloud computing is basically delivering computing at the Internet scale. Compute, storage, networking infrastructure as well as development and deployment platforms are made available on-demand within minutes. Sophisticated futuristic applications such as those described in the earlier sections are made possible by the abstracted, auto-scaling compute platform provided by cloud computing. A formal definition follows.

The US *National Institute of Standards* (*NIST*) has come up with a list of widely accepted definitions of cloud computing terminologies and documented it in the NIST technical draft [21]. As per NIST, cloud computing is described as follows:

> Cloud computing is a model for enabling **ubiquitous**, convenient, **on-demand** network access to a **shared pool** of configurable computing resources (e.g., networks, servers, storage, applications, and services) that can be **rapidly provisioned** and released with minimal management effort or service provider interaction.

To further clarify the definition, NIST specifies the following five essential characteristics that a cloud computing infrastructure must have.

On demand self-service: The compute, storage or platform resources needed by the user of a cloud platform are self-provisioned or auto-provisioned with minimal configuration. As detailed in Chapter 2, it is possible to log on to Amazon Elastic Compute Cloud (a popular cloud platform) and obtain resources, such as virtual servers or virtual storage, within minutes. To do this, it is simply necessary to register with Amazon to get a user account. No interaction with Amazon's service staff is needed either for obtaining an account or for obtaining virtual resources. This is in contrast to traditional in-house IT systems and processes, which typically require interaction with an IT administrator, a long approval workflow and usually result in a long time interval to provision any new resource.

Broad network access: Ubiquitous access to cloud applications from desktops, laptops to mobile devices is critical to the success of a Cloud platform. When computing moves to the cloud, the client applications can be very light weight, to the extent of just being a web browser that sends an HTTP request and receives the result. This will in turn make the client devices heavily dependent upon the cloud for their normal functioning. Thus, connectivity is a critical requirement for effective use of a Cloud Application. For example, cloud services like Amazon, Google, and Yahoo! are available world-wide via the Internet. They are also accessible by a wide variety of devices, such as mobile phones, iPads, and PCs.

Resource pooling: Cloud services can support millions of concurrent users; for example, Skype supports 27 million concurrent users [22], while Facebook supported 7 million simultaneous users in 2009 [23]. Clearly, it is impossible to support this number of users if each user needs dedicated hardware. Therefore, cloud services need to share resources between users and clients in order to reduce costs.

Rapid elasticity: A cloud platform should be able to rapidly increase or decrease computing resources as needed. In a cloud platform called Amazon EC2, it is possible to specify a minimum number as well as a maximum number of virtual servers to be allocated. The actual number will vary depending upon the load. Further, the time taken to provision a new server is very small, on the order of minutes. This also increases the speed with which a new infrastructure can be deployed.

Measured service: One of the compelling business use cases for cloud computing is the ability to "pay as you go," where the consumer pays only for the resources that are actually used by his applications. Commercial cloud services, like Salesforce. com, measure resource usage by customers, and charge proportionally to the resource usage.

CLOUD DEPLOYMENT MODELS

In addition to proposing a definition of cloud computing, NIST has defined four deployment models for clouds, namely Private Cloud, Public Cloud, Community Cloud and Hybrid Cloud. A **Private cloud** is a cloud computing infrastructure that is built for a single enterprise. It is the next step in the evolution of a corporate data center of today where the infrastructure is shared within the enterprise. **Community**

cloud is a cloud infrastructure shared by a community of multiple organizations that generally have a common purpose. An example of a community cloud is OpenCirrus, which is a cloud computing research testbed intended to be used by universities and research institutions. **Public cloud** is a cloud infrastructure owned by a **cloud service provider** that provides cloud services to the public for commercial purposes. **Hybrid clouds** are mixtures of these different deployments. For example, an enterprise may rent storage in a public cloud for handling peak demand. The combination of the enterprise's private cloud and the rented storage then is a hybrid cloud.

Private vs. Public Clouds

Enterprise IT centers may either choose to use a private cloud deployment or move their data and processing to a public cloud deployment. It is worth noting that there are some significant differences between the two. First, the private cloud model utilizes the in-house infrastructure to host the different cloud services. The cloud user here typically owns the infrastructure. The infrastructure for the public cloud on the other hand, is owned by the cloud vendor. The cloud user pays the cloud vendor for using the infrastructure. On the positive side, the public cloud is much more amenable to provide elasticity and scaling-on-demand since the resources are shared among multiple users. Any over-provisioned resources in the public cloud are well utilized as they can now be shared among multiple users.

Additionally, a public cloud deployment introduces a *third party* in any legal proceedings of the enterprise. Consider the scenario where the enterprise has decided to utilize a public cloud with a fictitious company called NewCloud. In case of any litigation, emails and other electronic documents may be needed as evidence, and the relevant court will send orders to the cloud service provider (e.g., NewCloud) to produce the necessary emails and documents. Thus, use of NewCloud's services would mean that NewCloud becomes part of any lawsuit involving data stored in NewCloud. This issue is discussed in more detail in Chapter 7, titled *Designing Cloud Security.*

Another consideration is the network bandwidth constraints and cost. In case the decision is made to move some of the IT infrastructure to a public cloud [24], disruptions in the network connectivity between the client and the cloud service will affect the availability of cloud-hosted applications. On a low bandwidth network, the user experience for an interactive application may also get affected. Further, implications on the cost of network usage also need to be considered.

There are additional factors that the cloud user need to use to select between a public or private cloud. A simplified example may make it intuitively clear that the amount of time over which the storage is to be deployed is an important factor. Suppose it is desired to buy 10TB of disk storage, and it is possible either to buy a new storage box for a private cloud, or obtain it through a cloud service provided by NewCloud. Suppose the lifetime of the storage is 5 years, and 10TB of storage costs $X. Clearly NewCloud would have to charge (in a simplified pricing model) at least $X/5 per year for this storage in order to recover their cost. In practice, NewCloud would have to charge more, in order to make a profit, and to cover idle periods when this storage is not rented out to anybody. Thus, if the storage is to be used only temporarily for 1 year, it may be cost-effective to rent the storage from NewCloud, as the business would then only have to pay on the order of $X/5. On the other hand, if the storage is intended to be used for a longer term, then it may be more cost-effective to buy the storage and use it as a private cloud. Thus, it can be seen that one of the factors dictating the use of a private cloud or a public cloud for storage is how long the storage is intended to be used.

Of course, cost may not be the only consideration in evaluating public and private clouds. Some public clouds providing application services, such as Salesforce.com (a popular CRM cloud service) offer unique features that customers would consider in comparison to competing non-cloud applications. Other public clouds offer infrastructure services and enable an enterprise to entirely outsource the IT infrastructure, and to offload complexities of capacity planning, procurement, and management of data centers as detailed in the next section. In general, since private and public clouds have different characteristics, different deployment models and even different business drivers, the best solution for an enterprise may be a hybrid of the two.

A detailed comparison and economic model of using public cloud versus private cloud for database workloads is presented by Tak et al. [25]. The authors consider the intensity of the workload (small, medium, or large workloads), *burstiness*, as well as the growth rate of the workload in their evaluation. The choice may also depend upon the costs. So, they consider a large number of cost factors, including reasonable estimates for hardware cost, software cost, salaries, taxes, and electricity. The key finding is that private clouds are cost-effective for medium to large workloads, and public clouds are suitable for small workloads. Other findings are that vertical hybrid models (where parts of the application are in a private cloud and part in a public cloud) tend to be expensive due to the high cost of data transfer. However, horizontal hybrid models, where the entire application is replicated in the public cloud and usage of the private cloud is for normal workloads, while the public cloud is used for demand peaks, can be cost-effective.

An illustrative example of the kind of analysis that needs to be done in order to decide between a private and public cloud deployment is shown in Table 1.1. The numbers in the table are intended to be hypothetical and illustrative. Before deciding on whether a public or private cloud is preferable in a particular instance, it is necessary to work out a financial analysis similar to the one in Table 1.1. The table compares the estimated costs for deployment of an application in both a private and public cloud. The comparison is the total cost over a 3-year time horizon, which is assumed to be the time span of interest. In the table, the software licensing costs are assumed to increase due to increasing load. Public cloud service costs are assumed to rise for the same reason. While cost of the infrastructure is one metric that can be used to decide between private and public cloud, there are other business drivers that may impact the decision.

Table 1.1 Hypothetical Cost of Public vs. Private Cloud

(in USD)	Private Cloud			Public Cloud		
	Year 1	Year 2	Year 3	Year 1	Year 2	Year 3
Hardware	70,000	40,000	20,000			
Setup Costs	30,000			5,000		
Software (Licensing)	200,000	400,000	700,000			
Labor costs	200,000	200,000	200,000			
Service costs				300,000	600,000	1,000,000
WAN costs				15,000	30,000	56,000
Cost for year	500,000	640,000	920,000	320,000	630,000	1,056,000
Total	2,060,000			2,006,000		

BUSINESS DRIVERS FOR CLOUD COMPUTING

Unlike in a traditional IT purchase model, if using a cloud platform, a business does not need a very high upfront capital investment in hardware. It is also difficult in general to estimate the full capacity of the hardware at the beginning of a project, so people end up over-provisioning IT and buying more than what is needed at the beginning. This again is not necessary in a cloud model, due to the on-demand scaling that it enables. The enterprise can start with a small capacity hardware from the cloud vendor and expand based on how business progresses. Another disadvantage of owning a complex infrastructure is the maintenance needed. From a business perspective, Cloud provides high availability and eliminates need for an IT house in every company, which requires highly skilled administrators.

A number of business surveys have been carried out to evaluate the benefits of Cloud Computing. For example, the North Bridge survey [26] reveals that the majority of businesses are still experimenting with the cloud (40%). However, a significant minority does consider it ready even for mission critical applications (13%). Cloud computing is considered to have a number of positive aspects. In the short term scalability, cost, agility, and innovation are considered to be the major drivers. *Agility* and *innovation* refer to the ability of enterprise IT departments to respond quickly to requests for new services. Currently, IT departments have come to be regarded as too slow by users (due to the complexity of enterprise software). Cloud computing, by increasing manageability, increases the speed at which applications can be deployed, either on public clouds, or in private clouds implemented by IT departments for the enterprise. Additionally, it also reduces management complexity. *Scalability*, which refers to the ease with which the size of the IT infrastructure can be increased to accommodate increased workload, is another major factor. Finally, cloud computing (private or public clouds) have the potential to reduce IT costs due to automated management.

Well, what are the downsides of using the public clouds? Three major factors were quoted by respondents as being inhibiting factors. The first is **security**. Verification of the security of data arises as a concern in public clouds, since the data is not being stored by the enterprise. Cloud service providers have attempted to address this problem by acquiring third-party certification. **Compliance** is another issue, and refers to the question of whether the cloud security provider is complying with the security rules relating to data storage. An example is health-related data, which requires the appointment of a compliance administrator who will be accountable for the security of the data. Cloud service providers have attempted to address these issues through certification as well. These issues are discussed in Chapter 7. The third major inhibitor cited by businesses was *interoperability and vendor lock-in*. This refers to the fact that once a particular public cloud has been chosen, it would not be easy to migrate away, since the software and operating procedures would all have been tailored for that particular cloud. This could give the cloud service provider undue leverage in negotiations with the business. From a financial point of view, "pay per use" spending on IT infrastructure can perhaps be considered as an expense or liability that will be difficult to reduce, since reduction could impact operations. Hence, standardization of cloud service APIs becomes important and current efforts towards the same are detailed in Chapter 10.

INTRODUCTION TO CLOUD TECHNOLOGIES

This section gives an overview of some technology aspects of cloud computing that are detailed in the rest of the book. One of the best ways of learning about cloud technologies is by understanding the three cloud service models or service types for any cloud platform. These are Infrastructure as a Service (**IaaS**), Platform as a Service (**PaaS**), and Software as a Service (**SaaS**) which are described next.

The three cloud service types defined by NIST, IaaS, PaaS and SaaS, focus on a specific layer in a computer's runtime stack – the hardware, the system software (or platform) and the application, respectively.

Figure 1.4 illustrates the three cloud service models and their relationships. At the lowest layer is the hardware infrastructure on which the cloud system is built. The cloud platform that enables this infrastructure to be delivered as a service is the IaaS architecture. In the IaaS service model, the physical hardware (servers, disks, and networks) is abstracted into virtual servers and virtual storage. These virtual resources can be allocated on demand by the cloud users, and configured into virtual systems on which any desired software can be installed. As a result, this architecture has the greatest flexibility, but also the least application automation from the user's viewpoint. Above this is the PaaS abstraction, which provides a platform built on top of the abstracted hardware that can be used by developers to create cloud applications. A user who logs in to a cloud service that offers PaaS will have commands available that will allow them to allocate middleware servers (e.g., a database of a certain size), configure and load data into the middleware, and develop an application that runs on top of the middleware. Above this is the SaaS abstraction, which provides the complete application (or solution) as a service, enabling consumers to use the cloud without worrying about all the complexities of hardware, OS or even application installation. For example, a user logging in to an SaaS service would be able to use an email service without being aware of the middleware and servers on which this email service is built. Therefore, as shown in the figure, this architecture has the least flexibility and most automation for the user.

While the features offered by the three, service types may be different, there is a common set of technological challenges that all cloud architectures face. These

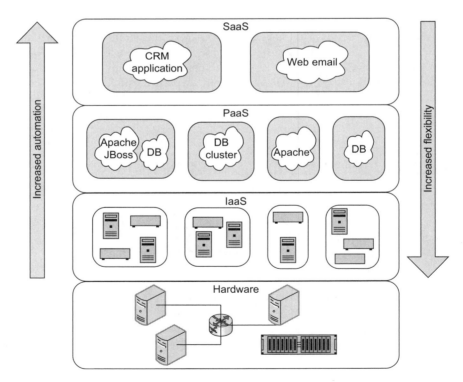

FIGURE 1.4

Cloud service models.

include computation scaling, storage scaling, multi-tenancy, availability, and security. It may be noted that in the previous discussion, the three different service models have been shown as clearly layered upon each other. This is frequently the case; for example, the Salesforce.com CRM SaaS is built upon the Force.com PaaS. However, theoretically, this need not be true. It is possible to provide a SaaS model using an over-provisioned data center, for example.

Infrastructure as a Service

The IaaS model is about providing compute and storage resources as a service. According to NIST [21], IaaS is defined as follows:

> The capability provided to the consumer is to provision processing, storage, networks, and other fundamental computing resources where the consumer is able to deploy and run arbitrary software, which can include operating systems and applications. The consumer does not manage or control the underlying cloud infrastructure but has control over operating systems, storage, deployed applications, and possibly limited control of select networking components (e.g., host firewalls).

The user of IaaS has single ownership of the hardware infrastructure allotted to him (may be a virtual machine) and can use it as if it is his own machine on a remote network and he has control over the operating system and software on it. IaaS is illustrated in Figure 1.5. The IaaS provider has control over the actual hardware and the cloud user can request allocation of virtual resources, which are then allocated by the IaaS provider on the hardware (generally without any manual intervention). The cloud user can manage the virtual resources as desired, including installing any desired OS, software and applications. Therefore IaaS is well suited for users who want complete control over the software stack that they

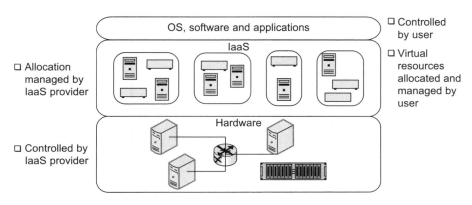

FIGURE 1.5

Infrastructure as a Service.

run; for example, the user may be using heterogeneous software platforms from different vendors, and they may not like to switch to a PaaS platform where only selected middleware is available. Well-known IaaS platforms include Amazon EC2, Rackspace, and Rightscale. Additionally, traditional vendors such as HP, IBM and Microsoft offer solutions that can be used to build private IaaS.

Platform as a Service

The PaaS model is to provide a system stack or platform for application deployment as a service. NIST defines PaaS as follows:

> *The capability provided to the consumer is to deploy onto the cloud infrastructure consumer-created or acquired applications created using programming languages and tools supported by the provider. The consumer does not manage or control the underlying cloud infrastructure including network, servers, operating systems, or storage, but has control over the deployed applications and possibly application hosting environment configurations.*

Figure 1.6 shows a PaaS model diagramatically. The hardware, as well as any mapping of hardware to virtual resources, such as virtual servers, is controlled by the PaaS provider. Additionally, the PaaS provider supports selected middleware, such as a database, web application server, etc. shown in the figure. The cloud user can configure and build on top of this middleware, such as define a new database table in a database. The PaaS provider maps this new table onto their cloud infrastructure. Subsequently, the cloud user can manage the database as needed, and develop applications on top of this database. PaaS platforms are well suited to those cloud users who find that the middleware they are using matches the middleware provided by one of the PaaS vendors. This enables them to focus on the application. Windows Azure, Google App Engine, and Hadoop are some well-known PaaS platforms. As in the case of IaaS, traditional vendors such as HP, IBM and Microsoft offer solutions that can be used to build private PaaS.

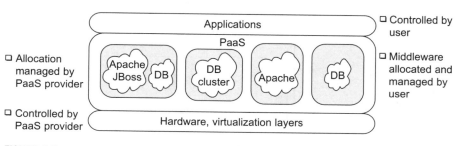

FIGURE 1.6

Platform as a Service.

Software as a Service

SaaS is about providing the complete application as a service. SaaS has been defined by NIST as follows:

The capability provided to the consumer is to use the provider's applications running on a cloud infrastructure. The applications are accessible from various client devices through a thin client interface such as a web browser (e.g., web-based email). The consumer does not manage or control the underlying cloud infrastructure including network, servers, operating systems, storage, or even individual application capabilities, with the possible exception of limited user-specific application configuration settings.

Any application that can be accessed using a web browser can be considered as SaaS. These points are illustrated in Figure 1.7. The SaaS provider controls all the layers apart from the application. Users who log in to the SaaS service can both use the application as well as configure the application for their use. For example, users can use Salesforce.com to store their customer data. They can also configure the application, for example, requesting additional space for storage or adding additional fields to the customer data that is already being used. When configuration settings are changed, the SaaS infrastructure performs any management tasks needed (such as allocation of additional storage) to support the changed configuration. SaaS platforms are targeted towards users who want to use the application without any software installation (in fact, the motto of Salesforce.com, one of the prominent SaaS vendors, is "No Software"). However, for advanced usage, some small amount of programming or scripting may be necessary to customize the application for usage by the business (for example, adding additional fields to customer data). In fact, SaaS platforms like Salesforce.com allow many of these customizations to be performed without programming, but by specifying business rules that are simple enough for non-programmers to implement. Prominent SaaS applications include Salesforce.com for CRM, Google Docs for document sharing, and web email systems like Gmail, Hotmail, and Yahoo! Mail. IT vendors such as HP and IBM also sell systems that can be configured to set up SaaS in a private cloud; SAP, for example, can be used as an SaaS offering inside an enterprise.

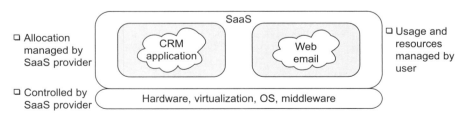

FIGURE 1.7

SaaS cloud model.

Technology Challenges

The technology challenges for cloud computing arise from the fact that the scale of cloud computing is much, much larger than that of traditional computing environments – as it will be shared by many users, many applications and in fact many enterprises! These challenges, therefore, impact all the three cloud service models described earlier. The rest of the book highlights the methods used by different cloud systems to overcome these challenges.

Figure 1.8 shows the traffic to the five most popular web sites. The continuously dropping curve is the fraction of all Web requests that went to that web site while the V-shaped curve is the response time of the web site. It can be seen that the top web site – Facebook.com – accounts for about 7.5% of all Web traffic. In spite of the high traffic, the response time – close to 2 seconds – is still better than average. To support such high transaction rates with good response time, it must be possible to scale both compute and storage resources very rapidly. **Scalability** of both compute power and storage is therefore a major challenge for all three cloud models. High scalability requires large-scale sharing of resources between users. As stated earlier, Facebook supports 7 million concurrent users. New techniques for **multi-tenancy**, or fine-grained sharing of resources, are needed for supporting such large numbers of users. Security is a natural concern in such environments as well.

Additionally, in such large-scale environments, hardware failures and software bugs can be expected to occur relatively frequently. The problem is complicated by the fact that failures can trigger other failures, leading to an avalanche of failures that can lead to significant outages. Such a failure avalanche occurred once in 2011 in Amazon's data center [28, 29, 30]. A networking failure triggered a re-mirroring (making a replica or mirror) of data. However, the re-mirroring traffic interfered with

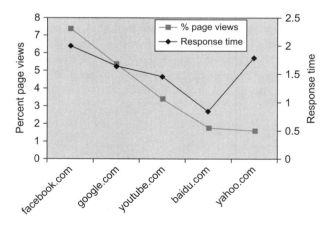

FIGURE 1.8

Traffic statistics for popular web sites.

(Data Source: Alexa.com [27])

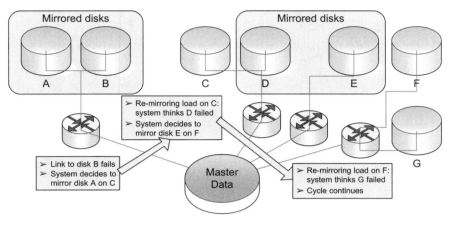

FIGURE 1.9

An example showing avalanche of failures.

normal storage traffic, causing the system to believe that additional mirrors had failed. This in turn triggered further re-mirroring traffic, which interfered with additional normal storage traffic, triggering still more re-mirroring (see Figure 1.9), bringing down the whole system. **Availability** is therefore one of the major challenges affecting clouds. Chapter 6 gives some approaches that can be used to address these challenges, but of course more research yet needs to be done to solve the issues completely.

SUMMARY

This chapter has focused on many concepts that will be important in the rest of the book. First, the NIST definition of cloud computing and the three cloud computing models defined by NIST (Infrastructure as a Service or IaaS, Platform as a Service or PaaS, Software as a Service or SaaS) have been described. Next, the four major cloud deployment models – private cloud, public cloud, community cloud, and hybrid cloud, were surveyed and described. This was followed by an analysis of the economics of cloud computing and the business drivers. It was pointed out that in order to quantify the benefits of cloud computing, detailed financial analysis is needed. Finally, the chapter discussed the major technological challenges faced in cloud computing – scalability of both computing and storage, multi-tenancy, and availability. In the rest of the book, while discussing technology, the focus will be on how different cloud solutions address these challenges, thereby allowing readers to compare and contrast the different solutions on a technological level.

Go ahead – enjoy the technology chapters now and demystify the cloud!

References

[1] Nicholas Carr, W W. The Big Switch: Rewiring the world, from edison to google. Norton & Company, 2009. ISBN-13: 978-0393333947.

[2] O'Reilly T, What is web 2.0? Design patterns and business models for the next generation of software, September 2005. http://oreilly.com/web2/archive/what-is-web-20.html 2005 [accessed 08.10.11].

[3] Facebook Now Has 750 Million Users. http://techcrunch.com/2011/06/23/facebook-750-million-users/ [accessed 08.10.11].

[4] Egypt's Facebook Revolution: Wael Ghonim Thanks The Social Network. http://www.huffingtonpost.com/2011/02/11/egypt-facebook-revolution-wael-ghonim_n_822078.html [accessed 08.10.11].

[5] Egyptians protesting Tahrir Square Cairo. http://www.youtube.com/watch?v=S8aXWT3fPyY [accessed 25.01.11].

[6] How Obama used social networking tools to win, INSEAD. http://knowledge.insead.edu/contents/HowObamausedsocialnetworkingtowin090709.cfm; [accessed 10.07.09].

[7] The Diverse and Exploding Digital Universe, IDC. http://www.emc.com/collateral/analyst-reports/diverse-exploding-digital-universe.pdf; 2008 [accessed 08.10.11].

[8] Internet Enemies, by Reporters sans Frontiers. http://www.rsf.org/IMG/pdf/Internet_enemies_2009_2_.pdf; [accessed 12.03.09].

[9] Google sees growing struggle over web censorship. http://www.reuters.com/article/2011/06/27/us-google-censorship-idUSTRE75Q4DT20110627 [accessed 08.10.11].

[10] Zanasi A. text mining and its applications to intelligence, CRM and knowledge management. WIT Press; 30 2007, p. 203.

[11] Gardner D. Cloud computing uniquely enables product and food recall processes across supply chains. http://www.zdnet.com/blog/gardner/cloud-computing-uniquely-enables-product-and-food-recall-processes-across-supply-chains/3163; [accessed 25.08.09].

[12] Mobile broadband subscribers overtake fixed broadband, Infonetics Research. http://www.infonetics.com/pr/2011/Fixed-and-Mobile-Subscribers-Market-Highlights.asp [accessed 08.10.11].

[13] Software that spills info by looking at your photo, Bangalore Mirror, 3 August 2011, p. 13.

[14] Gerrard G, Thompson R. Two million cameras in the UK, Cheshire Constabulary, CCTV Image, Vol. 42. http://www.securitynewsdesk.com/wp-content/uploads/2011/03/CCTV-Image-42-How-many-cameras-are-there-in-the-UK.pdf [accessed 08.10.11].

[15] J. R. Raphael, Apple vs. Android location tracking: Time for some truth, Computerworld. http://blogs.computerworld.com/18190/apple_android_location_tracking; [accessed 25.04.11].

[16] Rambam S. Privacy Is Dead - Get Over It, 8th www.ToorCon.org Information Security Conference, September 30, 2006, San Diego, California. http://video.google.com/videoplay?docid=-383709537384528624 [accessed 08.10.11].

[17] Ms Smith, Google CEO Schmidt: No Anonymity Is The Future Of Web, Network World. http://www.networkworld.com/community/blog/google-ceo-schmidt-no-anonymity-future-web; 2010 [accessed 08.10.11].

[18] Pogue D. Don't worry about who's watching. Scientific American. http://www.scientificamerican.com/article.cfm?id=dont-worry-about-whos-watching; [accessed 01.01.11].

[19] Suroweiki J, The Wisdom of Crowds, Anchor, 16 August 2005.

[20] What is HSX Anyway? http://www.hsx.com/help/ [accessed 08.10.11].

[21] The NIST Definition of Cloud Computing (Draft), Peter Mell, Timothy Grance, NIST. http://csrc.nist.gov/publications/drafts/800-145/Draft-SP-800-145_cloud-definition.pdf [accessed 08.10.11].

[22] Skype hits new record of 27 million simultaneous users in wake of iOS video chat release, Vlad Savov, Engadget. http://www.engadget.com/2011/01/11/skype-hits-new-record-of-27-million-simultaneous-users-in-wake-o/ [accessed 08.10.11].

[23] Erlang at Facebook, Eugene Letuchy. http://www.erlang-factory.com/upload/presentations/31/EugeneLetuchy-ErlangatFacebook.pdf; [accessed 30.04.09].

[24] Cloud storage will fail without WAN Acceleration, so FedEx to the rescue? Larry Chaffin, 6 December 2010, Networking World. http://www.networkworld.com/community/blog/cloud-storage-will-fail-without-wan-accelerat [accessed 06.12.11].

[25] Tak BC, Urgaonkar B, Sivasubramaniam A. To Move or Not to Move: The Economics of Cloud Computing. The Pennsylvania State University, Hot Cloud'11: 3rd Usenix Workshop on Hot Topics in Cloud Computing, June 2011, Portland, Oregon, http://www.usenix.org/event/hotcloud11/tech/final_files/Tak.pdf [accessed 08.10.11].

[26] 2011 Future of Cloud Computing Survey Results, Michael Skok, North Bridge Venture Partners. http://futureofcloudcomputing.drupalgardens.com/media-gallery/detail/91/286; [accessed 22.06.11].

[27] Alexa, The Web Information Company. http://alexa.com [accessed 08.10.11].

[28] Major Amazon Outage Ripples Across Web, April 21st, 2011 : Rich Miller, Data Center Knowledge. http://www.datacenterknowledge.com/archives/2011/04/21/major-amazon-outage-ripples-across-web/ [accessed 08.10.11].

[29] Kusnetzky D, Analyzing the Amazon Outage with Kosten Metreweli of Zeus, May 16, 2011, http://www.zdnet.com/blog/virtualization/analyzing-the-amazon-outage-with-kosten-metreweli-of-zeus/3069 [accessed 16.05.11].

[30] Phil Wainewright, Seven lessons to learn from Amazon's outage. http://www.zdnet.com/blog/saas/seven-lessons-to-learn-from-amazons-outage/1296; [accessed 24.04.11].

Infrastructure as a Service

INFORMATION IN THIS CHAPTER:

- Storage as a Service: Amazon Storage Services
- Compute as a Service: Amazon Elastic Compute Cloud (EC2)
- HP CloudSystem Matrix
- Cells-as-a-Service

INTRODUCTION

This chapter describes an important cloud service model called "Infrastructure as a Service" (IaaS), which enables computing and storage resources to be delivered as a service. This is the first of the three cloud computing service models described in the previous chapter. The other two models are studied in subsequent chapters. Under the IaaS cloud computing model, cloud service providers make computing and storage resources (such as servers and storage) available as a service. This offers maximum flexibility for users to work with the cloud infrastructure, wherein exactly how the virtual computing and storage resources are used is left to the cloud user. For example, users will be able to load any operating system and other software they need and execute most of the existing enterprise services without many changes. However, the burden of maintaining the installed operating system and any middleware continues to fall on the user/customer. Ensuring the availability of the application is also the user's job since IaaS vendors only provide virtual hardware resources.

The subsequent sections describe some popular IaaS platforms for storage as a service and then compute as a service. First, the section *Storage as a Service* (sometimes abbreviated as **StaaS**) takes a detailed look at key Amazon Storage Services: (a) **Amazon Simple Storage Service (S3)**, which provides a highly reliable and highly available object store over HTTP; (b) **Amazon SimpleDB**, a key-value store; and (c) **Amazon Relational Database Service (RDS)**, which provides a MySQL instance in the cloud. The second part of the chapter describes compute aspects of IaaS – i.e., enabling virtual computing over Cloud. Customers of these services will typically reserve a virtual computer of a certain capacity, and load software that is needed. There could also be features that allow these virtual computers to be networked together, and also for the capacity of the virtual computing to be increased or decreased according to demand. Three diverse instances of **Compute as a Service** are described in this chapter, namely **Amazon Elastic Compute Cloud (EC2)**, which is Amazon's IaaS offering, followed by HP's flagship product called CloudSystem Matrix and finally **Cells as a Service**, an HP Labs research prototype that offers some advanced features.

STORAGE AS A SERVICE: AMAZON STORAGE SERVICES

Data is the lifeblood of an enterprise. Enterprises have varied requirements for data, including structured data in relational databases that power an e-commerce business, or documents that capture unstructured data about business processes, plans and visions. Enterprises may also need to store objects on behalf of their customers, like an online photo album or a collaborative document editing platform. Further, some of the data may be confidential and must be protected, while others data should be easily shareable. In all cases, business critical data should be secure and available on demand in the face of hardware and software failures, network partitions and inevitable user errors.

> **NOTE**
>
> **Amazon Storage Services**
> - Simple Storage Service (S3): An object store
> - SimpleDB: A Key-value store
> - Relational Database Service (RDS): MySQL instance

Amazon Simple Storage Service (S3)

Amazon Web Services (AWS), from Amazon.com, has a suite of cloud service products that have become very popular and are almost looked up to as a de facto standard for delivering IaaS. Figure 2.1 shows a screen shot of AWS depicting its different IaaS products in multiple tabs (S3, EC2, CloudWatch). This chapter covers a good amount of detail of S3, SimpleDB, EBS, RDS, and EC2 and Chapter 8 describes CloudWatch.

Amazon S3 is a highly reliable, highly available, scalable and fast storage in the cloud for storing and retrieving large amounts of data just through simple web services. This section gives some preliminary details of the platform first and then, takes a simple example of using S3, followed by a detailed description of S3 features [1]. More advanced uses of S3 are described in a later section on Amazon EC2, with an example of how S3 APIs can be used by developers together with other Amazon compute services (such as EC2) to form a complete IaaS solution. First, a look at how one can use S3 as a simple cloud storage to upload files.

Accessing S3

There are three ways of using S3. Most common operations can be performed via the AWS console, the GUI interface to AWS (shown in Figure 2.1) that can be accessed

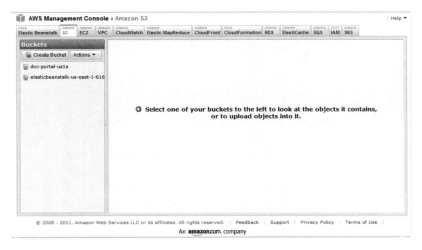

FIGURE 2.1

AWS console.

via http://aws.amazon.com/console. For use of S3 within applications, Amazon provides a REST-ful API with familiar HTTP operations such as GET, PUT, DELETE, and HEAD. Also, there are libraries and SDKs for various languages that abstract these operations.

> **NOTE**
>
> **S3 Access Methods**
> - AWS Console
> - Amazon's RESTful API
> - SDKs for Ruby and other languages

Additionally, since S3 is a storage service, several **S3 browsers** exist that allow users to explore their S3 account as if it were a directory (or a folder). There are also file system implementations that let users treat their S3 account as just another directory on their local disk. Several command line utilities [2, 3] that can be used in batch scripts also exist, and are described towards the end of this section.

Getting Started with S3

Let's start with a simple personal use-case. Consider a user having a directory full of personal photos that they want to store in the cloud for backup. Here's how this could be approached:

1. Sign up for S3 at http://aws.amazon.com/s3/. While signing up, obtain the **AWS Access Key** and the **AWS Secret Key**. These are similar to userid and

password that is used to authenticate all transactions with Amazon Web Services (not just S3).

2. Sign in to the **AWS Management Console** for S3 (see Figure 2.1) at https://console.aws.amazon.com/s3/home.

3. Create a **bucket** (see Figure 2.2) giving a name and geographical location where it can be stored. In S3 all files (called **objects**) are stored in a bucket, which represents a collection of related objects. Buckets and objects are described later in the section *Organizing Data in S3: Buckets, Objects and Keys*.

4. Click the *Upload* button (see Figure 2.3) and follow the instructions to upload files.

5. The photos or other files are now safely backed up to S3 and available for sharing with a URL if the right permissions are provided.

From a developer perspective, this can also be accomplished programmatically, in case there is a need to include this functionality in a program.

Organizing Data In S3: Buckets, Objects and Keys

Files are called **objects** in S3. Objects are referred to with keys – basically an optional directory path name followed by the name of the object. Objects in S3 are replicated across multiple geographic locations to make it resilient to several types of failures (however, consistency across replicas is not guaranteed). If object versioning is enabled, recovery from inadvertent deletions and modifications is

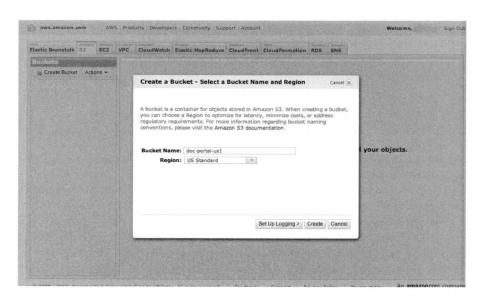

FIGURE 2.2

Creating a bucket.

FIGURE 2.3

Uploading objects.

possible. S3 objects can be up to 5 Terabytes in size and there are no limits on the number of objects that can be stored. All objects in S3 must be stored in a **bucket**. Buckets provide a way to keep related objects in one place and separate them from others. There can be up to 100 buckets per account and an unlimited number of objects in a bucket.

Each object has a key, which can be used as the path to the resource in an HTTP URL. For example, if the bucket is named `johndoe` and the key to an object is `resume.doc`, then its HTTP URL is http://s3.amazonaws.com/johndoe/resume.doc or alternatively, http://johndoe.s3.amazonaws.com/resume.doc By convention, slash-separated keys are used to establish a directory-like naming scheme for convenient browsing in S3 explorers such as the AWS Console, S3Fox, etc. For example, one can have URLs such as http://johndoe.s3.amazon.aws.com/project1/file1.c, http://johndoe.s3.amazon.aws.com/project1/file2.c, and http://johndoe.s3.amazon.aws.com/project2/file1.c. However, these are files with keys (names) `project1/file1.c`, and so on, and S3 is not really a hierarchical file system. Note that the bucket namespace is shared; i.e., it is not possible to create a bucket with a name that has already been used by another S3 user.

Note that entering the above URLs into a browser will not work as expected; not only are these values fictional, even if real values were substituted for the bucket and key, the result would be an "HTTP 403 Forbidden" error. This is because the URL lacks authentication parameters; S3 objects are private by default and requests should carry authentication parameters that prove the requester has rights to access the object, unless the object has "Public" permissions. Typically the client library, SDK or application will use the AWS Access Key and AWS Secret Key described later to compute a signature that identifies the requester, and append this signature to the S3 request. For example, the S3 *Getting Started Guide* is stored in the awsdocs bucket at the S3/latest/s3-gsg.pdf key with anonymous read permissions; hence it is available to everyone at http://s3.amazonaws.com/awsdocs/S3/latest/s3-gsg.pdf.

S3 Administration

In any enterprise, data is always coupled to policies that determine the location of the data and its availability, as well as who can and cannot access it. For security and compliance with local regulations, it is necessary to be able to audit and log actions and be able to undo inadvertent user actions. S3 provides facilities for all of these, described as follows:

Security: Users can ensure the security of their S3 data by two methods. First, S3 offers **access control** to objects. Users can set permissions that allow others to access their objects. This is accomplished via the AWS Management Console. A right-click on an object brings up the object actions menu (see Figure 2.4). Granting anonymous read access to objects makes them readable by anyone; this is useful, for example, for static content on a web site. This is accomplished by selecting the *Make Public* option on the object menu. It is also possible to narrow read or write access to specific AWS accounts. This is accomplished by selecting

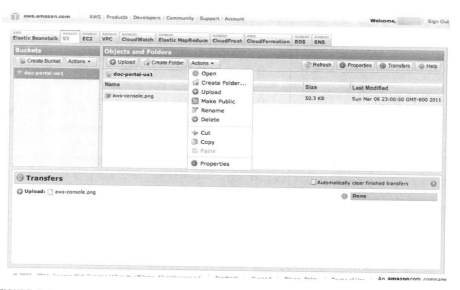

FIGURE 2.4

Amazon S3: Performing actions on objects.

the *Properties* option that brings up another menu (not shown) that allows users to enter the email ids of users to be allowed access. It is also possible to allow others to put objects in a bucket in a similar way. A common use for this is to provide clients with a way to submit documents for modification, which are then written to a different bucket (or different keys in the same bucket) where the client has permissions to pick up the modified document.

The other method that helps secure S3 data is to collect audit logs. S3 allows users to turn on **logging** for a bucket, in which case it stores complete access logs for the bucket in a different bucket (or, if desired, the same bucket). This allows users to see which AWS account accessed the objects, the time of access, the IP address from which the accesses took place and the operations that were performed. Logging can be enabled from the AWS Management Console (Figure 2.5). Logging can also be enabled at the time of bucket creation.

Data protection: S3 offers two features to prevent data loss [1]. By default, S3 replicates data across multiple storage devices, and is designed to survive two replica failures. It is also possible to request **Reduced Redundancy Storage(RRS)** for non-critical data. RRS data is replicated twice, and is designed to survive one replica failure. It is important to note that Amazon does not guarantee consistency among the replicas; e.g., if there are three replicas of the data, an application reading a replica which has a delayed update could read an older version of the data. The technical challenges of ensuring consistency, approaches to solve it and trade-offs to be made are discussed in detail in the *Data Storage* section of Chapter 5.

FIGURE 2.5

Amazon S3 bucket logging.

Versioning: If versioning is enabled on a bucket, then S3 automatically stores the full history of all objects in the bucket from that time onwards. The object can be restored to a prior version, and even deletes can be undone. This guarantees that data is never inadvertently lost.

Regions: For performance, legal and other reasons, it may be desirable to have S3 data running in specific geographic locations. This can be accomplished at the bucket level by selecting the region that the bucket is stored in during its creation. The region corresponds to a large geographic area, such as the USA (California) or Europe. The current list of regions can be found on the S3 web site [1].

Large Objects and Multi-part Uploads

The object size limit for S3 is 5 terabytes, which is more than is required to store an uncompressed 1080p HD movie. In the instance that this is not sufficient, the object can be stored in smaller chunks with the splitting and re-composition being managed in the application, using the data.

Although Amazon S3 has high aggregate bandwidth available, uploading large objects will still take some time. Additionally, if an upload fails, the entire object needs to be uploaded again. Multi-part upload solves both problems elegantly. S3 provides APIs that allow the developer to write a program that splits a large object into several parts and uploads each part independently [4]. These uploads can be parallelized for greater speed to maximize the network utilization. If a part fails to upload, only that part needs to be re-tried. S3 supported up to 10,000 parts per object as of writing of this book.

Amazon Simple DB

Unlike Amazon S3 that provides a file level operations, **SimpleDB** (**SDB**) provides a simple data store interface in the form of a key-value store. It allows storage and retrieval of a set of attributes based on a key. Use of key-value stores is an alternative to relational databases that use SQL-based queries. It is a type of NoSQL data store. A detailed comparison of key-value stores with relational databases, is found in the section *Scaling Storage* in Chapter 6. The next section provides a short overview of SDB.

Data Organization and Access

Data in SDB is organized into domains. Each item in a domain has a unique key that must be provided during creation. Each item can have up to 256 attributes, which are name-value pairs. In terms of the relational model, for each row, the primary key translates to the item name and the column names and values for that row translate to the attribute name-value pairs. For example, if it is necessary to store information regarding an employee, it is possible to store the attributes of the employee (e.g., the employee name) indexed by an appropriate key, such as an employee id. Unlike an RDBMS, attributes in SDB can have multiple values – e.g., if in a retail product database, the list of **keywords** for each item in the product catalog can be stored as a single value corresponding to the attribute `keywords`; doing this with an RDBMS

Storage as a Service: Amazon Storage Services **31**

would be more complex. More in-depth technical details of NoSQL data stores can be found in Chapter 5.

SDB provides a query language that is analogous to SQL, although there are methods to fetch a single item. Queries take advantage of the fact that SDB automatically indexes all attributes. A more detailed description of SDB and the use of its API is described with an example in a later section on Amazon EC2.

SDB Availability and Administration

SDB has a number of features to increase availability and reliability. Data stored in SDB is automatically replicated across different geographies for high availability. It also automatically adds compute resources in proportion to the request rate and automatically indexes all fields in the dataset for efficient access. SDB is schema-less; i.e., fields can be added to the dataset as the need arises. This and other advantages of NoSQL to provide a scalable store are discussed in Chapter 5, *Paradigms for Developing Cloud Applications*.

Amazon Relational Database Service

Amazon Relational Database Service (RDS) provides a traditional database abstraction in the cloud, specifically a MySQL instance in the cloud. An RDS instance can be created using the RDS tab in the AWS Management Console (see Figure 2.6).

FIGURE 2.6

AWS console: relational database service.

AWS performs many of the administrative tasks associated with maintaining a database for the user. The database is backed up at configurable intervals, which can be as frequent as 5 minutes. The backup data are retained for a configurable period of time which can be up to 8 days. Amazon also provides the capability to snapshot the database as needed. All of these administrative tasks can be performed through the AWS console (as in Figure 2.6). Alternatively, it is possible to develop a custom tool which will perform the tasks through the Amazon RDS APIs.

COMPUTE AS A SERVICE: AMAZON ELASTIC COMPUTE CLOUD (EC2)

The other important type of IaaS is Compute as a Service, where computing resources are offered as a service. Of course, for a useful compute as a service offering, it should be possible to associate storage with the computing service (so that the results of the computation can be made persistent). Virtual networking is needed as well, so that it is possible to communicate with the computing instance. All these together make up Infrastructure as a Service.

Amazon's Elastic Compute Cloud (EC2), one of the popular Compute as a Service offerings, is the topic of this section. The first part of this section provides an overview of Amazon EC2. This is then followed by a simple example that shows how EC2 can be used to set up a simple web server. Next, a more complex example that shows how EC2 can be used with Amazon's StaaS offerings to build a portal whereby customers can share books is presented. Finally, an example that illustrates advanced features of EC2 is shown.

Overview of Amazon EC2

Amazon EC2 allows enterprises to define a virtual server, with virtual storage and virtual networking. As the computational needs of an enterprise can vary greatly, some applications may be compute-intensive, and other applications may stress storage. Certain enterprise applications may need certain software environments and other applications may need computational clusters to run efficiently. Networking requirements may also vary greatly. This diversity in the compute hardware, with automatic maintenance and ability to handle the scale, makes EC2 a unique platform.

Accessing EC2 Using AWS Console

As with S3, EC2 can be accessed via the Amazon Web Services console at http://aws.amazon.com/console. Figure 2.7 shows the EC2 Console Dashboard, which can be used to create an **instance** (a compute resource), check status of user's instances and even terminate an instance. Clicking on the "Launch Instance" button takes the user to the screen shown in Figure 2.8, where a set of supported operating system images (called **Amazon Machine Images, AMI**) are shown to

FIGURE 2.7

AWS EC2 console.

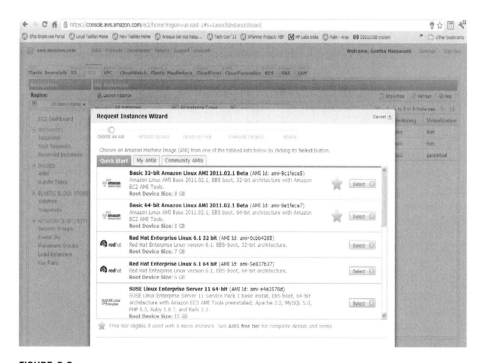

FIGURE 2.8

Creating an EC2 instance using the AWS console.

choose from. More on types of AMI and how one should choose the right one are described in later sections in this chapter. Once the image is chosen, the EC2 instance wizard pops up (Figure 2.9) to help the user set further options for the instance, such as the specific OS kernel version to use, whether to enable monitoring (using the CloudWatch tool described in Chapter 8) and so on. Next, the user has to create at least one key-value pair that is needed to securely connect to the instance. Follow the instructions to create a key-pair and save the file (say my_keypair.pem) in a safe place. The user can reuse an already created key-pair in case the user has many instances (it is analogous to using the same username-password to access many machines). Next, the security groups for the instance can be set to ensure the required network ports are open or blocked for the instance. For example, choosing the "web server" configuration will enable port 80 (the default HTTP port). More advanced firewall rules can be set as well. The final screen before launching the instance is shown in Figure 2.10. Launching the instance gives a public DNS name that the user can use to login remotely and use as if the cloud server was on the same network as the client machine.

For example, to start using the machine from a Linux client, the user gives the following command from the directory where the key-pair file was saved. After a

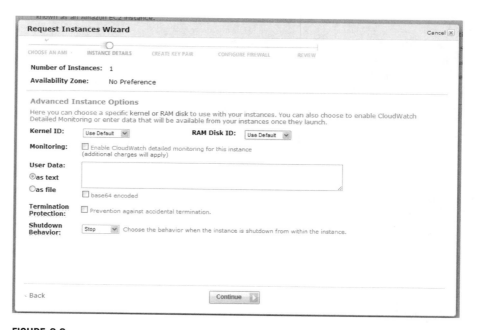

FIGURE 2.9

The EC2 instance wizard.

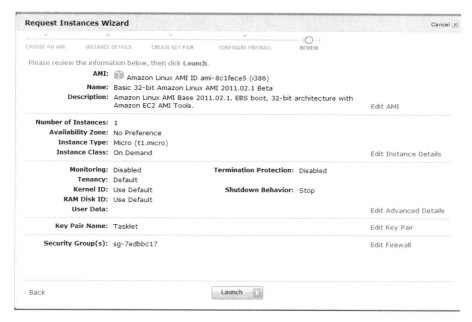

FIGURE 2.10

Parameters that can be enabled for a simple EC2 instance.

few confirmation screens, the user is logged into the machine to use any Linux command. For root access the user needs to use the `sudo` command.

```
ssh -i my_keypair.pem ec2-67-202-62-112.compute-1.amazonaws.com
```

For Windows, the user needs to open the `my_keypair.pem` file and use the "Get Windows Password" button on the AWS Instance page. The console returns the administrator password that can be used to connect to the instance using a Remote Desktop application (usually available at `Start-> All Programs -> Accessories -> Remote Desktop Connection`).

A description of how to use the AWS EC2 Console to request the computational, storage and networking resources needed to set up and launch a web server is described in the *Simple EC2 example: Setting up a Web Server* section of this chapter.

Accessing EC2 Using Command Line Tools

Amazon also provides a command line interface to EC2 that uses the EC2 API to implement specialized operations that cannot be performed with the AWS console. The following briefly describes how to install and set up the command line utilities. More details are found in *Amazon Elastic Compute Cloud User Guide* [5].

The details of the command line tools are found in *Amazon Elastic Compute Cloud Command Line Reference* [6].

NOTE

Installing EC2 command line tools

- Download tools
- Set environment variables (e.g., location of JRE)
- Set security environment (e.g., get certificate)
- Set region

Download tools: The EC2 command line utilities can be downloaded from *Amazon EC2 API Tools* [7] as a Zip file. They are written in Java, and hence will run on Linux, Unix, and Windows if the appropriate JRE is available. In order to use them simply unpack the file, and then set appropriate environment variables, depending upon the operating system being used. These environment variables can also be set as parameters to the command.

Set environment variables: The first command sets the environment variable that specifies the directory in which the Java runtime resides. PATHNAME should be the full pathname of the directory where the java.exe file can be found. The second command specifies the directory where the EC2 tools reside; TOOLS_PATHNAME should be set to the full pathname of the directory named ec2-api-tools-A.B-nnn into which the tools were unzipped (A, B and nnn are some digits that differ based on the version used). The third command sets the executable path to include the directory where the EC2 command utilities are present.

```
For Linux:
$export JAVA_HOME=PATHNAME
$export EC2_TOOLS=TOOLS_PATHNAME
$export PATH=$PATH:$EC2_HOME/bin
For Windows:
C:\>SET JAVA_HOME=PATHNAME
C:\>SET EC2_TOOLS=TOOLS_PATHNAME
C:\>SET PATH=%PATH%,%EC2_HOME%\bin
```

Set up security environment: The next step is to set up the environment so that the EC2 command line utilities can authenticate to AWS during each interaction. To do this, it is necessary to download an X.509 certificate and private key that authenticates HTTP requests to Amazon. The X.509 certificate can be generated by clicking on the "Account" link shown in Figure 2.7, clicking on the "Security Credentials" link that is displayed, and following the given instructions to create a new certificate. The certificate files should be downloaded to a .ec2 directory in the home directory on Linux/Unix, and C:\ec2 on Windows, without changing their names. The following commands are to be exe:uted to set up the environment; both Linux and Windows commands are given. Here, `f1.pem` is the certificate file downloaded from EC2.

```
$export EC2-CERT=~/.ec2/f1.pem
or
C:\> set EC2-CERT=~/.ec2/f1.pem
```

Set region: It is necessary to next set the **region** that the EC2 command tools interact with – i.e., the location in which the EC2 virtual machines would be created. AWS regions are described in a subsequent section titled *S3 Administration*. In brief, each region represents an AWS data center, and AWS pricing varies by region. The command `ec2-describe-regions` can be issued at this point to test the installation of the EC2 command tools and list the available regions.

The default region used is the US-East region "us-east-1" with service endpoint URL http://ec2.us-east-1.amazonaws.com, but can be set to any specific end point using the following command, where `ENDPOINT_URL` is formed from the region name as illustrated for the "us-east-1".

```
$export EC2-URL=https://<ENDPOINT_URL>
Or
C:\> set EC2-URL =https://<ENDPOINT_URL>
```

A later section explains how developers can use the EC2 and S3 APIs to set up a web application in order to implement a simple publishing portal such as the Pustak Portal (running example used in this book). Before that one needs to understand more about what a computation resource is and the parameters that one can configure for each such resource, described in the next section.

EC2 Computational Resources

This section gives a brief overview of the computational resources available on EC2 first, followed by the storage and network resources, more details of which are available at *EC2 Introduction* [8].

Computing resources: The computing resources available on EC2, referred to as EC2 instances, consist of combinations of computing power, together with other resources such as memory. Amazon measures the computing power of an EC2 instance in terms of EC2 Compute Units [9]. An **EC2 Compute Unit (CU)** is a standard measure of computing power in the same way that bytes are a standard measure of storage. One EC2 CU provides the same amount of computing power as a 1.0–1.2 GHz Opteron or Xeon processor in 2007. Thus, if a developer requests a computing resource of 1 EC2 CU, and the resource is allocated on a 2.4 GHz processor, they may get 50% of the CPU. This allows developers to request standard amounts of CPU power regardless of the physical hardware.

The EC2 instances that Amazon recommends for most applications belong to the **Standard Instance** family [8]. The characteristics of this family are shown in Table 2.1, *EC2 Standard Instance Types*. A developer can request a computing resource of one of the instance types shown in the table (e.g., a Small computing

Table 2.1 EC2 Standard Instance Types

Instance Type	Compute Capacity	Memory	Local Storage	Platform
Small	1 virtual core of 1 CU	1.7GB	160GB	32-bit
Large	2 virtual cores, 2 CU each	7.5GB	850GB	64-bit
Extra Large	4 virtual cores, 2 CU each	15GB	1690GB	64-bit

instance, which would have the characteristics shown). Figure 2.8 showed how one can do this using the AWS console. Selection of local storage is discussed later in the section titled *EC2 Storage Resources*.

Other instance families available in Amazon at the time of writing this book include the High-Memory Instance family, suitable for databases and other memory-hungry applications; the High-CPU Instance family for compute-intensive applications; the Cluster-Compute Instance family for High-Performance Compute (HiPC) applications, and the Cluster GPU Instance family which include Graphic Processing Units (GPUs) for HiPC applications that need GPUs [8].

Software: Amazon makes available certain standard combinations of operating system and application software in the form of **Amazon Machine Images (AMIs)**. The required AMI has to be specified when requesting the EC2 instance, as seen earlier. The AMI running on an EC2 instance is also called the **root AMI**.

Operating systems available in AMIs include various flavors of Linux, such as Red Hat Enterprise Linux and SuSE, the Windows server, and Solaris. Software available includes databases such as IBM DB2, Oracle and Microsoft SQL Server. A wide variety of other application software and middleware, such as Hadoop, Apache, and Ruby on Rails, are also available [8].

There are two ways of using additional software not available in standard AMIs. It is possible to request a standard AMI, and then install the additional software needed. This AMI can then be saved as one of the available AMIs in Amazon. The other method is to import a VMware image as an AMI using the `ec2-import-instance` and `ec2-import-disk-image` commands. For more details of how to do this, the reader is referred to [9].

Regions and Availability Zones: EC2 offers regions, which are the same as the S3 regions described in the section *S3 Administration*. Within a region, there are multiple availability zones, where each availability zone corresponds to a virtual data center that is isolated (for failure purposes) from other availability zones. Thus, an enterprise that wishes to have its EC2 computing instances in Europe could select the "Europe" region when creating EC2 instances. By creating two instances in different availability zones, the enterprise could have a highly available configuration that is tolerant to failures in any one availability zone.

Load Balancing and Scaling: EC2 provides the **Elastic Load Balancer**, which is a service that balances the load across multiple servers. Details of its usage are in the section *EC2 Example: Article Sharing in Pustak Portal*. The default load balancing policy is to treat all requests as being independent. However, it is also possible to have timer-based and application controlled sessions, whereby successive requests from the same client are routed to the same server based upon time or application direction [10]. The load balancer also scales the number of servers up or down depending upon the load. This can also be used as a failover policy, since failure of a server is detected by the Elastic Load Balancer. Subsequently, if the load on the remaining server is too high, the Elastic Load Balancer could start a new server instance.

Once the compute resources are identified, one needs to set any storage resources needed. The next section describes more on the same.

NOTE

EC2 Storage Resources
- Amazon S3: Highly available object store
- Elastic Block Service: permanent block storage
- Instance Storage: transient block storage

EC2 Storage Resources

As stated earlier, computing resources can be used along with associated storage and network resources in order to be useful. S3, which is the file storage offered by Amazon, has already been described in the *Amazon Storage Services* section. Use of the S3 files is similar to accessing an HTTP server (a web file system). However, many times an application performs multiple disk IOs and for performance and other reasons one needs to have a control on the storage configuration as well. This section describes how one can configure resources that appear to be physical disks to the EC2 server, called **block storage resources**. There are two types of block storage resources: Elastic Block Service, and instance storage, described next.

Elastic Block Service (EBS): In the same way that S3 provides file storage services, EBS provides a block storage service for EC2. It is possible to request an EBS disk volume of a particular size and attach this volume to one or multiple EC2 instances using the instance ID returned during the time the volume is created. Unlike the local storage assigned during the creation of an EC2 instance, the EBS volume has an existence independent of any EC2 instance, which is critical to have persistence of data, as detailed later.

Instance Storage: Every EC2 instance has local storage that can be configured as a part of the compute resource (Figure 2.8) and this is referred to as **instance storage**. Table 2.2 shows the default partitioning of instance storage associated with each EC2 instance for standard instance types. This instance storage is

Table 2.2 Partitioning of Local Storage in Standard EC2 Instance Types

	Small	Large	Extra Large
Linux	/dev/sda1: root file system /dev/sda2: /mnt /dev/sda3: /swap	/dev/sda1: root file system /dev/sdb: /mnt/ dev/sdc /dev/sdd /dev/sde	/dev/sda1: root file system /dev/sdb: /mnt /dev/sdc /dev/sdd /dev/sde
Windows	/dev/sda1: C: xvdb	/dev/sda1: C: xvdb xvdc xvdd xvde	/dev/sda1: C: xvdb xvdc xvdd xvde

Table 2.3 Comparison of Instance Storage and EBS Storage

	Instance Storage	EBS storage
Creation	Created by default when an EC2 instance is created	Created independently of EC2 instances.
Sharing	Can be attached only to EC2 instance with which it is created.	Can be shared between EC2 instances.
Attachment	Attached by default to S3-backed instances; can be attached to EBS-backed instances	Not attached by default to any instance.
Persistence	Not persistent; vanishes if EC2 instance is terminated	Persistent even if EC2 instance is terminated.
S3 snapshot	Can be snapshotted to S3	Can be snapshotted to S3

ephemeral (unlike EBS storage); i.e., it exists only as long as the EC2 instance exists, and cannot be attached to any other EC2 instance. Furthermore, if the EC2 instance is terminated, the instance storage ceases to exist. To overcome this limitation of local storage, developers can use either EBS or S3 for persistent storage and sharing.

The instance AMI, configuration files and any other persistent files can be stored in S3 and during operation, a snapshot of the data can be periodically taken and sent to S3. If data needs to be shared, this can be accomplished via files stored in S3. An EBS storage can also be attached to an instance as desired. A detailed example of how one does this is described later in the context of Pustak Portal.

Table 2.3 summarizes some of the main differences and similarities between the two types of storage.

S3-backed instances vs. EBS-backed instances: EC2 compute and storage resources behave slightly differently depending upon whether the root AMI for the EC2 instance is stored in Amazon S3 or in Amazon Elastic Block Service

(EBS). These instances are referred to as **S3-backed instances** and **EBS-backed instances**, respectively. In an S3-backed instance, the root AMI is stored in S3, which is file storage. Therefore, it must be copied to the root device in the EC2 instance before the EC2 instance can be booted. However, since instance storage is not persistent, any modifications made to the AMI of an S3-backed instance (such as patching the OS or installing additional software) will not be persistent beyond the lifetime of the instance. Furthermore, while instance storage is attached by default to an S3-backed instance (as shown in Table 2.2), instance storage is not attached by default to EBS-backed instances.

EC2 Networking Resources

In addition to compute and storage resources, network resources are also needed by applications. For networking between EC2 instances, EC2 offers both a public address as well as a private address [5]. It also offers DNS services for managing DNS names associated with these IP addressees. Access to these IP addresses is controlled by policies. The Virtual Private Cloud can be used to provide secure communication between an Intranet and the EC2 network. One can also create a complete logical sub network and expose it to public (a DMZ) with its own firewall rules. Another interesting feature of EC2 is the Elastic IP addresses which are independent of any instance, and this feature can be used to support failover of servers. These advanced features and how these can be used to set up a network are described in this section, after understanding the key terminologies next.

NOTE

EC2 Networking

- Private and public IP addresses per instance
- Elastic IP addresses not associated with any instance
- Route 53 DNS that allows simple URLs (e..g. www.mywebsite.com)
- Security groups for networking security policies

Instance addresses: Each EC2 instance has two IP addresses associated with it – the **public IP address** and the **private IP address**. The private IP address and DNS name can be resolved only within the EC2 cloud. For communication between EC2 instances, the internal IP addresses are most efficient, for the messages then pass entirely within the Amazon network. The public IP address and DNS name can be used for communication outside the Amazon cloud.

Elastic IP addresses: These IP addresses are independent of any instance, but are associated with a particular Amazon EC2 account and can be dynamically assigned to any instance (in which case, the public IP address is de-assigned). Therefore, they are useful for implementing failover. Upon failure of one EC2 instance, the Elastic IP address can be dynamically assigned to another EC2 instance. Unlike instance IP addresses, Elastic IP addresses are not automatically allocated; they have to be generated when needed.

Route 53: Enterprises may desire to publish a URL of the form http://www. myenterprise.com for EC2 instances. This is not possible by default, since the EC2 instances are inside the `amazon.com` domain. Route 53 is a DNS server that can be used to associate an Elastic IP address or public IP address with a name of the form `www.myenterprise.com`.

Security Groups: For networking security, it is common to define network security policies that restrict the ports through which any machine can be accessed, or the IP addresses that can access a server. The same can be achieved for EC2 instances using security groups, briefly mentioned earlier. Each security group is a collection of network security policies. Different security groups should be created for different server types; for example, the web server security group could specify that port 80 may be opened for incoming connections. The default security group when creating an EC2 instance allows the instance to connect to any outside IP address but disallows incoming connections.

Virtual Private Cloud: Enterprises that desire more control over their networking configuration can use **Virtual Private Cloud** (**VPC**). Examples of the advanced networking features offered by VPC include:

i. the ability to allocate both public and private IP addresses to instances from any address range
ii. the ability to divide the addresses into subnets and control the routing between subnets
iii. the ability to connect the EC2 network with an Intranet using a VPN tunnel.

Details of VPC are beyond the scope of this book and can be found in *Amazon Virtual Private Cloud* [11].

Simple EC2 Example: Setting up a Web Server

Now, all the terminologies and concepts learned in the previous two sections will be used in a simple example of creating a web server. The web server will be created as an EBS-backed instance, to avoid the necessity of having to periodically back up the storage to S3.

The process is broken down into four steps:

i. Selecting the AMI for the instance
ii. Creating the EC2 instance and installing the web server
iii. Creating an EBS volume for data, such as HTML files and so on
iv. Setting up networking and access rules.

It is assumed that the data needed for the web server (HTML files, scripts, executables, and so on) are available, and have been uploaded to EC2. Furthermore, to illustrate how to install custom software on a standard AMI, it is assumed that the web server needed also has to be uploaded to EC2 and then installed (in reality, a web server instance may be available as an image as well).

Selecting the AMI

Instructions to create a new EC2 instance using the AWS console were described earlier. The user may recall that one step during this process is selecting an AMI (discussed around Figure 2.8). More details of this phase to perform advanced functionality are described next.

Using the dropdown menus to select "Amazon Images" and "Amazon Linux" brings up a list of Linux images supplied by Amazon, as shown in Figure 2.11. Here, the root device column indicates whether the root device for the image is EBS or not. Some of the important parameters of the AMI are in the "Description" tag in the lower half of the figure. It can be seen that the image is a 64-bit Amazon Linux image with the root device /dev/sda1 in EBS. The value `true` in the "Block Devices" field is the `DeleteUponTerminate` flag and indicates that the device is not persistent; i.e., it will vanish if the EC2 instance terminates. Clicking the "Launch" button brings up the launch wizard, which goes through a number of steps (such as selecting the size of the machine, and possibly creating a new key pair) before launching the EC2 instance. However, at the time of this writing, there is no way to create an EC2 instance with a persistent root device through the AWS Console. Therefore, the next section describes how to launch the EC2 instance using the command line.

Creating the Example EC2 Instance

Two other important steps done during the creation of an instance are (i) generate a key pair that provides access to the EC2 servers that are created and (ii) create a

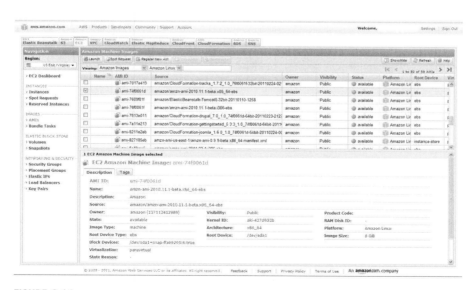

FIGURE 2.11

Selecting an AMI.

security group that will be associated with the instance and specify the networking access rules. In our example, since the instance created will not have the required software (web server) installed on it by default, the security group created will initially be an empty security group that disallows any incoming network access. Subsequently, the security group will be modified to allow HTTP access.

The key pair is generated from the EC2 console (see Figure 2.11) by clicking on the "Key Pair" link, following the instructions and downloading the resulting files (called f2.pem in this example). In the earlier section, there was a necessity to execute the remote shell command from the directory where the key-pair (.pem) file was stored. The following script shows how to set an environment variable named EC2-PRIVATE-KEY so as to make the downloaded key the default key-pair for EC2 instances.

```
For Linux:
$ export EC2-PRIVATE-KEY=~/.ec2/f2.pem
$ ec2addgrp "Web Server" -d "Security Group for Web Servers"
$ ec2run ami-74f0061d -b dev/sda1=::false -k f2.pem -g "Web Server"

For Windows:

C:\> set EC2-PRIVATE-KEY =C:\.ec2\f2.pem
C:\> ec2addgrp "Web Server" -d "Security Group for Web Servers"
C:\> ec2run ami-74f0061d -b "xvda=::false" -k f2.pem -g "Web Server"
```

In the above example, the ec2addgrp command (short for ec2-create-group) creates a security group called "Web Server" and disallows all external access. As stated earlier, this rule will later be modified to allow HTTP access. Next, the ec2run command (short form for ec2-run-instances command) is used to start the instance with a persistent EBS root volume. The first parameter is the AMI id of the AMI selected in Figure 2.11. The value false in the -b flag (which controls the behavior of the root volume) indicates that the DeleteUponTerminate flag for this volume is to be set to false. This implies that the volume will not be deleted even if the EC2 instance terminates. The -k and -g parameters specify the keypair that can be used to communicate with the instance and the security group for the instances, respectively. The number of instances to be launched defaults to 1. A range can be explicitly specified using the -instance-count parameter. More details of all the command line options for EC2 are available at *Amazon Elastic Compute Cloud Command Line Reference* [6].

The DNS name for the newly created instance is available from AWS console. Alternatively, the ec2-describe-instances command (ec2din is the short form) can be also used to get the public DNS name of the instance. Subsequently, ssh, PuTTY or Remote Desktop Connection can be used to login to the instance and download the software to be installed (via yum, for example). After installing the additional software, the image can be saved on EBS as an AMI using the ec2-create-instance command. The parameter instanceId is the instance id of the EC2 instance, and the command returns the AMI Id of the newly created EBS AMI. These steps are shown in the following script:

```
For Linux :
$ ec2din
$ ssh -i f2.pem instance-id
$ ec2-create-instance -n "Web Server AMI" instanceId

For Windows:

C:\>ec2-describe-instances
C:\putty
C:\>ec2-create-instance -n "Web Server AMI" instanceId
```

Attaching an EBS Volume

Since the HTML pages to be served from the web portal need to be persistent, it is required to create an EBS volume for holding the HTML pages that are to be served by the web server. EBS volumes can be created from the EC2 console (see Figure 2.11) by clicking on the "Volumes" link. This brings up a listing of all EBS volumes currently owned by the user. Clicking the "Create Volume" button brings up the screen shown in Figure 2.12, where the size of the needed volume can be specified before being created.

The new volume that has been created is shown on the "Volumes" screen with a status of available (see masked content on Figure 2.13). Clicking on the "Attach Volume" button brings up the "Attach Volume" screen (Figure 2.13), which has drop-down menus for the EC2 instance to be used, as well as the device name (xvdf to xvdp for Windows, /dev/sdf to /dev/sdp for Linux). After making the appropriate selections, clicking the "Attach" button will virtually

FIGURE 2.12

Creating an EBS volume.

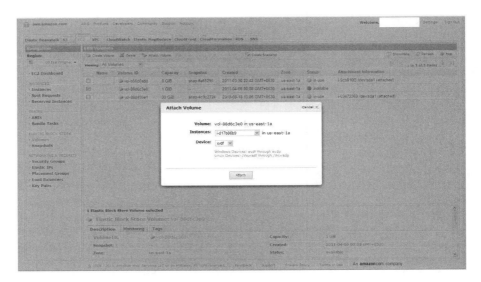

FIGURE 2.13

Attaching an EBS volume to an EC2 instance.

attach the volume to the selected instance. At this stage, an EC2 instance has been created, the web server has been installed and a separate persistent store on EBS has been attached.

Allowing External Access to the Web Server

Since the web server is now ready for operation, external access to it can now be enabled. Clicking on the "Security Groups" link at the left of the EC2 console brings up a list of all security groups available. Figure 2.14 shows the available security groups, which consist of the newly created group "Web Server" and two default groups. By clicking on the "Inbound" tab, it is possible to input rules that specify the type of traffic allowed. Figure 2.14 shows how to add a new rule that allows traffic on port 80 from all IP addresses (specified by the 0 IP address). A specific IP address can also be typed in to allow a specific IP address to be allowed. Clicking the "Add Rule" button adds this particular rule. After all rules are added, clicking the "Apply Rule Changes" button activates the newly added rules. By permitting external access to the web server, it is effectively in a DMZ (which is a region in an Intranet where external access is allowed) [12, 13]. Similarly, by disallowing external access from outside to other servers, they are effectively kept out of the DMZ.

This completes the deployment of a simple web server on EC2 and EBS. The next section makes this example much more complex allowing Web 2.0 style usage and applies it to the Pustak Portal case study.

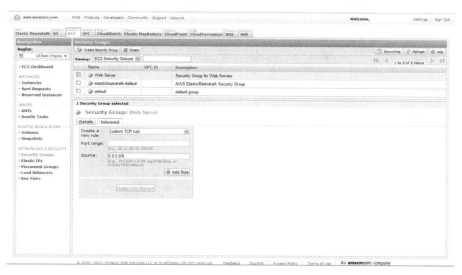

FIGURE 2.14

Modifying a security group.

Using EC2 for Pustak Portal

The following section describes a more complex case of deploying the running example of Pustak Portal (a simple book publishing portal detailed in the Preface). The Portal is enhanced to allow authors to upload and share book chapters or short articles in various formats with readers, who have to be registered with the portal. This kind of functionality is similar to portals of online newspapers and magazines. For this, it is necessary to store the documents, together with metadata such as the file type, and an access control list of readers who have been given access permission. Since a particular article may become very popular due to its topical nature, the load on the portal could vary greatly, and it is necessary that the number of servers scale up and down with usage. This motivates the use of Amazon EC2.

The high-level architecture of the enhanced Pustak Portal is shown in Figure 2.15. The articles are stored in S3, while the associated metadata, such as article properties, the list of users the document is shared with, etc., are stored in Simple DB. The portal web site runs on EC2 and automatically scales up and down with usage. Example code for this will be written in Ruby [14].

NOTE

S3 APIs illustrated

- Read object
- Write object
- Delete object

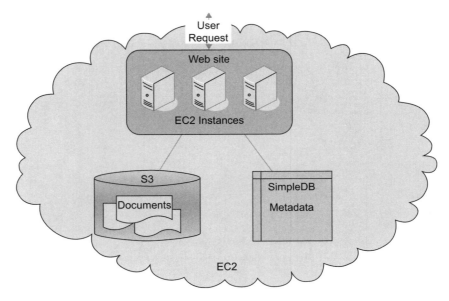

FIGURE 2.15

Article sharing portal architecture.

Document Store for the Article Portal

RightScale has developed some Ruby Gems (packages) for AWS. First, these open source gems are imported using the require statement.

```
require 's3/right_s3'
```

Next, initialize the S3 client with authentication credentials so that it is possible to access S3 using RightScale AWS API [15]. Recall from the *Getting Started* section of the S3 section that authentication keys are generated when creating an Amazon account.

```
def initialize(aws_access_key_id, aws_secret_key)
    @s3 = RightAws::S3.new(aws_access_key_id, aws_secret_key);
    @bucket = @s3.bucket('document_portal_store', true)
end
```

Assume that each author has their own bucket. In that case, they can upload their articles using a unique identifier that they assign to the article.

```
def save(doc_id, doc_contents)
    @bucket.put(doc_id, doc_contents)
end
```

Similarly, the opening of existing objects is done as follows:

```
def open(doc_id)
    @bucket.get(doc_id).data
end
```

When an article is no longer relevant, the authors can delete it as follows:

```
def delete(doc_id)
    @bucket.get(doc_id).delete
end
```

Storing the Article Metadata

> **NOTE**
>
> **SimpleDB APIs illustrated**
> - Connect to database
> - Read data
> - Write data
> - Search database

Assume that the following metadata has to be stored for each article: the name of the article, author, and a list of readers. This information can be stored in Simple DB as key value pairs. Recall that SimpleDB allows one to store attributes associated with a key. The first step is to initialize a SimpleDB client.

```
require 's3/right_sdb_interface'

class DocumentMetadata
    def initialize(aws_access_key_id, aws_secret_key)
        @domain = 'document_portal_metadata'
            @sdb = RightAws::SdbInterface.new(aws_access_key_id,
            aws_secret_key)
        @sdb.create_domain(@domain)
    end
```

To store the metadata for a new article, it is necessary to create an entry for this article and write the corresponding attributes to Simple DB. Since Pustak Portal created a bucket for each author, and the article names are unique within the bucket, the combination of the author name and bucket will be unique and can be used as the key to store and retrieve data, and is the variable doc_id. Note that SDB values are always arrays, so name and author have to be converted to an array.

```
def create(doc_id, doc_name, author, readers, writers)
    attributes = {
        :name => [ doc_name ],
        :owner => [ owner ],
```

```
          :readers => readers,
          :writers => writers,
      }

      @sdb.put_attributes(@domain, doc_id, attributes)
  end
```

The metadata can be retrieved as follows:

```
def get(doc_id)
    result = @sdb.get_attributes(@domain, doc_id)
    return result.has_key?(:attributes) ? result[:attributes] : {}
end
```

The following procedures can be used to grant or revoke access for readers:

```
def grant_access(doc_id, access_type, user)
    attr_name = access_type == :read_only ? :readers : :writers
    attributes = { attr_name => [ user ] }
    @sdb.put_attribute(@domain, doc_id, attributes)
end

def revoke_access(doc_id, access_type, user)
    attr_name = access_type == :read_only ? :readers : :writers
    attributes = { attr_name => [ user ] }
    @sdb.delete_attribute(@domain, doc_id, attributes)
end
```

It may also be necessary to find the articles that a user has access to. These could be articles that were created by the user (owned) or those that other users have granted him access to. We can use SimpleDB's Query feature as follows:

```
def documents(user)
    docs = { :owned => [], :read_only => [], :write => [] }
    query = "['owner'='#{user}'] union ['readers'='#{user}'] union
    ['writers'='#{user}']"
    @sdb.query(@domain, query) do |result|
        result[:items].each do |doc_id, attributes|
            access_type = nil
            if attributes["owner"].include?(user) then
            access_type = :owned
            elsif attributes["readers"].include?(user) then
            access_type = :read_only
            end

            docs[access_type] << { doc_id => attributes } if
            access_type

            true # tell @sdb.query to keep going
        end
    end

    return docs
end
```

This basic data model can be used to write the views and controllers for a Ruby-on-Rails web application that is part of Pustak Portal and allows authors to upload, and share documents with readers. AWS also provides SDKs for Java, .NET, PHP and also mobile platforms like Android and iOS, so the Pustak Portal application can be developed in other languages as well as for mobile platforms.

EC2 Example: Auto-Scaling the Pustak Portal

The starting point for an AWS-based auto-scaling web site is the bundle for the web application that captures all the dependencies for the application. For example, the portal needs a web application and a Web Application Archive (WAR) if the application is written in Java. Similarly, the Ruby gems if the program is written in Ruby. Using an application bundle, one can enable auto-scaling in two ways:

i. Using AWS Beanstalk
ii. Application-based auto-scaling.

Both approaches are discussed in the following section.

Auto-Scaling using AWS Beanstalk

AWS Beanstalk [16] is a part of EC2 that provides auto-scaling. Beanstalk automates the auto-scaling deployment process. The application developer just provides the application WAR, configures the load balancer, sets auto-scaling parameters and Tomcat/Java parameters and also an email address for notifications. All of this can be done at the AWS Console. When Beanstalk finishes deploying, it creates a fully functioning, auto-scaling, load-balanced web site at http://<app-name>.elasticbeanstalk.com.

Figure 2.16 shows the Beanstalk console for the sample application provided by Amazon. The application is running in the default environment, which consists of Linux and Tomcat (this is actually the AMI described earlier in the chapter). Buttons for launching a new environment (AMI) or importing a new application in to AWS are shown in the top right of the screen. Graphs showing the performance statistics of the application are also shown in the figure.

At the time of this writing, AWS Beanstalk only supported WAR deployments, so it was not suitable for the Pustak Portal application described earlier in Ruby. The next section describes how one can auto-scale such (non Beanstalk) application solutions on EC2, for a general case.

Application-controlled Auto-Scaling

If the application deployment cannot be auto-scaled using Beanstalk, then it is necessary for the developer to develop the auto-scaling infrastructure. This can be done in three steps as follows.

1. **Select an AMI:** As stated earlier, an AMI consists of the combination of the OS and software needed by the application. A large number of AMIs, including AMIs provided by software vendors such as IBM and Oracle, are available at *Amazon Machine Images (AMIs)* [17]. If no suitable AMIs are

FIGURE 2.16

Amazon web services console for beanstalk.

available, it is necessary to create a custom AMI. This process is described in the section "Creating a Custom AMI." Make a note of the AMI Id.

2. **Set up an Elastic Load balancer:** From the EC2 Section of the AWS Console (see Figure 2.16), select "Load Balancers" ->"Create Load Balancer" and fill out the values requested. It is possible to start without any instances initially; they will be started when auto-scaling is enabled. Make a note of the new load balancer name.

3. **Set up Auto-scaling:** This is done in the command line that follows (since it is not currently available from the AWS console). The `as-create-launch-config` command creates a launch configuration using the AMI ID obtained earlier and an EC2 instance (`m1.small` in this case). The `as-create-auto-scaling` command creates a group of instances that will scale from 1 to a maximum of 10, covered by the load balancer created earlier. Upon execution, the minimum specified number of instances will be created automatically.

Auto-scaling is controlled by an auto-scaling policy. An auto-scaling policy specifies the conditions under which the number of instances is to be scaled up or down. The policy is specified by the `as-put-scaling-policy` command. The following code snippet states that the number of instances should be increased by 1, with a 300-second wait time between consecutive runs to allow instances to launch. Running this will return a policy ID, which must be noted. A scale-down policy similar to the scale-up policy can also be specified.

The conditions under which the scale-up policy is to be executed are specified by the `mon-put-metric-alarm` command. This is a CloudWatch CPU alarm set to execute the policy when CPU utilization exceeds 75%. More details about CloudWatch, the EC2 monitoring tool, are described in Chapter 8. Finally, the script needed to do all of the steps is as follows.

```
$ as-create-launch-config DocPortalLaunchConfig -image-id <image ID> -
instance-type m1.small

$as-create-auto-scaling-group DocPortalGroup -launch-configuration
DocPortalLaunchConfig -availability-zones us-east-1a -min-size 1 -max-
size 10 -load-balancers <loadbalancer name>

$ as-put-scaling-policy DocPortalScaleUp -auto-scaling-group
MyAutoScalingGroup -adjustment=1 -type ChangeInCapacity -cooldown 300

$ mon-put-metric-alarm DocPortalCPUAlarm -comparison-operator
GreaterThanThreshold -evaluation-periods 1 -metric-name CPUUtilization -
namespace "AWS/EC2" -period 600 -statistic Average -threshold 75 -alarm-
actions <policy ID> -dimensions "AutoScalingGroupName=DocPortalGroup"
```

NOTE

HP CloudSystem Automation Suite

- CloudSystem Matrix: A product that enables IaaS as a private cloud solution as well as basic application deployment and monitoring.
- CloudSystem Enterprise: A product that enables IaaS as a private or hybrid cloud solution; supports a single services view, heterogeneous infrastructure, bursting and bridging to a public cloud if desired, and advanced life cycle management.
- CloudSystem Service Provider: A product that enables public or hosted private cloud; meant for service providers to provide SaaS; includes aggregation and management of those services.

HP CLOUDSYSTEM MATRIX[1]

While Amazon EC2 is an example of public IaaS cloud, **HP CloudSystem Matrix** is an important IaaS offering from HP for Enterprises to build private or hybrid clouds. CloudSystem Matrix is part of the **CloudSystem Automation Suite** of products, which includes three IaaS products, namely, CloudSystem Matrix, CloudSystem Enterprise and CloudSystem Service Provider. CloudSystem Matrix, as mentioned earlier, is a is private cloud IaaS offering. It allows customers to perform basic infrastructure and application provisioning and management very rapidly. **CloudSystem Enterprise** includes Matrix and advanced IaaS features, such as the ability to manage hybrid clouds, with support for cloud-bursting (described in Chapter 6) and the ability to allocate resources from a public cloud to supplement

---

[1]Contributed by Mr. Nigel Cook, Hewlett-Packard Laboratories, USA

private cloud resources during a peak period. Therefore, CloudSystem Enterprise can draw upon resources both from public clouds (such as Amazon) as well as private resources belonging to the enterprise to create an optimal hybrid service. **CloudSystem Service Provider** is targeted at service providers and provides the infrastructure needed to build a PaaS or SaaS service that can be offered to customers. This section describes the key technology of all three products, the CloudSystem Matrix software. Built on market leading HP BladeSystem, the Matrix Operating Environment, and Cloud Service Automation for Matrix, CloudSystem Matrix offers a self-service infrastructure portal for auto-provisioning and built-in lifecycle management to optimize infrastructure, monitor applications and ensure uptime for cloud and traditional IT. In this section, the basic features of CloudSystem Matrix are described first, following which there is a description of how a portal such as Pustak Portal can be set up using the Web GUI interface. CloudSystem Matrix also offers APIs which allow the infrastructure to be managed programmatically; these APIs are illustrated with an example in Chapter 8, *Managing the Cloud*.

Since Amazon EC2 has been described in detail, the description in this section will be limited to key features of CloudSystem Matrix and internal implementation details, rather than the user view of IaaS as was done for EC2. This will enable the reader to appreciate the features that one can expect in a generic IaaS platform and also give a sense of the potential architecture and implementation of Amazon EC2 or similar systems.

Basic Platform Features

CloudSystem Matrix [18] is an HP product that combines server, network, storage and management components in an integrated offering. The inbuilt management provides a web-based graphical user interface, as well as an exposed web service API that provides infrastructure as a service (IaaS) capabilities. The fundamental elements of the CloudSystem Matrix IaaS interfaces are:

1. Service Catalog
2. Consumer Portal (self-service interface)
3. One or more shared resource pools
4. Service template design and authoring tools
5. Administrator Portal containing tools for group, resource capacity, usage and maintenance management.

In combination, these elements allow infrastructure to be easily consumed and administered. A typical example is the case of a consumer who wants to create and administer a service. The consumer can browse the **Service Catalog**, which lists the available infrastructure offerings. The catalog entries serve as a blueprint template for new service creation by the consumer. To create a new service, the consumer uses the **Consumer Portal**, which is a **self-service interface**, to select the desired catalog entry and nominate the desired shared resource pool to be used as a source of capacity for the new service. **Self-service** means, as the name implies, that a cloud user who wishes to set up a service can set it up without interacting with a cloud administrator. Recall from Chapter 1 that self-service is defined by NIST as one of the fundamental characteristics of a cloud service. The shared resource pool consists of a collection of similar resources, such as storage LUNs, and virtual machines. Subsequently, the consumer uses the Consumer Portal to perform on-going management operations over the lifetime of the service. This could be simple activities including re-boot or console access to their environment, or more advanced activities such as adjusting the resources assigned to the service – expanding to meeting demand growth, as well as quiescing resources for savings during low utilization periods.

Entries in the Service Catalog need to be authored, tested and published with tools to support the process. This is done via the **Service Template Designer Portal** and the **Workflow Designer Portal.** The administrator of the environment uses the **Administrator Portal** to manage the groups of consumers, setting policies associated with their catalog access, and resource pool consumption. Administrator tools also need to support capacity planning associated both with demand growth as well as the impacts of maintenance schedules.

CloudSystem Matrix treats all resources in a uniform manner; i.e., as objects with **attributes** that are grouped into **resource pools**. For servers, the virtual servers can have attributes such as the speed of the CPU, the OS available, and the cost. Similar virtual servers can be grouped into resource pools of servers. Similarly, virtual storage devices can also have attributes such as their speed, RAID configuration, and cost per byte and can also be grouped into resource pools. Network configuration allows specification of various policies such as the IP address assignment policy (Static, DHCP, or Auto-allocation). During service instantiation, resources are allocated from the appropriate pools based upon user specification.

Implementing the Pustak Portal Infrastructure

CloudSystem Matrix can be used for several IaaS usecases [19]. A portal like Pustak Portal can be implemented using the CloudSystem Matrix service catalog templates and self-service interfaces previously described. CloudSystem Matrix service templates are typically authored with a built-in graphic designer and then published into the catalog in an XML format. It is also possible to create the XML representations using other tools and import the templates using the CloudSystem Matrix APIs.

Template Design for Pustak Portal

As stated earlier, service template design is the first step in service setup using CloudSystem Matrix. Subsequently, the template can be used to instantiate the service [20]. The template design for the Pustak Portal is shown in Figure 2.17. The design uses a combination of virtual machines and physical servers to realize the service in order to leverage the flexibility conferred by virtualization. This is illustrated in Chapter 8 *Managing the Cloud* where scaling the service up or down is considered.

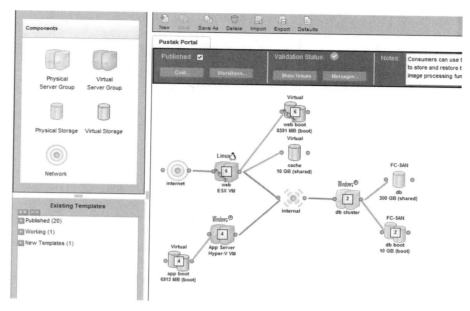

FIGURE 2.17

CloudSystem Matrix service template example.

The service is realized in a conventional three tier application. In the example template, the web tier is connected to the Internet and contains six ESX host VMs running a Linux operating system realized as a set of linked clones. These VMs share a file system used as a cache for frequently used web data. The web tier connects to a private service internal network that is used for communication between the web tier servers and the application and database servers. The App Server tier contains four HyperV VMs running windows, while the database tier contains two physical servers also running Windows. The physical server database cluster shares a 300GB Fibre Channel disk.

Resource Configuration

After template definition, it is necessary to configure the resources (server, storage, network) used in the service template. These attributes are set in the Service Template Designer Portal. As an example for a virtual server configuration (see Figure 2.18), it is possible to set:

- Cost Per Server used for charge back
- Initial and Maximum number of servers in the tier
- Option to deploy servers as linked clones
- Number of CPUs per VM

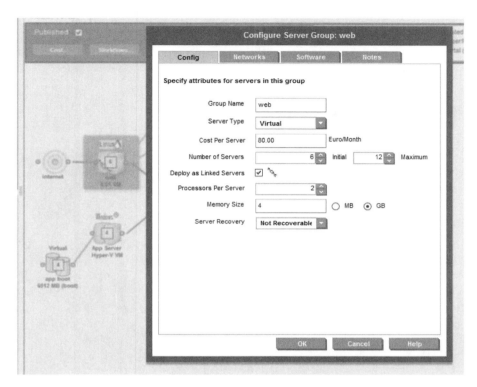

FIGURE 2.18

CloudSystem Matrix server configuration example.

- VM Memory size
- Server recovery automation choice

For the configuration of the physical servers there is an additional configuration parameter regarding processor architecture and minimum clock speed. The software tab in the designer allows configuration of software to be deployed to the virtual or physical server.

Similarly for disk configuration, Figure 2.19 shows an example of a Fibre Channel disk, with the following configuration parameters:

- Disk size
- Cost Per GB used for charge back
- Storage type
- RAID level
- Path redundancy
- Cluster sharing
- Storage service tags

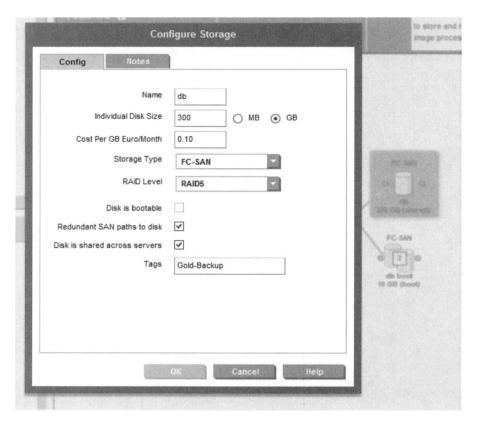

FIGURE 2.19

CloudSystem Matrix storage configuration example.

Storage service tags are used to specify the needs for storage security, backup, retention and availability requirements.

Network configuration allows the service network requirements to be specified including requirements regarding:

- Public or private
- Shared or exclusive use
- IPV4 or IPV6
- Hostname pattern
- Path redundancy
- IP address assignment policy (Static, DHCP or Auto-allocation)

For example, specifying a private, exclusive-use network would provide the servers a network isolated from other servers in the environment.

Pustak Portal Instantiation and Management

Once the Pustak Portal templates have been created, the self-service interface of CloudSystem Matrix can be used by consumers to perform various **lifecycle operations** on the cloud service. Lifecycle operations are major management operations, such as creation, destruction, and addition and removal of resources. More specific details of lifecycle operations as per DMTF reference architecture can be found in Chapter 10. Consumer lifecycle operations are available either from a browser-based console or via the published web service APIs. The browser-based console provides a convenient way for the consumer to view and access their services, browse the template catalog and create new services and delete existing ones, view the status and progress of the infrastructure requests they have initiated, examine their resource pool utilization, and view their resource consumption calendar.

The lifecycle operations include the ability to adjust the resources associated with a particular service. Referring back to Figure 2.18 as an example, the number of servers in the web tier was initially specified to be 6 servers, with 12 as maximum number of servers in the tier. From the self-service portal the consumer has the ability to request additional servers to be added, up to the maximum of 12 servers. The consumer also has the ability to quiesce and reactivate servers in a tier. For example, in a tier that has 6 provisioned servers, the consumer can request 3 servers be quiesced, which will cause those servers to be shut down and the associated server resource released. However, a quiesced server disk image and IP address allocation is retained, so that the subsequent re-activate operations can occur quickly, without requiring a server software re-provisioning operation.

In order to maintain service levels and contain costs, the owner can dynamically scale the resources in the environment to make sure that the service has just enough server and storage resources to meet the current demand, without the need to be pre-allocated and have a lot of idle resources. The service scaling can be performed depending on the number of concurrent users accessing the system. As stated previously, this can be done manually via the Consumer Portal. In Chapter 8, *Managing the Cloud*, there is a detailed description of how this can be accomplished automatically using the CloudSystem Matrix APIs.

Cells-as-a-Service[2]

This section describes a novel IaaS technology called **Cells-as-a-Service**, which is a research prototype from Hewlett-Packard Laboratories. The Cells-as-a-Service prototype (simply referred to as **Cells** for short) was built to support multi-tenanted services for complex services. In any complex realistic service, there are various components such as a ticketing service, billing service, logging service, etc. that may be required to be hosted on an infrastructure service. A unique feature of the Cells prototype is its ability to define templates for such complex

---

[2]Contributed by Dr. Badrinath Ramamurthy, Hewlett-Packard, India.

systems and enable easy deployment. Cells has been evolving, and currently supports many of the properties mentioned previously. As before, this section first introduces some simple concepts defined by the platform, explains the usage through a simple example and then describes the advanced features of the platform with Pustak Portal.

Introduction to Cells-as-a-Service

In order to understand what the Cells-as-a-Service platform enables, one needs to look at a cloud service from a different perspective. In any complex realistic service, there are various stakeholders and components, which are distinguished to clarify the exposition:

- **Cell** is an abstraction for a set of virtual machines interconnected to deliver a service.
- A **Service Template (ST)** is a template describing the infrastructure (including both software and hardware) that is required to realize a service. Since it is a template, various parameters, such as the number of servers needed, may not be specified.
- A **Service User (SU)** is the consumer of a service
- **Service Provider (SP):** The person who acquires the resources to host the service, and then configures and runs the service is a Service Provider (SP).
- **Compute Service Provider (CSP):** The entity from which the service provider acquires the resources by supplying the Service Template is called the Compute Service Provider (CSP).

A **Cell Specification (CS)** specifies the structure of a particular cell that implements a service. If a particular type of service is instantiated multiple times, it is useful to have an ST that describes the service, and then derive a CS from it as needed. In some cases, the SU and the SP are the same, as in the case of an individual renting some machines for running a computation. The Amazon EC2 and the CaaS prototype are examples of CSPs.

Example: Setting Up a Web Portal

To make the ideas from the previous section more concrete, consider a simplified situation where Cells is used to set up a web service for accessing HTML documents available on the node.

The Cells Portal is the primary entry point for a user. The first thing that the user (likely to be an SP) does is to request for a sign-on. Once the user fills out the requisite details and signs into his account he sees all the resources he has permissions to access. Among these resources are the Cells that the user has created.

For an example, let us assume he is a new customer and has no cells to his name. To start with, the user first creates a (empty) cell, and then populates it. The process of creation of a cell makes an **initial controller service**, specific to the cell, available to him. He can now interact with the cell controller to populate the cell. If the user already has a file containing the specification of a cell (more on that in a moment), he can use an option to simply submit the specification to the cell. Alternately, the specification may be graphically created using a drag and drop user interface to create the elements, their connectivity and specify the element properties.

The cell specification contains the details of all the (virtual) resources used by the cell. For instance, consider creating a cell with two nodes – one is a web server and the other runs a backend database for the web server. One way to specify this is to say that one wants two VMs – a WebVM and a DBVM on a private network (see Figure 2.20). Both have local disks. The WebVM has an additional interface to connect to the external world; and the DBVM has an additional large disk to store the data in the database. Figure 2.20 shows a schematic of this configuration.

Assume for simplicity that the two VMs' specialized OS images are provided as two different images already available to the user, just as a specification, and also that the IaaS console or portal provides a tool to author such a specification graphically (Figure 2.21). The user then just submits the specification, causing the service to deploy the required resources and *power on* the cell.

On the IaaS portal, the user will now see the cell being populated with elements specified in the specification and also virtual machines popping up to life along with the disks and the network elements. In a few seconds, the nodes are up and the user can now log in to the node that has the external facing network interface. By simply clicking on that node the user can see the externally resolvable name and routable IP address (see Figure 2.21).

The user can also log into the WebVM server and DBVM (via WebVM) and do any customizations on the server, as needed. The configured services become ready to use for the SUs as an application service end-point on the WebVM.

The power of template-based service deployment that Cells provides can be seen by contrasting this to the multiple configurations and scripts that are necessary in a typical IaaS system. These template specifications can also be shared and therefore are easy to replicate.

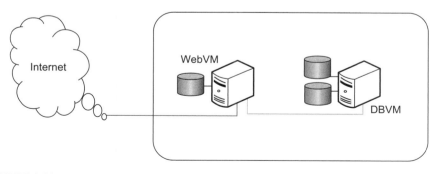

FIGURE 2.20

An example cell.

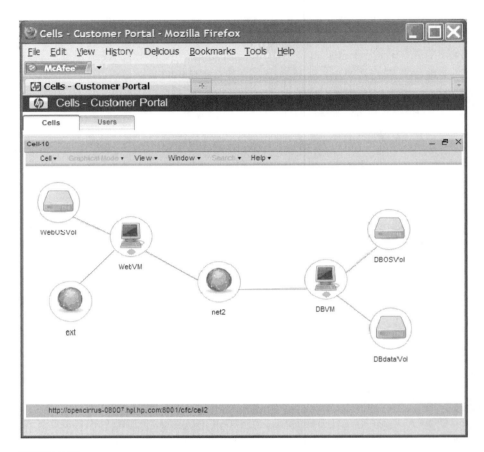

FIGURE 2.21

An example interface to the cell.

Cell Specification for the Example

As previously stated, the user submits a template specification to realize they require cell contents or infrastructure deployment. This section describes a sample specification to understand the platform better. The starting point is a skeleton of the specification for the cell schematically shown earlier in Figure 2.20.

In this example, the specification has an all-encompassing <cell> element that contains two network elements (XML node network), a storage volume (XML node volume) and a virtual machine (XML node vm). These three are the common basic resources in a cell. The network element specifies the name of the network and optionally one can specify what the subnet id should be. This subnet id is a resource and is only visible within the cell. Another cell can use the same subnet id but that will represent a different subnet, limited to that cell. In this example the two networks have subnet ids 2 and 15, representing the two networks on which the NICs of the node will sit.

For `volume`, there is a name associated with the volume and a URL describing the image location. The local volume `webVol` is initialized with the contents of the image specified by the resource `urn: sup: vol-0-1-27`. Independently, one should expect that the specified resource has already been made available to the controller with this resource name. Perhaps this is a volume either created by the same user or by someone else but made visible to this user. In the example this is the volume containing the OS and any other configuration data that will be the image on which the WebVM will run.

```
<?xml version="1.0" ?>
<cell>
- <network def="ext">
    <subnet>15</subnet>
</network>
- <network def="net2">
    <subnet>2</subnet>
</network>
- <volume def="webOSVol">
    <imageUrl>urn:sup:vol-0-1-27</imageUrl>
    <size>256</size>
</volume>
- <vm def="webVM">
    <vbd def="vbd0">
        <volUrl>sup:/webOSVol</volUrl>
    </vbd>
    <vif def="vif0">
        <netUrl>sup:/ext</netUrl>
        <external>true</external>
    </vif>
    <vif def="vif1">
        <netUrl>sup:/net2</netUrl>
    </vif>
</vm>
...
</cell>...
```

The last item in this skeleton is a virtual machine. This VM is for the WebVM of the example. The `VM` specification simply mentions that the VM's block device should be connected to the volume `webVol`, mentioned earlier, and that the two interface NICs `vif0` and `vif1` should be connected appropriately to the network elements mentioned earlier. Further, the specification on the interface qualifies the interface `vif0` to be externally routable.

Clearly, this only specifies part of the whole specification for the cell shown in Figure 2.20. The DBVM and its two volumes (for the OS and the database) would also need to be specified. The NIC on the DBVM would also connect to net2, allowing the two VMs to communicate. With the addition of these elements, the specification would be complete.

Note that only a few attributes, such as size of volumes and the external connectivity attribute for a network interface, have been shown. There are many more attributes that may be specified, such as the trailing part of the IP address of the individual interfaces, called the `host` part. The specification may also contain elaborate rules that describe which VMs in which cells may connect over the network. There are also rules that govern disk image sharing.

Multi-tenancy: Supporting Multiple Authors to Host Books

The previous section showed how a simple cell is created. This section contains a more elaborate example. This example also shows how a cell may be flexed-up by invocations from applications running in VMs within a cell.

Assume that Pustak Portal (a **service provider** or **SP**) is creating a service to give authors the ability to create portals for their books and provide a search service for anyone who wishes to search for terms in the author's portal. Thus the author's portal would contain the books written by the author. In addition, it must also contain an index which can be searched. The example describes how construction of this complex system would be automated using Cells.

Figure 2.22 illustrates the structure of the kind of cell that is needed. Assume that the service provider starts with a specification for a cell with two VMs. One is the **Controller Service VM (CVM)** that hosts the main service which is the interface to prospective authors; the second, the **Search Engine VM (SVM)** which hosts the service that has indexed content of author books and provides users a search service over the books' contents. This specification looks very much like the specification for the simple cell in the earlier example, but has one main difference – both VMs are in external facing as well as internal facing subnets. Thus, each of the VMs has two NICs. See Figure 2.22a.

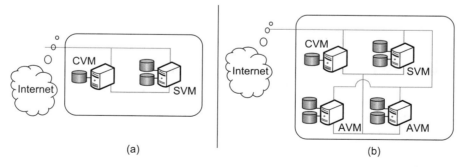

(a)   (b)

FIGURE 2.22

Author web site cell. Structure of the cell to support websites for each author.

The author acquires a web site by making a web request to the CVM via its portal. For the application in the CVM to make a request to the controller so that the request is honored, the application needs to hold an appropriate certificate – this is the certificate provided by Cells to the SP when creating the SP user. The result is that an **Author VM (AVM)** gets created on the backend and returns an **Author URL (AURL)** by which he can access his web site (which is inside the AVM). Among other information, the negotiation between the CVM portal and the author to create an author web site includes creating certificates to authenticate the author to the portal in the AVM. This is at the application level and is handled entirely by the logic of the application in the CVM. Any method may be used by the CVM service to establish identity with the service in the AVM. Figure 2.22(b) shows the cell after two AVMs have been added.

Now the author uses the AURL to do anything that the service allows. Among them will be the ability to upload the book content. Another feature will be the ability to contact the SVM and post a request to it to index its contents for any end user search. Also note that every author gets a new AVM – a nice complex use case that requires multi-tenancy at the infrastructure level that this platform handles very well. So, the cells architecture is not just an IaaS but enables customized cloud services to be built over it.

Note that all the logic to accept requests for a web portal from an author allows the author the facility to edit his web portal; the logic to access and index the books and other such features are logic embedded in the corresponding web services, which are already part of the OS image that those corresponding AVMs are created from.

The initial specification submitted to create the cell contains the CVM and AVM specifications along with the required subnets and volumes that are sketched in Figure 2.22(a). At some point in the web application logic of the CVM, a decision is taken to create an AVM. At this point it, the CVM, dynamically submits a specification to create an AVM from the corresponding image. The Cells architecture provides a way of updating a cell specification by submitting a specification change or a `delta` to the controller. The `delta` is a specification that specifies what has changed. This specification is shown in the following code segment.

```
<?xml version="1.0" ?>
<delta>
- <set>
    <path> volAVM02a </path>
    <spec>
       <volume>
          <imageUrl>urn:sup:vol-0-1-30</imageUrl>
          <size>250</size>
       </volume>
    <spec>
</set>
- <set>
    <path> volAVM02b </path>
```

```
    <spec>
        <volume>
        <imageUrl>urn:sup:vol-0-1-35</imageUrl>
        <size>1000</size>
        </volume>
    </spec>
</set>
- <set>
    <path> vmAVM02</path>
<set>
<vm>
    <vbd def="vbd0">
        <volUrl>sup:/volAVM02a</volUrl>
    </vbd>
    <vbd def="vbd2">
        <volUrl>sup:/volAVM02b</volUrl>
    </vbd>
    <vif def="vif0">
        <netUrl>sup:/net2</netUrl>
    </vif>
    <vif def="vif1">
        <netUrl>sup:/net15</netUrl>
        <external>true</external>
    </vif>
</vm>
</set>
</delta>
```

In this specification, a new VM has been added that has two disks (`volAVM02a` and `volAVM02b`). One volume will be used for the OS and the web service and the other to host the book and all other content for the portal. The AVM, like the CVM and SVM, has NICs on both the predefined internal and external subnets (`net2` and `net15`).

Isolation of Multiple Tenants

One can optimize the solution by enhancing the cell design (implementation of the backend) in several ways too. One option is to ensure that each AVM is not a new VM in the existing cell, but is a separate cell on its own. Rules can also be added to allow only communication between the SVM and the corresponding AVM. The advantage of this model is that since each VM is in a separate cell, if one AVM is compromised and becomes a rogue VM for some reason, it cannot affect the other AVMs by creating spurious traffic on any of the attached subnets. Then one can even give full root access to the VM itself to the author and let him enhance it in any further way he wishes. In this scenario, probably he will host a bunch of different applications unconstrained by what the default AVM provides.

Load Balancing the Author Web Site

Another interesting enhancement to the cell could be to allow load balancing. Consider the case where it is necessary to balance the load coming into an AVM. Among other things, load-balancing requires triggering the submission of a `delta` specification to the controller service to add an AVM, just as in the case of adding a new author VM. This design is explained in greater detail next.

Assume that the WebVM in Figure 2.20 is overloaded, perhaps because of all the processing it has to do. One of the advantages of using an IaaS is that the infrastructure may be dynamically flexed to meet performance requirements. To do this one may modify the infrastructure to look as described in Figure 2.23.

Here the load is arriving into the system at the node **LBVM** that is a load-balancer. The load-balancer then forwards the request to one of two WebVMs as shown in the figure. The reverse proxy facility as provided in, for example, the Apache web server supports this. In a simple case, the load-balancer does a round robin forwarding of requests. Further, when the load at all servers reaches a point that the SLA drops, the logic may submit a request to the underlying cell to bring up a new node running a WebVM to forward the requests to. In order to do this the LB needs to submit a delta request to add a server. One can write out the delta specification by looking at the delta specification in the previous section.

Note that application level logic is needed to reconfigure the LB so that it recognizes that the new node is a valid target for forwarded traffic. It is possible to use a similar delta to specify the removal of a WebVM in case the load is low

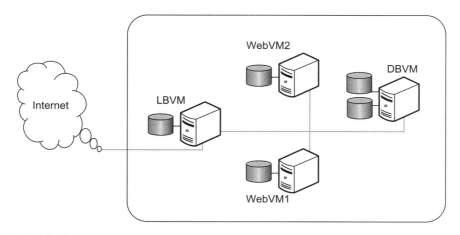

FIGURE 2.23

A load-balancing configuration.

enough that it can be handled by one fewer WebVM. In that case, the delta for deleting the identified node and its volume is shown here:

```
<delta>
<set>
    <path> WebVM2 </path>
    <spec> </spec>
</set>
<set>
    <path> WebOSVol2 </path>
    <spec> </spec>
</set>
</delta>
```

Another popular way to flex scale-out the web service is to add a WebVM and then use infrastructure using DNS-based load balancing. Details of how the DNS server responds to requests and balances loads is beyond the scope of this description and can be found in *DNS Name Server Load Balancing* [21].

In some cases it is the data service that is the bottle neck and not the web server. One way to address this is to have data that is distributed across nodes, as in the case of a distributed hash table or a distributed column store. In this case, there is no separate DB server. The LB makes a decision on where to forward the request depending on the data being requested. When a node is created by flexing up, the LB additionally needs to redistribute data so that the new node is also used. Consistent hashing techniques may be used to minimize the amount of data movement.

With that design, infrastructure service provides the core ability to flex the infrastructure. If this is coupled with the right application logic to restart application instances and allows some configuration and possibly data movement to actually distribute the load, then it makes a highly scalable Pustak Portal built almost as a platform to enable authors to host their book web sites.

In summary, the Cells technology and research lays a strong emphasis on simplicity of interface and modularity of design to build a reliable, scalable implementation of Infrastructure as a Service. Note the interesting fact that all the operations on the cell can be done just by posting appropriate specifications to modify the resources within a cell. The whole process is simply specification driven. While this section focused on providing a user perspective of the Cells prototype, the reader may wish to look at associated HP Labs Technical Reports [22, 23, 24] to get an idea of some internal workings of the networking and storage aspects.

SUMMARY

As detailed in this chapter, the IaaS cloud computing model offers virtual computing resources (servers, storage and networking) as a service. The advantage of this model is the flexibility it offers in allowing customers to create any desired computing environment by installing software of their choice. The disadvantage of this model compared to PaaS and SaaS models is that the burden of upgrading (in general, managing) the software falls upon the user. Since the IaaS model offers virtual computing resources that mimic a physical data center, the techniques used to upgrade software in a traditional data center can be used.

The IaaS services discussed in this chapter have two major functionalities: service creation, and service management. Important functions in service management include load balancing, failover, and monitoring and metering. Service creation in Amazon EC2 can be done using the AWS console for simple use cases. For more complex configurations involving S3 and EBS, one can use programming or scripting methods to set up the infrastructure needed. Service creation in HP Cloud-System Matrix is a two-step process. First, the service can be defined via the Service Catalog, Service Template Designer Portal and the Workflow Designer Portal These definitions are then saved in XML format in the Service Catalog, where they can be used for instantiating the service. The next step after service definition in CloudSystem Matrix is service instantiation. Similar to Amazon EC2, the Consumer Portal can be used by a naïve user to select an existing service template (say, 3-tier architecture) and instantiate it using resources from a resource pool. This console-based usage can be used to build or replicate complex infrastructures and is not just limited to simple templates.

In Amazon EC2, service definition is accomplished through the AMI definition, which includes specification of the software and hardware needed for the server. EC2 offers a wide variety of standardized computing environments (e.g., Windows, Linux, Solaris, Ruby on Rails), as well as a number of popular software packages (e.g., Hadoop, Apache, and DB2). This software environment can be customized, either by installing additional software on the EC2 virtual systems, or by importing a virtualized VMWare server image from the customer's servers as a custom AMI. The AMI also specifies additional EBS virtual disks needed. Following this, the AMI can be instantiated on servers of pre-specified size (e.g., small). After the AMI is instantiated, the software on the AMI can be configured (if needed) manually or using scripts.

In addition to the AMI, EC2 also allows storage (via S3 files, SimpleDB – a key-value store, or RDB – a relational database) to be associated with EC2 instances. Networking allows the creation of two types of addresses: private addresses for communication with EC2, and public IP addresses for external communication. Additionally, hybrid clouds can be created using EC2's Virtual Private Clouds, which creates a VPN that encompasses resources from an enterprise data center as well as EC2.

Since Amazon EC2 is a public cloud, it supports the notion of regions, which are specific geographic locations from which the needed computing resources can be drawn. This is for the purpose of performance or satisfying legal requirements. In CloudSystem Matrix as well it is possible to partition the resource pool into geographic regions, and specify allocation from specific regions.

Service management is the other important factor in IaaS offerings. Load balancing and failover is an important feature of service management. In EC2, load balancing and scaling can be accomplished by Elastic Beanstalk [16] and the Elastic Load Balancing service, which will distribute incoming requests over multiple servers. The load balancers also support the notion of a session, which may be application-defined. Load balancing and scaling in CloudSystem Matrix is accomplished through APIs, as described later in Chapter 8, titled *Managing the Cloud*.

Finally, the Cells architecture is a very interesting piece of research, which enables very easy creation of complex infrastructure – using just a simple XML specification that can be authored on a graphical user interface as well. This approach enables one to create a complex infrastructure and share and replicate the same as another instance. The example also described how one can even use the platform to host multi-tenanted service providers using the Pustak portal. This is a promising research in the right direction of enabling simplified deployment and management of cloud infrastructure.

Storage as a Service acts as an important complementary functionality by providing highly available and reliable persistent storage. Multiple services from Amazon Web Services were studied, and those provided diverse interfaces – block device interface (EBS), database interface(RDS), key-value stores (SimpleDB) or simple file system (S3) interface. These and other storage platform services are studied in the section describing storage aspects of PaaS in Chapter 3. Additional background concepts to enable efficient use of cloud storage are available in Chapters 5 and 6.

IaaS models allow virtual resources in the cloud to be provisioned for enterprise applications. These can, if desired, be an extension of the enterprise data center leading to a hybrid cloud model. The IaaS model, therefore, is suitable for enterprises that consider the cloud to be a natural extension of their data centers. More in-depth discussion on how one can use the IaaS platforms to address the scalability, availability and other technical challenges of the cloud can be found in Chapter 6.

References

[1] Amazon Simple Storage Service (Amazon S3), http://aws.amazon.com/s3 [accessed 16.10.11].

[2] s3cmd: command line S3 client, http://s3tools.org/s3cmd [accessed 10.11].

[3] Standalone Windows .EXE command line utility for Amazon S3 & EC2, http://s3.codeplex.com/ [accessed 10.11].

[4] API Support for Multipart Upload, http://docs.amazonwebservices.com/AmazonS3/latest/dev/index.html?uploadobjusingmpu.html [accessed 01.11].

[5] Amazon Elastic Compute Cloud User Guide, http://docs.amazonwebservices.com/AWSEC2/latest/UserGuide/ [accessed 10.11].

[6] Amazon Elastic Compute Cloud Command Line Reference, http://docs.amazonweb services.com/AWSEC2/latest/CommandLineReference/ [accessed 01.11].

[7] Amazon EC2 API Tools, http://aws.amazon.com/developertools/351?_encoding= UTF8&jiveRedirect=1 [accessed 10.11].

[8] EC2 Introduction, http://aws.amazon.com/ec2/ [accessed 10.11].

[9] EC2 FAQs, http://aws.amazon.com/ec2/faqs/ [accessed 10.11].

[10] Elastic Load Balancing, http://aws.amazon.com/elasticloadbalancing/ [accessed 10.11].

[11] Amazon Virtual Private Cloud, http://aws.amazon.com/vpc/ [accessed 10.11].

[12] AWS Security Best Practices, http://awsmedia.s3.amazonaws.com/pdf/AWS_Security_ Whitepaper.pdf; 2011 [accessed 10.11].

[13] Fernandes R. Creating DMZ configurations on Amazon EC2, http://tripoverit.blogspot. com/2011/03/creating-dmz-configurations-on-amazon.html [accessed 10.11].

[14] Ruby Programming Language, http://www.ruby-lang.org/en/ [accessed 10.11].

[15] http://docs.amazonwebservices.com/AmazonS3/latest/API/ [accessed 10.11].

[16] AWS Elastic Beanstalk, http://aws.amazon.com/elasticbeanstalk [accessed 10.11].

[17] Amazon Machine Images (AMIs): Amazon Web Services, *Amazon Web Services*, http://aws.amazon.com/amis [accessed 10.11].

[18] HP CloudSystem Matrix, http://www.hp.com/go/matrix [accessed 10.11].

[19] Server and Infrastructure Software - UseCases, http://www.hp.com/go/matrixdemos [accessed 10.11].

[20] HP Cloud Maps, http://www.hp.com/go/cloudmaps [accessed 10.11].

[21] DNS Name Server Load Balancing, http://www.tcpipguide.com/free/t_DNSName ServerLoadBalancing.htm [accessed 10.11].

[22] Cabuk S, Dalton CI, Edwards A, Fischer A. A Comparative Study on Secure Network Virtualization, HP Laboratories Technical Report, HPL-2008-57, May 21, 2008.

[23] Edwards A, Fischer A, Lain A. Diverter: a new approach to networking within virtualized infrastructures. In: Proceedings of the first ACM workshop on research on enterprise networking, WREN '09, 2009. p. 103–10.

[24] Coles A, Edwards A. Rapid Node Reallocation Between Virtual Clusters for Data Intensive Utility Computing. IEEE International Conference on Cluster Computing 2006.

Platform as a Service

INFORMATION IN THIS CHAPTER:

- Windows Azure
- Google App Engine
- Platform as a Service: Storage Aspects
- Mashups

INTRODUCTION

The previous chapter provided a description of Infrastructure as a Service (IaaS), the first model of cloud computing that provides hardware resources on demand by offering reliable compute and storage resources as a cloud service. This chapter looks at **Platform as a Service (PaaS)**, the second model of cloud delivery. This model provides a platform on which users can directly develop and deploy their applications without worrying about the complexity of setting up the hardware or system software. PaaS systems usually support the complete life cycle of an application – starting from helping in application design, PAPIs for application development, supporting the build and test environment as well as providing the application deployment infrastructure on cloud. Additional features during application execution for persistent data usage, state management, session management, versioning and application debugging are also provided by certain PaaS solutions.

IaaS offerings provide only raw computing power, and customers purchase instances of virtual machines, install the requisite software, and host their applications on them. In contrast, PaaS offerings provide completely managed platforms for applications hosted on the cloud. PaaS customers manage **instances of applications** – specifying the details of instances of the application required and the cloud service will guarantee that the instances will be created and maintained without user intervention. For example, a PaaS solution will ensure the availability of the application despite downtime of the underlying virtual machine by automatically creating a new instance of the application on a new virtual machine when the machine goes down. In order to facilitate automated application management, PaaS solutions provide a more restricted environment than IaaS for its customers, with fewer choices for operating systems and programming environments. However, it clearly results in lesser management burden on the customer.

PaaS systems can be used to host a variety of cloud services. They can be used by online portal-based applications like Facebook that need to scale to thousands of users. They can be used by a startup that wants to host their new application in a Software-as-a-Service model without any upfront cost for hardware or system software, as well as benefit from the flexibility in scaling to a large number of users. PaaS systems can also be used for massively parallel computations typically found in High Performance Computing applications and Internet-scale file hosting services. In addition, enterprises can deploy their Line-of-Business applications in the cloud, taking advantage of the scale and availability while still maintaining security and privacy of data.

This section takes a deeper look at a few popular PaaS systems, namely Windows Azure Platform from Microsoft and Yahoo! Pipes, for developing mashup applications, and Hadoop, an Internet-scale **big data** platform. A separate section in this chapter deals with the storage aspects of Platform as a Service, specifically detailing a few cloud services from IBM that provide data-oriented platform services (pureXML and Data Studio) as case studies. As in earlier chapters, the application developer perspective of PaaS is described first, so as to provide a quick guide to get the developer started on the platform. Next, the chapter describes the underlying technology of PaaS systems and the components that make up the platform to enable the developer to create efficient applications by leveraging the more advanced features of the PaaS solution. The reader is encouraged to study Chapter 5 to get some deeper insights into application design and development for the Cloud, by introducing new paradigms of application design that is best suited for Cloud platforms.

WINDOWS AZURE[1]

The **Azure Services Platform** is a popular application platform for the cloud that allows Windows applications and web-services to be hosted and run in Microsoft datacenters. A simplistic view of Azure can be as a cloud deployment platform for applications developed for Windows using .NET. While Azure is primarily designed for PaaS capabilities, it also includes certain features for **Data-as-a-Service** (**DaaS**) and Infrastructure-as-a-Service (IaaS). However, this section focuses primarily on the PaaS features of the platform and gives only a high-level overview of the DaaS and IaaS features of Azure.

The rest of the section is organized as follows: First, a simple "Hello World" example that shows how to get started with Windows Azure is presented. Next, the example is made slightly more complex by showing how to pass messages between two of the application components – one of the primary ways of integrating components in Azure. The second example is also used to illustrate how to test and debug under Azure. This is followed by an overview of the basic and advanced features of Windows Azure, such as Azure storage, queues, tables and, security.

---

[1]Contributed by Mr. Gopal Srinivasa from Microsoft Research, India.

The examples and screenshots in this section are based on version 1.2 of the Windows Azure SDK. They may differ slightly for newer versions, whose documentation can be found on the Microsoft web site [1]. For decision makers contemplating the move to Windows Azure, the web site also provides a *Guide for Decision Makers* and a TCO calculator that can be used as a pricing guide. The business end of Windows Azure is presented in *The Business of Windows Azure Pricing* [2]. The portal and the PDC site also provide white papers and talks from customers on their experiences moving applications to the cloud.

A "Hello World" Example

The usage of the Windows Azure service is best demonstrated with a simple example. This example shows how to develop a Web application that displays a custom homepage, accepts the visitor's name, and welcomes him/her. To simplify the development of this application, Visual Studio templates included in the freely downloadable [3] Visual Studio Web Developer 2010 Express edition are used.

The first step is to download and install development tools required to develop Azure applications. At the time of this writing, the Windows Azure SDK with all required software was available for download free of cost from http://www.microsoft .com/windowsazure/learn/get-started/?campaign=getstarted.

Like any other cloud-hosted application, Windows Azure applications typically have multiple instances running on different virtual machines. However, developers need not create nor manage these virtual machines explicitly. Instead, developers just write applications either as a **Web role** and/or **Worker role**, and tell Windows Azure the number of instances of each role that should be created. Windows Azure silently creates the requisite number of virtual machines, and hosts instances of the roles on them. The two roles supported by Azure depict the common types of applications that are hosted on .NET systems. The **Web role** mirrors Web applications that are hosted on IIS servers and provide external interactivity while the **Worker role** mirrors the heavy-duty processing that is typically done by Windows services and applications. These roles are described in more detail in a subsequent section. A typical Azure application consists of multiple components (Web and Worker roles) that exchange messages and that forms a fundamental design paradigm used in Azure.

The first step in developing an application is to create a Visual Web Developer cloud project. For this, the "File" menu on Visual Studio is used to select "New project", and then the option "Cloud" is selected in the left pane with the option of "Windows Azure Cloud Service." Figure 3.1 shows a screenshot of this process. On clicking "OK" in the dialog box, the developer is presented with another dialog that offers the choice of roles (Web and Worker roles briefly described above). For this example, one Web role and one Worker role will be selected as shown in Figure 3.2.

Note that the number of roles selected here is independent of the number of **instances** of the roles that can be created on the cloud. Windows Azure will allow

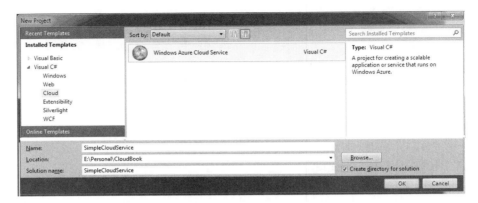

FIGURE 3.1

Creating a new Cloud project in Azure Visual Studio.

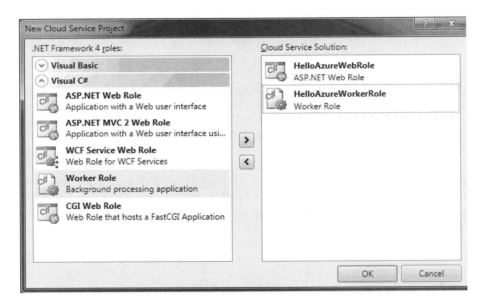

FIGURE 3.2

Choosing Web and Worker roles.

creation of multiple instances of any role that is to be deployed on the cloud. However, at the time of this writing, a single application could only have a maximum of 25 roles defined.

After the roles are selected, Visual Studio automatically creates two projects for developing each role. Additionally, a **Visual Studio Cloud Service Solution** is created for the two Azure roles, as seen in the Figure 3.2. A Visual Studio Solution is a collection of related projects grouped as logical entities. The Web role is essentially an ASP.NET web application, with additional features for cloud-based deployment. The Worker role is a simple C# program. While for this example C# will be used as the programming language, software development kits for Java and Php are available at http://www.windowsazure4j.org/ [4] and http://phpazure.codeplex.com/ [5], respectively. Additionally, VisualBasic and IronRuby can be used. A full list of supported programming languages can be found in [6].

The next step is to modify the "Default.aspx" page to add a custom message as shown in Figure 3.3. It is now possible to build the solution to create a simple Azure application which consists of two files – a **service package** (*.cspkg) that contains the binaries, and a **service configuration** (*.cscfg) that is used to configure the application. One can test this application through Visual Studio by using the "F5" key which brings up the web site, which at this point just shows a welcome message. The first Azure application is ready! Additional simple examples can be found in many books and sites [7].

Example: Passing a Message

In a cloud environment, message passing between components is a basic functionality, since cloud applications are built from simpler components that communicate with each other via messages. The following section shows how messages can be passed from one component to another. For this example, the Web role will prompt the user for his/her name and pass that to the Worker role and print back the result got from the Web role. For this, first some additional markup is introduced in the default ASPX page to add a simple submit button with an input text box and some additional labels, as shown in the following snippet.

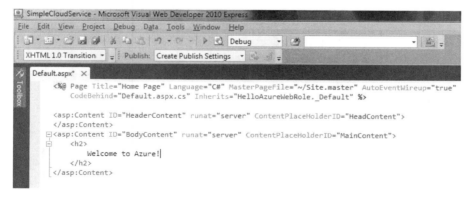

FIGURE 3.3

Modifying the default page to write a custom message.

```
<asp:Label ID="MsgLabel" runat="server"> Enter your name and click
submit. </asp:Label>
<br />
<asp:TextBox ID="NameTextBox" runat="server" > </asp:TextBox>
<asp:Button ID="Button1" runat="server" CausesValidation="true" Text =
"Submit" OnClick="OnSubmitBtnClick" />
<br />
<asp:Label ID="ResponseLabel" runat="server"> </asp:Label>
```

The input string from the default page is transmitted from the Web role to the Worker role and in return, the worker sends back a string (may be the current time). For this, the handler OnSubmitBtnClick for the "Submit" button needs to pass the input string as a message to the Worker role. To enable this communication between the Web role and Worker role, it is necessary to use the message-passing features of Azure. Message passing on the Azure cloud can be done through queues that form part of Azure storage. Other different types of Azure storage are described in subsequent sections. Here, the example code will describe simple usage of some APIs for managing queues. Following is an implementation of the OnSubmitBtnClick method.

```
protected void OnSubmitBtnClick(object sender, EventArgs e)
{
    //Select the storage account to use. Account information is specified
    in the
    //service configuration file, as a key-value pair. Default behavior is to
    //use the dev store
    CloudStorageAccount account = CloudStorageAccount.
    FromConfigurationSetting("AzureStorageConnectionString");
    //Now we create a client that can operate queues on the account.
    CloudQueueClient client = account.CreateCloudQueueClient();
```

To use the message-passing APIs, it is necessary to create a **storage account object**, and that is specified in the configuration file with the key AzureStorageConnectionString. Among other things, the application configuration file stores such settings used by the program in the form of key-value pairs. The value associated with the above key is used as the storage account connection string. During development, this value can be set to use development storage to facilitate tracing/debugging of the program. In production, this should be set to the storage account of the developer.

Next, it is necessary to get a reference to the queue to transmit messages to the worker. This is needed for the two-way communication between the Worker role and Web role introduced for this example. For this, two queues are used, the first one named webtoworker and the second named workertoweb. This is accomplished by the GetQueueReference method, which returns a reference to the queue. The CreateIfNotExist() function is used to create the queue when the code is executed for the first time. Attempting to access a queue without creating it will throw an exception.

```
//We request access to a particular named queue. The name of the queue
//must be the same at both the web role and the worker role.
//container name must be lowercase!
webToWorkerQueue = queueClient.GetQueueReference("webtoworker");
//Create the queue if it does not exist.
webToWorkerQueue.CreateIfNotExist();
workerToWebQueue = queueClient.GetQueueReference("workertoweb");
workerToWebQueue.CreateIfNotExist();
```

It is now possible to add a message to the queue for the Worker role – simply send the string typed by the user as the message to the Worker role. This message is added to the `webtoworker` queue as shown in the following code snippet. Messages can be objects of any serializable type.

```
webToWorkerQueue.AddMessage(new
CloudQueueMessage(this.NameTextBox.Text));
```

The sent message will now reach the Worker role. To process the response from the worker, it is necessary to listen to the messages on the `workertoweb` queue. The following code snippet demonstrates the process. The code loops while checking the queue for an available message. As the name suggests, the `PeekMessage()` method checks if a queue has an unprocessed message. If such a message exists, it returns the message, otherwise it returns null. The loop breaks once the worker has written a message into the `workertoweb` queue.[2]

```
//Wait for a response from the worker
while ((response = workerToWebQueue.PeekMessage()) == null)
    ;
//There is a message. Get it.
response = responseQueue.GetMessage();
if (response != null) {
    //Show the response to the user
    ResultLabel.Text = response.AsString;
    //Always delete the message after processing
    //so that it is not processed again.
    responseQueue.DeleteMessage(response);
}
```

The reply from the queue is obtained by using the `GetMessage()` function. There are two differences between the `GetMessage()` and `PeekMessage()` functions:

i. the former is a blocking function that blocks if the queue is empty, while the latter is a non-blocking function

---

[2]Version 1.5 of the Windows Azure SDK has introduced many additional features to message handling.

ii. the `GetMessage()` function marks the messages as invisible to other roles accessing the queue, which is similar to obtaining an exclusive lock on the message for a particular time period, while the `PeekMessage()` does not.

Once the message is retrieved, we delete the message from the queue, so that the same message is not processed twice, and show the reply to the user by setting the `ResultLabel` field to the text returned by the Worker role. Note that we can use the `AsString` function because we know that our messages are strings. For other, custom data types, we would have to invoke the `AsByte` property, which returns a serialized representation of the message, and deserialize the bytes returned into the object. Of course, for real-world applications, it is better to use AJAX or an ASP.NET `UpdatePanel` to poll for arrived messages instead of waiting indefinitely as the previous example does. That would give a better user experience as the backend request to the Worker role will not block.

NOTE

.NET terminology used

- **Property:** A property is a member, usually with public access, that provides a flexible mechanism to read, write, or compute the value of a private field of a class.
- **Serialization:** Process of converting an object into a string or binary form for transmission over a network or to save to disk. The reverse process of creating an object from such a saved copy is de-serialization.

Now, the Worker role in the example is studied in detail. The Worker role has to monitor the incoming message queue for new messages, and when it gets a message, it has to respond back with a message, say, the server time. So, in the example, the worker appends the server time to the received message, and adds it to the outgoing queue.

Recall that Visual Studio has already generated a template Worker role. This template has two public methods: `OnStart` and `Run`. The `OnStart()` method is invoked by the runtime when an instance of the Worker role is started. This is for one-time startup activity, such as creation of the two message queues. The `Run()` method is also invoked once and it does the processing for the Worker role. Please note that the `Run()` method should never return – the Azure agent detects if the role terminates (be it with an exception or regular function return) and starts a new instance of the Worker role. This feature of the Azure agent ensures availability of the application and minimal downtime of the cloud-hosted application.

The `Run()` method for the example is as follows:

```
Trace.WriteLine("HelloAzureWorkerRole entry point called",
"Information");
while (true) {     //Get the next message from the incoming queue
   CloudQueueMessage message =
webToWorkerQueue.GetMessage();
if (message != null) {
```

```
//Say, the message is the username. Other fields in the message
//like ID help map responses to requests.
string userName = message.AsString;
Trace.WriteLine("Got message with user: " + userName + " id: " +
message.Id, "Information");
//Create the response to the web-role.
CloudQueueMessage messageToSend = new CloudQueueMessage("Hello, " +
userName + ". The server time is: " + DateTime.Now.ToString());
//Send the message to the web role.
workerToWebQueue.AddMessage(messageToSend);
Trace.WriteLine("Sent message: " + messageToSend.AsString + " with
id: " + messageToSend.Id, "Information");
//delete the message that we are going to process. This prevents other
workers from processing the message.
webToWorkerQueue.DeleteMessage(message);
}
```

The infinite while loop to get the message is typical of all Worker roles, indicating that the function should never terminate. Unlike the Web role, the Worker role directly calls the GetMessage() function to look for new messages. The Worker role can block because it does nothing until it gets a message. The remaining code is similar to that of the Web role. The worker reads requests from the webtoworker queue, creates a string with the server time and adds it to the workertoweb queue to send to the Web role.

This concludes the walkthrough of most of the example code for both Worker and Web roles.

One additional step is required – a ConfigurationSettingPublisher must be set for both the Web role and Worker role so that the correct configuration files are read. The following lines of code are added to the Application_Start function (which is the event handler that is invoked when an ASP.NET application is started by the web server). This function is present in the Global.asax.cs file (which is an auto generated file that contains global declarations in an ASP.NET project) in the Web role project, and to the OnStart() function in the WorkerRole.cs file in the Worker role project.

```
CloudStorageAccount.SetConfigurationSettingPublisher((configName,
configSetter) =>
{
    string connectionString;
    if (RoleEnvironment.IsAvailable) {
        connectionString = RoleEnvironment.
        GetConfigurationSettingValue(configName);
    }else {
        connectionString = ConfigurationManager.AppSettings[configName];
    }
    configSetter(connectionString);
});
```

Azure Test and Deployment

The application developed in the previous example will be used for demonstrating testing and debugging features of Azure. When the cloud service is started in debug mode, Visual Studio brings up the window shown in Figure 3.4. The left pane shows the result of the program (Web role) and the right pane shows the source code of the application. One can add breakpoints, step through the code, and watch variables just as is done in a regular Visual Studio project. Please note that Visual Studio must be started in administrator mode to debug cloud applications. The application is now running on the local machine on top of a Windows Azure emulator known as the **development fabric**. The development fabric provides the functionality of Windows Azure on the local machine so that users can debug the logic of their services in the familiar environment provided by Visual Studio.

The final result of the application is shown in Figure 3.5, where the Web role received an input string from the user, sent that to the Worker role, and then received back a server timestamp to display to the user.

One can also view the message queues and trace statements for both Web role and Worker role. For this, the development fabric view shown in Figure 3.6 is used. One can select a role on the left pane and see the messages and trace output for the selected role on the right pane. A more detailed description about the development fabric from a technical standpoint is in the next section.

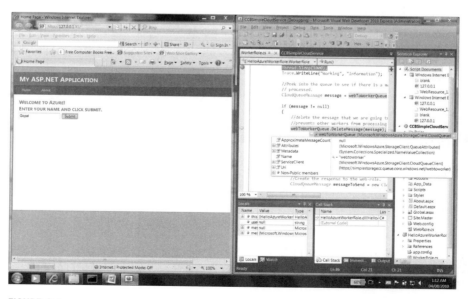

FIGURE 3.4

Side-by-side windows showing live debugging of an Azure application.

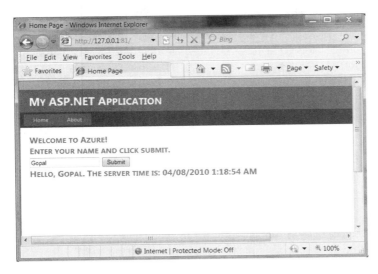

FIGURE 3.5

The output of the sample Azure application.

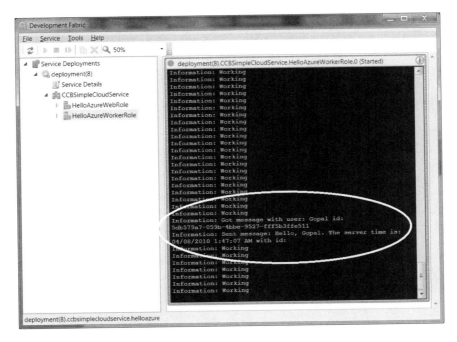

FIGURE 3.6

Trace messages of the Worker role shown in the development fabric UI.

Deploying Azure applications: So far, the development and testing of the new application happened on the local machine. The same now needs to be deployed on the cloud. For this, one needs to obtain an **Azure subscription** from the Microsoft Online Customer Portal [8]. The process of obtaining the subscription is documented on Microsoft Technet [9].

Once a subscription is created, a developer login is available to the Windows Azure developer portal at http://windows.azure.com, where the developer can create a new project. Figure 3.7 shows the Azure portal page with the project added.

Once a subscription has been obtained in the developer portal, the next step is to create a **hosted service** and a **storage account** for the new application. The hosted service creates the end points for accessing the application. The unique service URL that is selected here will be used by clients to access the application. Similarly, the storage account exposes the endpoints for accessing cloud storage for the application. Figure 3.8 depicts the creation of the hosted service and the unique URL chosen here is `simpleazureservicecc`. This implies that the web page will be available to users at http://simpleazureservicecc.cloudapp.net. For this example, the application and storage are assumed to be hosted in the US region – other options for geo-distribution are Europe or Asia Pacific. Different regions have different cost implications and the details of the different costs are available on the Azure pricing web-page.

Windows Azure allows us to request that multiple roles of an application and the shared data be deployed in an efficient manner to get good performance. This is done through **affinity groups** – applications and data that work together can be placed in an affinity group so that they are hosted in the same region. For this

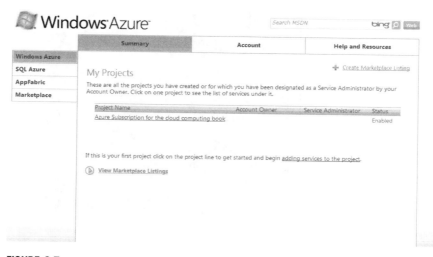

FIGURE 3.7

Login page of the developer portal.

FIGURE 3.8

Creating a hosted service.

example application, the default values for the affinity group will be used. Clicking on the "Create" button creates a placeholder service using the settings provided.

Since the example application uses message queues for communication, a storage account is also created on the portal. Figure 3.9 shows the portal after the storage account is created. Three endpoints have been defined for the storage account for different types of storage that one can use in Azure, namely **blobs**, **tables**, and **queues**. The example uses queues. Other models will be examined in the next section. Similar to a hosted service, the name of the storage account forms part of each endpoint and defines the highest level namespace for them.

There are two access keys that are generated – either key can be used to obtain access to the storage endpoints. Microsoft recommends that the keys be changed regularly to avoid the pitfalls of a leaked key. The observant reader will notice the term affinity groups in the screenshot and this is similar to the case of the hosted service, to provide geographic proximity to data and applications. Windows Azure also offers the option of enabling a **content delivery network** (**CDN**) for the data – this allows applications to serve data from locations that are closest to the end user. At the time of writing there were 18 data-centers around the world that are part of the Azure CDN. Since the example content consists of only the messages transmitted between the Web and Worker roles, this option will not be selected.

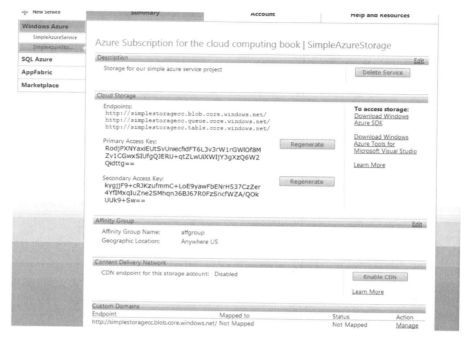

FIGURE 3.9

Storage portal information.

After creating a storage account, the configuration should be modified to use the cloud storage for messages. This is accomplished by modifying the `AzureStorageConnectionString` configuration parameter in the service configuration (`.cscfg`) file to use cloud storage for application data. Recall that this parameter was initially configured to use development storage; the new setting is:

```
"DefaultEndpointsProtocol=[http|https];
AccountName=<storage_account_name>;
AccountKey=<key>".
```

The application is now rebuilt. Figure 3.10 shows the development fabric view with the application accessing cloud storage instead of the development storage. The example is almost complete. In order to host the Web and Worker roles on the cloud, it is necessary to create a package by using the "Publish" context menu, shown in Figure 3.11. Choose the "Create Service Package" option to create the application's service package (`.cspkg`) file.

Next, we return to the home page of the hosted service shown in Figure 3.12. The page shows two deployment environments – **production** and **staging**. Both environments host the application on the cloud, but the staging environment creates

FIGURE 3.10

Development fabric running on cloud storage.

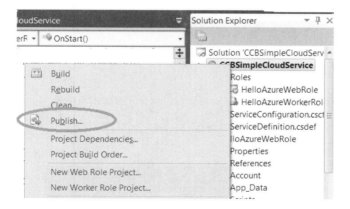

FIGURE 3.11

Publish menu.

the deployment with a temporary URL as the end point, while the production deployment uses the service URL.

Applications can be moved from production to staging and vice-versa at any time. First, the application will be deployed in the staging environment, as shown in Figure 3.13. Green bars next to the Web and Worker roles indicate that they

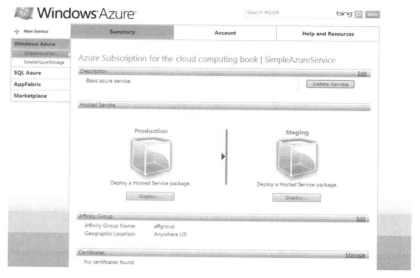

FIGURE 3.12

Home page of the hosted service portal.

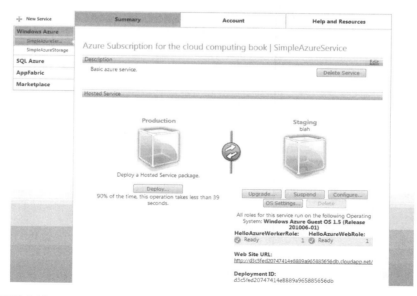

FIGURE 3.13

HelloAzure application after upload to the staging environment.

are executing. The staging application is hosted on a temporary URL, one that is nearly impossible to discover accidentally. This allows developers to deploy their applications on the cloud and test them before making them publicly available.

> **NOTE**
>
> **CPU Time Billing**
>
> Windows Azure starts billing for CPU time when applications are deployed in the staging environment and continues billing when applications (either in staging or production) are suspended. Applications must be deleted from the portal for billing to stop.

Finally, the deployment switch icon is selected to move the service into production. The application is now available on http://simpleazureservicecc.cloudapp.net. If more instances of the Web or the Worker role are needed, the service configuration from the configuration page in the portal can be modified. The configuration is an XML file which is similar to the one shown here:

```
<ServiceConfiguration serviceName="CCBSimpleCloudService"/>
  <Role name="HelloAzureWebRole">
    <Instances count="1" />
    <ConfigurationSettings>
    </ConfigurationSettings>
  </Role>
  <Role name="HelloAzureWorkerRole">
    <Instances count="1" />
    <ConfigurationSettings>
    </ConfigurationSettings>
  </Role>
</ServiceConfiguration>
```

The `Instances` node specifies the number of instances of each role. This can be set to higher values if more instances of either role are required. A method called `RoleEnvironmentChanging` is the handler that is invoked in the Web or Worker role whenever its settings are modified. The source code for this handler is automatically generated by Visual Studio, but can be modified to perform custom actions when the role settings are changed. Recall that this handler was added to the `OnStart()` and `Application_Start()` methods earlier.

The service configuration file can also be used to set the size of the VM to be used to run the role. Table 3.1 shows the sizes that were available at the time of writing this book. Additionally, each storage account can have a maximum of 100TB of storage on the cloud, and overall, the Azure storage system is designed to provide a bandwidth of 3GB/s, servicing 5000 requests per second for a single storage account. These are current numbers and are subject to change in the future.

To summarize, the following were the steps needed to build an Azure application. First the Web and Worker roles for the new application were created and

Table 3.1 VM Sizes Offered by Windows Azure

Compute Instance Size	CPU	Memory	Instance Storage	I/O Performance	Cost Per Hour
Extra Small	1.0 GHz	768 MB	20 GB	Low	$0.05
Small	1.6 GHz	1.75 GB	225 GB	Moderate	$0.12
Medium	2 × 1.6 GHz	3.5 GB	490 GB	High	$0.24
Large	4 × 1.6 GHz	7 GB	1,000 GB	High	$0.48
Extra Large	8 × 1.6 GHz	14 GB	2,040 GB	High	$0.96

tested in the development environment. Then an Azure subscription was obtained and used to create a hosted service and storage account. Next, the application was tested in the development environment but using cloud storage. Further testing of the application was performed, this time running live on the cloud, but in a staging environment. In the end, the staging environment was switched to production making the application globally accessible at the desired URL. While all the preceding steps are not mandatory, the pattern is a useful one to follow as it improves the overall development experience by allowing a large part of the debugging to be done in the development environment where there is better tool support. Figure 3.14 shows the portal after the application is switched to production mode.

This simple example demonstrates the power of the Azure platform. Web roles provide scalable front-ends to access applications – developers can host web sites or web services as Web roles and obtain high availability and scale for their applications. Worker roles are more powerful – developers can use them for large-scale data processing in conjunction with Azure storage, and for other compute-intensive tasks without needing investments in servers, data centers, cooling, and manpower to manage operations. They can scale up or scale down their applications on the go – with little or no downtime in-between. Commercial enterprises can use Azure to host e-commerce portals, with the ability to scale according to user load, with just a change in configuration settings. The application thus hosted can seamlessly interact with on-premise data and applications using the Windows Azure App Fabric (previously known as .NET Services).

Technical Details of the Azure Platform

At a high level, Windows Azure can be thought of as a Cloud Operating System over Microsoft blade servers. This operating system handles provisioning,

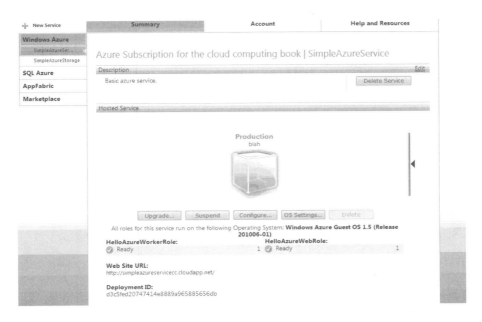

FIGURE 3.14

Final production deployment of the HelloAzure application.

monitoring and complete management of hardware. It provides a shared pool of compute, disk and network resources to the applications. The operating system also manages the application life-cycle on the platform and provides reliable building blocks for authoring applications such as storage, queuing, caching, access control and connectivity services. Individual applications are run in virtual machines that offer a Windows Server 2008-compatible environment and are managed by the cloud operating system.

In addition, the platform offers a relational database (SQL Azure) and a set of services called **AppFabric** (formerly known as .NET services) that allow on-premise applications to interoperate with applications hosted in the cloud with secure connectivity, messaging, and identity management. **On-premise applications** are applications hosted on machines within enterprise firewalls. A schematic diagram showing the interactions among these components is shown in Figure 3.15.

The following sections describe the next level details of the Azure runtime environment, SQL Azure and AppFabric.

Windows Azure Runtime Environment

The Windows Azure runtime environment provides a scalable compute and storage hosting environment along with management capabilities. It has three major components: **Compute**, **Storage** and the **Fabric Controller**.

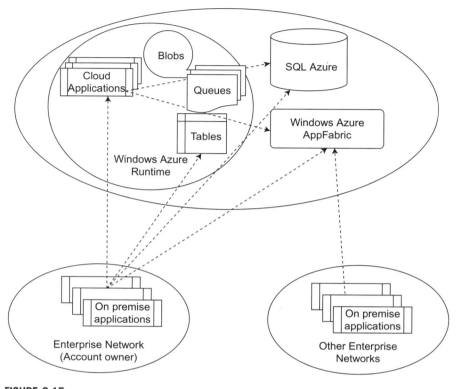

FIGURE 3.15

Schematic diagram of Azure platform services.

As depicted in Figure 3.16, Windows Azure runs on a large number of machines, all maintained in Microsoft data centers. The hosting environment of Azure is called the **Fabric Controller**. It has a pool of individual systems connected on a network and automatically manages resources by load balancing and geo-replication. It manages the application lifecycle without requiring the hosted apps to explicitly deal with the scalability and availability requirements. Each physical machine hosts an **Azure agent** that manages the machine – starting from boot up, installation of the operating system and then the application, application monitoring during its execution, and finally even attempting to fix the system if the agent detects any problems. Compute and storage services are built on top of this Fabric Controller. Note that the Fabric Controller is not the same as the AppFabric – the former manages machines in the cloud, while the latter provides services to connect on-premise applications with those in the cloud.

The **Azure Compute Service** provides a Windows-based environment to run applications written in the various languages and technologies supported on the

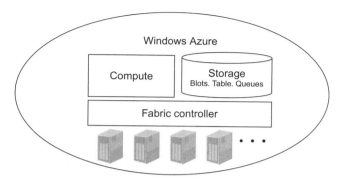

FIGURE 3.16

Windows Azure runtime environment components.

Windows platform. While any Windows-compatible technology can be used to develop the applications, the .NET framework with ASP.NET has the greatest tool and library support. Like most PaaS services, Windows Azure defines a programming model specific to the platform, which is called the **Web role-Worker role model**. This model was briefly referred to in the simple "Hello World" example and will be further detailed in *The Azure Programming Model* section later in this chapter.

The Windows Azure **storage service** provides scalable storage for applications running on the Windows Azure in multiple forms. It enables storage for binary and text data, messages and structured data through support for features called **Blobs, Tables, Queues** and **Drives**. The distinction between these types of storage is described in the section *Azure Storage Services*. For applications that require simple SQL-based access to traditional relational databases, SQL Azure provides a cloud-based RDBMS system. These are described later in this section.

Figure 3.17 shows a bird's-eye view of the internal modules of the platform. At the heart of the system are the storage and compute clusters – vast numbers of machines kept in Microsoft data centers. These machines, the operating systems running on them, and applications are managed by the Fabric Controller. The external interface of the Azure system consists of a set of REST APIs that perform service management and give users access to the storage system.

Fabric Controller

The **Fabric Controller** (**FC**) is a distributed program that manages the hardware and applications in a cluster internally used by Azure. The key task of the Fabric Controller is to assign the appropriate resources to an application based on the number of roles, number of role instances, and the upgrade and fault domains specified by the application. Each machine in the cluster runs a hypervisor which hosts virtual machines running Windows 2008-compatible OSes. The hypervisor is an Azure-specific version of Windows Operating System. The host operating

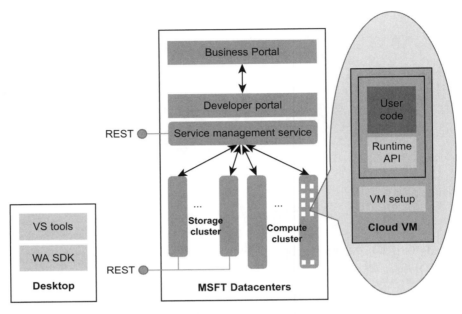

FIGURE 3.17

Windows Azure in one slide.

(Courtesy: Manuvir Das, Microsoft Corporation)

system has an Azure host agent that is responsible for monitoring the health of the physical machine, for starting virtual machine instances, and for reporting the health of the machine to the Fabric Controller. The FC monitors host agents through a heart-beat mechanism; if the FC detects that a host hasn't responded to a heartbeat within a pre-determined duration, it considers the machine to be down and takes measures to restore the machine. Guest operating systems have a guest Azure agent that monitors the role running on the VM. The guest agent restarts roles that terminate and keep the host agent informed about the status of the virtual machine. The host agent and the guest agent also communicate through a heartbeat; when the host detects that it hasn't received a heartbeat from a VM, it takes measures to restore the VM.

The FC also brings up new machines into the cluster when required, or when existing machines go down for any reason. Figure 3.18 shows how the FC works with multiple host agents running different parts of a single application. To prevent the FC from becoming a single point of failure, the FC itself runs on groups of machines.

Readers can look up the book *Programming Windows Azure* [10] for additional details about the Windows Azure architecture. Mark Russinovich's talk on Azure internals at the 2010 edition of Microsoft's Professional Developers Conference [11] is another good source for more information.

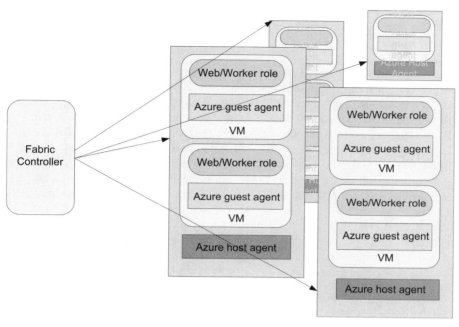

FIGURE 3.18

Fabric Controller architecture.

SQL Azure

SQL Azure provides a relational database on the cloud. While Azure Table storage service facilitates storing and querying of structured data, it does not provide full-relational capability provided by a traditional relational database management system (RDBMS). SQL Azure offers a cloud-based RDBMS system based on SQL Server with nearly all the features offered by on-premise versions of the RDBMS. The database thus hosted can be accessed using ADO.NET and other Microsoft data access technologies. In fact, most applications written for SQL Server will work unchanged when the database is deployed on SQL Azure. Customers can also use client-side reporting tools like SQL Server Reporting Services to work with cloud databases.

SQL Azure also frees customers from the operational details of managing large databases. Instead of focusing on service logs, configuration management, and backup, customers can now focus on what matters to their applications: data. The operational details of the infrastructure are handled transparently by the Microsoft data centers.

The programming model used for SQL Azure is very similar to that of existing database applications and, in a way, SQL Azure provides Database as a

Service. Readers interested in learning more about SQL Azure are referred to the documentation on the SQL Azure site [12].

Azure AppFabric

A common need in large IT companies is for applications to talk to each other. While this is hard to accomplish within an enterprise, it is even harder when some of the applications are hosted on the cloud. This is due to security requirements. The overall system needs to support **federated identity management**, where two distinct entities can trust each other's identity management systems. This is typically done either by configuring firewalls to allow for movement of data or building secure virtual private networks (VPN). Further complications arise when applications have to communicate between an organization and its vendors, partners, or customers, all of whom may operate in completely different environments with different identity management, security, and application policies and technologies. The **Azure AppFabric** is a middleware platform that developers can use to bridge existing applications/data to the cloud through secure, authenticated connectivity across network boundaries.

The Azure AppFabric consists of three main components: the Service Bus, Access Control, and Caching modules, briefly described here:

- The **Service Bus** provides secure messaging and connectivity between cloud and on-premise applications and data. It exposes on-premise data and services in a secure manner to selected cloud applications through firewalls, NAT gateways and other restrictive network boundaries.
- The **Access Control** component provides federated identity management with standards-based identity providers that includes Microsoft's Active Directory, Yahoo!, Google and Facebook. Using this Access Control module, developers can integrate their identity management systems and that of their partners/vendors with Windows Azure applications. This provides users across these organizations a single sign-on facility to access services hosted on Azure. In conjunction with the Service Bus, Access Control allows an organization to selectively expose its data and services to partners, vendors, and customers in a secure manner, with appropriate authorization at the access points.
- The **Caching component** provides an in-memory, scalable, highly available cache for application data, which includes data stored in Azure tables and SQL Azure. Caching improves the performance of both cloud applications and on-premise applications that access cloud resources through intelligent caching of managed objects.

The functionalities of all the AppFabric components are available as .NET libraries for use by developers. Both Service Bus and Access Control are essential parts of the AppFabric and are available in the Azure commercial release. At the time of writing, Caching was available as a technology preview, while Microsoft had announced two more services, Integration and Composite app, to provide more functionality to developers. Further details of the AppFabric are available in the AppFabric site [13]. Additionally, the Azure portal [1] has "deep dives" on many topics. These include the Service Bus, Access Control, Table storage, Blob storage, and Queues. The portal also has guides on SQL Azure – including introduction to SQL Azure, scaling it out, and development and deployment of SQL Azure databases.

Azure Programming Model

In the "Hello World" example described in the first section on Azure, the application used the concept of a **Web role** and a **Worker role**, and configured Windows Azure with the number of instances of each role that should be created. The Web role enables web applications to be hosted on IIS servers and provides external interactivity while the Worker role mirrors the heavy-duty processing that is typically done by Windows services and applications. These two roles supported by Azure depict the common types of application components that a developer needs to create to develop a full-fledged cloud application. The following looks at more details of these concepts that will help in producing a good design of cloud applications.

Web Role and Worker Role

As the name suggests, Web role instances accept and process HTTP (or HTTPS) requests that arrive through a web server hosted on the virtual machine in which it runs. Web roles can be implemented using any technology supported by Microsoft's web-server Internet Information Services (IIS) 7, which includes plain HTML/JS, ASP.NET, and Windows Communication Framework (WCF). Windows Azure provides in-built load-balancing to spread requests across Web-role instances of a single application. This has important implications for the application. Readers should note that there is no **affinity** for a particular instance of a Web role; i.e., requests from clients are randomly distributed over all the Web roles, and it is not possible to guarantee that requests from the same client go to the same Web role. Therefore, all Web roles must be stateless. Application state must be stored either in Windows Azure storage, or in SQL Azure.

Worker roles are similar to Web roles in that they can accept requests and process them, with the exception that they do not run in an IIS environment. Worker roles are used for the more heavy-duty processing that is typically done by Windows services in on-premise applications. Web roles and Worker roles communicate by either using message queues or by setting up direct connections via WCF or other technologies. Figure 3.19 illustrates an application with two Web roles and two Worker roles running in the cloud with a load balancer that directs clients' requests to one of the Web role instances. On similar lines, the Web role can contact either of the Worker role instances.

Microsoft provides Visual Studio project templates for creating Windows Azure Web roles, Worker roles, and combinations of the two, and developers are free to use any programming language supported on Windows. Eclipse for Java and PHP development are supported via plug-ins.

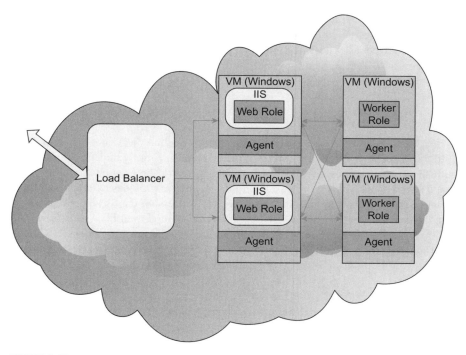

FIGURE 3.19

Compute service with two Web roles and two Worker roles.

The Windows Azure software development kit also includes the **Development Fabric** – a version of the Windows Azure environment that runs on the developer's machine. The development fabric contains the **dev store** which mimics Windows Azure storage, and a Windows Azure agent that provides much of the functionality provided by the cloud agent. Developers can create and debug their applications using this local simulation, then deploy the app to Windows Azure in the cloud when it is ready. These were depicted in Figures 3.4 to 3.6 earlier in this chapter.

Using Azure Cloud Storage Services

> **NOTE**
>
> **Azure Storage Services**
>
> **Blob service:** For large binary and text data
> **Azure Drives:** To use as mounted file systems
> **Table Service:** For structured storage of non-relational data
> **Queue Service:** For message passing between components

The Windows Azure platform offers four kinds of storage service for applications to store data – blobs, drives, tables and queues. The **Blob service** lets applications store and retrieve large binary and text data, called blobs (**Binary Large Objects**). It provides file-level storage and is similar to Amazon S3. It also allows developers to mount blobs as "cloud drives" for programmatic access from within the applications. Windows **Azure Drives** are used for mounting an NTFS volume to be accessed by an application, and are similar to Amazon EBS. The **Table service** is used for structured storage for non-relational data, and is similar to Amazon's SimpleDB. The **Queue service** can be used for storing messages that may be accessed by a client. We used this service in the "Hello World" example. The Queue storage provides reliable message-passing services for both applications that are completely within the cloud and also for applications that are partitioned between on-premise and cloud. Both on-premise and cloud applications can access all the capabilities of the storage service through a REST-based CRUD API (see sidebar).

NOTE

CRUD: Create, Read, Update and Delete functionality, typically offered by an API that deals with data

---

Access to each of the storage services is through an **Azure storage account** which acts as a namespace and defines ownership of data. All three services are accessible through REST-based endpoints (over HTTP/HTTTPs). Customers create storage accounts to avail the functionality of these services. Each storage account can store a maximum of 100TB of data across the different storage types. Customers can create additional storage accounts for higher storage needs. Access to data on the storage services is controlled by a pair of keys that are provided for each account.

Blob Service

Blobs are (typically large) unstructured objects like images and media, and are similar to Amazon S3. Applications deal with blobs as a whole, although they might read/write parts of a blob. Blobs can have optional metadata associated with them in the form of key-value pairs; for instance, an image could have a copyright notice stored as metadata. Blobs are always stored under **containers**, which are similar to AWS buckets. Every storage account must have at least one container, and containers can have blobs within them. Container names can contain the directory separator character ("/") – this gives developers the facility to create hierarchical "file-systems" similar to those on disks. This is similar to Amazon S3, except that in S3, object names (and not buckets) can have the "/" character.

The blob service defines two kinds of blobs to store text and binary data: A **page blob** and a **block blob**. Page blobs are blobs that are optimized for random read/write operations anywhere in the content of the blob, while block blobs are optimized for streaming and are read and written a block at a time. Multiple sets of blobs can be organized in containers that can be created within an **Azure storage account**.

In order to make data transfer more efficient, Windows Azure implements a content delivery network (CDN) that stores frequently accessed data closer to the applications that use it. The AppFabric's Caching component can also be used to improve read performance of applications while accessing Azure blobs.

As mentioned before, access to blob and storage services in Azure is through REST interfaces. Below is an example REST API for creating a block blob. Please note that the same blob can be accessed by a different application or different process in the application to enable sharing of text or binary data.

```
Request Syntax:
PUT http://myaccount.blob.core.windows.net/pustakcontainer/
mycloudblob HTTP/1.1
Request Headers:
x-ms-version: 2009-09-19
x-ms-date: Fri, 2 Sep 2011 12:33:35 GMT
Content-Type: text/plain; charset=UTF-8
x-ms-blob-type: BlockBlob
x-ms-meta-m1: v1
x-ms-meta-m2: v2
Authorization: SharedKey myaccount:YhuFJjN4fAR8/
AmBrqBz7MG2uFinQ4rkh4dscbj598g=
Content-Length: 29

Request Body:
Sold book ISBN 978-0747595823
```

If x-ms-blob-type header is PageBlob, a new page blob is created. On similar lines, to access a blob, one needs to use one of the following URI's in the GET method as below, depending upon whether the shared data is time varying or statically updated.

```
GET http://myaccount.blob.core.windows.net/pustakcontainer/mycloudblob
GET http://myaccount.blob.core.windows.net/pustakcontainer/
   mycloudblob?snapshot=<DateTime>
```

The response contains the contents of the blob that can be used by the application. Additionally, the response also contains an Etag response header which can be used in the next GET with If-Modified request header, for application optimization.

Table Service

For structured forms of storage, Windows Azure provides structured key-value pairs stored in entities known as **Tables**, which are similar to Amazon SimpleDB described in Chapter 2. The Table storage uses a NoSQL model based on key-value pairs for querying structured data that is not in a typical database. This concept of NoSQL and some guidelines for developers to design using key-value pairs are explained in Chapter 5.

Simply put, a **Table** is a bag of typed properties that represents an entity in the application domain. For instance, the following definition {EmployeeId: int,

`EmployeeName: string}` defines a table that could be used to store (minimal) employee data. It is important to note that these tables are not relational in nature, nor are table schemas enforced by the Azure framework. Data stored in Azure tables is partitioned horizontally and distributed across storage nodes for optimized access.

Every table has a property called the **Partition Key**, which defines how data in the table is partitioned across storage nodes – rows that have the same partition key are stored in a partition. In addition, tables can also define **Row Keys** which are unique within a partition and optimize access to a row within a partition. When present, the pair {partition key, row key} uniquely identifies a row in a table.

The access to the Table service is also through REST APIs similar to the Blob service described earlier. To create a table, an XML description (actually ADO. NET entity set) is sent as the request body to a `POST` method. To access specific records of data within a table, the application can use query entities operation in a `GET` method. Two examples of using the table query operation are given below. The first one does a search for a record with matching partition key and row key, while the second uses a condition over one of the fields to extract required data fields.

```
GET http://myaccount.table.core.windows.net/pustaktable
   (PartitionKey='<partition-key>',RowKey='<row-key>')
GET /myaccount.table.core.windows.net/Customers()?$filter=(Rating
   ge 3) and (Rating le 6)
```

Queue Service

Queues are the third kind of storage, provided for reliable message delivery within and between services. A storage account can have unlimited number of queues, and each queue can store an unlimited number of messages, with the restriction that messages are limited to 8KB in size at the time of this writing. Queues are used by Web roles and Worker roles for inter-application communication, and by applications to communicate with each other. An example program using message queues for communication between Web and Worker roles was seen earlier in this chapter.

The Azure SDK provides .NET wrappers for the REST APIs offered by the storage services. The `CloudStorageAccount` class provides authentication, while the `CloudBlobClient`, `CloudTableClient` and `CloudQueueClient` classes offer functionality required by clients of the Blob, Table and Queue storage, respectively.

Channel 9 [14] and Microsoft's Professional Developers' Conference (PDC) [15] are great sources of talks and deep dives on Windows Azure. Both sites have developers and program managers from the Windows Azure team presenting and demonstrating different features of the Azure platform.

Handling the Cloud Challenges

Chapter 1 had mentioned that all cloud platforms have to handle certain common technical challenges, namely scalability, multi-tenancy, security and availability. The following discussion shows how these challenges are handled in Azure.

Scalability

The major resources that need to be scaled are compute resources and storage resources.

Scaling Computation: In any cloud application, it is a requirement for the application to be able to scale up and down in response to the load. To scale Worker roles, developers can use shared queues with multiple Worker roles reading off one or more queues as shown in Figure 3.20. One can also create the VM instances in an upgrade domain (with manual or automatic upgrade) using REST APIs, if needed. The upgrade domain operation is asynchronous and can be invoked with the following POST command, for example:

```
https://management.core.windows.net/<subscription-id>/services/
hostedservices/pustakService/deploymentslots/deployment/?comp upgrade
```

Windows Azure places Web roles behind a hardware load-balancer that provides load-balancing of incoming requests across the different instances of the Web role with a very high throughput. Each queue offers a throughput of nearly 500 transactions per second. For higher throughput, developers can create multiple queues between Web roles and Worker roles, and have the Worker roles pick up messages either at random, or based on some other scheduling strategy. Customers can use the monitoring API (described later in this section) to monitor load on their role instances and choose to add new instances on the fly when required. It can be seen that this is similar to the load balancing possible in Amazon and HP CloudSystem Matrix.

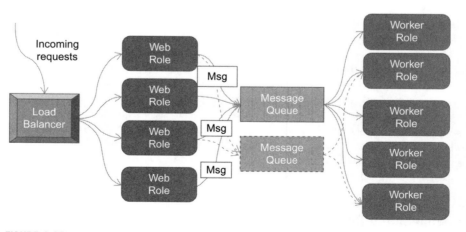

FIGURE 3.20

Scaling Web and Worker roles using shared queues.

Scaling Storage: In Azure, storage is scaled by partitioning the data, with each partition being stored and accessed as a separate entity. As stated previously, to facilitate scaling data, Windows Azure allows the specification of a partitioning key that is used to partition blobs, tables and messages across machines in the Azure storage. Hence, the partitioning key determines how well data is distributed across machines, which makes it a crucial design decision while designing Azure applications. For blobs and queues, the names of the blob or queue serve as the partition key, while developers can define a partition key for the tables they create.

Security and Access Control

There are four aspects of security that need to be handled well for secure access control and the solutions used by Azure and those are described below.

Identity and authentication: First, the methods used to identify and authenticate the users should be easy to use and secure. Windows Azure uses Live ID to provide identity and authentication services. Actions that users perform on the portal are authenticated using this service.

Message encryption: Communications between different entities must be ensured to be secure. For all secure HTTP endpoints, including those for storage and roles, Windows Azure automatically verifies and decrypts requests (and encrypts messages for internally initiated traffic) using customer-provided certificates. Additionally, the service management API uses SSL to encrypt communication between the customers and the service, using a certificate uploaded by the customer in the Azure portal. This process also allows account owners to delegate service administration to a group of people as follows – first, the account owner uploads the certificate (with the private key) and provides administrators with the public key. Administrators now need to sign their requests (if done programmatically) with the public key provided. Thus, the account owner's credentials and private key remain private, and the service administration can be delegated to others.

Multi-tenancy: Since the cloud is a shared infrastructure, methods used to enforce isolation between processes running on the same server are important. The Windows Azure trust boundary terminates at the host operating system. Everything that executes above the host operating system is untrusted. This creates a boundary where trusted code (host operating system) is in charge of the physical machine, and untrusted code is run on virtual machines, with a secure hypervisor controlling the boundary between the two. Both the hypervisor and the host operating system have undergone intensive scrutiny, including proof techniques to provide a strong barrier against malicious applications. Virtual machines are thus isolated from each other and the host operating system. Further, the host Azure agents in conjunction with the host operating system implement mechanisms to ensure that the VMs running on them cannot spoof other machines, cannot receive traffic not directed to them (also known as **promiscuous mode** in network packet sniffer terminology), and cannot send or receive broadcast traffic from inappropriate sources.

Storage security: To protect customer data, Windows Azure provides **storage account keys (SAKs)** which are required for most data accesses. These SAKs are available from the Azure Portal. Storage requests can additionally be encrypted with customer certificates, which protect customer communication from eavesdropping attacks. When data is deleted from the store, the storage subsystem makes the customer data unavailable – delete operations are instantly consistent, and all copies of deleted data are removed. In the event of hardware repair, personnel at the data center will de-magnetize hard drives to ensure that customer data never leaves the data center.

For security and privacy, *Windows Azure Security Overview* [16] is a good guide to the security and privacy features of Windows Azure. "Azure Security Notes" [17] provides detailed discussions on cloud security, and securing Azure applications. *Security Best Practices for Developing Windows Azure Applications* [18] provides best practices on designing secure Azure applications. Further, Chapter 7 describes the design considerations for a secure cloud platform.

Reliability and Availability

This section describes the measures taken by Windows Azure to ensure the availability of both services and storage.

Service Availability: To provide a reliable service, Windows Azure introduces the concepts of fault domains and upgrade domains. Two virtual machines are in a single **fault domain** if a single hardware fault, network or power outage can bring down both machines. When a role has multiple instances, Windows Azure automatically distributes the instances across different fault domains so that a single outage does not bring down the role. Upgrade domains are used to make service upgrades to a running application. When an in-place upgrade is done to an existing application, Windows Azure rolls out one upgrade domain at a time – thus ensuring that some instances of the service are always available to serve user requests. A similar strategy is used for OS upgrades – each domain is updated individually. Together, fault domains and upgrade domains ensure high availability of customer applications. The SLA for Windows Azure guarantees that when customers deploy two or more role instances in different fault and upgrade domains, their Internet facing roles will have external connectivity at least 99.95% of the time.

Storage Availability: Windows Azure keeps three copies of user data in three separate nodes in different fault domains to minimize the impact of hardware failures. Similarly, when customers choose to run more than one instance of their application roles, the instances are run in different fault and upgrade domains, ensuring that instances of the roles are always available. The SLA guarantees 99.95% uptime for applications that have more than one role instance. Further, mechanisms to mitigate Denial of Service attacks are provided by the platform – the details are too intricate to be mentioned here, and can be found in documented security best practices [18].

Interoperability

A major focus of the Windows Azure cloud has been interoperability of cloud-based applications with on-premise services and resources. Interoperability is important, since organizations may migrate a subset of their applications to the cloud. These applications, which are designed to be hosted on premise, may need other services to function correctly. For example, a payroll application may need access to an internal employee database and the authentication service of the enterprise, such as Active Directory. Many challenges need to be overcome in order to provide such access. Firewalls and NAT devices make it difficult for external services to initiate communication with services that are behind these barriers. Authentication and authorization of users is another issue, as the external and internal services might use disparate authentication mechanisms. Finally, discovery of the internally hosted services in a secure and reliable manner is a challenge.

The Azure AppFabric is focused on interoperability. As described earlier, the **Service Bus** component provides bidirectional communication between on-premise and on-cloud applications. The Access Control component is a service that mediates access control between Windows Azure and internal services residing in a data center. Both components are exposed through the Azure AppFabric SDK, and are available to developers as paid services. Details of the service are beyond the scope of this chapter. Readers interested in the topic should read the *Windows Azure AppFabric Overview* [13] document on the Azure web site.

Designing Pustak Portal in Azure

This section illustrates the features of Azure by considering the design of Pustak Portal, the running example described in the Preface of this book. Consider implementing a self-publishing feature in Pustak Portal which allows authors to upload books and perform document and image processing functions to prepare the books for publication. The portal provider (owner of Pustak), uses the IaaS and PaaS features of the cloud platforms to scale to the huge number of users manipulating their documents on the cloud. The portal provider is also interested in monitoring the usage of the portal and ensuring maximum availability and scalability of the portal.

As per the description of the Pustak Portal in the Preface, component developers can add additional document manipulation/processing functionality on the portal and will get paid by the portal owner if consumers use their document services. To enable this feature and for ease of integration, a standard interface for components can be defined as follows. Components are expected to adhere to a design where they obtain the source URLs from a message queue, read the contents of the URL from Azure storage, perform the processing and write the result to a target URL which is also specified in the initial message. The component is then expected to return a message indicating the target URL and whether the operation was successful.

This portal can be implemented on the Windows Azure platform by using a Web-role, Worker-role pair for each distinct service feature, with multiple instances of each role for scale. For example, if one of the features is to index the book, the Web role could have a button that causes the book to be submitted to a Worker role for indexing. In other words, each document processing application will correspond to a Worker role (and an optional Web role) in the system. The examples presented previously in the chapter illustrated how to write such pairs.

The Windows Azure Guidance project on CodePlex [19] has many documents related to developing and architecting Windows Azure projects. The PDC talk [20] is another good source of information. The Microsoft Patterns and Practices Developer Center has a detailed guide on architecting applications for Azure [21]. Another useful guide is the book *Windows Azure Platform Articles from the Trenches* [22].

Storage for Pustak Portal

The Windows Azure storage services can be used for different aspects of Pustak Portal. The documents and images for the books can be stored in blob storage, while storing structured data like user information and billing details in table storage or SQL storage. The main entities in the system are shown in Figure 3.21 (these are the same regardless of whether the information is to be stored in SQL or tables). The User entity stores information about the authors in the system. The Application entity stores information about the document processing applications in the system. The Developer entity stores information about the developers of the various applications. The UserFiles entity contains information

FIGURE 3.21

Entities in the Pustak portal.

about the books written by the authors, and the `UserApplicationActivity` entity stores data about the usage of applications by the authors. A detailed description of the various fields in these entities will be presented in the later parts of this section together with a description of the functionality implemented by these fields.

SQL Azure: SQL Azure is a better fit for storing relational data like the `User` entity and `Developer` entities. Unlike other Azure storage services (tables, queues and blobs), SQL Azure does not have REST APIs. The `sqlcmd` utility can be used to send standard SQL commands to operate on relational tables, create tables, insert data and so on. An example command is shown here:

```
C:\>sqlcmd -U guestLogin@hplabserver.net -P simple -S hplabserver.net -d master
1> CREATE DATABASE pustakDB;
```

In general, the entities shown in Figure 3.21 can be created either in Azure Table storage or in SQL Azure. An important consideration for choosing one over the other is whether the application requires strong consistency and other ACID properties.

Security: As seen in Figure 3.21, the data stored for each user in Pustak Portal include the name of the user, the Live ID of the user, and a Live ID authorization token that is returned by the Live ID authentication services when a user is successfully authenticated.

For scaling Pustak Portal data, partitioning keys can be used. The key icon in Figure 3.21 indicates the partitioning keys for each table. For `UserApplicationActivity`, `User`, and `UserFiles` tables, `UserLiveIdAuthToken`, the LiveID authorization token of the user serves as the natural partitioning key because it partitions data and activity on a per-user per session basis. For the Developer and Application tables, the `DeveloperLiveID` and `ApplicationId` fields serve as a natural partitioning key since they partition the data on the basis of the developer and the application, respectively.

Tracing and Monitoring: While the Windows Azure SDK provides a wide gamut of debugging and profiling facilities in the simulation environment, most real-world applications will need debugging and profiling in the deployment environment. However, debugging on the Azure cloud is difficult because the cloud is a dynamic environment with distributed transactions and applications that are dynamically switched between virtual machines. This makes it crucial to have sufficient support for tracing and diagnostics in the Azure system, particularly the ability to centrally manage diagnostics on the various role instances, to store logs in reliable data stores that are available off the cloud, and to fine-tune the diagnostics setup. More details on Azure cloud management are available in Chapter 8. Additionally, an excellent overview of Windows Azure Diagnostics and Monitoring features can be found on the PDC10 portal [23] and the complete documentation on the MSDN web site [24].

GOOGLE APP ENGINE

Google App Engine is a PaaS solution that enables users to host their own applications on the same or similar infrastructure as Google Docs, Google Maps and other popular Google services. Just like Microsoft Azure provides a platform to build and execute .NET applications, Google App Engine enables users to develop and host applications written using Java, Python and a new language called Go [25]. The platform also supports other languages that use JVM (Java Virtual Machine) runtime such as JRuby, JavaScript (Rhino), and Scala programming languages.

The applications hosted on Google App Engine can scale both in compute and storage just like other Google products. The platform provides distributed storage with replication and load balancing of client requests. The applications can be easily built using Eclipse Integrated Development environment that many developers will be familiar with. This section gives a simple overview and key highlights of the platform.

Getting Started

Step by step instructions for using Google App Engine are described here, based on the procedure available as of the writing of this book [26]. The developer first signs up for a Google App Engine account using his/her gmail credentials. Figure 3.22 shows the first screen when the application is being configured.

Google App Engine allows a newly developed application to be served from the developer's own domain name. For example, if the developer chooses myapp as an application name, then the application will be served at http://myapp.appspot.com. This URL can be shared publicly or selectively shared with a small group of members. Every developer can host up to 10 applications for free with 500 MB of complimentary storage. The developer needs to pay a nominal amount for the storage and bandwidth resources used by the application beyond these limits. A simple dashboard showing the usage metrics for each application can be seen on the portal, a screenshot of which is shown in Figure 3.23.

NOTE

Developing and Deploying on Google App Engine

1. Download the SDK (Eclipse plug-in)
2. Create a new "Web Application Project"
3. Configure the application
4. Develop code
5. Test in simulated App Engine environment
6. Deploy to Google App Engine

Developing a Google App Engine Application

To develop Java applications, the App Engine SDK (software development kit) needs to be installed. The SDK is an Eclipse plug-in (Figure 3.24) that includes

FIGURE 3.22

Google App Engine: Application configuration.

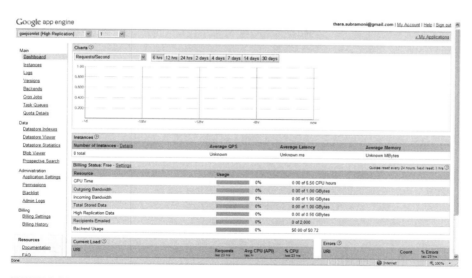

FIGURE 3.23

Application dashboard of Google App Engine.

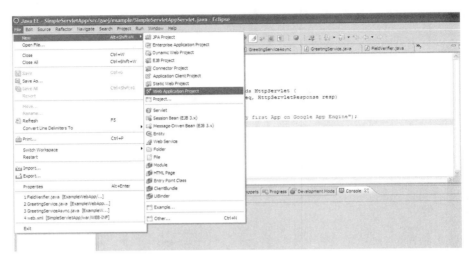

FIGURE 3.24

Google App Engine Eclipse plug-in.

build, test and deployment environments and is available at http://dl.google.com. eclipse/plugin/3.x. To get started, one should create a new project as a "Web Application Project"; right click the project and select "Google" in the preferences and enter a valid application id for the project. After developing (programming) the application, during the deployment stage one needs to specify an app id for the application. To deploy onto the App Engine, similar to creating the application, one needs to just right click on the project and select the "Deploy to App Engine" option and the application gets uploaded onto the App Engine and gets deployed!

Another interesting option during application configuration, is an option to create a **GWT (Google Web Toolkit)** application. GWT basically allows one to create interactive applications with drag and drop facility to author a custom graphical interface. The toolkit then automatically converts the UI portion into JavaScript with AJAX [27] (asynchronous) calls to access the backend logic on the server. It may be noted that since Javascript runs within a browser (client-side) and Ajax provides a non-blocking way of accessing the backend, the overall effect is a good experience with quick response for interactive applications. A skeleton code for GWT can be created using the following command.

```
webAppCreator -out myFirstApp com.cloudbook.myFirstApp
```

The developer can also check the "Generate GWT Sample Code" option during application creation to get a default "Greeting" project created (Figure 3.25). If this option is unchecked one could write their own Java servlet code and deploy it on the App Engine as discussed earlier. So, literally any web application written in Java can be deployed on the App Engine.

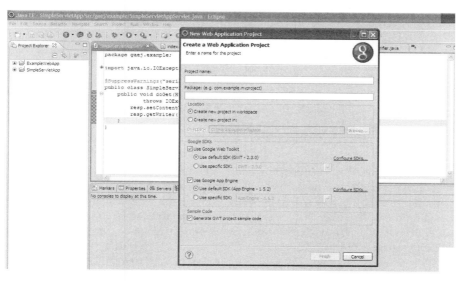

FIGURE 3.25

Google App Engine App deployment.

The SDK comes with a local web server for test deployment. This local web server simulates the secure runtime or App Engine sandbox environment with limited access to the underlying operating system. For example, the application can only be accessed using HTTP on specific ports. It cannot write to the file system and can read only files that were uploaded along with application code. An additional restriction with the sandbox environment is that the application when accessed over HTTP should return back with a response code within 30 seconds. These restrictions are mainly to prevent one application from interfering with another.

Using Persistent Storage

As mentioned before, an App running within the sandbox environment of Google App Engine cannot write to the file system and has other restrictions on using OS calls. However, in reality, two apps may want to communicate or two components may want to share data or two requests may fall under a single session of the application and hence need persistent data. In order to use such persistent data across requests, the application must use special App Engine services such as **datastore,** and **memcache**, described in the following. Figure 3.26 gives a pictorial view of using the persistence mechanisms over a simple application to manage book information.

The datastore service provides a distributed data storage with a query engine that supports transaction semantics. The datastore is a key-value storage similar to Amazon SimpleDB and Windows Azure Table Service. Every data record is an

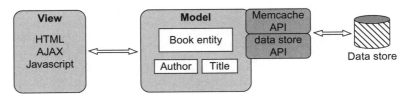

FIGURE 3.26

Using persistent stores in Google App Engine.

entity and is identified using a key and a set of properties. Operations on groups of entities can also be performed if a transaction requires it. The App Engine datastore provides high availability by replicating the data in multiple copies and providing a well-proven algorithm (called Paxos algorithm) to synchronize the multiple copies and provide **eventually consistent** responses (eventual consistency is explained in detail in Chapter 6).

The following code snippet exemplifies use of the App Engine APIs for datastore. This Java code will be part of a servlet and handles the POST method for uploading book information. For simplicity, only the title, author and publisher are added. To bring in some variety in data types used, the current date is also added into the book record. The snippet first retrieves the form submission information, creates a new Entity and adds in new key-value pairs into the `Entity` using `setProperty` call. Finally, after all the operations on the `Entity` are performed, `datastore.put` method is used to upload that information. Along similar lines, one can develop the GET method to list details (properties) of a selected book or all the books in the store.

```
package guestbook;

import com.google.appengine.api.datastore.DatastoreService;
import com.google.appengine.api.datastore.DatastoreServiceFactory;
import com.google.appengine.api.datastore.Entity;
import com.google.appengine.api.datastore.Key;
import com.google.appengine.api.datastore.KeyFactory;

import java.io.IOException;
import java.util.Date;

import javax.servlet.http.HttpServlet;
import javax.servlet.http.HttpServletRequest;
import javax.servlet.http.HttpServletResponse;

public class SetBookDataServlet extends HttpServlet {
    public void doPost(HttpServletRequest req, HttpServletResponse resp)
    throws IOException {

        String bookTitle = req.getParameter("title");
        Key bookKey = KeyFactory.createKey("book", bookTitle);
        String author = req.getParameter("author");
        Date date = new Date();
```

```
Entity book = new Entity("BookData", bookKey);
book.setProperty("author", author);
book.setProperty("date", date);
book.setProperty("publisher", publisher);

DatastoreService datastore = DatastoreServiceFactory.
getDatastoreService();
datastore.put(book);
resp.sendRedirect("/book.jsp?title=" + bookTitle);
    }
}
```

The **memcache** service can be used to speed up the datastore queries by having a local cache. For example, if a book is newly published and has become a hot seller, instead of going to the datastore for updating the sales data, the developer may wish to keep that entity information in cache, update it locally and write back to datastore later. Similarly, when multiple clients are requesting the same, it helps to serve the response from the cache instead of a datastore. Usual rules of caching principles apply here as well; any record may get replaced by another entity if cache is low on memory.

A code snippet to use an implementation of memcache in Java called JCache follows.

```
import java.util.HashMap;
import java.util.Map;
import net.sf.jsr107cache.Cache;
import net.sf.jsr107cache.CacheException;
import net.sf.jsr107cache.CacheFactory;
import net.sf.jsr107cache.CacheManager;
import com.google.appengine.api.memcache.jsr107cache.GCacheFactory;
Cache cache;
public void initCache() {

        Map bookprops = new HashMap();
        bookprops.put(GCacheFactory.EXPIRATION_DELTA, 1600);

        try {
           CacheFactory cacheFactory = CacheManager.getInstance().
           getCacheFactory();
           bookcache = cacheFactory.createCache(bookprops);
        } catch (CacheException e) {
           System.out.println("Error in caching"); return;
        }
// ... other code.
}
public byte[] getFomCache()
{
        // Get the value from the cache.
           value = (byte[]) cache.get(key);
}
```

```
public void putCache(String key, byte[] value){
        // Put the value into the cache.
        cache.put(key, value);
}
```

In addition to the previously described APIs for efficient persistent data storage, there are other very useful libraries supported for task management, user data management, developing collaborative applications and so on. For example, the channel API provides a persistent connection between the browser clients and server for real time interactivity without polling. The interested reader is encouraged to visit the official Google web site to get the latest list of APIs and sample codes from *App Engine Java Overview - Google App Engine - Google Code* [28].

As mentioned earlier, the applications hosted on the App Engine run within a sandbox. Though the sandbox of App Engine does not allow the developer to write to the file system, it is possible to read files that are packaged as a part of the WAR file. Additionally, access to certain file types can trigger applications while some can be static. Accesses to **static files** are allowed and result in simple file access; whereas accessing files called **resource files** will result in application execution (such as execution of JSP files in web application servers). One can specify the files that need to be treated as static files and those that need to be treated as resource file by editing a simple configuration file named appengine-web.xml. A snippet of the configuration file is the following.

```
<static-files>
      <include path="/**.png" />
      <exclude path="/data/**.png" />
   </static-files>
<resource-files>
      <include path="/**.xml" />
      <exclude path="/feeds/**.xml" />
   </resource-files>
```

In summary, Google App Engine is an excellent platform for developers who want to host their first application on the cloud. All they need to do is to develop applications just like web applications, and then the App Engine development tool (Eclipse plug-in) takes care of deploying it on the cloud. The usage policy of the App Engine cloud platform also makes it easy for developers to try out creating cloud applications, as the first 10 applications are hosted free of charge. This should give the reader a great reason to start off right away.

PLATFORM AS A SERVICE: STORAGE ASPECTS

This section describes Cloud platforms that provide PaaS solutions just for accessing Cloud storage. In the previous section, we looked at the overall platform provided by Azure, where some storage services (with Tables, Blobs, queues and SQLAzure) could be used along with the compute platform. Some cloud platforms provide special features to handle scalable storage needs of cloud applications, and can be used independent of the platform used for computation. Such special storage services offered by PaaS vendors are surveyed in this section with IBM data services and Amazon Web Services as case studies.

Amazon Web Services: Storage

Amazon Web Services (**AWS**) is again at the forefront when it comes to offering storage services on the cloud. It caters to most common storage and data needs of a cloud application by offering services for accessing files, storage blocks/volumes, relational databases with SQL-query support and even simple key-value pairs (NoSQL). A detailed description of these data-oriented services was presented in Chapter 2 and an example of using those services along with cloud-hosted compute services was described. A brief overview of these services is given here for continuity.

Amazon Simple Storage Service (S3)

The reader may recall from Chapter 2 that Amazon S3 offers file storage in the cloud. Users create buckets and drop objects or files within them. These files are accessible using URLs of the form http://s3.amazonaws.com/<bucket>/<key> or http://bucket.s3.amazonaws.com/<key>, where "bucket" generally is a name chosen by the user to refer to the collection of files (similar to containers in Azure) and "key" is the name of the file. S3 therefore offers a single-level directory, in some sense. RESTful APIs with HTTP methods such as GET and PUT are provided to retrieve and upload files. Client libraries exist to invoke these operations from many programming languages such as Java and Ruby.

Data files can also be placed in specific geographic locations called **regions**. By default, each file is replicated, and the architecture is designed to survive multiple replica failures ensuring good availability of the file. Additionally, S3 offers versioning and access controls to files and also offers logging to track file changes. Clearly, Amazon S3 is a very useful service as it provides a persistent file system support for cloud applications. It can also be used just as a platform service from on-premise applications that require large-scale shared file systems.

Amazon Simple DB

Amazon Simple DB (**SDB**) is a highly scalable key-value store that allows easy access to semi-structured data with attributes stored and retrieved on the basis of a key. A set of key-value pairs are organized in the form of domain. For example, in Pustak Portal, the different attributes of a book can be accessed by a key that identifies the book (ISBN for example). SDB also provides SQL-like methods for searching the database. Unlike relational databases, records in SDB need not have a fixed schema. This makes it simple to use SDB as a method of sharing and integrating data across applications or components of a cloud application where each component can update key-value pairs relevant to its functionality and use others as needed.

Amazon Relational Database Services

AWS also provides traditional relational databases as a cloud service. In fact, a number of relational databases have been hosted on EC2 and are available as web services. These include MySQL, which is provided under the name **Relational Database Service** (RDS) and IBM DB2. These databases can be instantiated and managed through the Amazon Web Services console. Amazon provides many administrative capabilities to take a snapshot and backup the database as well. The database can be used either by an on-premise application or a cloud application hosted on EC2 or any other infrastructure provider.

A complete description of the Amazon Storage services described above was provided in Chapter 1. Additionally, some fundamental issues of data storage and theory behind them are discussed in greater detail in the *Data Storage* section of Chapter 5 and the *Scaling Storage* section of Chapter 6.

IBM SmartCloud: pureXML[3]

SmartCloud is the set of cloud products and services available from IBM, that include IaaS, PaaS and SaaS solutions. This section describes a platform for enabling XML Data as a Service using IBM Data Studio and pureXML – a storage service that allows cloud services to store and retrieve XML documents [29]. Many cloud services require flexibility in data storage schema, and one way to get that is to use XML databases. XML has also been used as a data exchange payload between multiple components of an application. For example, IBM DB2, pureXML and IBM Data Studio can be used to create a microblogging application with an Adobe FLEX® frontend [30, 31]. In this example, the author shows how pureXML capabilities of IBM DB2 allow storage of XML natively in a database, while Adobe FLEX applications can read XML directly and populate FLEX user interfaces. Additionally, as described in Chapter 6, XML databases enable support of multi-tenancy in storage.

This section looks at the basic concepts of pureXML, how pureXML can effectively support hybrid applications and touches upon the kind of query languages supported for ease of programmability. The first part of the section describes how XML data is stored in DB2. Subsequently, the section describes how pureXML is made available as a web service using IBM Data Studio and its usage.

pureXML

As stated previously, there is a need for vendors to support XML data so that applications can benefit from the robustness and scalability of traditional database systems while continuing to use XML as a flexible data format. However, XML is not well-tuned for traditional relational database systems. Hence, storing and querying XML data via non-relational database techniques may result in the

---

[3]Contributed by Dr. Dibyendu Das, Principal Technical Staff, AMD India.

strengths of relational database like performance, scalability, availability and reliability being compromised. pureXML is designed to marry the strengths of traditional DB2 with techniques for effective access of XML data.

Conceptual Overview: Following is a simple XML snippet describing the attributes of a document. Table 3.2 shows a corresponding record of an equivalent database that may be used to store all the data about books. One can clearly see the parallels between the two. Each attribute in an XML node becomes a field in the schema. An important thing to note is that if the user wants to add any additional information about the book (e.g., getting an award), then the fixed schema of the database will make it difficult to handle, whereas it is almost no effort for XML data. Nevertheless, it can be seen that it is possible to store XML data in relational databases (like DB2).

```
<book>
        <title> Angela's Ashes </title>
        <author> Frank McCourt </author>
        <genre> Fictionalized Biography </genre>
        <publisher> Scribner </publisher>
        <synopsis> includes anecdotes and stories of Frank McCourt's
childhood and early adulthood </synopsis>
</book>
```

Management of XML data in traditional database systems is usually carried out using one of the following techniques:

i. **Stuffing**: Here the XML data is stored in large objects using BLOBs (Binary Large Objects type) in relational databases. In this case, the XML data is usually stored or retrieved in its entirety.

ii. **Shredding**: Here the XML data is decomposed into multiple relational columns and tables and is somewhat similar to the example shown in Table 3.2.

iii. **Native XML Database** (**NXD**) where the internal data model of the database is based on XML documents which are not necessarily stored as text files. Even the query syntax such as XQuery will be supported.

Table 3.2 Database Equivalent of the XML Example

Title	Author	Genre	Publisher	Synopsis
Angela's Ashes	Frank McCourt	Fictionalized Biography	Scribner	includes anecdotes and stories of Frank McCourt's childhood and early adulthood

While some of these approaches may be effective for certain kinds of data storage, hybrid applications that want to use both XML and non-XML data may face a myriad of issues when such techniques are employed. For example, stuffing XML data in large objects may not be effective if queries on parts of the data need to be supported, as the entire document needs to be retrieved in such cases. Even decomposing data into regular relational database rows and columns may result in loss of flexibility and high conversion times. Finally, native XML databases are not yet mature and may not provide the reliability that is already built into traditional relational databases. pureXML tries to overcome these drawbacks by storing XML documents as a DB2 column which is marked with an XML data type.

NOTE

pureXML Summary
- Stores XML documents as a DB2 column of type XML
- Data stored in original hierarchical form
- Efficient storage and retrieval methods
- Query via XQuery

The XML data type in pureXML is just SQL data which can be stored, queried and accessed quickly. In this data type, the XML data is stored in its original hierarchical form. pureXML is thus capable of the following:

i. efficiently storing and managing hierarchical structures seen in XML documents
ii. efficiently transforming XML data into relational databases or creating a relational view.

Additionally, pureXML can be queried using a standards-based query language (**XQuery**) typically used to query XML, and can be accessed via popular APIs and frameworks including JDBC, ODBC, PHP, .NET, Ruby on Rails, and Zend [32].

The hybrid database structure under pureXML can be viewed as shown in Figure 3.27. Here, a client application can access either a regular relational database table and/or XML data transparently using different types of queries: SQL queries, a combination of SQL/XML queries, XQuery or a combination of SQL/XQuery. The XML parser and the relational parser interfaces send the queries to a common query compiler and optimization engine which subsequently accesses the relevant part of the hybrid database (the table part or the hierarchical tree part) for insertion, deletion, updates and queries.

Storage Architecture: In pureXML, the XML documents are stored on disk pages as tree structures that reflect the XML data model [33]. XML data are usually stored separately from the original table objects. In every row of the XML an **XDS** (**XML data specifier**) object is stored that contains information on how to access the tree structure on the disk (see Figure 3.28). Storing XML data separately removes the requirement of stuffing or shredding the XML data,

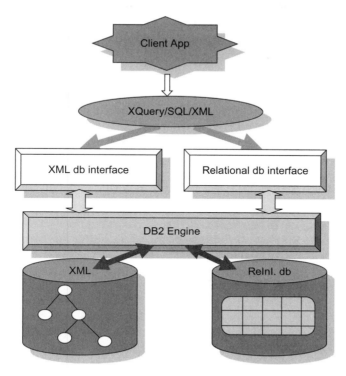

FIGURE 3.27

A view of a hybrid database.

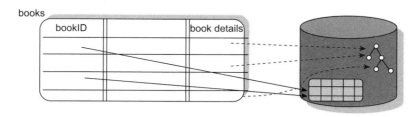

FIGURE 3.28

Storage mechanism in pureXML.

maintaining its natural and versatile hierarchical structures. Thus, XML is a data type in DB2, just like any other SQL data type, except its storage mechanism. It may be noted that XML schema is not required in order to hold an XML column and schema validation is optional.

Creating a database table with XML datatype: To illustrate with a simple example, take the hypothetical case of a hybrid database that stores information about books for Pustak Portal. For every book, in addition to an identification number, certain information about every book is stored as XML data. Such a hybrid database can be created using the following command:

```
CREATE table books ( bookID char(32),. . . , bookDetails xml);
```

After creating the database, the following are details about entering data into the database, querying the database, and updating records [34, 35].

Entering XML data into the database: XML data can be entered into a table created with XML data types using the INSERT statement. If the database needs to be populated with a large number of XML documents, the IMPORT command can be used. For example, the following code fragment demonstrates how an XML document can be inserted into an XML column of a DB2 database on-the-fly.

```
INSERT INTO books ( bookID,...,bookDetails) VALUES (ISBNxxxxx, ...,
    XMLPARSE(' <book>
      <title> Angela's Ashes </title>
      <author> Frank McCourt </author>
      <genre> Fictionalized Biography </genre>
      <publisher> ... </publisher>
      <synopsis> ... </synopsis>
        </book>'
    ) );
```

While inserting data into a column of DB2 which is of XML data type, it is checked whether the data is well-formed; that is, whether it conforms to certain syntax rules specified in the W3C standard for XML. The XMLPARSE keyword is used to enforce this. However, the XMLPARSE keyword is optional as it is implicitly called every time XML data is populated in the database. When used explicitly, certain additional options can be specified (e.g., to preserve/strip whitespace) along with the keyword.

Querying XML data: As stated earlier, DB2 supports query languages that help access data using either SQL, XQuery (a functional language which is built on XPath), a combination of SQL/XML or a combination of XQuery and embedded SQL. An application can employ both SQL and XQuery/XML and a single query can encompass both kinds of queries. The results of queries can either be relational, XML or a combination of both. DB2 also contains a set of built-in functions to be used for XML data. They fall into the categories of DB2-defined and XQuery-defined functions. Examples of each of these combinations are given in the subsequent examples.

DB2-defined functions need to use db2-fn as a prefix to use the proper namespace. The two main functions available are called xmlcolumn and sqlquery. xmlcolumn is used to extract XML documents from a XML column of a DB2 table while sqlquery enables SQL queries to be embedded inside XQuery. For example, the following code retrieves the entire column of bookDetails from the books database.

```
XQUERY db2-fn: xmlcolumn('BOOKS.BOOKDETAILS')
```

To access the author names from the XML documents stored in the books table, the following XQuery can be used:

```
XQUERY
    for $d in db2-fn: xmlcolumn('BOOKS.BOOKDETAILS')/book/author
    return $d;
```

The query returns the following answer:

```
<author> Frank McCourt </author>
```

The following is an example of embedded SQL within XQuery, where the author for a book with a particular bookID can be selected. Here, the sqlquery function provides the option to give the SQL full select as an input.

```
XQUERY db2-fn: sqlquery (
    'SELECT bookDetails FROM books WHERE bookID = ...'
    )/book/author;
```

XQuery-defined functions do not need a prefix. The functions supported fall broadly in the categories of string functions (e.g., compare, concat), boolean functions (e.g., not, zero-or-one), number functions (e.g., abs, floor, ceiling), date functions (e.g., current-date, implicit-timezone), sequence functions (e.g., count, last-index-of), *QName* functions and node functions. XQuery also supports FLWOR (for, let, where, order by and return) expressions. We can also query via a combination of SQL/XML commands which allows XQuery expressions and commands to be embedded in SQL. Some of the useful commands under this include XMLQUERY and XMLTABLE. While XMLQUERY allows an XML query to be embedded in SQL, XMLTABLE generates tabular output from XML data, which is useful for providing a relational view. An example of XMLQUERY follows, where XMLEXISTS returns a boolean value depending on whether a certain attribute is present or absent.

```
SELECT bookID, XMLQUERY('$c/book/author'
                        passing books.bookDetails as "c")
    FROM books
        WHERE XMLEXISTS('$d/book/title'
                        passing books.bookDetails as "d")
```

Updating XML data: In order to update the full XML document stored in the XML column of a DB2 database, one can use the UPDATE command available in SQL as shown below:

```
UPDATE books SET bookDetails = XMLPARSE( DOCUMENT (
    ...
    ) )
WHERE bookID = ...
```

To update parts of the XML document one can retrieve the entire document, modify it as required and consequently use the SQL UPDATE command to replace with the new version.

NOTE

Advanced pureXML Features

- XML indexing
- XML validation
- XML shredding
- Full-text search

Advanced Features of pureXML

In addition to the basic database operations described previously, pureXML provides several features for better manageability, correctness and speed and efficiency of access of the stored XML data. This includes the use of XML indexing, validating the XML data against a pre-defined XML schema, shredding XML data into relational tables and allowing for powerful XML full-text search.

XML indexing is a mechanism to speed up queries for XML documents. These indexes provide direct access to intermediate nodes of the hierarchical tree structure instead of at the root of the tree. This speeds up the queries but may slow down other operations like insert, delete and update. In addition, extra storage is required to store information for indexing.

The **XML validation** process checks whether the structure, data types, and content of an XML document are valid. The XML validations are carried out against a pre-registered XML schema. The following command shows how a document can be validated against a pre-registered schemaID.

```
INSERT INTO books (bookID,...,bookDetails) VALUES (..., ...,
XMLVALIDATE( XMLPARSE (
    '<book> ... </book>' ) ACCORDING TO XMLSCHEMA ID schemaID ) )
```

XML shredding: DB2 provides the functionality to decompose XML data such that they can be stored in regular columns as part of the relational database table. It uses an annotated XML schema document that describes the decomposition rules. The annotations point to which part of the traditional relational database table the corresponding parts of the XML data should reside in. As in schema validation, the schema documents that describe the decomposition must also be registered in the **XML Schema Repository (XSR)**. The following command can then be issued to decompose an XML document:

```
DECOMPOSE XML DOCUMENT <xml-doc-name> XMLSCHEMA <xml-schema-
document>
```

In addition to supporting XQuery where text searches are simple substring matches, DB2 supports an advanced full-text search mechanism via the **Net Search Extender (NSE)** engine. NSE can search full-text documents stored in a DB2 database using SQL queries. NSE does not employ sequential searching of the text which can become inefficient. Instead, using a text index, which typically consists of significant terms that are extracted from the text document, it can carry out efficient and fast searches over large volumes of text. For full-text search on its XML columns, one needs to run the command:

```
DB2TEXT ENABLE DATABASE FOR TEXT CONNECT TO booksdb
    DB2TEXT CREATE INDEX ind FOR TEXT ON books(bookDetails) CONNECT TO
    booksdb
```

Using IBM Data Studio to Enable DaaS

As seen from the description in the previous section, pureXML enables the developer to have a data abstraction at the semantic or application layer with operations using XML data used in the application. This section describes how one can now enable the pureXML-enabled DB2 to be hosted on the cloud, in the form of **Data As A Service (DaaS)**. Before describing the details of IBM Data Studio, a brief overview of service-oriented architectures is called for.

NOTE

IBM Data Studio Components

- Data Project Explorer: develop and deploy DaaS services and clients
- Data Source Explorer: by the database administrators for managing DB2 instances and databases.

Service-oriented Architectures

Every application hosted on the cloud exposes web service APIs (using protocols such as HTTP, REST, SOAP) for web clients (either on-premise applications or other co-operating applications) to access its functionality. While this is common, most of these applications also follow a **Service-oriented Architecture** where the internal components of the application too are exposed as web service APIs (though may not be publicly available). The communication among these components will be using web service calls and so any internal change in the individual components will not affect the rest of the modules. It also enables independent maintenance and versioning. More importantly, this design is key to achieving scale out of the application as seen in Chapter 6.

Web services interoperate with a formal contract that is defined using **Web Services Description Language (WSDL)**. WSDL is language independent and implementations based on C# and Java EE for working with WSDL are already available. In fact, legacy systems written in COBOL can also be web service enabled with WSDL. WSDL includes knowledge on how to structure request/response messages, how to interpret these messages, and what kind of protocol (SOAP/REST/HTTP) to use in order to invoke the service. Traditionally SOAP (Simple Object Access Protocol), a protocol that defines the structure of the data payload while invoking an other service as an RPC (remote procedure call) mechanism, has been used to implement web service interfaces. More recently, there is a drive towards using REST (Representational state transfer) which uses well known standard HTTP methods of GET, PUT, POST, DELETE to provide a Web API. Most often Web API implementations in both SOAP and REST use XML for specifying the parameters of the remote procedure call.

Data as a Service (DaaS) is a service delivery model that provides structured data as a service. So, an application designed with service-oriented architecture can now share data among the different components by enabling DaaS over a database. pureXML can be hosted as a DaaS and therefore enables web clients (either on-premise or cloud-hosted applications) to manipulate data stored in a DB2 hybrid database. pureXML uses a software framework called **Web Services Object Runtime Framework (WORF)**.

WORF and DADX

WORF is a software environment provided by IBM to create simple XML-based web services to access DB2. It uses Apache SOAP 2.2 and its protocol extension called **Document Access Definition Extension (DADX)**. A DADX document can be defined by SQL commands and each document defines a web service under WORF. WORF supports **resource-based deployment**, wherein a web service is just defined in a resource file and placed in a specific directory of the web application. When a client requests that resource file, WORF loads the file and enables a web service as per the specification in the resource file. Users familiar with Servlet programming can see an analogy of this to WAR files deployed in web application servers. If the resource file is edited, WORF detects that there were changes to the file and so recreates a new version of the web service. This makes web service deployment very simple. The resource file is in DADX format, which is described later in this section.

DADX is an XML file that describes the web services that the users can access. When the web application server receives a request (in the form of a call to a method/query) from a client, WORF looks up the DADX file, and tries to locate the requested method in the file. After the requested method is located, the queries or stored procedures associated with the requested method are executed. The following code fragment demonstrates a sample DADX file consisting of a method name `getAuthor`. A client request with the method name `getAuthor()` is routed through this DADX file by WORF, which subsequently results in the answer "Frank McCourt" to be sent to the client. Here `XMLSERIALIZE` converts the query output as a string for consumption by the client.

```
<operation name = "getAuthor">
    <query>
        <SQL_query>
            SELECT XMLSERIALIZE ( XMLQUERY('$c/book/author/text()'
                        passing books.bookDetails as "c") as VARCHAR
                        (64) )
            FROM books
                WHERE XMLEXISTS('$d/book/title'
                        passing books.bookDetails as "d")
```

```
        </SQL_query>
      </query>
    </operation>
```

> **NOTE**
>
> **Summary of WORF functionality**
> * Connect to the DB2 database
> * Execute the query statements and stored procedures to access the hybrid database
> * Generate WSDL, XML schema and test pages for use and verification of the created web service

WORF supports an environment by which XML-based web services can be used to access DB2 data and stored procedures. WORF uses the DADX definition file to provide an implementation of a web service. This is done using a servlet that accepts a web service invocation over SOAP, an HTTP GET, or an HTTP POST. This servlet implements the service by accessing DB2, invoking the SQL/XML/XQuery operation defined in the DADX file, and returning the results as a response. WORF works on Websphere Application Server and Apache Tomcat. The framework allows developers to bypass the effort of writing and developing the web services ground-up, thereby increasing their productivity. WORF is used not only at runtime for wrapping a database query/access operation as a web service in the context of an invocation; it also generates all that are required to deploy the required service. WORF can automatically generate a Web Services Description Language (WSDL) file which can be published in a UDDI registry. A view of how WORF/DADX/DB2 interacts with each other is given in Figure 3.29. IBM has a tool that implements WORF and supports generation of DADX, called **IBM Data Studio**.

IBM Data Studio

IBM Data Studio [36, 37] is a tool for database administration and database development with an Eclipse-based GUI. It can run on Linux and Windows and is part of the IBM Integrated Data Management portfolio of products. The **Data Project Explorer** component of Data Studio can be used for developing SQL scripts, writing XQuery, stored procedures and subsequently deploying on an application server like Websphere Application Server (WAS). The **Data Source Explorer** is used by the database administrators for managing DB2 instances and databases. One can experiment with pureXML by downloading DB2 Express-C, Websphere Application Server and Data Studio [38]. DB2 Express-C is a version of DB2 Universal Database Express Edition (DB2 Express) for the community, which is completely free to download, develop, deploy, test, run, embed and redistribute. DB2 Express-C is available for Linux and Windows running 32-bit or 64-bit hardware. The WebSphere Application Server Community Edition is available at [39]. Pre-built Amazon Machine Images of IBM DB2 Express-C are available at http://www.ibm.com/developerworks/downloads/im/udbexp/cloud.html [40].

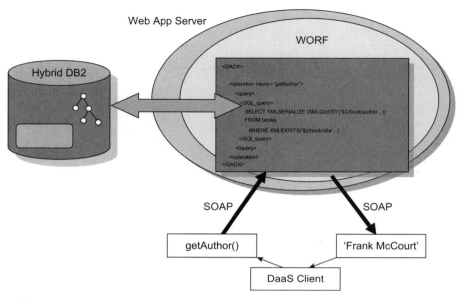

FIGURE 3.29

WORF/DADX interaction around pureXML.

Data Studio takes care of all the JDBC code required to access/query DB2 data. It also (internally) generates a WSDL file for each Data Web Service that is created. In addition, it creates the runtime tooling required for clients to access the deployed web service using SOAP/HTTP/REST-style bindings, generate the code necessary to look up the operation names in WSDL for the corresponding DB2 access queries. And dispatch results. The deployed service can also be tested before being published for use by a larger community. Thus, IBM Data Studio provides a unified framework to the user in which (s)he can develop web services and database applications very quickly and easily. Functionalities like WORF and specification of files like DADX are transparently handled. Finally, the generated web services are packaged in the form of a ready-to-use web application for clients to exploit. The Web Services Explorer component of Data Studio can be used to test the generated web services. It can test the invocation of these services over SOAP or other protocols.

APACHE HADOOP

One of the best-known cloud platforms for big data today is **Apache Hadoop**. Many research papers have been written describing the experiences of porting large data-intensive applications onto this platform. Hadoop solves a specific class of data-crunching problems that frequently comes up in the domain of Internet computing and high-performance computing. At the time of this writing, Hadoop held the world record for the fastest system to sort large data (500 GB of data in 59 sec and 100 terabytes of data in 68 seconds). Along with the ability to analyze large data sets, Hadoop provides a solution for storing these datasets efficiently, and in a way that is highly available. Hadoop is optimized for batch-processing applications, and scales to the number of CPUs available in the cluster.

Hadoop was first started as a part of the Apache Nutch project, an open source web search engine with developer APIs. After Google published information about its MapReduce technology behind its search engine [41, 42], Nutch was rewritten to use MapReduce. Later, the MapReduce parts were extracted into a separate project called Hadoop, as it was found that MapReduce was a widely applicable technology. The creators of this initial version of Hadoop were Doug Cutting and Mike Cafarella in 2004. So, in 2006, the Hadoop project was officially announced as a standalone open source project, hosted by Apache Software Foundation and sponsored with many developers from Yahoo!.

NOTE

Key Subprojects of Hadoop
- Hadoop Common
- Hadoop Distributed File System
- MapReduce
- Pig, Hive, Hbase

Overview of Hadoop

Hadoop has three components – the **Common** component, the **Hadoop Distributed File System** component, and the **MapReduce** component. Each of these components is a sub-project in the Hadoop top-level project. The Common sub-project deals with abstractions and libraries that can be used by both the other sub-projects. A widely used and a widely implemented interface in the Common sub-project is the FileSystem interface. The Hadoop Distributed File System is a file system for storing large files on a distributed cluster of machines. Hadoop MapReduce is a framework for running jobs that usually does processing of data from the Hadoop Distributed File System. Frameworks like **Hbase, Pig** and **Hive** have been built on top of Hadoop. **Pig** is a dataflow language and execution environment over Hadoop. **Hbase** is a distributed key-value store which supports SQL-like queries similar to Google's BigTable [43] and **Hive** is a distributed data warehouse to manage data stored in the Hadoop File System. There are many real-life applications of Hadoop. Please refer to http://wiki.apache.org/hadoop/PoweredBy for a complete list of applications and organizations using it.

This section gives an introduction to the MapReduce platform with a simple example and high-level architectural details of MapReduce and the Hadoop Distributed File System (HDFS). A detailed description of MapReduce from a programming perspective is given in Chapter 5, where hints and approaches to design an application to work efficiently on the MapReduce framework are described with multiple examples. A further detailed description of the internal architecture of MapReduce and HDFS is presented in Chapter 6 on *Addressing the Cloud Challenges*.

MapReduce

Hadoop requires the cloud applications written on its platform to use a new programming model called **MapReduce** [42]. This model is very useful to express the inherent parallelism within an application and take advantage of the parallel processing support provided by Hadoop for fast and efficient execution. MapReduce works in two phases – the **Map phase** and the **Reduce phase**. To write an application using the MapReduce framework, the programmer just specifies two functions – the **Map function** and **Reduce function**. The inputs to these two functions are simple key-value pairs.

The processing flow for a MapReduce program is given below:

- The input data is split into chunks, each of which is sent to different Mapper processes. The output of the Mapper process includes key-value pairs.
- The result of the Mapper process is partitioned based on the key and is sorted locally.
- The Reduce function gets this sorted key-value data for one key, processes it and generates the output key-value pairs.

An example will make things clear.

A Simple Example of MapReduce

An example that uses MapReduce APIs in Java to analyze sales data of Pustak Portal is described next. The program described finds the total sales of each book and picks the book that has the maximum number of sales per day. The input is a log file that lists the sales of every book from different dealers (one book per line) and the MapReduce program finds the total sales per book. The Map function gets key-value pairs where key is the line number, and it outputs key-value pairs with key as the ISBN of the book. The shuffle sorts the key-value pairs and hands over all the sales data per book (per ISBN) to the reduce function, which computes the sum based on its input key-value pairs. More detail follows.

Let us assume that the data found in the log file is in the following format:

```
ISBN1234, name of book1, author, dealer name, location, 10, ...
ISBN3245, name of book2, author, dealer name, location, 20, ....
...
ISBN9999, name of book1111, author, dealer name, location, 32, ...
```

The application works in two phases. In the map phase, the log file is preprocessed to extract only the interesting fields of the record. The preceding lines in the log file are presented to the Map function in the form of key-value pairs as shown in the code that follows. Here the keys are the line offsets within the file which is ignored by the Map function.

```
(0, "ISBN1234, name of book1, author, dealer name1, location, 10, ...")
(101, "ISBN3245, name of book2, author, dealer name, location, 20, ....")
(250, "ISBN1234, name of book1, author, dealer name2, location, 110, ...")
...
(1189, "ISBN9999, name of book1111, author, dealer name, location, 32")
```

So, the Map function is very simple in this case. A sample output of the Map function will be:

```
(ISBN1234, 10)
(ISBN3245, 20)
(ISBN1234, 110)
...
(ISBN9999,32)
...
```

Now, the MapReduce framework processes the output of the Map function before sending it to the Reduce function. It sorts and groups the key-value pairs by key. So, the Reduce function gets consolidated data for each book (based on the ISBN), like this:

```
(ISBN1234, [10,110])
(ISBN3245, [20])
...
(ISBN9999, [32,22,112])
```

The Reduce function just needs to go through one line at a time and add up the different elements in the list to create the final key-value pair of results.

The actual Java code to do the functions that were listed previously is given in the Map function code that follows. There three key methods in the application – the Map function that implements the `Mapper` interface to define the `map()` method, the Reduce function that implements the `Reducer` interface to define the reduce method and the Main method that fires the map reduce job.

```java
import java.io.IOException;
import java.util.Iterator;

import org.apache.hadoop.io.IntWritable;
import org.apache.hadoop.io.Text;
import org.apache.hadoop.mapred.MapReduceBase;
import org.apache.hadoop.mapred.OutputCollector;
import org.apache.hadoop.mapred.Mapper;
import org.apache.hadoop.mapred.Reporter;

public class SalesConsolidatorMap extends MapReduceBase
        implements Mapper<LongWritable, Text, Text, IntWritable>
{
```

```
public void map (LongWritable key, Text value,
        OutputCollector<Text, IntWritable> output, Reporter
reporter)
        throws IOExcpetion {
    String line = value.toString();
    String [] splitStr = line.split(",");
    String isbn = splitStr[0];
    int count = Integer.parseInt(splitStr[5]);
    // Output key value pairs with selective information
    output.collect(new Text(isbn), new IntWritable(count));
    }
}
```

The Mapper interface has four formal parameters for input key, input value, output key and output value. Instead of using built-in Java types, Hadoop provides its own set of basic types to support network serialization (and hence optimized distributed application execution). The map method is passed a key and a value, along with additional parameters for outputting information. The output of the Map function is realized in the call to output.collect method, which writes out the ISBN to count key-value pairs.

The reduce method is also written along similar lines. The input parameters of reduce correspond to output parameter types of the map method (Text and IntWritable) as shown in the following snippet. The summation inside the loop is performing the reduce function and again the output.collect method is used to output the consolidated key-value pairs. Please note that the output format of this reduce function can actually be passed to another reduce function for hierarchical consolidation.

```
import java.io.IOException;
import java.util.Iterator;

import org.apache.hadoop.io.IntWritable;
import org.apache.hadoop.io.Text;
import org.apache.hadoop.mapred.MapReduceBase;
import org.apache.hadoop.mapred.OutputCollector;
import org.apache.hadoop.mapred.Reducer;
import org.apache.hadoop.mapred.Reporter;

public class SalesConsolidatorRed extends MapReduceBase
        implements Reducer<Text,IntWritable, Text, IntWritable>
{

    public void reduce (Text key, Iterator<IntWritable> values,
            OutputCollector<Text, IntWritable> output, Reporter
reporter)
            throws IOExcpetion {
        int sum = 0;
        while (values.hasNext()) {
          // Reduce function is performed here
            sum = sum + values.next().get();
        }
```

```
    // Output key value pair
    output.collect(key, new IntWritable(sum));
    }
  }
```

The following code snippet gives the code to execute the MapReduce task. The description of the job is specified in the `JobConf` object. The mapper and reducer classes are also set in the same `Jobconf` object and the `runJob` method starts off the map-reduce activity.

```
import java.io.IOException;
import org.apache.hadoop.fs.Path;
import org.apache.hadoop.io.IntWritable;
import org.apache.hadoop.io.Text;
import org.apache.hadoop.mapred.FileInputFormat;
import org.apache.hadoop.mapred.FileOutputFormat;
import org.apache.hadoop.mapred.JobClient;
import org.apache.hadoop.mapred.JobConf;

public class SalesConsolidator {
    public static void main(String[]args) throws IOException {

    if (args.length != 2) {
        System.err.println("Please give input path and output path as
        arguments");
    System.exit(-1);
    }
    // Define the new job
    JobConf job = new JobConf(SalesConsolidator.class);
    job.setJobName("Sales Consolidation");

    FileInputFormat.addInputPath(job, new Path(args[0]));
    FileOutputFormat.addOutputPath(job, new Path([args[1]]);

    // Set Mapper and Reducer functions for this job
    job.setMapperClass(SalesConsolidatorMap.class);
    job.setReducerClass(SalesConsolidatorRed.class);

    job.setOutputKeyClass(text.class);
    job.setOutputValueClass(IntWritable.class);

    // Run the MapReduce job
    JobClient.runJob(job);
    }
  }
```

The previous sample code uses Release 0.20.0 of MapReduce API. Please refer to http://hadoop.apache.org for the latest version of the API, download and installation instructions. Now, to test and execute the previous sample application, one can use the following commands. The input log files are in the directory data/sales/input **and output will be in the** data/sales/consoled directory,

```
% export HADOOP_CLASSPATH=build/classes
% hadoop SalesConsolidator data/sales/input data/sales/consolid
```

Running non-Java MapReduce applications

The MapReduce framework in Hadoop has native support for running Java applications. It also supports running non-Java applications in Ruby, Python, C++ and a few other programming languages, via two frameworks, namely the **Streaming** framework and the **Pipes** framework. The Streaming framework allows MapReduce programs written in any language, including shell scripts, to be run as a MapReduce application in Hadoop. The basic assumption that is made here is that the programs can consume their input via stdin and they output via stdout. The MapReduce framework forks the Streaming program, sends the keys/values on the process's stdin, and captures output from the process's stdout. The Pipes library in MapReduce, on the other hand, provides C++ APIs for writing MapReduce applications. This is believed to provide better performance than Streaming. It is very useful when there are legacy applications written in C or C++, and one wants to move them to the MapReduce model.

Dataflow in Map Reduce[4]

In Hadoop MapReduce, inputs are referred to as **splits**. It is the job of the application writer to define the splits for his application. For example, if the log file containing sales information is a large file on which sales consolidation needs to be performed (as in the previous example), the application writer can define the splits as reasonably large chunks of the file. The splits information is included in the job submission request. Each Map task gets to work on one split, and produce the output. Each Map task produces the outputs for all Reduce tasks. Furthermore, the output per Reduce task is **sorted** via a user provided comparator on the Map output key data type. The number of outputs is equal to the number of Reduce tasks. As Map tasks complete, their outputs are made available to the Reduce tasks of the job. The process of transferring Map outputs to the Reduce tasks is called **Shuffle**. In the Shuffle phase, the Reduce tasks pull sections of the Map outputs relevant to them (typically all pairs with same key value). Reduce tasks process their inputs, and produce the final output (see Figure 3.30).

MapReduce can be viewed as a distributed sort engine. If the input were just passed through the framework with an Identity Map function and an Identity Reduce function defined for the corresponding job, the output would be sorted. More details of this and other such important algorithms are described in the section titled *Map Reduce Revisited* in Chapter 5.

The main advantage of using the MapReduce paradigm is that the application is now written in a manner that explicitly identifies portions of the application that can be executed in parallel. For example, as seen in Figure 3.30, the

---

[4]Contributed by Mr. Devaraj Das from Apache Hadoop PMC.

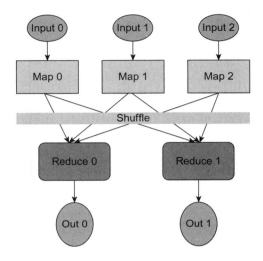

FIGURE 3.30

Dataflow in MapReduce.

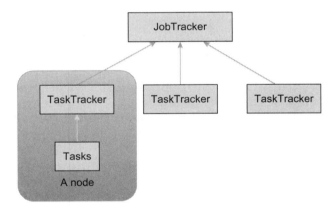

FIGURE 3.31

Architecture components of MapReduce.

operations on key-value pairs with the different keys can be done in parallel. Similarly Map tasks if working on different splits can work in parallel. The different Map and Reduce tasks can therefore be executed as independent threads or processes on a cluster of compute nodes to get maximum performance.

Hadoop MapReduce Architecture

The architectural components of Hadoop MapReduce that orchestrate the different Map and Reduce tasks to work in parallel are shown in Figure 3.31. The key processes in the system are the JobTracker, the TaskTracker and the different Tasks. These are described next.

- **The JobTracker:** The JobTracker is the central authority for the complete MapReduce cluster, and is responsible for scheduling and monitoring MapReduce jobs, to keep track of the node membership status of a MapReduce cluster, and to respond to client requests for job submissions and job status. The JobTracker can be configured to have multiple queues and a chosen job scheduler. Some schedulers that are in use are the **CapacityScheduler,** and the **FairScheduler**. The FairScheduler is a simple scheduler with a single queue while the CapacityScheduler supports multiple queues with different priority and guaranteed resource capacities [44].
- **The TaskTracker:** The TaskTrackers are the workers. The TaskTracker accepts Map and Reduce tasks from the JobTracker, launches them and keeps track of their progress over time. The TaskTracker reports the progress of the tasks to the JobTracker. The TaskTracker keeps track of the resource usage of tasks (currently only memory), and kills tasks that overshoot their memory limits.
- **The Tasks:** Tasks run as separate processes. They have framework code that does some setup and teardown, between which runs the user code. The tasks are expected to report progress periodically to their parent TaskTracker. The tasks run in their own sandboxed environment.

Since the Map and Reduce tasks execute in parallel, the computation of MapReduce can be scaled up as many more nodes are added into the cluster (see Chapter 6 to understand the theoretical limits of scale up). Now, since all tasks operate on key-value pairs, the storage has to be efficient and high performing with high throughput. That is the motivation of another Hadoop project called **Hadoop Distributed File System (HDFS)**, a distributed file system that enables a fast retrieval amd updates, described next.

Hadoop Distributed File System

To store the input, output and intermediate key value pairs Hadoop uses a file system interface that can be implemented by anyone and plugged in as a file system in Hadoop. There are a number of file systems already part of the Hadoop distribution. They include the Hadoop Distributed File System, S3 file system, Kosmos file system, and others. Each file system serves some specific lower level storage. The Hadoop Distributed File System is based on ideas in *The Google file system* [41].

The Hadoop Distributed File System (HDFS) is a distributed file system that provides high throughput access to data. The applications of HDFS include MapReduce and other such platforms where a large storage based on commodity hardware is required. The system is optimized for storage of very large files, high availability and reliability of data. This section gives an overview of HDFS with details of its architecture and API for accessing it.

HDFS API

Applications can use HDFS file systems using the standard file system APIs. One of the main differences of HDFS with respect to other distributed file systems is that it provides simple IO centric APIs and does not attempt to provide a full-blown Posix API set. In particular, HDFS does not provide consistency over reads and writes; i.e., if multiple nodes read and write the file at the same time, the data seen by the various nodes may not be consistent, unlike a POSIX compliant file system. Additionally, it exposes the location of blocks of the files. This feature is leveraged by Hadoop's MapReduce implementation to co-locate computations with data needed for the computation.

As mentioned before, Hadoop uses a file system interface that can be implemented by anyone and plugged in as a file system in Hadoop. Applications specify the file system using the file system's URI. For example, `hdfs://` is used to identify the HDFS filesystem.

HDFS Example: Finding the Location of Data Blocks

As HDFS is written in Java, HDFS files can be read and written just like any other Java file using Java `DataInputStream` and `DataOutputStream` APIs such as `readUTF()`. As noted earlier, one of the key features of Hadoop is to schedule tasks at nodes where the data is stored. The HDFS client also tries to read data from the nearest node in order to minimize network traffic. The following code fragment illustrates how to find the hosts that have a particular data block.

```
import java.io.File;
import java.io.IOException;
import org.apache.hadoop.conf.Configuration;
import org.apache.hadoop.fs.FileSystem;
import org.apache.hadoop.fs.FSDataInputStream;
import org.apache.hadoop.fs.FSDataOutputStream;
import org.apache.hadoop.fs.Path;
public class HDFSExample {
public static void main (String [] args) throws IOException {
   String exampleF = "example.txt";
   int BlockNo = 0;
/*1*/Configuration conf = new Configuration();
   FileSystem fs = FileSystem.get(conf);
/*2*/Path fPath = new Path(exampleF);
/*3*/FileStatus fStat = fs.getFileStatus (fPath);
/*4*/int fLen = fStat.getLen();
/*5*/BlockLocation[] blockLocs = fs.getFileBlockLocation (fPath,
      0, fLen);
}
```

Statement 1 and the following statement initialize the interface to the HDFS file system. Statement 2 gets a pointer to the desired file (called "exampleF"). Statement 3 gets a `FileStatus` object. One of the methods of this object is the getlen() method, which is invoked in statement 4 to get the length of the file in blocks. Statement 5 then invokes the getFileBlockLocation () method, which has three parameters. The first parameter, fPath, specifies the file about which information is desired. The second and third parameters specify the region of the file (start block and end block) for which the information is desired, In the example, information about the whole file is queried. The getFileBlockLocation() method returns an array of BlockLocation. After the call, blockLocs[i] contains information about the location of the ith block; blockLocs[i].getHosts() returns an array of String that contains the names of the host nodes which have a copy of the ith block in the region. This information can now be used to move computation to those nodes if that is possible in the system. More information about these APIs is available at [45].

As mentioned before, this section only gave an introduction to usage of Map-Reduce and HDFS platforms. An in-depth study of the MapReduce **programming paradigm is given in Chapter 5** and some advanced topics in the **internal architecture** of MapReduce and HDFS are discussed in **Chapter 6**.

MASHUPS

Thus far, this chapter described multiple platforms meant for advanced developers to develop cloud applications. This section looks at simple ways of creating cloud applications using platforms that provide visual programming – that even a non-expert end user can use to develop personally relevant applications. The Web has a plethora of data and services and end users may want to integrate these to make it usable in a manner that they find most useful. As an example, when planning a trip, a web site may provide a list of flights between certain destinations, and the user may want to now sort them by flight time or price – but only for airlines that he usually travels with. Another example could be a user who wants to combine data from various sources with map information to visualize, say, available apartments on a world map and be notified when a certain type of apartment is available for sale. Data **Mashups**, a technology that enables such simple integration of information from multiple web sources to enable end users to create Cloud-hosted personal applications, is described in this section.

Mashups are web sites or software applications that merge separate APIs and data sources into one integrated interface/experience. They thus democratize data access by moving control closer to users who then combine existing data sources without owners being involved [46]. Such situational (short-lived) applications filter, join and aggregate data from multiple sources to serve a specific need. An important factor enabling Mashups is that many web services (e.g., Yahoo!, eBay and Amazon) have opened their systems to external use through public APIs and Web feeds (e.g., RSS or Atom). This enables third-party developers to integrate the basic data and services that Web platforms provide and make information more useful than it would be on its own. Yahoo! Pipes is one such platform for end-users to create Mashups via visual programming, and is described next.

Yahoo! Pipes

Yahoo! Pipes (or **Pipes** for short) is an interactive tool that enables combining many data feeds (e.g., RSS Atom and RDF) into a single aggregate and then transforming them through web service calls (e.g., language translation, and location extraction). They are conceptually similar to the well-known process communication tool in Unix called **pipes**. In the same way that Unix pipes allow data to be piped in sequence through multiple programs, Yahoo! Pipes can also be used to perform a series of data operations on multiple data sets. However, with Yahoo! Pipes, developers can manipulate data that's available on the web, and not just data locally available on the system. Yahoo! Pipes are also not just limited to one input and one output (like Unix pipes). Certain operators can have more than one input.

While Unix pipes allow for the sequential processing of data, Yahoo! Pipes allow users to define a data processing pipeline, which can be a data flow graph, as illustrated in the examples later in this section. The graph is produced by interconnecting data sources and operators. The data sources for a Pipe consist not only of data feeds from a web site, but also any data that can be converted into a feed (such as a file, or user input). The operators are pre-defined by Pipes, each performing a certain task (e.g., looping, filtering, regular expressions, or counting). Once a pipe is built, it can be re-used as a component in another pipe until the ultimate mashup is created. One can also store the pipe and attach it as a module to MyYahoo! page or Yahoo! front page.

It is common to create Pipes for combining interesting news feeds. Other examples include feeds containing (i) all the apartment listings near parks or schools; (ii) all eBay listings within a certain price range; (iii) process the Craigslist feed and identify location information (geocodes) to augment the feed with a link that displays a property's address by passing it to Google Maps. More details on how one can create such simple personalized integration of information is described next.

Figure 3.32 gives the screenshot of the Yahoo! Pipes web page, with insets showing an enlarged version of the menus for better readability. The rest of this section describes a simple example first and then provides a more comprehensive description of the various data sources and operations that Pipes enables.

A Simple Yahoo! Pipe to Generate City News

The following example pipe is called CityNews and generates a feed containing news about a city. It is very simple but demonstrates the power of Pipes. The first step is to go to the Yahoo! Pipes web site at `http://pipes.yahoo.com`, and click on the `My Pipes` link. If there are no pipes yet, this will bring up an editing webpage for the Pipes UI where the first pipe can be created, as shown in Figure 3.32.

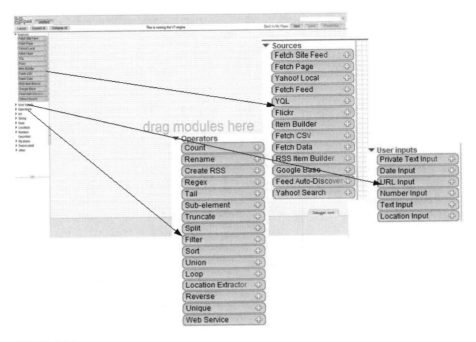

FIGURE 3.32

Pipes editor UI.

Select RSS feeds: The next step is to choose the web feeds to be combined, and aggregate them into a single feed. On the left-side menu bar, under `Sources` is a box called `Fetch Feed`. Dragging this box onto the editing field will cause a URL box to appear as shown in Figure 3.33, into which the URL of the desired RSS feed can be entered.[5] In the example, news about a city is needed, so the URL of the RSS feed of the government web site can be used (see Figure 3.34). The example shows how to add the RSS feed of California. After the feed has been added, the debugger says there are 45 items in the feed. Additional URLs can be added either by dragging the `Fetch` box or by clicking on the + sign in the `Fetch` box.

Combine RSS feeds: Finally, all the feeds can be combined using a `Union` box. Such a box can be created by dragging the `Union` box under `Operators` in the left side menu on to the editing field. The outputs of the `Fetch` boxes can then be connected to the `Union` box as shown in Figure 3.34 by clicking and dragging the mouse from point to point. The example uses Wikipedia as a source, thus exemplifying the versatility of Pipes. The debugger now shows 112 items after the union operation on the feeds.

---

[5]The URL of a site's RSS feed can be found by clicking on the RSS icon in the URL box at any web site with a feed.

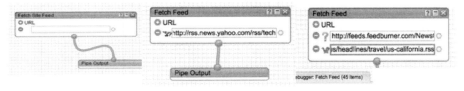

FIGURE 3.33

Getting started.

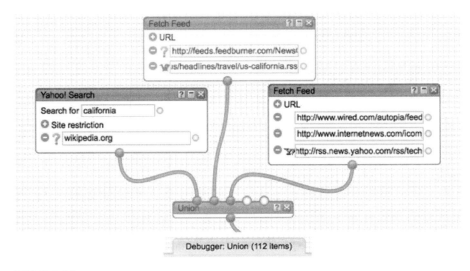

FIGURE 3.34

Combining feeds.

Filtering the Pipe: At this point, the pipe has four feeds, all with a hefty array of daily headlines. That's a lot of information to wade through every day. To limit the data flow down to a manageable level, the Pipe can be filtered. This can be done by dragging a `Filter` box onto the editing field from the `Filter` box under the `Operators` category on the left-side menu bar. The output of the `Union` box is connected to the input of the `Filter` box, and the output of the `Filter` box with the input of the Pipe Output. The choices in the `title` drop-down menu on the `Filter` box update when this connection is made. The `Filter` box allows filtering of the content in numerous ways which can be selected by clicking on the `title` and `contains` boxes. Assume that it is desired to monitor articles concerning unemployment rate, technology, and California. The example in the picture shows how to show feeds that contain these keywords. The debugger now shows 24 items after filtering from 112 items (see Figure 3.35).

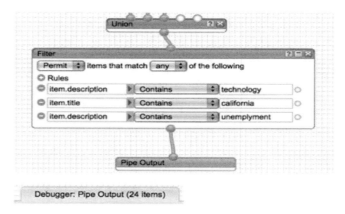

FIGURE 3.35

Filtering the feed.

The Pipe can be saved by clicking Save near the top of the editing field, and naming the Pipe. On the MyPipes page, clicking Publish allows the Pipe to be made public.

Pipes Data Sources and Operations

To describe the operations and data sources Pipes provides, the Pipes editor UI is used (see inset with heading operators in Figure 3.32), as it lists all the data sources and operations available in the left side pane. The important and frequently used sources and operations are described; a comprehensive list can be found in the Yahoo! documentation as described later.

Sources: The sources available are shown expanded in Figure 3.32 as inset. These include Fetch Feed, which takes as input a feed URL and returns the items in the feed [47], as well as Feed Auto-Discovery, which takes as input the URL for a web site, and returns the URLs of all the feeds discovered on the web site. The Fetch Data module takes as input the URL of an XML or JSON file, attempts to parse it, and extracts specified fields. The Fetch Page module returns the HTML page specified by a URL as a string; while the Fetch CSV module allows the conversion of a CSV file into a feed. Finally, the Yahoo! Local module allows searching for services in a location (e.g., gyms in San Francisco) while the Yahoo! Search module provides an interface to Yahoo Search.

An important source is the **YQL source** listed earlier. YQL is an SQL-like query language that can be used to develop programs that process data available on the web, where the native processing functionality present in Pipes is not sufficient. An example is where it is desired to find an apartment in a town that also contains a Pizza Hut. The most efficient way to do this would be to generate a list of apartments and locations and Pizza Huts and locations, sort both on locations and merge. YQL is described in detail in a later section.

User Inputs: Figure 3.32 also shows the user inputs that can be used in Pipes. For brevity, only the expanded `User Inputs` part of the Pipes editor GUI are shown; the rest are in Figure 3.32. The `Text Input` module takes text input by the user and outputs a text string that can be used as input by other modules or operators [48], while the `Private Text Input` module is used for the input of confidential text that should not be displayed, such as a password. The `URL Input` module takes a URL input by the user and outputs a URL that can be used as input to a module that expects a URL. The `Location` module accepts user input and outputs a `Location` datatype that can be used as input to another pipe module. The `Location` module also displays the quality of the location, which describes the accuracy on a scale of 0 to 100 (with 100 being the most accurate).

Operators: Figure 3.32 shows the operators available in Pipes. It can be seen that Pipes provide a powerful set of operators needed for string and data structure manipulation. The `Count` operator counts the number of items in a feed. The `Create RSS` operator creates an RSS feed from a non-RSS structure [49]. `Regex` allows pattern matching and substitution based upon regular expressions; for details please see *Module Reference: Operator Modules* [49]. The `Union` and `Filter` operators have already been described in the example earlier. The `Tail` and `Truncate` operators return the last and first *N* items from an RSS feed, respectively. The `Split` operator splits a feed into two identical feeds. The `Web Service` operator sends Pipes data to a web service in JSON format.

Similarly, the `URL` operators build a URL from various fields in Pipes data [50]. The `String` operators perform string manipulations, such as tokenization, substring, and pattern match [51]. The `Date` operators perform data extraction and formatting [52]. The `Location` operators extract and format location information [53], while the `Number` operators perform simple mathematical functions [54].

Yahoo! Query Language

The previous section describes Yahoo! Pipes, which allows combining and filtering of data from the Web. While this is very powerful, for some applications, it may be desirable to have data processing power comparable to that provided by relational databases. The present section describes **Yahoo! Query Language (YQL)**, a service that allows developers to perform more powerful processing that is comparable in power to relational databases.

YQL was developed by Yahoo! to encourage the creation of a developer community around Yahoo! data. There are thus YQL services for all Yahoo! data (e.g., Contacts from Yahoo! Mail). Additionally, non-Yahoo! services can also be mapped to YQL. YQL is used internally by Yahoo! in a large number of Yahoo! services (e.g., Yahoo! Homepage, and Search). This helps ensure its quality and comprehensiveness.

The rest of this section first provides an overview of YQL, including a description of the `YQL Console`, which allows testing of YQL statements. This is followed by a YQL example that shows how to generate tweets about

New York Times bestsellers published by Pustak Portal. The example also illustrates how YQL can be incorporated into Pipes.

YQL Overview

In the same way that relational databases view data as being stored in tables, YQL allows the manipulation of data stored in **Open Data Tables (ODT)**. To allow the data in Yahoo! services to be processed by YQL, Yahoo! provides a mapping from Yahoo! services to ODT. For example, the list of photographs stored on Flickr, Yahoo!'s photo service, is available as an ODT. Many external web services, such as Twitter, are also available as ODTs. A full list of such services can be found from the YQL Console, as described in the rest of this section.

Figure 3.36 shows the YQL Console [55], which allows users to execute YQL statements and examine the results. It is thus an important debugging and learning tool. At the top of the console, there is an area where YQL statements can be typed in. The figure shows the YQL statement `show tables`, which displays the tables available. Below is a radio button which allows selecting XML or JSON as the output. The output area contains a list of tables available. By default, it shows only the Yahoo! tables; clicking on the `Show Community Tables` link on the right-hand side shows the non-Yahoo! tables as well, including Facebook and Twitter. The `nyt` (*New York Times*) menu item has been expanded to show the various tables available, including the *New York Times* bestsellers (see Figure 3.37).

FIGURE 3.36

YQL console.

FIGURE 3.37

Web services available as open data tables.

YQL Example: Tweeting about New York Times Bestselling Books

To illustrate the usage of YQL and Yahoo! Pipes, the rest of this section describes how to write a pipe that (i) pulls the list of bestsellers from the *New York Times*; (ii) filters the books published by Pustak Portal; (iii) generates tweets about these books (for purposes of publicity).

> **NOTE**
>
> **YQL Example**
> - Access NYT ODT documentation
> - Get authorization
> - Test YQL statements in console
> - Create pipe to get bestsellers
> - Create pipe to loop over bestsellers and generate Tweets

```
<results>
    <table name="nyt.bestsellers" security="ANY" src=http://www.
datatables.org/nyt/nyt.bestsellers.xml>
        <meta>
            <author>Sam Pullara</author>
```

```
        <documentationURL> http://developer.nytimes.com/docs/
best_sellers_api</documentationURL>
        </meta>
        <request>
            <select usesRemoteList="true">
                <key name="apikey" required="true" type="xs:string"/>
                <key name="listname" required="true" type="xs:string"/>
                <key name="date" required="true" type="xs:string"/>
                <key name="sort_order" type="xs:string"/>
                <key name="sort_by" type="xs:string"/>
        </select>
```

Access ODT documentation, get authorization: As shown in Figure 3.37, the *New York Times* bestseller list is available as the ODT nyt.bestsellers in YQL. To extract the list of bestsellers, it is necessary to understand the API provided for accessing the table. This can be achieved by typing the YQL statement desc nyt.bestsellers into the YQL console and pressing the Test button, or by hovering the mouse over the nyt.bestsellers item and clicking the desc button that appears. Either method produces the output shown in the code segment *Description of nyt.bestsellers table*, where only the YQL console output is shown for clarity. The documentationURL tag shows that the documentation for accessing this table can be found in *The Best Sellers API* [56]. By accessing the documentation web site, it can be seen that it is necessary to register at the web site in order to use the web site. Additionally, the parameters needed to formulate the query (shown later) and their format can also be found. In addition to the name of the bestseller list (various bestseller lists, such as Hardcover Fiction are available), it can be seen that an api_key(needed for authentication) needs to be specified. The web site specifies that the api_key is generated during registration.

Test YQL statements: Based upon the documentation earlier, the YQL statement to retrieve the list of best sellers can now be written and tested in the YQL Console. The list is retrieved using a SELECT statement [57] as shown in the following code:

```
SELECT * FROM nyt.bestsellers WHERE listname='Hardcover Fiction' AND
apikey='
```

This statement is similar to the SQL SELECT statement and retrieves records that meet a selection criterion (specified by the WHERE clause). In this case, the statement retrieves all the fields of the selected records, specified by the *. As in SQL, selected fields can be retrieved by naming the fields, separated by commas. The WHERE clause contains two conditions. The first condition states that the Hardcover Fiction list is desired. The lists available, as well as the field name (listname), can be found in the ODT documentation [56]. The final condition specifies the api_key, which authenticates to the web site. The api_key is specified in the blank space between the single quotes. The output is shown in the console (see code segment *Testing Query to*

Retrieve NYT Bestsellers, where only the output is shown for clarity), and includes a list of books, together with other information, such as the publisher.

```
<list_name>Hardcover Fiction</list_name>
<display_name>Hardcover Fiction</display_name>
<bestsellers_date>2011-04-23</bestsellers_date>
<published_date>2011-05-06</published_date>
<rank>1</rank>
<rank_last_week>0</rank_last_week>
<weeks_on_list>1</weeks_on_list>
<asterisk>0</asterisk>
<dagger>0</dagger>
<isbns>
    <isbn>
        <isbn10>0446573108</isbn10>
        <isbn13>9780446573018</isbn13>
    </isbn>
    <isbn>
        <isbn10>0446573078</isbn10>
        <isbn13>9780446573078</isbn13>
    </isbn>
</isbns>
<book_details>
    <book_detail>
    <title>The Sixth Man</title>
    <description>The lawyer for an alleged serial killer is murdered, and
    two former Secret Service agents...</description>
    <contributor>by David Baldacci</contributor>
    <author>David Baldacci</author>
    <contributor_note/>
    <price>27.99</price>
    <age_group/>
    <publisher>Grand Central</publisher>
    <primary_isbn13>9780446573018</primary_isbn13>
```

Create Pipe to get bestsellers: A Pipe that retrieves the bestsellers using the YQL query shown earlier can be generated as follows. First, clicking on the YQL box in the Sources list brings up a pipe module, as seen in Figure 3.38. The same YQL query that was executed in the previous step can be typed in to the module to create a pipe that gets the list of bestsellers from the *New York Times*. The output from the pipe needs to be filtered to get the books published by Pustak Portal. The publisher name is available in the field publisher in the XML document (see previous code segment). Filtering can be achieved either by (i) adding an additional condition to the WHERE clause selecting records where the publisher is Pustak Portal; or (ii) connecting the output of this module to a Filter module that does the filtering.

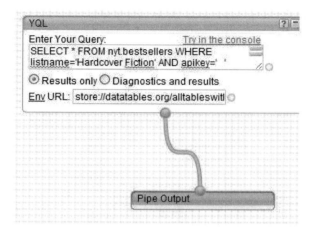

FIGURE 3.38

Pipe for YQL select.

Create Pipe to generate tweets: Twitter messages are also available through an ODT that makes the messages appear to be rows in a data table. The APIs and fields available can be found in the same way as the NYT APIs starting from the YQL console, and hence is not repeated here. Twitter messages will be generated via the YQL INSERT statement [58], which, like its SQL counterpart, inserts a row into a table. However, the YQL INSERT statement can also trigger actions; in the case of the Twitter ODT it causes generation of a new Twitter message, as shown in the following code segment.

```
INSERT INTO twitter.status (message, userid, password) VALUES ("<book>
is on the New York Times bestseller list!", "userid", "password")
```

Since multiple books from Pustak Portal may be on the bestseller list, it is necessary to loop over all the books and generate an INSERT for each book as shown in the code segment. In the statement, userid and password are the Twitter userid and password and are used for authentication. The message parameter represents the tweet that will be generated, and the <book> parameter has to be replaced by the name of the book.

To generate the INSERT statements needed, a Loop Pipe module can be used. The Loop module is created in the Pipes editor by clicking on the Loop menu item in the Operators menu (see Figure 3.39). By dragging a String Builder module inside the Loop module, and filling in the parameters as shown in Figure 3.40, it is possible to generate the INSERT statements needed as strings. These strings are then passed to another Loop module that has a YQL module embedded in it. This Loop module iterates over all the strings, and invokes the YQL module with each string, resulting in the generation of the needed tweets.

FIGURE 3.39

Loop Module.

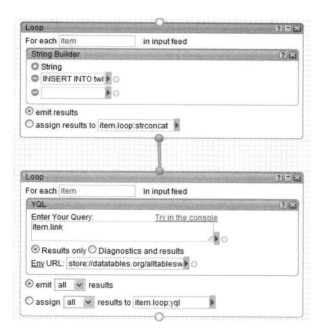

FIGURE 3.40

Loops to generate tweet.

YQL Update and Delete Statements

In addition to SELECT and INSERT statements, YQL also provides UPDATE and DELETE statements as well, which update fields of selected records, and delete records, respectively [58]. The syntax of these statements is shown here:

- UPDATE <ODT> SET field=value WHERE filter
- DELETE FROM <ODT> WHERE filter

The UPDATE statement sets the value of the field attribute to the specified *value* in the rows selected by filter from the ODT. The DELETE statement deletes the selected rows. As with INSERT, the update or delete could trigger an action, depending upon the ODT being used.

Thus as described in this section, one can see that diverse PaaS solutions are possible and now available – those that enable existing applications to be hosted on the cloud (Azure, Google AppEngine), those that require a whole new redesign of the application (MapReduce) and those that allow even technically inexperienced end users to create cloud applications (Yahoo! Pipes).

SUMMARY

This chapter described an important cloud model that is very relevant to developers. As seen, Platform as a Service provides an application development as well as deployment environment for cloud-hosted applications. Diverse types of PaaS systems were studied. On one hand, Windows Azure and Google App Engine, which enable traditional applications (.NET and Java) to directly execute on the cloud, were detailed and at the other end, Hadoop, which provides a completely new paradigm for cloud applications, was also described. Just as any traditional computer application has compute, storage and data resources, PaaS systems should also provide support for cloud applications for these three key aspects. The chapter, therefore, also described the PaaS features for enabling cloud storage services and special data services that enable applications to manipulate data in a more structured form – either in XML (pureXML) or relational (SQL Azure). Each section not only described the developer APIs, but also included some internal technical architectural details that would enable a developer to better understand the system to develop more efficient applications.

The most important advantage of the Windows Azure platform is the programming model it supports. By making the application the center of operation, instead of the virtual machine, it provides a higher level of abstraction that is simpler for developers. The rich tooling and API support offered by Visual Studio, .NET framework and the Windows platform together make the platform very appealing. The ease of development and debugging is another attraction. Management is simple, through an API, and there are a wide range of third-party tools that can be used to manage the service. Another benefit is the ServiceBus and AccessControl APIs that allow developers to mix and match cloud applications with on-premise ones, using the same authentication and authorization mechanisms that they have on-premise. Applications can be scaled easily, data partitioning is available. However, developers need to tune their applications to utilize these features. A drawback of Windows Azure is that the platform is limited to supporting applications that run on the Windows operating system. At the time of writing, it wasn't possible to host applications that run on other operating systems.

Though Azure is usually described as a PaaS system, in the Professional Developers' Conference 2010, Microsoft announced the public availability of "VM Role" which essentially provides IaaS-like services on the Windows Azure environment [59]. The VM role allows users to provision virtual machines with full administrative privileges. Images can be prepared on-premise and uploaded to Azure storage for application onto the virtual machines. Windows Azure makes shadow copies of these images before applying them to the virtual machines. Changes made by the programs to the operating system or the disks are maintained in differencing disks – these changes can be saved or rolled back easily. This is an example of a case where vendors enhance their core strength in their cloud offering to provide an end-to-end cloud solution.

Hadoop has become the de facto cloud platform for researchers to work on their Big Data computing applications. The new programming paradigm introduced by Hadoop – MapReduce – stems from the features of olden day parallel programming and distributed programming enthusiasts. It is interesting to see strongly researched technologies come back and be more relevant to present day computing systems. Use of the MapReduce paradigm requires the user to think differently about his/her application. Chapter 5 will equip the developer with fundamental concepts to help them decompose the application design in MapReduce format.

Google App Engine, on the other hand, seems to target a developer who is well-versed in programming for traditional systems and would like to move onto the cloud. The development system is very similar to traditional development (Eclipse IDE), the programming is very similar (Java, Python) and deployment also very similar (from Eclipse IDE)! Once the developer is able to create a few cloud applications, the other advanced features of App Engine for data persistence (datastore), channels, memcache and so on, are available. The datastore is also very simple and emulates other cloud platforms, with the use of key-value pairs (NoSQL).

Finally, use of cloud storage from an application can be in multiple forms. The application developer may want to use only simple and traditional relational databases to store persistent data across different runs of the application. In this case, SQL Azure or database offerings from Amazon can be used. Alternatively, more abstract ways of using a relational system in the form of key-value pairs can be used with Amazon SimpleDB. On the other side of the spectrum, the application can use filesystem or block storage (as one would have done in a non-cloud application using a local file system). In this case Amazon S3 or EBS can be used. Moving higher up in the application stack and semantics, if the application wants to use XML-like structured data, services such as pureXML will be very handy. So, the user can use the most relevant form of cloud storage applicable to the problem domain being solved by the cloud application.

References

[1] Windows Azure. http://www.microsoft.com/windowsazure/ [accessed 08.10.11]

[2] The Business of Windows Azure Pricing: What you should know about Windows Azure Platform Pricing and SLAs.

[3] http://www.microsoft.com/windowsazure/sdk/ [accessed 08.10.11]

[4] http://www.windowsazure4j.org/ [accessed 08.10.11]

[5] http://phpazure.codeplex.com/ [accessed 08.10.11]

[6] http://www.microsoft.com/windowsazure/sdk/ [accessed 08.10.11]

[7] http://code.msdn.microsoft.com/windowsazure [accessed 08.10.11]

[8] https://mocp.microsoftonline.com/site/default.aspx [accessed 08.10.11]

[9] http://www.microsoft.com/windowsazure/learn/tutorials/setup-and-install-tutorial/2-signup/ [accessed 08.10.11]

[10] Programming Windows Azure: Programming the Microsoft Cloud, Sriram Krishnan, O'Reilly Media, 24 May 2010.

[11] Inside Windows Azure, Mark Russinovich, Microsoft Professional Developers Conference 2010, 29 October 2010, http://channel9.msdn.com/Events/PDC/PDC10/CS08 [accessed 08.10.11]

[12] SQL Azure. http://www.microsoft.com/windowsazure/sqlazure/ [accessed 08.10.11]

[13] Windows Azure AppFabric Overview. http://www.microsoft.com/windowsazure/appfabric/ [accessed 08.10.11]

[14] Channel 9. http://channel9.msdn.com [accessed 08.10.11]

[15] Microsoft's Professional Developers' Conference. http://www.microsoftpdc.com/2009 [accessed 08.10.11]

[16] Windows Azure Security Overview, Kaufman and Venkatapathy. http://go.microsoft.com/?linkid=9740388 [accessed 08.10.11]

[17] Meier JD. Windows Azure Security Notes, http://blogs.msdn.com/cfs-file.ashx/__key/CommunityServer-Blogs-Components-WeblogFiles/00-00-00-48-03/0572.AzureSecurity-Notes.pdf [accessed 08.10.11]

[18] Security Best practices for Developing Windows Azure Applications. http://download.microsoft.com/download/7/3/E/73E4EE93-559F-4D0F-A6FC-7FEC5F1542D1/Security-BestPracticesWindowsAzureApps.docx [accessed 08.10.11]

[19] Codeplex. http://www.codeplex.com [accessed 08.10.11]

[20] Developing Advanced Applications with Windows Azure, Steve Marx. http://www.microsoftpdc.com/2009/SVC16 [accessed 08.10.11]

[21] Moving Applications to the Cloud on the Microsoft Windows Azure Platform. http://msdn.microsoft.com/en-us/library/ff728592.aspx. [accessed 08.10.11]

[22] Windows Azure platform Articles from the trenches. http://bit.ly/downloadazurebookvol1 [accessed 08.10.11]

[23] Kerner K. Windows Azure Monitoring Logging and Management APIs. http://www.microsoftpdc.com/2009/SVC15 [accessed 08.10.11].

[24] Collecting Logging Data by Using Windows Azure Diagnostics. http://msdn.microsoft.com/en-us/library/gg433048.aspx [accessed 08.10.11]

[25] http://golang.org/doc/go_tutorial.html. [accessed June 2011].

[26] http://code.google.com/appengine/. [accessed June 2011].

[27] Ajax learning guide. http://searchwindevelopment.techtarget.com/tutorial/Ajax-Learning-Guide. [accessed June 2011].

[28] http://code.google.com/appengine/docs/java/overview.html. [accessed June 2011].

[29] Chen WJ, Chun J, Ngan N, Ranjan R, Sardana MK. 'DB2 9 pureXML Guide', in IBM Redbooks® (http://www.redbooks.ibm.com/redbooks/pdfs/sg247315.pdf); 2007. [accessed June 2007].

[30] Lennon J. 'Leveraging pureXML in a Flex Microblogging Application, Part 1: Enabling Web Services with DB2 pureXML', IBM developerWorks® article (http://www.ibm.com/developerworks/xml/library/x-db2mblog1/); 2009. [accessed June 2011].

[31] Lennon J. 'Leveraging pureXML in a Flex Microblogging Application, Part 2: Building the Application User interface with Flex', IBM developerWorks® article (http://www.ibm.com/developerworks/xml/library/x-db2mblog2/index.html?ca=drs-); 2009. [accessed June 2011].

[32] Chen, WJ, Sammartino, A, Goutev, D, Hendricks, F, Komi, I, Wei, MP, Ahuja, R, 'DB2 Express-C: The Developer Handbook For, XML, PHP, C/C++, Java and .NET', In: IBM Redbooks® http://www.redbooks.ibm.com/redbooks/pdfs/sg247301.pdf; 2006 [accessed June 2011].

[33] Nicola, M, Linden, BV, 'Native XML Support in DB2 Universal Database', Proceedings of the 31st Annual, VLDB http://www.vldb2005.org/program/paper/thu/p1164-nicola.pdf; 2005 [accessed June 2011].

[34] Nicola, M, Chatterjee, P DB2 pureXML Cookbook: Master the Power of the IBM Hybrid Data Server. IBM Press; 2009 [accessed June 2011].

[35] Zhang, G. Introduction to pureXML in DB2 9. http://www.hoadb2ug.org/Docs/Zhang0812.pdf [accessed June 2011].

[36] Bruni, P, Schenker, M 'IBM Data Studio', IBM Redpaper®. http://www.redbooks.ibm.com/redpapers/pdfs/redp4510.pdf [accessed June 2011].

[37] Eaton, D, Rodrigues, V, Sardana, MK, Schenker, M, Zeidenstein, K, Chong, RF. Getting Started with IBM Data Studio for DB2. http://download.boulder.ibm.com/ibmdl/pub/software/data/sw-library/db2/express-c/wiki/Getting_Started_with_Data_Studio_for_DB2.pdf; 2010 [accessed June 2011].

[38] Chong, R, Hakes, I, Ahuja, R. Getting Started with DB2-Express. http://public.dhe.ibm.com/software/data/sw-library/db2/express-c/wiki/Getting_Started_with_DB2_Express_v9.7.pdf; 2009 [accessed June 2011].

[39] WebSphere Application Server Community Edition, IBM. http://www-01.ibm.com/software/webservers/appserv/community/ [accessed 14.10.11].

[40] Free: IBM DB2 Express-C. http://www.ibm.com/developerworks/downloads/im/udbexp/cloud.html. IBM [accessed 14.10.11].

[41] Ghemawat, S, Gobioff, H, Leung, S-T. The Google file system.SOSP'03. Proceedings of the nineteenth ACM symposium on Operating Principles, New York: 2003. [accessed June 2011].

[42] Dean, J, Ghemawat, S. MapReduce: Simplified Data Processing on Large Clusters. OSDI '04: 6th Symposium on Operating Systems Design and Implementation USENIX Association. http://www.usenix.org/event/osdi04/tech/full_papers/dean/dean.pdf; 2004 [accessed June 2011].

[43] Chang, F, Dean, J, Ghemawat, S, et al., 2008. Bigtable: A distributed storage system for structured data. ACM Trans Comput Syst (TOCS) 2008;26 (2) [accessed June 2011].

[44] http://hadoop.apache.org/common/docs/r0.19.2/capacity_scheduler.html [accessed June 2011].

[45] Using HDFS Programmatically. http://developer.yahoo.com/hadoop/tutorial/module2.html#programmatically [accessed June 2011].

[46] Enals R, Brower E, et al., Intel Mash Maker : Join the Web, Intel Research, 2007 [accessed June 2011].

[47] Module Reference: Source Modules. http://pipes.yahoo.com/pipes/docs?doc=sources [accessed June 2011].

[48] Module Reference: User Input Modules. http://pipes.yahoo.com/pipes/docs?doc=user_ inputs [accessed June 2011].

[49] Module Reference: Operator Modules. http://pipes.yahoo.com/pipes/docs?doc=operators [accessed June 2011].

[50] Module Reference: URL Modules. http://pipes.yahoo.com/pipes/docs?doc=url [accessed June 2011].

[51] Module Reference: String Modules. http://pipes.yahoo.com/pipes/docs?doc=string [accessed June 2011].

[52] Module Reference: Date Modules. http://pipes.yahoo.com/pipes/docs?doc=date [accessed June 2011].

[53] Module Reference: Data Types. http://pipes.yahoo.com/pipes/docs?doc=location [accessed June 2011].

[54] Module Reference: Number Modules. http://pipes.yahoo.com/pipes/docs?doc=number [accessed June 2011].

[55] http://developer.yahoo.com/yql/console [accessed June 2011].

[56] The Best Sellers API. http://developer.nytimes.com/docs/best_sellers_api [accessed June 2011].

[57] YQLSelect. http://developer.yahoo.com/yql/guide/select_syntax.html [accessed June 2011].

[58] Syntax of I/U/D. http://developer.yahoo.com/yql/guide/iud-syntax.html [accessed June 2011].

[59] Migrating and Building Apps for Windows Azure with VM Role and Admin Mode, Mohit Srivastava. http://channel9.msdn.com/events/PDC/PDC10/CS09; October 2010. [accessed June 2011].

Software as a Service

INTRODUCTION

The previous two chapters have studied how computing resources can be delivered as a service through the model of Infrastructure as a Service (IaaS), as well as how application deployment platforms can be delivered as a service through the model of Platform as a Service (PaaS). Clearly, these are generic services that can be used by developers for creating new applications which can themselves be accessed as a service and that is the topic of this chapter. These cloud services which deliver application software as a service fall into the category of Application as a Service, more commonly known as Software as a Service (SaaS).

There are many advantages of delivering an application as a service. First of all, users can directly use these applications without any new software installations on their local machines, as these applications will now execute within a web browser (YouTube, for example). The required software will be available on multiple platforms and can be used from any of the user's devices (say, home PC, office PC, mobile device). If the application is needed only for a short period of time, the user can simply pay per use (say a home modeling software is used only when someone is renovating/buying a house). Further, these applications can be customized for different users both in terms of user interface and selected features, so there is no loss in flexibility. From the application vendor's point of view, there are many advantages as well. Many service providers find it economically viable to offer a new application as a service instead of creating packages and distribution channels. More importantly, it helps to ensure that the software is not pirated. With SaaS, the application vendor need not worry about distributing updates of newer versions of the application; only the cloud application needs to be changed and the new version will now be used the next time the consumer accesses it. By ensuring that the latest version of the software is always used, the SaaS model lowers support costs. The application vendor also gets better insight into the needs of the customers by analyzing the usage data collected at a central location. Due to these reasons and more, the SaaS model will make the adoption of Cloud Computing much wider.

This chapter studies some examples of popular SaaS applications that not only provide service-enabled solutions but also provide a platform where developers can rapidly create and customize newer applications in the same domain. The first section describes Salesforce.com, one of the very well-known SaaS cloud applications that delivers a CRM service. This is followed by a description of social computing services and then Google Docs, which are important consumer applications. Each section discusses both the straightforward use of the application as well as the use of the platform APIs to extend the functionality. Each section also contains a brief overview of the underlying technology and how it can be applied to Pustak Portal, the running example of the book.

CRM AS A SERVICE, SALESFORCE.COM

Salesforce.com [1] is a well-known Customer Relationship Management (CRM) application used for financial, delivery and staffing related to business systems operations. A CRM application consists of a set of workflows (business processes) together with software that helps to manage customer-related activities and information. These activities could be related to sales (such as using customer information to generate future leads), marketing tasks (like using historical sales data to develop sales strategies) or to provide better customer service (by using call center data). Salesforce.com provides a comprehensive list of features for all of these three types of activities. This section, however, focuses on the features of Salesforce.com for customer support representatives as a case study of SaaS usage.

A Feature Walk Through

Before a business can start using Salesforce.com, there is a small setup phase where the business user can customize Salesforce.com for their business requirements. This involves first obtaining a Salesforce.com account. Second, the system administrator belonging to the business has to import their existing customer data into Salesforce.com, customize the various Salesforce.com screens, and give access rights for the appropriate screens to the employees of the business. The description following does not go into the details of this setup, and assumes that the required configuration has already been set up.

After the Salesforce.com portal has been set up, customer support representatives can log in and go to the `Call Center` web page, shown in Figure 4.1. This contains functionality for handling customer requests, such as recording customer calls, assigning the cases to support personnel, and searching for solutions. The web page contains a number of tabs. Figure 4.1 shows the `Cases` tab, which helps support representatives to keep track of, and handle, customer complaints. It can be seen that the web page allows one to search for a particular case, look at recent cases, and

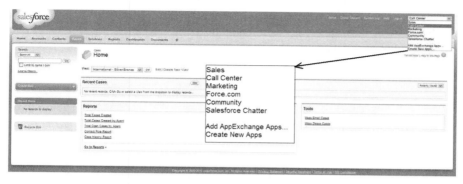

FIGURE 4.1

Salesforce.com.

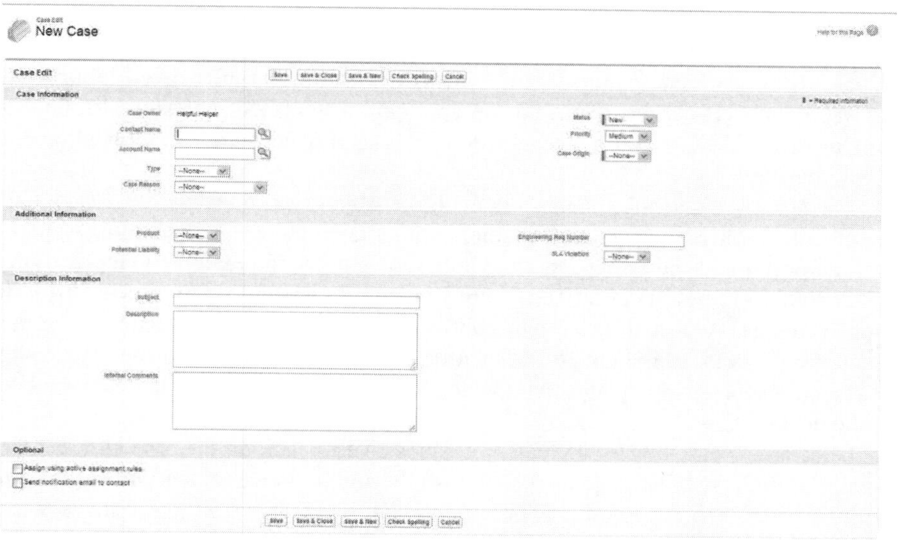

FIGURE 4.2

Salesforce.com: *New Case* screen.

generate useful reports such as the total number of cases. The tool `Mass Email` allows one to send an email to the email id associated with each case. The default fields for a case can be seen by clicking on the `Create New` bar to the left of the web page. This brings up the screen shown in Figure 4.2, which can be used by support (call center) personnel who are generating a new case from a phone call. The `Contact Name` and `Account Name` fields can be found by searching the `Contacts` and `Accounts` database. Many of the fields, example, `Priority`, and `Case Origin`, are values selected from a pull-down menu. In Salesforce.com, this is referred to as a **picklist**. Additional fields can be added to the case record by the administrator, thus customizing this page to the needs of each enterprise.

> **NOTE**
> To test the functionality presented here, readers can visit *www.salesforce.com* and sign up for a free account.

The other tabs on the page contain some interesting functionality useful for employees handling customer calls. For example, the Solutions tab provides access to a database containing earlier solutions to customer problems. This database is searchable, allowing employees to quickly resolve customer problems. The full list of tabs can be found by clicking on the "+" sign. The administrator can customize the tabs visible on each screen. The Sales and Marketing web pages contain functions useful for sales and marketing, respectively, and are similar to the Call Center page. Furthermore, the Community and Salesforce Chatter web pages allow for instant messaging, forums, and other types of collaboration between users. It can be seen that the application interface is designed to suit a typical business need and hence can be customized to reuse as an application for a new business.

The Add App Exchange App tab (Figure 4.5) enables users to extend the functionality of Salesforce.com by installing applications from the Salesforce.com. AppExchange portal and the Create New App tab allows users to create new applications (over Salesforce.com) and offer them for free download or purchase through AppExchange. Access to these tabs can be controlled by the administrator for the enterprise. Advanced features of the platform can be accessed using the Force.com link, a complete featured platform on which Salesforce.com executed that is described in the next section.

Once a new case has been created, it is possible to click on the case id to get the details of the case. The page also contains a button to create an activity associated with the case, which could be a task or an event (such as a meeting to discuss the case). Figure 4.3 shows the screen for creating a new task. This screen contains fields for assigning a task to another agent, setting a deadline, and so on.

It is not always necessary to manually enter cases. Salesforce.com has features to automatically create cases from the Web as well as custom emails. For creating cases automatically from a self-service web page, the administrator can create a web script using the Salesforce.com application that can be included in the web site belonging to the business. Salesforce.com has other advanced features for assisting customer support representatives. For example, cases can also be automatically generated by extracting fields from customer emails. There are also features to support soft phones, case teams consisting of employees with different roles, and creating case hierarchies. Details of these advanced features are beyond the scope of this book, but can be found under the link Cases in the Help page [2].

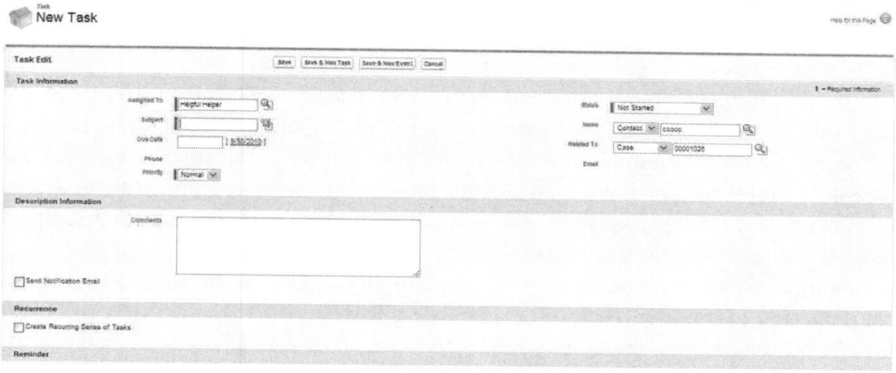

FIGURE 4.3

Salesforce.com new task screen.

Customizing Salesforce.com

In the earlier paragraphs, the standard features and web pages in Salesforce.com were described. However, businesses will want to customize Salesforce.com to suit their business processes. This is a very important aspect of supporting **multi-tenancy** in a SaaS application. A brief overview of some important customizations and details are presented next.

> **NOTE**
>
> **Customizing the application**
>
> - Change field names
> - Set conditions for field updates
> - Set conditions for email alerts
> - Customize UI

As stated earlier, Salesforce.com allows renaming fields of all Salesforce.com database objects as well as addition of custom fields. For example, businesses can add fields to the case record shown in Figure 4.2 to keep track of data unique to the business. Fields like the `Product` field, which are selected via a picklist, can be set to product codes for the business. Workflows (business processes) are captured in Salesforce.com by means of a series of rules. For example, **assignment rules** shown in Figure 4.2 can be used to automatically assign cases to support representatives. By updating assignment rules, customer case workflow can be tailored to business needs. Apart from task rules, other types of rules that can be implemented are (i) email alerts, which send an email alert under certain condition, (e.g., confirmation of a sale), (ii) field updates (e.g., when a contract is about to expire) (iii) outbound messages that interface to an external system (e.g., send a message to a finance system when an invoice is approved). Details can be found on the portal describing the creation of Workflow Rules web site [3].

Finally, both administrators and users can customize the look and feel of the user interface. This includes items such as the placement and content of text and graphics, names and numbers of tabs on each screen, and the overall layout of the screen. Administrators can set an overall look and feel for the business, and give employees rights to personalize their individual views. More details of this aspect can be found under the link Customize on the Help page [2].

Another SaaS application whose functionality is similar to Salesforce.com is Sugar CRM [4], which is an Open Source CRM suite. A comparison of Sugar CRM and Salesforce.com by the Salesforce.com team is in [5].

Force.com: A Platform for CRM as a Service

Salesforce.com is built on a software platform called **Force.com**. When customers use Salesforce.com, they are really using a sophisticated application built on the Force.com platform, where the application stores its data and execution logic in Force.com (for example, the data used for different Case records). Users of Force.com can build their own applications, which are either standalone or integrated with Salesforce.com. In fact as described later in this section, the reader can see that Force.com has several features studied in Chapter 3 and can, in fact, be considered as a PaaS solution on its own. This section reviews the architecture and high-level components of Force.com, to show to the reader the complexity of developing a really configurable SaaS application.

Architecture Overview

Figure 4.4 shows the architecture of Force.com which is detailed in this subsection. The lowest layer is the Force.com database, which stores the CRM data for users, as well as the associated metadata (such as user privileges). It is a distributed, reliable database that is shared among all the users of Force.com. In order to ensure privacy of data for each user and give an effect of each having their own database, the data from different users are securely isolated from one another. Further, the administration and maintenance of the database is automated and controlled by Force.com administrator, thus reducing the IT management overhead on the users. The next layer above the database is the **Integration** layer. This supports SOAP (Simple Object Access Protocol) based **Web Services API** [6] for accessing the database, and hence can be used by any development environment that interfaces to SOAP, such as Java and .Net. The Web Services API has also been used to develop connectors that connect to other cloud services such as Amazon, as well as other enterprise software such as SAP and Oracle.

Above the Integration layer is the **Logic** layer, which contains workflow and business logic. This contains the workflow logic for Salesforce.com and also allows customers to extend the functionality of Salesforce.com or write their own

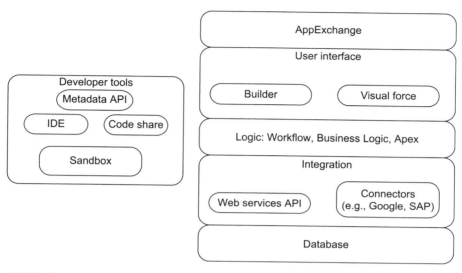

FIGURE 4.4

Key components of Force.com architecture.

cloud applications. Like the database, it is built on a scalable platform. This is transparent and virtualized to the platform user, i.e., the user will not be aware of the number of processors being used to execute the workload or even the type of processors being used. The workflow engine contains common scheduling functionality such as timed events and tasks. More sophisticated logic can be built using the Apex programming language [7].

The **User Interface** (**UI**) layer sits above the Logic layer. There are two components that can be used to create the UI. The **Builder** component provides a simple drag-and-drop interface which allows simple manipulations of the default UI, such as changing the layout of the default display. The **Visualforce framework** allows building of a custom UI and is described in more detail later in this section. The AppExchange layer (web page) allows customers of Salesforce.com to install third-party applications that integrate with and extend the functionality of Salesforce.com (see Figure 4.5).

Additionally, Force.com offers a set of developer tools to enable testing and debugging of programs. Programs can be run in isolation and debugged inside a runtime environment called **Sandbox.** The Sandbox also provides a full-fledged test environment and even allows copying of data from a customer's production data to the Sandbox for testing purposes. This is similar to the sandbox provided by Google App Engine described in Chapter 2. The **IDE** (Integrated Development Environment) is based on Eclipse, and contains tools such as a schema browser, Apex code editor and tools to organize code and build the final program. The Developer tools also contain **Code Share**, a source code management system that allows more than one programmer to jointly work on code. The developer tools also include the **Metadata API**, which allows developers to manipulate metadata, such as the structure of objects. This is useful, for example, for enhancing the application to use additional data fields without requiring major edits to the application. Some of the above key modules of Force.com are described next.

Force.com Database

As stated earlier, the Force.com database stores CRM data, together with metadata, such as user rights and privileges. It is not a relational database. It is a database that stores records, with each record corresponding to an object. For example, any new cases created would be stored as records. Similarly, each task, account or other object in the system would have a corresponding record in the Force.com database.

NOTE

Force.com database

- Record-oriented, not relational
- Each record corresponds to a Force.com object
- Each record has a unique ID
- Relationships to other records are represented by relationship fields: Master-Detail, Parent-Child
- Data types include Number and Text, as well as specialized types such as Picklist, Email, Phone, and Checkbox.

Each record can have three types of fields:

1. **Identity, or ID field:** created for every record when it is first generated. The ID field uniquely identifies the record and is 15 characters long.
2. The **data fields:** contain each field corresponding to an attribute of the object. There are a large number of data types as described subsequently.
3. The **Relationship field** captures the relationship across objects. For example, each Case can have a Contact associated with it. So, the record for a case would contain the ID field for the Contact. This type of relationship is called a **Lookup** relationship. A relationship called **Master-Detail** relationship captures the parent-child relation, where deletion of the parent record removes all the child records. This is somewhat similar to Delphi database concepts [8].

Additionally, there are **System** fields such as the creation date and modification time, and **Help** fields that can store help associated with the record. More detailed information about the architecture is available in the Force.com White Paper [9].

The Force.com database supports a large number of data types. In addition to common types such as Number and Text, there are also some special data types to help simplify programming. These include: Picklist and Multi-Select Picklists, which allow the selection of one value from a list of values (such as the Product field). The Checkbox data type represents Boolean values. There are also values for

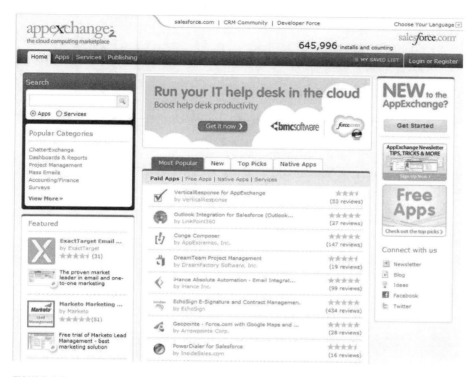

FIGURE 4.5

Salesforce.com AppExchange.

Email, Phone, and URL. A full list is available in *A Comprehensive Look at the World's Premier Cloud-Computing Platform* [9].

Programming on Salesforce.com and Force.com

This section describes how to develop some simple programs on the Salesforce.com platform. It starts with a simple program to load existing data in bulk into the Force.com database. Bulk loading of data is where multiple records, such as customer records, are batched together, and loaded together into Force.com. Clearly, bulk loading can be more efficient than individual loads, as each load operation incurs a network overhead.

A Force.com Example: Bulk Load of Data

To allow users to quickly get started, a simple Java program is used to bulk load data into Salesforce.com. This program can also be used to upload test data that is used to test and run the hosted programs later. Since the program is slightly complicated, it will be explained method by method.

> **NOTE**
>
> **This example shows**
> - Use of Force.com Web Services Connector
> - Bulk insert, delete or update of data into Force.com database
> - Use of Web Services API
> - Background tasks

First, the code imports the Java classes and the Salesforce.com classes needed. The required jar files are available in the Force.com Web Services Connector (WSC) kit downloadable from http://code.google.com/p/sfdc-wsc/downloads/list. Executing the command "ant all" generates the jar files [10].

```
Import com.sforce.async.AsyncApiException;
import com.sforce.async.BatchInfo;
import com.sforce.async.BatchStateEnum;
import com.sforce.async.CSVReader;
import com.sforce.async.ContentType;
import com.sforce.async.JobInfo;
import com.sforce.async.JobStateEnum;
import com.sforce.async.OperationEnum;
import com.sforce.async.RestConnection;
import com.sforce.soap.partner.PartnerConnection;
import com.sforce.ws.ConnectionException;
import com.sforce.ws.ConnectorConfig;

package com.hindustan.crm;

import java.io.*;
import java.util.*;
```

The following code shows the Java source code for the bulk load example that was described above. The implementation of the methods called in BulkLoad method are detailed.

```
public class BulkLoad {
private static final String apiVersion = "19.0";
private static final String authEndpoint = "https://login.salesforce.
   com/services/Soap/u/" + apiVersion;
private RestConnection restConnection = null;

public static void main(String[] args) throws ConnectionException,
AsyncApiException, IOException {
    if (args.length != 3) {
        System.out.println("User ID, Password and/or Security Token are
        not provided.");
        return;
    }
    String userId = args[0];
    String pw = args[1];
    String securityToken = args[2];
```

```
BulkLoad bl = new BulkLoad();
ConnectorConfig soapConnectorConfig = bl.establishSoapSession
    (userId, pw, securityToken);
bl.getRestConnection(soapConnectorConfig.getSessionId(),
                        soapConnectorConfig.getServiceEndpoint());
JobInfo jobInfo = bl.createInsertJob("Account");
BatchInfo batchInfo = bl.addBatch2Job(jobInfo, "myAccounts.csv");
bl.closeJob(jobInfo.getId());
bl.waitTillJobIsComplete(jobInfo);
bl.checkStatus(jobInfo, batchInfo);
}
```

The program logs in to Force.com using the establishSoapSession call with the user id and password from the command line. The next line creates a REST connection to the server using getRestConnection. The createInsertJob method creates a jobInfo object which specifies that Account records are to be inserted into the Force.com database. As this example is about uploading data, a jobinfo object that specifies an insert job has been created. The jobInfo object can also specify bulk update, and delete of records. The records to be loaded (or updated and deleted) are recommended to be loaded in batches of 1,000 to 10,000 records. A job can also be performed in multiple batches. The addBatch2Job call specifies the import of a batch of records by specifying the source (in this case, a comma separated variable (CSV) file), and submits the job for processing as a batch (background) task. The job (sequence of batches) is then closed by closeJob. In the subsequent lines, the program waits for the job to complete and prints out the number of objects inserted.

The next few code snippets show the implementation of the other methods called in BulkLoad method.

```
private ConnectorConfig establishSoapSession(String userId, String pw,
String securityToken) throws
ConnectionException {
    ConnectorConfig soapConnectorConfig = new ConnectorConfig();
    soapConnectorConfig.setUsername(userId);
    soapConnectorConfig.setPassword(pw + securityToken);
    soapConnectorConfig.setAuthEndpoint(authEndpoint);
    new PartnerConnection(soapConnectorConfig);
    return soapConnectorConfig;
}

private void getRestConnection(String sessionId, String soapEndPoint)
throws AsyncApiException {
    int soapIndex = soapEndPoint.indexOf("Soap/");
    String restEndPoint = soapEndPoint.substring(0, soapIndex) + "async/" +
    apiVersion;
    ConnectorConfig cc = new ConnectorConfig();
    cc.setSessionId(sessionId);
    cc.setRestEndpoint(restEndPoint);
    restConnection = new RestConnection(cc);
}
```

Consider the code fragment that shows the implementation of the establishSoapSession method. This returns a new ConnectorConfig object, after setting the userid and password. From the code that implements the getRestConnection method, it can be seen that the method returns a newly created RestConnection from the SOAP session id and service endpoint obtained from the SOAP session created by establishSoapSession [11, 12].

The createInsertJob method returns a new asynchronous (background) job. The setObject method specifies that Account objects are to be inserted; the setOperation method specifies that the operation being done is insertion (or import) of data. The complete code for these two methods is shown next. addBatch2Job uses the createBatchFromStream method to import a batch of records from the file passed in as input.

```java
private JobInfo createInsertJob(String sobjectType) throws
AsyncApiException {
    JobInfo jobInfo = new JobInfo();
    jobInfo.setObject(sobjectType);
    jobInfo.setOperation(OperationEnum.insert);
    jobInfo.setContentType(ContentType.CSV);
    jobInfo = restConnection.createJob(jobInfo);
    System.out.println(jobInfo);
    return jobInfo;
}

private BatchInfo addBatch2Job(JobInfo jobInfo, String filename) throws
IOException, AsyncApiException {
    FileInputStream fis = new FileInputStream(filename);
    try {
        BatchInfo batchInfo = restConnection.createBatchFromStream
        (jobInfo, fis);
        System.out.println(batchInfo);
        return batchInfo;
    } finally {
        fis.close();
    }
}
```

waitTillJobIsComplete gets the state of the job by using the getState method, and exits if the job is done. The following checkStatus method computes the number of objects that have been inserted (to detect if any errors occurred) and also displays relevant information on screen.

```java
private void closeJob(String jobId) throws AsyncApiException {
    JobInfo job = new JobInfo();
    job.setId(jobId);
    job.setState(JobStateEnum.Closed); // Here is the close
    restConnection.updateJob(job);
}
```

```
private void waitTillJobIsComplete(JobInfo jobInfo) throws
AsyncApiException {
    long waitTime = 0L; // first time wait time is 0
    boolean jobDone = false;
    BatchInfo batchInfo = null;
    do {
        try {
        Thread.sleep(waitTime);
        } catch (InterruptedException e) {
        }
        BatchInfo[] biList = restConnection.getBatchInfoList(jobInfo.
        getId()).getBatchInfo();
        batchInfo = biList[0];
        BatchStateEnum bse = batchInfo.getState();
        jobDone = (bse == BatchStateEnum.Completed || bse ==
        BatchStateEnum.Failed);
        waitTime = 10 * 1000; // next time onwards wait time is 10 seconds
    } while (!jobDone);
}

Private void checkStatus(JobInfo job, BatchInfo batchInfo) throws
AsyncApiException, IOException {
    CSVReader cvsReader = new CSVReader(restConnection.
    getBatchResultStream(job.getId(), batchInfo.getId()));
    List<String> headerLine = cvsReader.nextRecord();
    int colCount = headerLine.size();
    List<String> row;
    while ((row = cvsReader.nextRecord()) != null) {
        Map<String, String> result = new HashMap<String, String>();
        for (int i = 0; i < colCount; i++) {
            result.put(headerLine.get(i), row.get(i));
        }
        Boolean success = Boolean.valueOf(result.get("Success"));
        Boolean created = Boolean.valueOf(result.get("Created"));
        String id = result.get("Id");
        String error = result.get("Error");
        if (success) {
            if (created) {
                System.out.println("Created row with id " + id);
            } else {
                System.out.println("Problem in creating row with row " + id);
            }
        } else {
            System.out.println("Failed with error: " + error);
        }
    }
}
```

A sample input for the bulk data is shown in the following:

```
Account Number, Name, Contact
1. Acme Corporation, 1022238676868ab
2. XYZ Enterprises, aaabx1234fygher
```

The first line shows that each line in the file contains the `Account Number`, the `Name` and the `Contact`. While the `Account Number` and `Name` are human-understandable fields, the `Contact` field is not. The `Contact` field is really a reference or pointer to an already existing `Contact` record (if the contact data has not yet been loaded, it should be left empty). As stated earlier, each record in the Force.com database has a 15 character ID, and the Contact field in the `Account` object should contain the ID of the `Contact` record for the account.

This implies that generating the test data set is really a two-step (or multi-step) process. First, it is necessary to extract a list of Contacts and their IDs from the Force.com database. Then, the appropriate `Contact` IDs have to be inserted into the file to be used as input for the `Account` import program. Any other IDs in the `Account` object have also to be similarly inserted.

Bulk data loading of data in Force.com is more efficient than loading records individually. However, there are possible side effects as well, such as increased lock contention. There is a set of valuable performance tips present in documentation from Salesforce.com [13, 14, 15]. Some examples are (i) to use the `retrieve()` call, using HTTP/1.1 connections to allow for long-lasting sessions (ii) using compression in SOAP messages (iii) suspending triggers if possible on bulk load (to improve speed of load) (iv) ensuring that the data being loaded does not have lock conflicts with other transactions and (v) partitioning data for speed of processing.

Force.com – A More Complex Example

The following is a more complex example of programming Force.com that involves the use of alerts. Consider the running example of Pustak Portal, the hypothetical document portal owned by a publishing house. The publishing house keeps track of the inventory of each book that is in print. When a bookstore needs to order a book, it can enter a request for the book at the Pustak portal. If sufficient copies of the book exist, the portal satisfies the request. Otherwise if satisfying the request implies that the number of books would fall below a threshold, it triggers a workflow to print more copies of the book (subject to approval) and sends an email to the appropriate person in the publishing house.

The UI for this application is developed using the Force.com Builder UI. Figure 4.6 shows the `Accounts` tab in Pustak Portal. Since Pustak Portal is a publisher, the various bookstores are their customers. Therefore, the bookstores have been defined as Accounts in the Pustak Portal.

The list of books published by Pustak Portal is shown in Figure 4.7. Books have been defined as a new type of object in the Force.com database, which have `Inventory` and `ISBN` as attributes. By default, the Force.com Builder UI creates a tab for each object; this tab has been renamed to "Published Books".

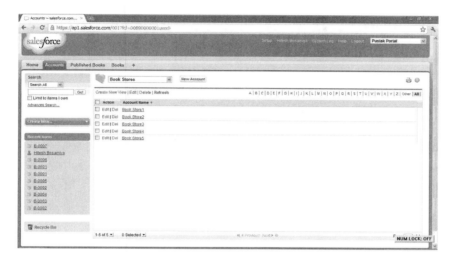

FIGURE 4.6

Accounts tab of Pustak Portal.

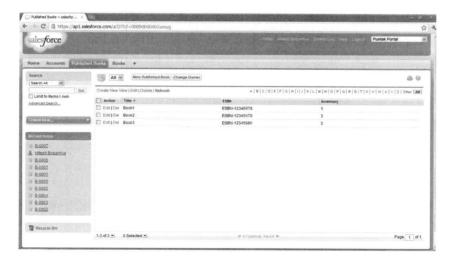

FIGURE 4.7

Force.com tab showing published books.

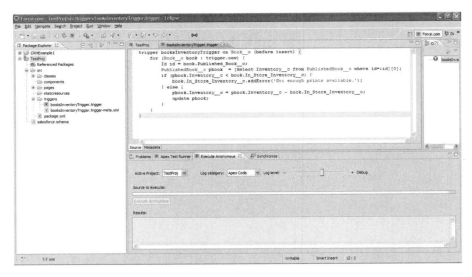

FIGURE 4.8

Force.com development environment showing triggers for Pustak Portal.

To implement a special workflow when the inventory of books falls below a threshold, one can implement a **trigger**, which executes automatically upon certain conditions (database operations such as insert, delete). The trigger is implemented in the Apex programming language. Apex is modeled after Java, but encapsulates many features of the Force.com platform [16]. For example, Force.com events are exposed in Apex; also, if there are conflicts due to concurrent updates, these are resolved by Apex runtime. For a list of more differences, see the wiki.

The trigger is defined using the Force.com IDE, shown in Figure 4.8. The IDE is a plug-in to Eclipse, and is downloaded from Force.com [17]. The trigger is defined as a class in the package "Triggers".

The same code shown in Figure 4.8 has been extracted here,

```
Trigger booksInventoryTrigger on Book__c (before insert) {
        for (Book__c book : trigger.new) {
                Id id = book.Published_Book__c;
                PublishedBook__c pbook = [Select Inventory__c from
                PublishedBook__c where id=:id][0];
                if (pbook.Inventory__c < book.In_Store_Inventory__c) {
                        book.In_Store_Inventory__c.addError('Not
                        enough prints available.');
                } else {
```

```
pbook.Inventory__c = pbook.Inventory__c -book.
In_Store_Inventory__c;
update pbook;
            }
        }
    }
```

The first statement defines the trigger `booksInventoryTrigger`which is invoked when a database operation is performed on a record of type `Book__c` (which represents a book). The phrase `before insert` indicates that the trigger is a **before trigger** that executes before the database operation. The other kind of trigger is an **after trigger**. The phrase also indicates that the database operation is an insert. More detailed description of triggers and other Apex features can be found in a White Paper from Salesforce.com [18].

The second line iterates over all records being inserted, with `book` being the loop variable. This kind of for loop is called a **set iteration** loop. The next line finds the id (ISBN) of the book being ordered by the bookstore. The next line is a Salesforce Object Query Language (SOQL) query. The query finds the `Inventory` for the book by looking at the `PublishedBook__c` objects and comparing the requested book's ISBN to the ISBN of the object (`id=:id)`, where the ':' before the `id` indicates that we are referencing the variable. Since the result is always a set of objects, we take the first member, as indicated by the `[0]`. For more details on SOQL, see [19]. The `if` statement that follows checks if the request would make the inventory less than the threshold, and signals an error if true.

By associating the trigger with database inserts, it would be possible to have it execute during every invocation. However, to demonstrate the capabilities of Force.com, we define a trigger through the Force.com Builder UI.

Figure 4.9 shows how a workflow can be defined from the Salesforce UI. The `Object` field indicates that this is a rule that applies when an object of type `Published Book` is modified. The `Rule Criteria` field indicates that the criterion for firing the rule is that the `Inventory` is less than 5. The workflow action is that an email alert should be sent.

Finally, the screen for setting up an email alert is shown in Figure 4.10. It names the alert "Low on prints" (which was invoked by the workflow in Figure 4.10 and sends a message that the inventory of a particular book is low). Note that the email message allows use of Force.com variables.

This section took a detailed look at one of the well-known SaaS solutions for CRM applications. It was observed that Salesforce.com is not just a web portal that hosts a CRM application so that a small business can use it for their daily business activity, but also includes a platform and a set of developer APIs that can be used to build more sophisticated applications with a CRM module hosted on Force.com. This is typical about any SaaS application that needs to be largely customized for different users. In the process of making the features customizable,

FIGURE 4.9

Introducing a workflow trigger.

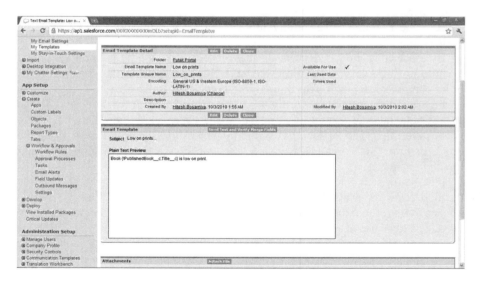

FIGURE 4.10

Configuring an email alert.

the underlying application architecture evolves to become a platform and starts looking like a PaaS solution, blurring the boundary between a configurable SaaS versus a simplistic PaaS, especially when the platform is also exposed to developers for enhanced applications. However, all SaaS solutions may not follow this route especially when the application itself can be used by multiple users without much customization – as will be seen in *Google Docs*. In the next section, another class of customizable SaaS applications that have evolved around the Web 2.0 style of computing are explored.

SOCIAL COMPUTING SERVICES[1]

Social computing has transformed the Web from being an industrial and technological infrastructure to something resembling a digital universe that is a replica of the physical universe. In retrospect, the World Wide Web was always intended as "a collaborative medium, a place where users [could] all meet and read and write" [20]. However, around 2006, there was a distinguishable trend when the amount of **User Generated Content** (**UGC**) started to explode across the Web. Further, cloud-based services like Facebook and Wikipedia provided a platform for users to create their own web-presence and content [21, 22]. These web sites go beyond just providing an infrastructure in the cloud but also leverage the content created by users in order to add value to others through collective intelligence. Hence, social computing on the Web introduces a revolutionary and unique set of challenges and opportunities.

The aim of the section on social computing has been twofold: (a) To introduce social computing as a paradigm: what it means, the underlying concepts and some of the recent trends; (b) To familiarize a developer with the social APIs that are available from some of the popular web sites which can be useful for writing social applications. Three popular social computing services are explored as case studies, namely Facebook (a social network), Picasa (a social media web site) and Twitter (a micro-blogging web site). Diverse programming languages and usage patterns will be used to exemplify the different APIs for the three web sites. Finally, an overview of Open Social API is given, which is an attempt to create a single API interface that programmers can use to interface this application with multiple social web sites and discuss the privacy implications of social networking.

What Constitutes "Social" Computing?

The term "social computing" is used to refer to a broad spectrum of cloud-based services which encourage and exploit the active participation of users and the content they create. Examples of web services that may qualify as "social computing"

---

[1]Contributed by Mr. Praphul Chandra, Hewlett-Packard Laboratories, India

include online social networking platforms like Facebook and LinkedIn; content sharing sites like YouTube and Flickr; content creation sites like Blogger and Wikipedia. As is obvious from these examples, not all social computing services are similar. In some cases, the focus is on providing a space in the cloud where social interactions can occur (example Facebook). In other social computing services, the focus is on providing a platform for sharing user-generated content (example YouTube). In yet other instances, social computing tools are embedded in a primary service (example Amazon.com) wherein the web-based retailer creates collective intelligence by mining user-created content to get user recommendations, seller and buyer reputations and so on. Each social computing service is unique in its focus – what is common among them is that each of them intelligently mines the content created by users to create key differentiators. Therefore, we define social computing[2] as the interplay between users, the content they create and approaches to mine this content.

The notion of **user as contributor** is, of course, fundamental to social computing. As stated earlier, User Generated Content (UGC) can take many forms for example social media (videos on YouTube, photographs at Flickr), user opinion (Reviews at Amazon, Feedback at eBay) or self-expression (personal pages at Facebook, Blogs). The recent emergence of **micro-blogging** services like Twitter is also interesting. The fact that real-world events get picked up by bloggers before they show up on traditional media such as news web sites makes blogs and micro-blogs a very attractive source for real-time search. In each of these cases, content created by users form the data on which computing algorithms operate to provide collective intelligence. These applications mine the content created by multiple users and use it for creating usable knowledge such as a user's reputation, the importance of a web page, product recommendations for a user and so on.

Social Networks on the Web

The popularity of Facebook has made the term "social network" commonplace in today's parlance. Most of us use the term to refer to our friends and family. Though this is broadly correct, a more formal definition can be:

> *A social network is a graph made up of persons or individuals (or organizations) as "nodes," and an "edge" representing relationship between two individuals. Edges can be created for different types of interdependency, such as friendship, kinship, common interest, financial exchange, dislike, sexual relationships, or relationships of beliefs, knowledge or prestige.*

The important thing to note from this definition is an understanding that the nodes and links in a network (graph) can be used to represent a variety of actors and relationships among them. It may be noted that, when nodes represent people

---

[2]The terms "social computing" and "Web2.0" are sometimes used interchangeably in the literature [23].

and links represent friendship, we get a social network which is ideally suited for social computing services like Facebook. There are two types of social networks. Consider a social network where each node in the graph represents a user's blog and the links between them represent hyperlinks between blogs. This is an example of a **socio-centric network**, i.e., a network representation where the programmer had access to all nodes and their inter-relationships. Now consider another social network where each node in the graph represents a user's email id and the links between them represent email communications (such as the one found in [24]). This graph was created from the perspective of one particular user. Such network representations, known as **ego-centric networks**, represent the network from a particular user's perspective and hence operate on a smaller set of information. For example, if Alice is a friend of Bob and Carol, she may or may not be aware whether there exists a link between Bob and Carol.

Case Study: Facebook

Facebook has grown to be one of the most popular online social networking web sites, as of the writing of this book. In addition to **social applications** that allow users to upload photographs and "friend" each other, Facebook also pioneered the **Open Graph API** which allowed developers to leverage the social networking data that is present in Facebook.

Social Applications on Facebook

There is a wide variety of features offered for users on Facebook. Here is a brief overview of the different types of social applications:

Newsfeed: Introduced in September 2006, this feature creates the signature user experience for users on Facebook and serves as the backbone of many other features. When users log in to their account, they see a *constantly updated* list of their friends' activity. Based on the privacy settings of the user, these updates may include information about changes in friends' profile, upcoming events, conversation among mutual friends, etc. Critics have focused on the cluttered nature of the user experience and the privacy implications of this feature but users can control the extent of newsfeed content they receive and share with others.

Notification: This feature can be thought of as the real-time version of Newsfeed. For certain key events (example a friend shares a link on the user's wall, someone commenting on a post that the user previously commented on), the user is notified as soon as these events occur. This feature too continues the *constantly updated* or *constantly in touch with friends* flavor of Facebook.

Photos: This is one of the most popular applications on Facebook. According to Facebook, it hosts more than 50 billion user photos (as of July, 2010), and more than 3 billion of these photos are viewed every day. This is a very simple application: users are allowed to upload their photographs and share them with other users – the challenge really is in the scale. Creating an application that can scale reliably and efficiently to such large usage scales is a key challenge for some social applications.

Beacon: Introduced in November 2007 and shut down in September 2009, this feature is a good example of the conflict between commercial opportunities and privacy concerns in online social networks. Facebook partnered with 44 web sites (including eBay® and Fandango®) so that a user's activity on any one of these web sites was automatically shared with the user's friends. For example, if a user listed an item for sale on eBay or purchased movie tickets and Fandango, this information would be automatically relayed to the users' friends via Newsfeed. For online retailers, this offered a great opportunity for targeted advertising, and for Facebook, an opportunity for additional revenue. However, the feature faced strong opposition from users and privacy activists and was finally shut down.

Like: This is a very interesting and ambitious feature. In some ways, it is a follow-up to the Beacon feature in that it seeks to expand the scope of Facebook beyond just the Facebook web site. Web site developers can insert the Facebook Like button on a web page (which has a URL, say http://www.cloudbook.com) as follows:

```
<fb:like href="http://www.cloudbook.com" font="arial"></fb:like>
```

If a Facebook user clicks on a Like button on a web page, a URL of this web page is posted on user's friends' wall via Newsfeed. From a user perspective, it allows users to share content they "like" on the Web – a feature very similar to social bookmarking and offered by web sites like delicious® and Digg®. From the perspective of the web site owner who inserted the Like button on his web page, it allows a potential for popularity (and increasing traffic on his web site) by exploiting the social network of users who like the page. Finally, it allows Facebook to create a much richer profile of the user and potential to become *the* single repository of user's content on the Web. The functionality of the Like feature can be further enhanced if the web site owner who inserts the Like button on his web page also adds metadata tags that describe the entity described by the web page.

Facebook Social Plug-ins

Facebook Login: Some readers would have noted that the Like feature is architecturally distinct from other features mentioned above. It is in fact, a plug-in that any web site can insert on its web page. Another social plug-in is the **Facebook Login**-button. If a web site developer inserts the Login button on his web page, a visitor will see pictures of those friends who have already signed-up on this web site. This of course, assumes that the user is logged onto Facebook – if not, the user can use this button to login. For the user, this social plug-in can help generate a level of trust and implicit-recommendation for the web site (since their friends are already using this service) and for the web site, it helps build on its reputation by leveraging the social network of existing users.

Adding a Facebook Login-button, on a web page can be done by adding the following code:

```
<fb:login-button show-faces="true"></fb:login-button>
```

Please note that the Facebook developer site will automatically generate the code if a URL is entered in the user interface.

Recommendations: Yet another social plug-in is **recommendations**. This plug-in considers all the interactions a user's friends have had with URLs from the given web site (via other social plug-ins), and highlights these objects on these URLs. This plug-in can then help users to focus their attention on specific parts of the web site by leveraging information about which parts the user's friends have interacted with in the past. This plug-in can be useful as a navigation aid added on complex web sites or in the discovery of new features. To add a recommendation plug-in, on a web page (which has a URL, say `http://www.cloudbook.com`), it is necessary to add code as follows:

```
<fb:recommendations site="http://www.cloudbook.com" font="arial"
border_color="light"></fb:recommendations>
```

An exhaustive coverage of all the social plug-ins supported is not in the scope of this book. The aim here is to familiarize the user with the concept of a social plug-in. A **social plug-in** is a piece of code which can be embedded in a web page so that users' interaction with that web page can be recorded and shared with other users. It also makes the web page become a standalone entity on an online social networking platform like Facebook, thus leveraging the services and functionality offered by the platform.

Open Graph API

Social plug-ins are a simple way to start integrating social features into any web site. However, they offer a limited set of functionality. To create a social application with custom functionality, Facebook's Open Graph API [25] which enables access to a very rich source of user content can be used. As the name suggests, the core content that this API exposes is represented as a social graph. As discussed earlier in this section, a social network representation contains nodes and the links between them. What exactly the nodes and links represent depends on the implementation and context. It is common to represent people (or email addresses or blogs) as nodes and "social relationships" (or email communication or hyperlinks) as links in a social network representation. Facebook's **social graph** has extended this notion, with every entity on Facebook being represented as a node in their social graph. This approach simplifies the API and makes it easier to use, as seen next.

Entities: Using a REST-based architecture, every entity (example, people, photos, events) on Facebook is represented as a node in the social graph. Every node is also assigned a unique ID and URL which makes accessing an entity on Facebook as simple as issuing a HTTP `GET` command (or typing the URL in your browser). To access the data associated with an entity having identifier ID, the URL is `https://graph.facebook.com/ID`. Note that the identifier (ID) may be system generated or may be the username as created by the user and `https://graph.facebook.com/me` refers to the current user. Some examples are shown in Table 4.1.

Accessing a URL of the type `https://graph.facebook.com/ID` returns all data associated with the entity with the identifier ID. If you want only a subset of the data, you can qualify this in the URL; for example, `https://graph.facebook.com/`

`bgolub?fields=id,name,picture` will only return the id, name, and picture of the user with ID `bgolub`.

Connection Types: Since the social graph contains nodes of different types, it follows that the links between nodes also need to be "typed" too. In Facebook, these are referred to as `CONNECTION_TYPE`. For a user with identifier `my_ID`, some examples of connection types are given in Table 4.2.

If the developer doesn't know all the different types of connections available for a particular entity, adding `metadata=1` to the object URL results in a JSON object that includes a metadata property that lists all the supported connections for the

Table 4.1 Facebook Entity Information.

Entity	URL	Comments
Users	https://graph.facebook.com/userid	Data for user possessing userid
Pages	https://graph.facebook.com/pepsi	Data for Pepsi and other products
Events	https://graph.facebook.com/5282952746	London Facebook Developer Garage, event id = 5282952746
Groups	https://graph.facebook.com/8450870046/	Cloud Computing user group; group id = 8450870046
Applications	https://graph.facebook.com/2439131959	Graffiti application; application id = 2439131959
Photos	https://graph.facebook.com/10150232972314050	Picture of Pepsi cans from Pepsi page; photo id = 10150232972314050
Profile photo	https://graph.facebook.com/10150309766585619	Profile photo of the *Royal Challengers Bangalore* cricket team, profile photo id = 10150309766585619

Table 4.2 Facebook Connection Types

URL	Comments
https://graph.facebook.com/my_ID/books	Books of user
https://graph.facebook.com/my_ID/events	Events user has participated
https://graph.facebook.com/my_ID/groups	Groups user is member of
https://graph.facebook.com/my_ID/likes	Likes for user
https://graph.facebook.com/my_ID/movies	Movies of user
https://graph.facebook.com/my_ID/home	News Feed for user
https://graph.facebook.com/my_ID/notes	Notes of user
https://graph.facebook.com/my_ID/photos	Photos of user
https://graph.facebook.com/my_ID/albums	Photo albums for user
https://graph.facebook.com/my_ID/videos	Videos uploaded by user
https://graph.facebook.com/my_ID/feed	Wall for user

given object. For example, to see all of the connections for the London Developer Garage event, the following URL can be used:

```
https://graph.facebook.com/5282952746?metadata=1
```

This outputs (some of the output has been deleted for brevity):

```
{
    "id": "5282952746",
    "version": 0,
    "owner": {
        "name": deleted
        "id": deleted
    },
    "name": "Facebook Developer Garage London",
    "description": deleted
"metadata": {
        "connections": {
            "feed": "https://graph.facebook.com/5282952746/feed",
            "members": "https://graph.facebook.com/5282952746/members",
            "picture": "https://graph.facebook.com/5282952746/picture",
            "docs": "https://graph.facebook.com/5282952746/docs"
        },
        "fields": [
            {
                "name": "id",
                "description": "The group ID. generic 'access_token',
                'user_groups', or 'friends_groups'. 'string'."
            },
            {
                "name": "version",
                "description": "A flag which indicates if the group was
                created prior to launch of the current groups product in
                October 2010. generic 'access_token', 'user_groups',
                or 'friends_groups'. 'int' where '0' = Old type Group,
                '1' = Current Group"
            },
            {
                "name": "icon",
                "description": "The URL for the group's icon.    generic
                'access_token', 'user_groups', or 'friends_groups'.
                'string' containing a valid URL."
            },
            {
                "name": "privacy",
                "description": "The privacy setting of the group.    generic
                'access_token', 'user_groups', or 'friends_groups'.
                'string' containing 'OPEN', 'CLOSED', or 'SECRET'"
            },
        ]
    },
```

Location (Entity and Connection Type): An entity type that deserves a special mention is location. Certain locations have their own Facebook page (for example, the Eiffel Tower). Such locations are also represented in the social graph as nodes and assigned a unique ID and URL `https://graph.facebook.com/` `14067072198` is the node for the Eiffel tower. The **connection type** between a user and a location is known as **checkin** and represents the notion of users having visited a particular location in the real world. This information can be accessed as follows:

```
GET https://graph.facebook.com/my_ID/checkins
```

If `my_ID` represents the ID of a user, the above API shows all the locations that the user has visited and checked into. If `my_ID` represents the ID of a location page, the above API shows all users that have visited this location and checked in.

Search: Facebook's architecture of the social graph subsumes not only people and their social relationships with other people but entities and the various relationships between these entities. From a user-centric view point, different connection types enable a user to be linked to diverse different entities in the social graph; for example, what movies a user likes, which groups a user belongs to, his photographs, and what events the user attended. This is an extremely rich set of data which can enable multiple applications but sometimes this data can get overwhelming and it becomes difficult to find what you are looking for. The default method for accessing information about an entity works if the ID or the username of the entity is known. It is also possible to use a URL to find an entity in the social graph; for example, to find the movie *The Magnificent Ambersons* on Facebook, if the movie's URL is `http://www.imdb` `.com/title/tt0035015/`, then the following refers to this entity in Facebook's social graph:

```
https://graph.facebook.com/?ids=http://www.imdb.com/title/tt0035015/
```

However, users of Facebook probably realize that this is not the way users find entities on Facebook – rather they use the Search feature available on Facebook. The Open Graph API also exposes the Search API for programmers. The structure of the search API along with some examples is given in the following code.

The Search API is a powerful tool for social applications that seek to leverage social content which is not associated with a single user but can be categorized according to other criteria; for example, finding groups on Facebook related to programming, finding all locations that allow users to check-in, or finding all conferences that have a presence on Facebook. The generic form of the Search API is as follows

```
https://graph.facebook.com/search?q=QUERY&type=OBJECT_TYPE
```

For example, the query

```
https://graph.facebook.com/search?q=network&type=post
```

produces the following result, which is the list of posts that contain the word "network" (note that only the first result is shown):

```json
{
    "data": [
        {
            "id": "100002366911800_140673586021538",
            "from": {
               "name": "New Labor",
               "id": "100002366911800"
            },
            "link": "http://www.facebook.com/notes/new-labor/ouralp-
               is-a-communication-network/140673586021538",
            "name": "OurALP is a communication network,",
            "description": "\nOurALP is a communication network, not a
               faction. We have no official executive or leader. We are a
               group of rank and file members of the ALP who consult
               together and then each of us acts as we see fit...",
            "icon": "http://static.ak.fbcdn.net/rsrc.php/v1/yY/r/
               1gBp2bDGEuh.gif",
            "type": "link",
            "application": {
               "name": "Notes",
               "id": "2347471856"
            },
            "created_time": "2011-08-12T08:49:59+0000",
            "updated_time": "2011-08-12T08:49:59+0000"
        },
```

Similarly, the query

```
https://graph.facebook.com/search?q=network&type=page
```

produces the following output:

```json
{
    "data": [
        {
            "name": "Cartoon Network",
            "category": "Tv network",
            "id": "84917688371"
        },
        {
            "name": "Food Network",
            "category": "Tv network",
            "id": "20534666726"
        },
```

This is the list of pages with the word "network" in their name; only the first two results are shown. Table 4.3 shows the other acceptable OBJECT_TYPE values.

Table 4.3 Facebook Search API

Entity type	Query
User with <userid> in name	https://graph.facebook.com/search? q=<userid>&type=user
Events with string <eee> in name; e.g., <eee> = conference	https://graph.facebook.com/search? q=<xxx>&type=event
Groups with string <ggg> in name	https://graph.facebook.com/search? q=<ggg>&type=group
Check-ins	https://graph.facebook.com/search?type=checkin

Extending Open Graph

In the section *Social Plug-ins* earlier, Facebook Like and other social plug-ins were described. The `Like` button can be embedded on any web page. It was also noted that the Like plug-in seeks to expand the scope of Facebook beyond just the Facebook web site. As per Facebook, if the web site developer adds some Facebook-recommended metadata (referred to as **Open Graph tags**) to his page, the web page can become the "equivalent of a Facebook page". What this means is that the Facebook social graph described in the section "*Open Graph API*" can contain any web page as a node if Open Graph tags are added. Open Graph tags contain metadata by which Facebook can understand the web page. They provide a structured representation of the webpage to Facebook. The following code example shows the metadata that Facebook recommends web site developers must add to their web page to integrate it into Facebook's social graph. The metadata being added is self-explanatory.

```
<html xmlns:og="http://opengraphprotocol.org/schema/"
      xmlns:fb="http://www.facebook.com/2008/fbml">
  <head>
    <title>The Magnificent Ambersons (1942)</title>
    <meta property="og:title" content="The Magnificent Ambersons"/>
    <meta property="og:type" content="movie"/>
    <meta property="og:url" content="http://www.imdb.com/title/
    tt0035015/"/>
    <meta property="og:image" content="http://ia.media-imdb.com/images/
    M/MV5BMTg3NjE2OTIwNl5BMl5BanBnXkFtZTYwODk5MTM5._V1._SY317_.jpg "/>
    <meta property="og:site_name" content="IMDb"/>
    <meta property="fb:admins" content="USER_ID"/>
    <meta property="og:description"
        content="The spoiled young heir to the decaying Amberson
        fortune comes between his widowed mother and the man she has
        always loved."/>
    ...
  </head>
  ...
</html>
```

Additional metadata like location and contact information can also be added. The set of recommended metadata tags is consistent with Facebook's claim that they are optimized for integrating those web pages that represent real-world things like movies, sports teams, restaurants, etc.

A quick word on how a web page becomes a part of the Open Graph. The first step is to add the `Like` button social plug-in to the web page. Next, add the recommended metadata tags as explained above. Now, when a user clicks on the `Like` button on the web page, a connection is made between the page and the user – and the web page is now part of the social graph. Functionally, the web page (a) appears in the Likes and Interests section of the user's profile, (b) can push content (example ads) to the user's wall and (c) shows up in Facebook searches.

Social Media Web Site: Picasa

Picasa focuses on social media experience centered on personal media. Picasa allows users to share their photographs with family and friends. Additionally, it allows users to create albums from photographs, add tags and other metadata like location, comment on photographs of other users, etc.

The Picasa API

The Picassa API [26] is similar in spirit to the Facebook API though there is no notion of Open Graph or social plug-in. As can be seen in Table 4.4, the REST APIs are very similar in intent to that of Facebook APIs. The fields which are parameters to the API are enclosed in '< >'. For example <userID> is the userid of the user. Picasa uses Google's userid's for <userID> and when it is set to default, the activity refers to the current user. The other parameters, such as <albumID>, are unique ids generated by Picasa. These ids are returned as a result of various calls; for example, the API shown in the first row of Table 4.4 returns a list of <albumID>, which can then be used to find a list of <photoID> in the album. Examples of these ids can be found in the example code segment shown next for a use case of searching for pictures of the Taj Mahal.

http://picasaweb.google.com/data/ is the common part of the APIs shown above. The term feed in the URL specifies that the result should be returned in the format of an ATOM feed. A snippet of an example ATOM feed that one such REST API returns is shown in the following code. As can be seen, this data is a rich source of information for photographs as it contains information about location, EXIF metadata, comments, tags, title, etc.

```
<?xml version='1.0' encoding='utf-8'?>
<feed xmlns='http://www.w3.org/2005/Atom'...
<updated>2011-08-13T06:32:18.072Z</updated>
<title type='text'>Search Results</title>...
<openSearch:totalResults>158377</openSearch:totalResults>...
<entry>...
```

```
<id>http://picasaweb.google.com/data/entry/api/user/<deleted>/
albumid/5114761574886048065/photoid/5114761725209903490</id>...
<title type='text'>DSC00675.JPG</title>
<summary type='text'>Taj Mahal, from the 2006 trip. </summary>
<content type='image/jpeg'
src='http://lh6.ggpht.com/-7FDWt-hEeUO/RvtIsJ3mgYI/AAAAAAAAAcE/
TrmtAzW1x88/DSC00675.JPG'/>...
<gphoto:id>5114761725209903490</gphoto:id>...
<gphoto:position>0.9782609</gphoto:position>...
<gphoto:commentCount>40</gphoto:commentCount>...
<exif:tags>
    <exif:fstop>5.0</exif:fstop><exif:make>SONY</exif:make><exif:
    model>DSC-H2</exif:model>
    <exif:imageUniqueID>4e7378f98016420d001c7269504db13b</exif:
    imageUniqueID>
</exif:tags>
</entry>
</feed>
```

In addition to ATOM feeds, other types of simple HTTP responses are also supported. The following APIs show how to update a photo and metadata, or

Table 4.4 Picasa API

Query	REST API
Requesting a list of albums for a particular user	GET http://picasaweb.google.com/data/feed/api/user/<userID>
Listing photos in an album with the id <albumID>, belonging to user <userID>	GET http://picasaweb.google.com/data/feed/api/user/<userID>/albumid/<albumID>
Listing tags that user <userID> has used in photos in their albums	GET http://picasaweb.google.com/data/feed/api/user/<userID>?kind=tag
Listing tags for photo <photoID>	http://picasaweb.google.com/data/feed/api/user/default/albumid/<albumID>/photoid/<photoID>?kind=tag
Listing comments for photo <photoID>	http://picasaweb.google.com/data/feed/api/user/default/albumid/<albumID>/photoid/<photoID>?kind=comments
Searching for photos tagged with both "tag1" and "tag2" and belonging to <userID>	GET http://picasaweb.google.com/data/feed/api/user/<userID>?kind=photo&tag=tag1,tag2
Searching for photos uploaded by other users (Context=all), matching a search for "Taj Mahal", maximum of 10 photos	GET http://picasaweb.google.com/data/feed/api/all?q=Taj%20Mahal&max-results=10

photo only, or metadata only. The photo and/or metadata should be in the body of the PUT statement. Only the full metadata can be replaced with this API.

```
Updating a photo and metadata or photo only
PUT http://picasaweb.google.com/data/media/api/user/<userID>/albumid/
<albumID>/photoid/<photoID >

Updating a photo's metadata only
PUT http://picasaweb.google.com/data/entry/api/user/<userID>/albumid/
<albumID>/photoid/<photoID >
```

The API part of the URL specifies that all metadata associated with the object should be returned and should be read-write enabled. The remaining part of the URL is specific to the particular REST API functionality. As an example, a complete post message which enables posting a photo with metadata is shown next.

```
Content-Type: multipart/related; boundary="END_OF_PART"
Content-Length: 4234766347
MIME-version: 1.0

Media multipart posting
-END_OF_PART
Content-Type: application/atom+xml

<entry xmlns='http://www.w3.org/2005/Atom'>
    <title>Taj Mahal.jpg</title>
    <summary>Wife and I in front of Taj Mahal 2009</summary>
    <category scheme="http://schemas.google.com/g/2005#kind"
    term="http://schemas.google.com/photos/2007#photo"/>
</entry>
-END_OF_PART
Content-Type: image/jpeg
...binary image data...
-END_OF_PART-
```

Wrapper Libraries

Most programmers prefer not to work directly with the REST APIs and instead use libraries that abstract out most of the common processing needed across multiple calls. It is common for libraries to provide functionality which parses the content received from GET calls. It is also common for these libraries to provide functionality which adds some default content in POST messages.

Libraries are available in many programming languages. The python library for Picasa is used as an example here. To start using any library, it first needs to be initialized. For the python Picasa library, initialization will look something like this:

```
import gdata.photos.service
import gdata.media
import gdata.geo
gd_client = gdata.photos.service.PhotosService()
```

Once you have initialized the interface, the application needs to be authenticated (while that is not shown here, the next section describes OAuth API for Facebook, to give the reader an idea of what is done). Now social applications can be written using the library. The following code segments show python library calls corresponding to the REST API calls described in the beginning of this section. Note that the python functions process the data returned by GET calls. As a programmer, it is not necessary to parse the Atom feed every time. Instead, the library parses and stores this data in a nice class structure.

The code for requesting a list of albums for a particular userID is as follows.

```
albums = gd_client.GetUserFeed(user=username)
for album in albums.entry:
print 'title: %s, number of photos: %s, id: %s' % (album.title.text,
    album.numphotos.text, album.gphoto_id.text)
```

Listing photos in an album with the id albumID, belonging to user userID, is done as follows:

```
photos = gd_client.GetFeed(
    '/data/feed/api/user/%s/albumid/%s?kind=photo' % (
        username, album.gphoto_id.text))
for photo in photos.entry:
print 'Photo title:', photo.title.text
```

Listing tags that user userID has used in photos in their albums:

```
tags = gd_client.GetFeed('/data/feed/api/user/%s?kind=tag' % username)
for tag in tags.entry:
    print 'Tag', tag.title.text
```

Listing tags by photo:
```
tags = gd_client.GetFeed('/data/feed/api/user/%s/albumid/%s/photoid/%
s?kind=tag' % (username, album.gphoto_id.text, photo.gphoto_id.text))
for entry in feed.entry:
print 'Tag', entry.title.text
```

The way to list comments by photo is as follows:

```
comments = gd_client.GetFeed(

    '/data/feed/api/user/%s/albumid/%s/photoid/%s?kind=comment&max-
    results=10' % (
    username, album.gphoto_id.text, photo.gphoto_id.text))
for comment in comments.entry:
print 'Comment', comment.content.text
```

Searching photos using tags tagged with both "foo" and "bar" and belonging to userID is as follows:

```
photos = gd_client.GetTaggedPhotos('foo,bar', user=username)
for photo in photos.entry:
    print 'Title of tagged photo:', photo.title.text
```

Searching photos uploaded by other users, matching a search for "puppy":

```
photos = gd_client.SearchCommunityPhotos('puppy', limit='10')
for photo in photos.entry:
print 'Community photo title:', photo.title.text
```

Micro-Blogging: Twitter

Twitter is a micro-blogging and social networking site. Like a blog it allows its users to write anything. However, the trigger line 'What's happening' suggests that users mostly write about in-the-moment experiences – like a self-created status message. Unlike typical blog sites, Twitter users are restricted to 140 characters or less (hence "micro"). Also, like other blogging services, Twitter allows users to subscribe to blogs of other users so that users can **follow** other users and read their micro blogs (also known as **status** or **tweets** in twitter lingo).

Consider the example shown in Figure 4.11: Three Twitter users, Alice, Bob and Carl, where Bob and Carl subscribe to Alice's tweets but Alice does not subscribe to anyone's tweets. Bob and Carl are therefore called **followers** of Alice. When Alice posts a micro-blog (or tweet) on twitter, Bob and Carl are notified and can read Alice's tweet. Note that when Bob posts a tweet, Alice is not notified, though the tweet is public. Alice may access or search for it later. One interesting aspect of Twitter's social network, which is created by users following other users, is its asymmetric nature. In the example, the Twitter social graph (Figure 4.11) will have a directed link from Bob to Alice and from Carl to Alice but there would be no links originating from Alice. In Twitter terminology, Alice has two followers but no friends. Bob has Alice as a friend and Carl has Alice as a friend.

Another important thing to note about Twitter is its real-time feature. Tweets are distributed in real-time; i.e., a tweet is delivered almost as soon as it is posted. A lot of interest in Twitter is due to the real-time nature of the information that traverses Twitter. This has led to innovations centered around analysis of tweets on a timeline to determine trends, changes in users' preferences and so on.

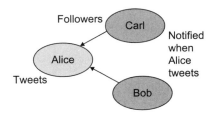

FIGURE 4.11

The Twitter social graph for the example.

> **NOTE**
>
> **Summary of Twitter APIs**
> - Lists of followers and friends
> - Real-time: last *n* tweets
> - Streaming: continuous feed of tweets
> - Geo-tagged: tweets from one or more locations

Twitter API

The REST APIs that allow developers to access the preceding Twitter data are specified in Twitter Developer Documentation [27]. Twitter supports both JSON and XML responses from its REST API. First, Table 4.5 contains code snippets that show the difference between accessing friends and followers described earlier.

There are also many APIs available to access the real-time features of Twitter. Some APIs that support time-based analysis of tweets (or statuses) are shown in Table 4.6.

Yet another set of APIs which exploit the real-time nature of Twitter are called **Streaming API**s [28]. These are useful when an application that uses social networking data depends on the analysis of real-time data. One way to do this is to call an API to retrieve the needed data iteratively in a loop. A more efficient way is to use a stream API which will stream data to the application in real-time. To quote the official documentation, this Twitter API allows "high-throughput near-real-time access to various subsets of public and protected Twitter data."

Consider another example of a social application that tracks and analyzes tweets about some topic (for example, sports) in real time. To receive JSON updates about keywords related to the topic, it is necessary to create a file called

Table 4.5 Twitter APIs

Operation	REST API
Get extended information of a given user (including latest status), specified by screen name	`GET http://api.twitter.com/1/ users/show.xml? screen_name=praphulcs`
Search API (search for a user specified by screen name)	`GET http://api.twitter.com/1/ users/search.xml?q=Praphul% 20Chandra`
Get list of user's friends, each with current status inline	`GET http://api.twitter.com/1/ statuses/friends.xml? screen_name=praphulcs`
Returns the user's followers, each with current status inline	`GET http://api.twitter.com/1/ statuses/followers.xml? screen_name=praphulcs`

Table 4.6 Twitter Time-Dependent APIs

Get the 20 most recent statuses from non-protected users	GET http://api.twitter.com/ version/statuses/ public_timeline.json
Get the 20 most recent statuses posted by screen_name	GET http://api.twitter.com/ version/statuses/user_timeline. json?screen_name=praphulcs
Get the 20 most recent mentions for the authenticated (current) user	http://api.twitter.com/version/ statuses/mentions.json

sportstracking that contains "track=cricket, soccer, tennis, badminton" and then do:

```
curl -d @sportstracking http://stream.twitter.com/1/statuses/filter.
json -u<appUserId>:<password>
```

curl is a command line tool for transferring data with URL syntax and it supports HTTP and other common protocols [29]. Of course, appUserID and password are the userid and password the application uses to retrieve data. Similarly, consider a social application which tracks and analyzes tweets from a particular location in real time. Twitter has an API called the **Geotagging API** (which specifies the latitude and longitude where the tweet was generated), and some twitter clients generate messages which are geo-tagged. To receive JSON updates about tweets geo-tagged with a particular location, it is necessary to create a file called 'locations' that contains a bounding box for the desired location. The bounding box is a pair of latitudes and longitudes that defines a rectangular box on the map. The locations file can contain multiple bounding boxes to track tweets from multiple locations. For example, locations = 16.786, −3.018, 16.76, −2.997 is a bounding box for Timbuktu (Tombouctou) in Mali, where 16.786 and −3.018 are the latitude and longitude, respectively, of one corner of the bounding box, and 16.76, −2.997 specifies the other corner (see Figure 4.12).

The statement locations = 16.786, −3.018, 16.76, −2.997, 16.726, −3, 16.714, −2.972 is a pair of bounding boxes for Timbuktu and the nearby town of Kabara. Using the above statement in the locations file, one can get tweets for Timbuktu and Kabara as follows:

```
curl -d @locations
http://stream.twitter.com/1/statuses/filter.json -u<appUserid>:<password>
```

There is another interesting way to add location information to tweets. Instead of simply adding latitude, longitude information, tweets may add a more semantic notion of location, i.e., the city or the neighborhood from which the tweet was made. To aid this, twitter provides an API (reverse_geocode) which searches for places (cities and neighborhoods) that can be attached to a tweet. Given latitude

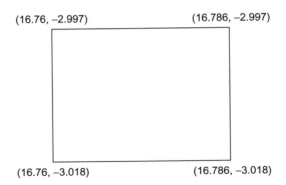

(16.76, –2.997)   (16.786, –2.997)

(16.76, –3.018)   (16.786, –3.018)

FIGURE 4.12

Bounding box for Timbuktu.

and longitude pair, or an IP address, this API returns a list of all the valid cities
and neighborhoods that can be used as a place_id in a tweet post:

```
http://api.twitter.com/1/geo/reverse_geocode.json?lat=16.786&long=-
3.018
```

A client application can use this API with user's lat, long location information
to retrieve a list of "places", have the user validate the location where he or she
is, and then send this place_id with a call to statuses/update.

Open Social Platform from Google

So far in this section, three popular social web sites which provide APIs for the development of social applications have been described. Though all the three web sites provided REST APIs, the conventions used in each of the three web sites were different.
There are many more such social web sites with their own conventions. This diversity
is probably important for providing a choice to users and to drive innovation in this
emerging field. However, from a programmer's perspective, this diversity provides a
challenge. How many different APIs can their application support? There is a need for
some uniformity. Google's Open Social platform [30] tries to provide a uniform API
to interact with many web sites. It is basically a set of APIs which serves as an
abstraction layer over multiple social web sites and services or **containers** in the terminology of Open Social. This approach has had some success but it is not guaranteed
that every social platform will support this (though most likely). The reader is directed
to the Open Social developer web site [30] for more information.

Privacy Issues: OAuth

One of the key aspects when programming for social computing is to keep in
mind the aspect of privacy. By definition, social computing is about users, their

relationships with other users and the content they create. When programming using this content, an appreciation for user's expectations for privacy would be key in understanding the underlying architecture of many "social applications" and also for ensuring that an application does not violate a user's privacy expectations.

The following examples illustrate some of the issues. Consider a social application that has been downloaded by user Alice. If Alice is linked to Bob in the application's social network, and Bob has marked a video as a favorite on YouTube, does the application (in-use by Alice) have the right to access and use Bob's favorite video? Again, assume Alice is a friend of Bob's on an online social networking site (for example, Facebook). Bob is also a friend of Carol; however, Alice is not a friend of Carol. Can Alice's application access information about Carol's profile? Actually, there is no right or wrong answer here. Different users have different expectations of privacy. More importantly, different social networking portals enforce different privacy policies. These policies are reflected in what the APIs do and do not expose to the programmer. Even when online social networking portals do allow applications to access user's content, they require that the application explicitly take permission from the user before accessing their content.

Consider another example, that of a social application for Facebook that seeks to create a movie recommendation application based on what movies a user and her friends like. Now, suppose a particular user Alice wants to use the application. To function, the application needs to access the movies that Alice likes, her list of friends and the movies they like. How does the application get this information? The application can ask Alice to provide her Facebook username and password which can be used to then access all of the desired information. This approach, though simple, has significant security loopholes. First, Alice has no reason to trust the application, which may actually use her username and password to acquire her personal photographs and misuse them. Alice has no way of ensuring that the application does not do the latter. Second, once Alice has given the application her username and password there is no way for her to take it back. The application can now and in the future access all of Alice's private information on Facebook. Of course, Alice can change her username and password to block the application but this approach does not scale very well – expecting the user to change her username and password after a single use of a social application will only ensure that no one uses such applications. Hence, what is needed is a security architecture that enables social applications to access specific content for specific periods of time without requiring the user to share her username and password with this application. There are multiple security architectures that achieve this: for example, Google AuthSub, Yahoo! BBAuth, Flick API and the OAuth protocol. Among them the growing open standard architecture is OAuth, explained next.

Overview of OAuth

OAuth provides a method for users to grant applications access to their "resources" without sharing their passwords. It also provides a way to grant limited access (in scope, duration, etc.) Though an intensive coverage of the OAuth security protocol is beyond the scope of this chapter, this section is intended to give the readers an overview of the architecture so as to develop an appreciation of the authentication flow which their application will undergo so as to help debug their code, in case of any errors.

The key architecture change introduced in OAuth is the notion of a **resource owner**. In the traditional client-server authentication paradigm, the client uses her security credentials (username & password) to authenticate herself to the server. OAuth introduces a third role in this model – the resource owner. The separation between the resource owner and the client is significant – the client acts on behalf of the resource owner but is NOT the resource owner. For our purposes, the terminology mapping mentioned in Table 4.7 would be helpful. With this mapping, it becomes easier to understand the use of OAuth for social applications.

In order for a social application to access resources from a server (social network site, e.g., Facebook) on behalf of a resource owner (user), it has to obtain permission from the resource owner. OAuth enables this permission in the form of a **token** and a matching **shared secret**. The purpose of the token is to make it unnecessary for the resource owner to share her username and password with the client. OAuth protocol can be used for applications other than social networking. The data flow for using OAuth protocol (Figure 4.13) in the context of social computing is as follows.

1. User makes a request to a social application.
2. Social application redirects user to Social networking (SN) site with a redirect_uri.
3. SN site informs user (via an user interface) about the resources the social application is requesting access for and asks for a confirmation.
4. User grants request by typing in her security credentials (username and password).
5. SN site authenticates the user's security credentials.
6. If correct, SN site sends a token & a shared secret to the social application and redirects user to redirect_uri. (Else request is rejected).
7. SN application uses token & shared secret to access resources which it has been granted access to.

Table 4.7 Terminology Mapping For OAuth	
Resource Owner	**User (human)**
Client	Social application (deployed on user's PC and / or a back-end server)
Server	A social networking site holding user's private data (e.g., Facebook)

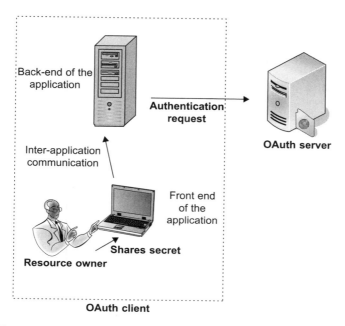

FIGURE 4.13

High-level architecture of OAuth.

Using OAuth in Facebook: As discussed, users can explicitly allow other applications to access their content on social networking sites without exposing user's Facebook username and password. This section shows use of Facebook APIs that use OAuth to do so. The following are the steps needed to authenticate an application that wants to access users' non-public content on Facebook.

1. Register the application to get an app ID and secret for the application. One can do this by clicking on `"Create New App"` and following the regular registration instructions at `http://www.facebook.com/developers/createapp .php`. At the end of the registration procedure, Facebook allocates an App Id and App Secret as below:

App ID:	275910438759498
App Secret:	20182e6931efd7939a01135e1baaa5d3

From OAuth perspective, from now on this Facebook app ID is the `client_id` and the Facebook application secret is the `client secret`.

2. The following URL redirects the users to Facebook so that they can login and grant access to the application and also specifies the URL that the user should be redirected to, after the completion of the authorization process

(redirect_uri). The user is now taken to a screen which looks as shown in Figure 4.14.

```
https://www.facebook.com/dialog/oauth?
client_id=<AppId>&redirect_uri=www.pustak.com&scope=email,
read_stream
```

3. If the user authorizes the application, Facebook redirects the user back to the redirect_uri specified with an additional argument (code=string) where string is the verification string (code or session authcode) that can be used to get the access token for the app.

4. The verification string must be exchanged to get an access token. This is done as with the following API, with exactly the same redirect_uri as in the previous step.

```
https://graph.facebook.com/oauth/access_token?client_id=<Facebook
AppId>&redirect_uri=http://www.pustak.com/oauth_redirect&client_
secret=<Facebook App Secret>&code=<session authcode>
```

The response to the above API is an access token (access_token parameter) together with the number of seconds until the token expires (the expires parameter). An example response can be as follows:

```
Access_token=12178242641841264|safkhjfsafh317813.jhffas.
244&expires=5108
```

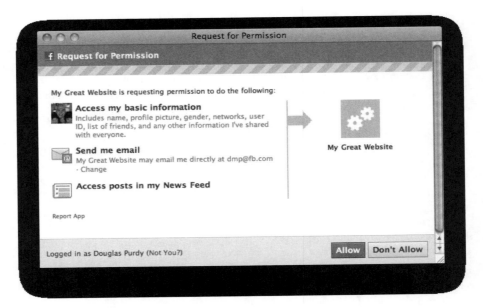

FIGURE 4.14

User authorizes the application to access his/her Facebook data.

5. The application then uses the access token returned by the request above to make requests on behalf of the user for Facebook details. If the application needs infinite time access, the application can request for offline_access permission.

In this section, the reader obtains a good understanding of the different APIs used to write social applications using data from popular social networking sites. There is a lot of literature on algorithms that can be used in these social applications and those are beyond the scope of this book. A good introduction to this topic is the book *Programming Collective Intelligence* by Toby Segaran [31]. It introduces some very interesting algorithms that can leverage data made available by social web services from a programmer's perspective. Analysis of social networks to understand user behavior is also a very interesting topic to study [32]. Finally, social computing is a highly dynamic and fast-growing area of research, so the reader has to refer to the latest research publications and API documentation to be current.

DOCUMENT SERVICES: GOOGLE DOCS

As mentioned in the *Social Networking* section, an important use of cloud computing is for sharing data. This sharing can be either with friends and colleagues as described before or just sharing for personal use across multiple devices. It is not uncommon for a consumer to own more than one computing device (an office laptop, a home computer and maybe even a mobile personal device). In those cases, use of a cloud service just to upload a document to a secure place, and using it across multiple personal devices anytime, anywhere is very valuable. Many such cloud services, e.g., www.dropbox.com, www.slideshare.com, www.scribed.com, exist. Over and above this, if the cloud service allows one to share these documents with a selected number of friends, and also allows a subset of them to modify and update, then it will be a very useful tool for collaboration as well. We'll look at more details of such features of document services using Google Docs as a case study.

Using Google Docs Portal

Google Docs is a popular cloud application and a very good example of a collaborative document service. It allows users to create and edit documents online as well as enables teams of people to share and work together on a single document. Its basic features are very simple – share, edit or simply store documents. However, this is now such a fundamental feature of society that Google Docs has become extremely popular in recent years.

Figure 4.15 shows a screenshot of the Google Docs home page after the user logs in. The page lists the files in the Test folder. The bar on the left shows

FIGURE 4.15

Google Docs home page.

other sets of files (e.g., those that meet a specific criterion – such as files Owned by me) or other folders (e.g., Folders shared with me). Action buttons on the top indicate actions that can be performed on selected or all files. The figure shows two files have been selected. In particular, the Share button allows the selected documents to be shared with other users. When sharing, the user will be asked whether to share just with "can view" permission or shared as "can edit" for each user. This will accordingly set the read and read-write permissions for each user.

These documents in the Test folder would have been either created fresh using Google Docs itself or created on the local computer and uploaded onto Google Docs. These two options are shown on the top left-hand menu. It is easy to create new documents using Google Docs. Figure 4.16 shows a screenshot of the page that appears for creating a presentation. It can be seen that the page is very similar to the view one would get with a presentation software package (such as Microsoft PowerPoint). A difference, however, is the Share button on the top right of the page. Clicking this button allows the presentation to be shared, so that multiple users can collaborate in the development of the document. In addition to presentations, users can also collaborate on documents, spreadsheets, and drawings.

There are desktop tools that simplify uploading of documents to Google Docs with just a simple drag-and-drop facility. An example of such tools is ListUploader for Windows or GDocsUploader for Mac OS X. The FireFox browser also supports a plug-in called GDocsBar, which supports a drag-and-drop upload onto the sidebar. Also, when a document is shared with a group of users, one can track who read the document by using Google Analytics. This is just a simple option that needs to be enabled in Google Docs. As the service becomes more and more popular, more such simpler usage modes will be established.

FIGURE 4.16

Google Docs create presentation.

Using Google Docs APIs

Google Docs also provides APIs that allow users to develop applications that upload documents to the Google Docs service and share documents [33]. When using any Google product, one should be aware that **Google Data Protocol (GDP)** is being used under the hood. GDP provides a secure means for new applications to let end users access and update the data stored by many Google products. Since GDP uses GET and POST requests, users may also use the protocol directly using any of the supported programming languages provided by HTTP client libraries. REST APIs similar to the one used for Facebook enable one to directly use the protocol. In this section, an example usage in Java is described. As an example, the Google Documents List API, that allows users to programmatically access and manipulate user data stored on Google Docs, is used [33].

> **NOTE**
>
> This example program demonstrates how one can upload and share documents using GData API.

The following is an example application that demonstrates several features of document sharing. The application first uploads a document onto Google Docs, and then shares the document to people on a mailing list (Google groups id), which also sends an email notifying those people about the document. Since the complete program runs to multiple pages, only the key snippets of the program will be described in this section.

First of all, the main Google Docs packages that one needs to import are the following.

```
import com.google.common.*;
import com.google.gdata.util.*;
import com.google.gdata.client.uploader.*;
import com.google.gdata.data.docs.*;
import com.google.gdata.data.media.*;
import com.google.gdata.data.acl.*;
```

A Simple Example

First, consider a very simple example that uploads a file without taking care of upload errors. Below is a snippet of Java code for doing this. This method throws an IOException when there is a communication or network error during upload. The uploadURL (hardcoded here for simplicity) points to the Google Docs URL for upload. Then a DocService object is created, and the user credentials are set for that object. After that, it is simple to upload a file – just set the filename, and title, and then call the insert method of the service.

```
public DocumentListEntry uploadFile(String filepath, String title)
                  throws IOException, ServiceException,
                  DocumentListException {
        URL createUploadUrl = new URL
            ("https://docs.google.com/feeds/upload/default/private/
            full");

        DocsService service = new DocsService("Pustak Portal");
        service.setUserCredentials(gmail_user, gmail_pass);

        File myfile = new File(filepath);
        String mimeType = DocumentListEntry.MediaType.fromFileName(
                            file.getName()).getMimeType();

        DocumentEntry myDocument = new DocumentEntry();
        myDocument.setFile(myfile, mimeType);
        myDocument.setTitle(new PlainTextConstruct(title));

        return service.insert(createUploadUrl), myDocument);
    }
```

The following code snippet shows how the methods of DocumentListEntry can be used to print out the details of the uploaded file.

```
public void printDocumentEntry(DocumentListEntry doc) {
        StringBuffer buffer = new StringBuffer();
        buffer.append(" -?- " + doc.getTitle().getPlainText() + " ");
        if (!doc.getParentLinks().isEmpty()) {
            for (Link link : doc.getParentLinks()) {
                buffer.append("[" + link.getTitle() + "] ");
            }
        }
    }
```

```
buffer.append(doc.getResourceId());
output.println(buffer);
}
```

TIP

If ResumableGDataFileUploader is used to upload data, then even connection disruptions are handled well.

Handling Disruptions in the Network

Uploading huge files takes a long time and one cannot expect that the client will be always connected during the upload time interval. The upload may fail in the middle because of disruptions in the network. Unfortunately, HTTP does not provide any guidance for reliably restarting failed uploads. However, Google Docs has APIs to handle such disruptions, and for that it is necessary to use the Java class called ResumableGDataFileUploader. For this, the following code should be executed in a Java thread, and the Listener pattern used to wait for the completion of the upload.

```
int MAX_CONCURRENT_UPLOADS = 10;
int PROGRESS_UPDATE_INTERVAL = 1000;
int DEFAULT_CHUNK_SIZE = 10485760;

// Create a listener
FileUploadProgressListener listener = new FileUploadProgressListener();
// Pool for handling concurrent upload tasks
ExecutorService executor =
        Executors.newFixedThreadPool(GDataConstants.
        MAX_CONCURRENT_UPLOADS);

// Get the file to upload
File file = new File(fileName);
URL createUploadUrl = new URL
        ("https://docs.google.com/feeds/upload/default/private/
        full");

DocsService service = new DocsService("Pustak Portal");
service.setUserCredentials(gmail_user, gmail_pass);

MediaFileSource mediaFile = new
    MediaFileSource(file,DocumentListEntry.MediaType.fromFileName
                                    (file.getName()).
                                    getMimeType());

// Fetch the uploader for the file
ResumableGDataFileUploader uploader = new
        ResumableGDataFileUploader(createUploadUrl, mediaFile,
        service,
            DEFAULT_CHUNK_SIZE, executor, listener,
            PROGRESS_UPDATE_INTERVAL);
```

```
// attach the listener to the uploader
listener.listenTo(uploader);
// Start the upload
uploader.start();
while (!listener.isDone()) {
    try {
        Thread.sleep(100);
    } catch (InterruptedException ie) {
        listener.printResults();
        throw ie; // rethrow
    }
}
```

Sharing the Document with a Mailing List

Finally, consider a more complex example that uses a **delegate** to login to Google Docs (class GDataServiceDelegate) and associates write permission to a Google Groups mailing list (SHARING_GROUP_NAME). The Java code for the same follows, with the important methods highlighted in bold. The ACLFeed class (Access Control List [34]) is used to add a new entry and set the right scope and role for the group.

```
private void shareUploadedDocumentWithGroup() {
            try {
        GDataServiceDelegate delegate = new GDataServiceDelegate(
                        GDataConstants.APPLICATION_NAME);
        delegate.login(username, password);
        DocumentListFeed resultFeed = delegate.getDocsListFeed
        ("documents");
        List<DocumentListEntry> listEntries = resultFeed.getEntries();
        DocumentListEntry entry = null;
        if (listEntries.size() > 0)
            entry = listEntries.get(0); //firstentry
        else
            return;

        AclFeed aclFeed = delegate.getAclFeed(entry.getResourceId());
        for (AclEntry aclEntry : aclFeed.getEntries()) {
            AclScope scope = new AclScope(AclScope.Type.GROUP,
            SHARING_GROUP_NAME);
            aclEntry.setScope(scope);
            aclEntry.setRole(new AclRole("writer"));
            aclEntry = aclEntry.update();

            printMessage(new String[] { aclEntry + ","
                    + aclEntry.getScope().getValue() + " ("
                    + aclEntry.getScope().getType() + ") : "
                    + aclEntry.getRole().getValue() });
        }
        printMessage(new String[] {"Your document has been shared"});
    } catch (Exception e) {e.printStackTrace();}
}
```

Embedding Google Docs in Other HTML Pages

Consider a scenario where Pustak Portal pages need to embed Google Docs; i.e., clicking on a link would display a document that is actually stored in Google Docs. Such a situation may arise if Pustak Portal decides to use Google Docs as a back-end store. It is possible for Pustak Portal to use the same APIs described earlier to upload documents to Google Docs and use Google Docs as a repository to store Pustak documents. The problem is that if a user of Pustak Portal wants to open a file, and that file takes the user to the Google Docs Service with user login just to view the document there, then the experience of using Pustak Portal is broken. So, is it possible to stay on Pustak Portal, but comfortably use Google Docs at the back-end? This use case is also elegantly supported by Google Docs.

In order to embed a Google Docs document into another HTML file, the unique URL of the document to be inserted is needed. To get this unique URL, the file needs to be published as a web page. For this, on Google Docs web page, click on "Share" and select "Publish As Webpage". A window as in Figure 4.17 will become visible, which not only shows the public URL, but also displays HTML code similar to the following, which should be inserted into Pustak Portal.

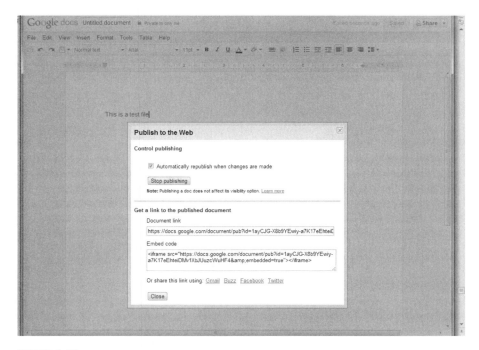

FIGURE 4.17

Publishing a document as a web page.

```
<iframe src="https://docs.google.com/document/pub?id=1ayCJGX8b9YEwiya
7K17eEhteiDMv
1Xb JUuzcWuHF4&amp;embedded=true"></iframe>
```

In addition to being able to retrieve documents by name, Google Docs also has APIs to search the list of documents [35]. The APIs allow search not only by a text string, but also by attributes of the file such as the type of the file and when it was last accessed. It is also possible to extract text from images and translate documents from one language to another [36].

Google Docs is a simple document management SaaS application that has been designed to enable uploading and sharing of documents using a cloud service as a persistent repository of information. Like all SaaS applications, all the features of Google Docs can be accessed using a portal. Additionally, the developer APIs enable the usage of this cloud application from within other applications. There are many such useful features provided by Google Docs that are helpful for collaborative tasks, such as writing this book! For full features of the Google Docs both through portal and API, the reader is referred to Google Docs [37] and Google Documents List Data API [38], respectively. As seen, even simple upload functionality is nontrivial to implement an API in such a way that it is resilient to disconnections in the network. Finally, the section showed how one can use the features of this SaaS in the running Pustak Portal example.

SUMMARY

In this chapter, the focus was mainly on the technical aspects of SaaS applications rather than the business benefits or the marketing hype. However, no SaaS chapter is complete without talking about the large change in the computing model that SaaS brings in for a user or an application vendor. The following briefly elaborates on this topic and evaluates the approaches followed in the different case studies described in this chapter.

Historically, the notion of SaaS existed even before the term "Cloud Computing" was coined. For example, most of the discussion about SaaS back in 2001 [39] is relevant even today. The SaaS term then created much interest and awareness of the benefits of delivering computing as a service over the Internet. There were many application service providers who turned into SaaS vendors by just hosting their application on a web portal. However, when the number of users of the application increased, they soon realized that in addition to providing a new application delivery model, SaaS also requires quite a few challenges to be solved at the hardware and platform level to address the scale, multi-tenancy and reliability issues. Thus, the first real cloud offerings came from companies such as Salesforce, Google and Amazon, who could be considered as SaaS vendors offering CRM as a service, search as a service and bookstore as a service, respectively. In order to be successful, these vendors were forced to develop technologies that would allow their services to scale to very large sizes quickly, as well as to support multiple customers on their infrastructure while still maintaining isolation (multi-tenancy). Thus, the SaaS model eventually expanded to become the cloud model.

In addition to technology, social computing applications delivered as SaaS have had a major impact on the Web. As stated in the *Introduction*, these applications have driven the evolution of the Web into the digital universe that it is today. It is likely that a major driving factor in the further evolution of cloud computing will be the generation of increasing user content, and the growing ability of users to access and modify this content from mobile devices. Additionally, this rich content will be mined by enterprises so that they can personalize their responses to users. Metaphorically, one can say that the Internet will change from being a passive entity (like the ocean which is unaware of the fishes swimming in it) to being an intelligent cloud which is aware of the users who inhabit it.

From an application delivery perspective, SaaS enables the end user view of the vision of cloud computing, where applications are no longer installed on a local machine but are available on the Internet. For customers, the advantages of SaaS include the ability to focus on using the application rather than having to spend effort in installing and maintaining it. For small businesses, SaaS makes the sophisticated enterprise applications used by larger enterprises affordable. For medium and large businesses, as stated in the *Introduction*, it is necessary to conduct a financial study to identify cost-saving opportunities between application delivery via SaaS versus deployment of a private cloud. There are also multiple benefits that application vendors see from the SaaS model. Rapid time to market of any new application without having to set up distribution channels or service channels to ensure that critical bug fixes reach their users is a great value, particularly to startups.

Technically speaking, unlike PaaS, SaaS systems are very diverse with different levels of usage of cloud technology, reflecting the diversity of possible applications. Vendors can deliver a novel application experience, or deliver a single but most used feature to multiple users (such as document upload and sharing as in Google Docs), or deliver a common application that can be customized to different business scenarios (as seen in Salesforce), or provide a platform to create newer applications around a particular domain (social computing). In each of these examples, the extent of configurability of the application and the flexibility provided by the system to different users largely varies. It is interesting to analyze these differences further.

In SalesForce.com, users were not only able to use the portal interface to tweak the look and feel but also could write their own programs to use the platform components of Salesforce to develop new applications. To provide the needed flexibility and configurability for developing sophisticated applications, Salesforce evolved into Force.com, which is a PaaS, where the user has access to individual application components (the database, the logic, workflow) and can develop applications even for other domains (not restricted to CRM). So, if a SaaS application is intended to provide different feature sets to different users, or expose underlying configurable elements to the user, a platform centric approach would be the right thing to do (though only limited functionality of the platform may eventually be exposed to the user). However, exposing the PaaS to users may not always be necessary, especially when the SaaS application itself can be used by multiple users without much special customization – as we saw in the section *Google Docs*.

The Google Docs example produced some additional insights. Though this SaaS application can be considered as a simple portal which enables hosting, sharing and viewing of documents, the extra features to support interoperability and reliability are interesting. The Google APIs can be used to support client-side applications that can use the Cloud as a persistence store and if needed as a document sharing and distribution mechanism, enabling a whole new class of applications to be developed. An important aspect of this SaaS use case is that extra care was taken to ensure reliability of the dependent applications. Given that the access to any SaaS application requires network connection, and given that this network is likely to break, the upload APIs had special features to ensure session management across disconnections. Another such feature in Salesforce.com is the ability to bulk load data [12, 40]. Incorporating such features to compensate for any gaps or limitations due to cloud-hosted application will be critical to the success of any SaaS application, as exemplified by the several debates about superiority of Google Doc versus Microsoft Office.

Though each SaaS application is focused on a specific domain and enables users to customize or develop newer applications in that specific domain, there are many opportunities to combine multiple SaaS applications and make it much simpler for the end user. For example, FaceConnector is a combination of Salesforce.com and Facebook – a mashup that pulls Facebook profile and friend information into a Salesforce CRM application [41]. Similarly, use of Salesforce and Google Docs together as an integrated solution claims to make it possible to manage an entire office in the Web [42], and integration between Amazon Web Services and Facebook allows development of applications that leverage Amazon together with Salesforce.com [43]. SaaS therefore forms a very important aspect of Cloud Computing.

References

[1] SalesForce.com. http://www.salesforce.com [accessed October 2011].

[2] https://na3.salesforce.com/help/doc/user_ed.jsp?loc=help [accessed March 2011].

[3] Creating Workflow Rules. https://login.salesforce.com/help/doc/en/creating_workflow_rules.htm [accessed October 2011].

[4] SugarCRM. http://www.sugarcrm.com/crm/ [accessed October 2011].

[5] White Paper. http://www.salesforce.com/ap/form/sem/why_salesforce_ondemand.jsp?d=70130000000EN1GandDCMP=KNC-Googleandkeyword=sugar%20CRMandadused=1574542173andgclid=CNfqoLK2uaQCFc5R6wod_R3TbQ [accessed March 2011].

[6] Force.com Web Services API Developer's Guide. http://www.salesforce.com/us/developer/docs/api/index.htm [accessed 08.10.11].

[7] Salesforce Apex Language Reference. https://docs.google.com/viewer?url=http://www .salesforce.com/us/developer/docs/apexcode/salesforce_apex_language_reference.pdf [accessed October 2011].

[8] A Beginner's Guide to Delphi Database Programming. http://delphi.about.com/od/ database/a/databasecourse.htm [accessed October 2011].

[9] A Comprehensive Look at the World's Premier Cloud-Computing Platform. http:// www.developerforce.com/media/Forcedotcom_Whitepaper/WP_Forcedotcom-InDepth_ 040709_WEB.pdf [accessed October 2011].

[10] Force.com Web Service Connector (WSC). http://code.google.com/p/sfdc-wsc/wiki/ GettingStarted [accessed October 2011].

[11] Salesforce API Reference. http://www.salesforce.com/us/developer/docs/api/index_ Left.htm# [accessed October 2011].

[12] Bulk API Developer's Guide. https://docs.google.com/viewer?url=http://www .salesforce.com/us/developer/docs/api_asynchpre/api_bulk.pdf [accessed October 2011].

[13] Performance tips by Simon Fell. http://sforce.blogs.com/sforce/2005/04/performance_ tip.html [accessed October 2011].

[14] http://blog.sforce.com/sforce/2005/05/sforce_performa.html [accessed 08.10.11].

[15] http://blog.sforce.com/sforce/2009/08/partitioning-your-data-with-divisions.html [accessed 08.10.11].

[16] http://wiki.developerforce.com/index.php/Apex_Code:_The_World's_First_On- Demand_Programming_Language [accessed 08.10.11].

[17] DeveloperForce Website. http://wiki.developerforce.com/index.php/Force.com_IDE_ Installation_for_Eclipse_3.3.x [accessed October 2011].

[18] Apex Code: The World's First On-Demand Programming Language. http://wiki. developerforce.com/images/7/7e/Apex_Code_WP.pdf [accessed October 2011].

[19] Salesforce Object Query Language (SOQL). http://www.salesforce.com/us/developer/ docs/api/index_Left.htm#CSHID=sforce_api_calls_soql.htmlStartTopic=Content% 2Fsforce_api_calls_soql.htm [accessed October 2011].

[20] Lawson M. Berners-Lee on the read/write web. http://news.bbc.co.uk/2/hi/technology/ 4132752.stm; 2005 [accessed 03.10.10].

[21] Eldon E. Facebook: 300 Million Monthly Active Users, "Free Cash Flow Positive". http://www.insidefacebook.com/2009/09/15/facebook-reaches-300-million-monthly- active-users/; 2009 [accessed 03.10.10].

[22] Voss, J. Measuring Wikipedia. In: Proceedings of the ISSI 2005. Stockholm, 2005.

[23] O'Reilly T. What is web 2.0: Design patterns and business models for the next generation of software. http://oreilly.com/web2/archive/what-is-web-20.html#mememap; 2005 [accessed 03.10.10].

[24] Baker C. My Map. http://christopherbaker.net/projects/mymap; [accessed 03.10.10].

[25] Graph API. http://developers.facebook.com/docs/reference/api/ [accessed 08.10.11].

[26] Picasa Web Albums Data API. http://code.google.com/apis/picasaweb/overview.html [accessed 08.10.11].

[27] Twitter developers. https://dev.twitter.com/ [accessed 08.10.11].

[28] Streaming API. http://dev.twitter.com/pages/streaming_api [accessed October 2011].

[29] CURL. http://curl.haxx.se/docs/ [accessed 08.10.11].

[30] OpenSocial. http://code.google.com/apis/opensocial/ [accessed 08.10.11].

[31] Segaran T. Programming collective intelligence: building smart web 2.0 applications, O'Reilly Media; 2007. ISBN-13: 978-0596529321.

[32] Wasserman S, Faust K. Social network analysis: methods and applications. Cambridge University Press; 1994. ISBN-13: 978-0521387071

[33] How to do stuff with Google Docs. http://www.labnol.org/internet/office/google-docs-guide-tutorial/4999/ [accessed 08.10.11].

[34] http://code.google.com/apis/documents/docs/3.0/developers_guide_java.html#Access ControlLists [accessed 08.10.11].

[35] http://code.google.com/apis/documents/docs/3.0/developers_guide_protocol.html# SearchingDocs [accessed 08.10.11].

[36] Translate a document, https://docs.google.com/support/bin/answer.py?answer=187189 [accessed October 2011].

[37] Google Docs homepage. http://docs.google.com [accessed 08.10.11].

[38] http://code.google.com/apis/documents/docs/3.0/developers_guide_protocol.html# SpecialFeatures [accessed 08.10.11].

[39] Software As A Service. A Strategic Backgrounder, Software & Information Industry Associatio, SIIA 2001, http://www.siia.net/estore/ssb-01.pdf [accessed October 2011].

[40] Got (lots of) Data? New Bulk API for High Volume Data. https://docs.google.com/viewer?url=http://www.salesforce.com/dreamforce/DF09/pdfs/ADVD009_Ferguson.pdf [accessed 08.10.11].

[41] http://sites.force.com/appexchange/listingDetail?listingId=a0330000003z9bdAAA [accessed 08.10.11].

[42] http://www.google.com/press/annc/20080414_salesforce_google_apps.html; 2008 [accessed 08.10.11].

[43] Force.com Toolkit for Amazon Web Services. http://aws.amazon.com/solutions/global-solution-providers/salesforce/ [accessed October 2011].

Paradigms for Developing Cloud Applications

INTRODUCTION

New platforms such as those studied as Platform as a Service in Chapter 3 enable developers to create efficient, scalable applications to be hosted on the Web. However, to effectively utilize these platforms, the developer who is just moving into developing cloud applications needs to learn new design methodologies for the application. This chapter describes these new methodologies and paradigms at a fundamental level with sufficient theoretical backing to enable the developer to consciously make the right choices for the application design.

The next section describes new concepts and techniques for handling large scale data storage during application execution. The use of both relational databases and NoSQL data stores to store cloud-hosted data is explained in detail. The Hadoop platform, described in Chapter 3, brings in a new notion of MapReduce programming that again requires rethinking on the application design. The next section explains the fundamental concepts of the MapReduce paradigm and guides the user in framing the problem statement as a MapReduce problem. This is particularly needed for so-called "Big Data" applications. The subsequent sections describe ways of developing rich client applications using client-side programming as well as visual programming with mashups for customized client interfaces for cloud-hosted applications.

SCALABLE DATA STORAGE TECHNIQUES

As stated in Chapter 1, cloud applications may have data storage requirements that exceed those of enterprise applications. For example, in 2009, Facebook required 1.5PB of storage for its photos, with a weekly growth rate of 25TB [1]. High capacities of this kind far exceed the needs of enterprise storage systems. In addition to high capacity, high throughput may also be a reason why conventional technologies cannot scale to the cloud. Netlog, a European social networking site, had 40 million active members, who generated 3000+ queries per second during peak time [2]. Additionally, the workload tended to be write-heavy, with a read-write ratio of 1.4:1. Similarly, a recent news report states that Google serves 2,000,000 requests per minute [3].

These examples show that conventional storage techniques may not be adequate for cloud applications. In this section, the question of how to scale storage systems to cloud-scale is discussed. The basic technique is to partition and replicate the data over multiple *independent* storage systems. The word *independent* is emphasized, since it is well-known that databases can be partitioned into mutually *dependent* sub-databases that are automatically synchronized for reasons of performance and availability. Partitioning and replication increases the overall throughput of the system, since the total throughput of the combined system is the aggregate of the individual storage systems.

The other technology for scaling storage described in this section is known by the name **NoSQL**.[1] NoSQL was developed as a reaction to the perception that conventional databases, focused on the need to ensure data integrity for enterprise applications, were too rigid to scale to cloud levels. As an example, conventional databases enforce a schema on the data being stored, and changing the schema is not easy. However, changing the schema may be a necessity in a rapidly changing environment like the cloud. For example, considering the Pustak Portal, it may be desired to capture additional information about the books being sold so as to enable the usage of more sophisticated recommendation algorithms requiring new columns to be added to the table. NoSQL storage systems provide more flexibility and simplicity compared to relational databases. The disadvantage, however, is greater application complexity. NoSQL systems, for example, do not enforce a rigid schema. The trade-off is that applications have to be written to deal with data records of varying formats (schema).

Partitioning and replication also increase the storage capacity of a storage system by reducing the amount of data that needs to be stored in each partition. However, this creates synchronization and consistency problems, and discussion of this aspect is deferred to Chapter 6.

The rest of this section is organized as follows: In the sub-section *Example: Pustak Portal Data*, some example data that is typical of a publishing portal is presented. The next section *Scaling Storage: Partitioning* describes how to scale storage systems by partitioning the example data discussed previously. The discussion is in the context of relational databases, but the same concepts apply to partitioning NoSQL systems as well. The next section describes NoSQL systems of the **key-value store** type. The following section describes the other type of NoSQL systems, known as **XML document databases**.

---

[1]The acronym NoSQL originally stood for *No SQL*. However, as some of the advantages of relational databases for the cloud became better known, NoSQL was re-interpreted to mean *Not Only SQL*.

Example: Pustak Portal Data

For illustrating the basic techniques of cloud storage and demonstrating the trade-offs, the following example is used. Assume that in Pustak Portal, the transactions on the books that have been sold have to be stored, as well as customer profiles and the current inventory of each book. The format of the data is shown in the entity-relationship diagram of Figure 5.1.

Table 5.1 shows the customer data that needs to be stored as well as the data on book sales. The customer data consists of a `Customer_Id` that uniquely identifies the customer, and `Name` and `Address` fields that specify the name and address of the customer, respectively. The `Total Bought` data contains the total amount of purchases by this customer from Pustak Portal. This data can be used, for example, to compute a customer membership level (e.g., Gold or Silver) that can be used to compute a discount or other membership benefits. Similarly, the inventory table (Table 5.2) contains the `Book_Id` and the `Warehouse_Id`, which together form the primary key, as well as `Inventory`, which is the number of copies of the book in stock at the warehouse. The sales data (Table 5.3) consists of a `Transaction_Id` that uniquely identifies the transaction, `Customer_Id` and `Book_Id` that uniquely identify the customer and book, respectively, together with the `Sale_Price`.

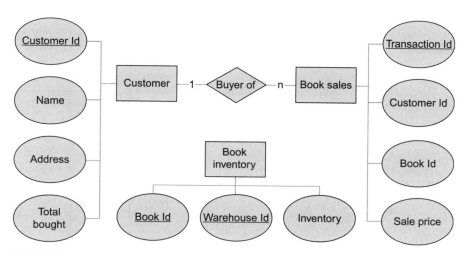

FIGURE 5.1

Example Pustak Portal data.

Table 5.1 Pustak Portal Customer Table

Customer_Id	Name	Address	Total_Bought
38876	Smith, John	15, Park Avenue, ...	$5,665

Table 5.2 Pustak Portal Inventory Table

Book_Id	Warehouse_Id	Inventory
1558604308	776	35

Table 5.3 Pustak Portal Transaction Table

Transaction_Id	Customer_Id	Book_Id	Sale_Price
775509987	38876	99420202	$11.95

We assume the sale price could vary because of discounts, for example, so it is necessary to store it in the book sale data. Finally, there is a one-to-many relationship between the customer data and the book sale data since a customer could have bought many books, but each sale is from only one customer. This database will be used as a running example in the rest of this chapter describing storage techniques.

Scaling Storage: Partitioning

Due to their widespread use and importance in enterprises, relational database technology has reached a high level of performance and reliability. Therefore, they form a natural choice for cloud storage. As of writing, many cloud applications were using MySQL for storing data. These include Wikimedia [4], Google [5], and Flickr [6]. However, databases in the terabyte range are currently considered very large [7]. As stated earlier, orders of magnitude larger storage are needed by cloud applications such as Facebook. So, traditional database deployments are not adequate for this purpose.

To scale both the throughput and the maximum size of the data that can be stored beyond the limits of traditional database deployments, it is possible to partition the data, and store each partition in its own database. For scaling the throughput only, it is possible to use replication. The rest of this section first describes partitioning and replication techniques used for scaling relational databases. Subsequently, these techniques are illustrated with the example described in the previous section. Finally, the disadvantages of a partitioning scheme are further detailed in the final subsection.

Recall that relational databases shown in Tables 5.1 to 5.3 depicted a simple way of storing the Pustak Portal data in relational tables. The first possible method is to store different tables in different databases (as in multidatabase systems). The second approach is to partition the data within a single table onto different databases. Further, two natural ways to partition the data from within a table are:

i. to store different rows in different databases and
ii. to store different columns in different databases.

The three techniques are discussed next. Since storing different columns in different databases is more common in NoSQL databases, it is discussed in the *NoSQL* sections.

Functional Decomposition

As stated previously, one technique for partitioning the data to be stored is to store different tables in different databases, leading to the storage of the data in a **multidatabase system (MDBS)** [8]. An example of a MDBS for a portal such as Pustak Portal is shown in Figure 5.2 [9]. Here, the data for the portal has been split into four databases. The Session Management database stores user information, such as the user profile, userid, and password. The eCommerce database stores customer transactions. The Content Management database stores information such as the goods to be sold, their photographs, and prices. The Data Warehousing database analyzes the transaction data and draws inferences about customer buying patterns. It is to be noted that these databases are not independent; for example, the Data Warehousing database periodically has to draw data from the eCommerce database. It can also be seen that since the number of functions into which a service is decomposed is in the order of 10s, this technique may not produce scaling beyond 10, which by itself would not be sufficient for a cloud-scale architecture.

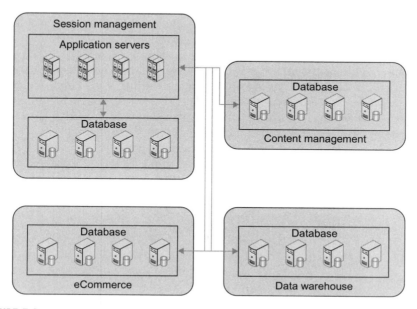

FIGURE 5.2

Functional decomposition of data.

Master-Slave Replication

To increase the throughput of transactions from the database, it is possible to have multiple copies of the database. A common replication method is **master-slave replication**, depicted in Figure 5.3 [9]. The master and slave databases are replicas of each other. All writes go to the master and the master keeps the slaves in sync. However, reads can be distributed to any database. Since this configuration distributes the reads among multiple databases, it is a good technology for read-intensive workloads. For write-intensive workloads, it is possible to have multiple masters, but then ensuring consistency if multiple processes update different replicas simultaneously is a complex problem. Additionally, time to write increases, due to the necessity of writing to all masters and the synchronization overhead between the masters rapidly becomes a limiting overhead.

Row Partitioning or Sharding

In cloud technology, **sharding** is used to refer to the technique of partitioning a table among multiple independent databases by row [10]. However, partitioning of data by row in relational databases is not new, and is referred to as **horizontal partitioning** in parallel database technology. The distinction between sharding and horizontal partitioning is that horizontal partitioning is done transparently to the application by the database, whereas sharding is explicit partitioning done by the application. However, the two techniques have started converging, since traditional database vendors have started offering support for more sophisticated partitioning strategies [11]. Since sharding is similar to horizontal partitioning, we first discuss different horizontal partitioning techniques. It can be seen that a good sharding technique depends upon both the organization of the data and the type of queries expected. A list of different sharding techniques follows.

Round-robin method: DeWitt et al. [12] describe three basic methods for horizontal partitioning. The **round-robin** method distributes the rows in a round-robin fashion over the different databases. In the example, we could partition the transaction table into multiple databases so that the first transaction is stored in the first database, the second in the second database, and so on.

The advantage of round-robin partitioning is its simplicity. However, it also suffers from the disadvantage of losing **associations** (i.e., related records are not likely to be stored in the same database). For example, suppose customers can log

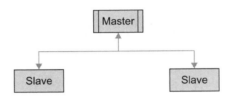

FIGURE 5.3

Master-slave replication.

on to the Pustak Portal and ask for a list of their recent orders in order to check on the status. Under round-robin partitioning, it is likely that these orders would be stored in different databases, so a query to find recent orders would have to query all databases.

NOTE

Sharding Techniques

- Round-robin by sharding attribute(s)
- Hash partitioning: hash on sharding attribute(s) to get the shard where record is stored
- Range partitioning: each shard stores a subrange of the sharding attribute(s)
- Directory-based: lookup sharding attribute(s) in a directory to find shard. Use memory cache to store directory for efficient lookup.
- Round-robin sharding loses data associations
- Range partitioning may be susceptible to load imbalance unless ranges are chosen carefully

---

Hash partitioning: Two techniques that do not suffer from the disadvantage of losing record associations are **hash partitioning** and **range partitioning** (see Figure 5.4.). In hash partitioning, the value of a selected attribute is hashed to

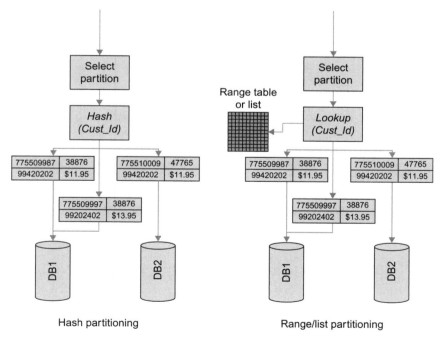

Hash partitioning   Range/list partitioning

FIGURE 5.4

Sharding methods.

find the database into which the tuple should be stored. If queries are frequently made on an attribute (such as `Customer_Id`), then associations can be preserved by using this attribute as the attribute that is hashed, so that records with the same value of this attribute can be found in the same database. This is illustrated in Figure 5.4 where transaction records with `Customer_Id` 38876 all hash to DB1.

Range partitioning: The range partitioning technique stores records with "similar" attributes in the same database. For example, the range of `Customer_Id` could be partitioned between different databases. Again, if the attributes chosen for grouping are those on which queries are frequently made, record association is preserved and it is not necessary to merge results from different databases.

Some web sites use **list partitioning**, which is a generalization of range partitioning [2]. Instead of partitioning on ranges of attributes of the record, each combination of attributes is looked up in a directory to find the database partition to which it belongs. For example, if `Customer_Id` is the partitioning attribute, it is looked up in a directory to find the database partition of interest (see Figure 5.4 which illustrates both range and list partitioning). To avoid performance bottlenecks, a memory-cached database can be used, since the amount of data is likely to be small (for example, if there are 20,000,000 customers, the database may be of the order of a few MB).

Range partitioning can be susceptible to load imbalance, unless the partitioning is chosen carefully. It is possible to choose the partitions so that there is an imbalance in the amount of data stored in the partitions (**data skew**) or in the execution of queries across partitions (**execution skew**). These problems are less likely in round robin and hash partitioning, since they tend to uniformly distribute the data over the partitions.

Case Study: Partitioning in Netlog

To illustrate these principles, this subsection describes sharding in Netlog [2]. The Netlog social networking site contains three databases – a database of users, a database of friendships between users, and a database of messages posted by users. The user database contains details about users such as their photos and videos. Initially, all these databases were stored in the same database server. As the I/O required grew beyond the capacity of a single database server, Netlog tried the following steps for scaling the I/O requirements.

Master-slave: The first scaling technology implemented for Netlog was master-slave replication (shown in Figure 5.3). Since the Netlog application has a high write/read ratio (1.4:1), the master eventually becomes a bottleneck.

Vertical partitioning: Since the writes to the user database were a bottleneck, the user database was partitioned vertically by putting independent columns on independent servers (e.g., photo details were stored in a separate database). However, the friendships and messages databases then became a bottleneck

Functional decomposition: The three databases – users, friendships, and messages – were put on separate database servers (the configuration being similar to the configuration shown in Figure 5.2). However, eventually with growth in load, the friendships and messages databases again became a bottleneck.

Master-slave: Initially, only the user database was set up in a master-slave configuration. Subsequently, the friendships and messages table were set up in a master-slave configuration as well, to increase the throughput. However, the messages database had a high write bandwidth and became a bottleneck.

Sharding: Some of the databases with high write traffic (messages database) were sharded on userid; i.e., data for a user were stored in database x where x is userid modulo the number of databases (see Figure 5.4). This is a hash sharding where the hash is simply the userid modulo the number of databases.

Example: Partitioning the Pustak Portal Data

To partition the Pustak Portal data shown in the previous case study, a combination of functional decomposition and sharding is used. The alternatives are discussed shortly, together with code fragments for implementing these alternatives. From the discussion that follows, it should be clear that there is no unique "best" partitioning alternative, and that the alternative chosen is strongly dependent upon the application (i.e., the queries that would be made against the database).

First, functional decomposition can be used to store the customer data, the transaction data, and the book inventory data in separate databases, and then shard each database separately (similar to the configuration in Figure 5.2). A simple scheme for further scaling is to shard the customer data and transaction data on `Customer_Id` (by, for example, hashing the `Customer_Id`). `Customer_Id` is selected as the sharding attribute because the assumption is that most of the online transactions would be related to individual customers (such as finding the status of a recent order, or updating the customer's profile). Other transactions (e.g., finding total sales of a book) are offline transactions where speed is not essential; therefore minimizing the response time for such a transaction is not essential (though the query should run efficiently). In that case, as stated previously, sharding the transaction database on the `Customer_Id` retains associativity, so that queries such as finding the outstanding orders for a customer need not span multiple servers, and hence reduces response time.

Before this sharding method can be implemented, one problem has to be solved. This problem is: sometimes, the `Transaction_Id` may be given, and since the transaction tables are sharded on `Customer_Id`, it is necessary to find the `Customer_Id` from the `Transaction_Id`. For example, a book may have been shipped to the customer, and it may be desired to notify the customer via an email that the book has shipped. The software that tracks the status of the order may send a message to an email module with the `Transaction_Id` of the order that just shipped. It is not possible to look up the transaction table to find the `Customer_Id`, since the transaction table is sharded on `Customer_Id`, so the shard to which the query is to be sent is unknown! This problem can be solved by modifying the transaction table as shown in Table 5.4. Here, the `Transaction_Id` has been decomposed into a pair (`Transaction_Num`, `Customer_Id`) which form a composite key for the table. The `Transaction_Num` can be some number which uniquely identifies the transaction for this customer, such as the seconds since a

Table 5.4 Transaction Table Modified for Sharding

Transaction_Id			
Transaction_Num	Customer_Id	Book_Id	Sale_Price
6732	38876	99420202	$11.95

particular date or a randomly generated number. Thus it can be seen that the sharding strategy may have an impact on the tables chosen.

```
CODE TO INITIALIZE CONNECTION TO TRANSACTION DATABASE SHARDS
import java.sql.*
class transDBs {
    public static final int NUM_TRANS_SHARD = 10;
    String dburl1 = "jdbc:mysql://transDB"    //First part of DB URL
    String dburl2 = ":3306/db"; //Second part of DB URL
    Connection[] transDBConns; // Array of transaction DB connections

    /* Return connection to transaction db shard for Customer_id */
    public Connection getTransShardConnection (int Customer_id) {
        return (transDBConns [Customer_id % NUM_DB]);
    }

    /* Load JDBC driver */
    Class.forName ("com.mysql.jdbc.Driver").newInstance();
    /* Initialize transaction DB shard connections */
    transDBConns = new Connection [NUM_DB];
    for (int i=0; i<NUM_DB; i++) {
        String dburl;
        /* transDBConns[0] points to jdbc:mysql://transDB0:3036/db */
        /* and so on */
        dburl = dburl1 + new Integer (i).toString() + dburl2;
        try {
            transDBConns[i] = DriverManager.getConnection (dburl,
            userid, pwd);
        } catch (Exception e) {
            e.PrintStackTrace();
        }
    } // for
} //transDBs
```

The preceding example code can be used to implement sharding in the transaction database. It is assumed that the database is sharded into NUM_TRANS_SHARD shards. The class transDBs maintains an array transDBConns of connections to the various database shards. The method getTransShardConnection can be used to get a connection to the database shard for a customer with a particular Customer_Id. Queries can then be performed against a shard as given in the next code sample, which shows how to retrieve all the transactions for a customer (assuming that the Customer_Id is a secondary index into the transaction table).

The statement starting `transDBConn =` gets a connection to the shard for a particular customer, and the subsequent `stmt.executeQuery` statement executes a query against the shard.

```
Executing a Query to a Transaction Database Shard
    Connection transDBConn; // Connection to transaction DB shard
    Statement stmt; // SQL statement
    ResultSet resset;
    transDBConn = transDBs.getTransShardConnection (Customer_Id);
    stmt = transDBConn.createStatement();
    resset = stmt.executeQuery ("SELECT * FROM transTable WHERE custID="
    + new Integer (Customer_Id).toString());
```

A more sophisticated method can be used if the customer base is geographically distributed. Assume that we can use the `Address` field to extract the continent that the customer lives in, and that Pustak Portal has servers in each continent. In that case, it may be useful to direct each customer's queries to a server in the continent the customer lives in. This can be achieved by hashing on both the continent as well as the `Customer_Id` as sharding attributes. For example, if the shard number is 3 digits (such as 342), the continent can be used to select the first digit of the number, and the `Customer_Id` to select the second two digits.

An intuitive method for sharding the inventory data is to use `Book_Id` as the sharding attribute. This would allow querying a single server to find all the warehouses in which a book is present, and to direct orders to the nearest warehouse to the customer. However, this would imply that some customer interactions, such as checkout, would span multiple shards. This is because when a customer checks out, the inventory of each book ordered would have to be updated, and this would generally span multiple servers, since the sharding is by `Book_Id`.

The need to update multiple servers upon checkout can be avoided by sharding in the following way. Assume there is a warehouse inventory management system under which a warehouse would have a very high (say 95%) probability of containing books wanted by customers who live close to it. Under that assumption, it is possible to shard by `Warehouse_Id`. When a customer checks out, there is a very high probability that all books ordered by the customer are in the nearest warehouse, so the transaction to update the inventory is very likely to involve only one server. If the book is not found in the nearest warehouse, the action taken depends on the inventory management system. For example, if there is a master warehouse that has copies of all books, the master warehouse can be queried.

Disadvantages of Sharding

As stated earlier, while sharding increases the scaling limits of the database, it creates additional complexity. Sharding creates additional consistency issues, as well as makes it difficult to re-shard in case the original sharding method does not create adequate throughput [13, 14]. More details follow.

Join complexity: When a single database is sharded across multiple servers, it is no longer simple to do joins, since this join has to be executed across multiple servers. A common solution to this problem is **denormalization**, whereby certain attributes are duplicated in multiple tables [15]. In the Pustak Portal example, suppose there are discussion forums containing topics that customers can initiate. When a customer logs in to the portal, consider the question of displaying a list of replies on all topics initiated by the customer. A common way to do this is to have a Topics table, which contains a list of topics, together with the userid of the customer who initiated the topic, and a Replies table, which has a list of replies, and topic ids. The desired list can be generated by joining the Topics table and the Replies table on the topic id and customer id. This is illustrated in Figure 5.5, which shows the case of generating a report for userid 999. From the Topics table, it can be seen that she is the initiator of topics 106 and 107; from the Replies table it can be seen that replies 10061 and 10062 are for these topics, and should be selected. Since the Replies table may be sharded, topics 106 and 107 could be in different shards, making this a complex operation. One way to handle this is to add the topic initiator userid (999 in this case) to the Replies table. This makes it possible to easily generate the report described earlier, but since the tables are no longer normalized, increases the database size and creates the problem of keeping the Topics table and Replies table consistent. If there is an inconsistency, it is possible that a customer may not see replies on topics she has initiated or vice versa.

Data consistency: The previous example is only one of the potential data consistency issues that could arise. Since the tables are split across multiple database servers, ensuring data consistency becomes the responsibility of the application.

Re-sharding: As the Netlog case study shows, an initial sharding design may not be sufficient for the throughput needed. In this case, the database may need to be re-sharded by increasing the number of shards or by using a different partitioning. This is very complex.

Reliability: Backups or snapshots become more complicated, since all shards have to be backed up in a synchronized manner to ensure consistency.

Auto-increment key complexity: Implementing auto-incrementing keys (where each inserted row gets a sequentially numbered key) has to be coordinated across shards.

Change in Database Schema
During the lifetime of a database deployment, it is not uncommon to have to re-organize the database. A white paper by Oracle [11] discusses many of the

Topic Id	Initiator		Reply Id	Topic Id	Reply
106	999		10059	76	...
107	999		10060	55	...
108	841		10061	107	...
109	263		10062	106	...

FIGURE 5.5

Denormalization example.

problems that arise when a database is reorganized, such as changing the schema, and introducing new indexes. The complexity of these changes increases with sharding.

Automatic Sharding Support

There are a number of efforts to add automatic sharding to MySQL by the use of a proxy. In these cases, the proxy sits between the client and the sharded database. After intercepting requests from the client, the proxy directs the request to the appropriate shard. Results are consolidated before being returned to the client. The proxy may also be able to transparently re-shard the database. Examples of such proxies include Scalebase [16], Spock proxy [17], and Hibernate Shards [18].

NoSQL Systems: Key-Value Stores

After the previous discussion on scaling relational databases, this section describes alternatives to relational databases. These alternatives were originally motivated by the desire to overcome the perceived constraints of relational databases that prevented scaling [19]. These include greater decentralization leading to greater reliability (i.e., avoiding the tight synchronization between replicas characteristic of databases), and a simplified interface compared to SQL. This subsection describes **key-value stores**, which simply store key-value pairs, and the only query interface is to use the key to get the corresponding value. **XML document databases** are described in the next section.

The rest of this section describes various well-known key-value stores. It can be seen that these have certain common features. First, the main API used for access is storage or retrieval of a value on the basis of a key. Second, the key-value stores offer automatic scaling by horizontally partitioning the store based on the value of the key. Thus sharding is an in-built feature of the key-value stores.

HBase

HBase, which is part of the Hadoop project, is one of the important scalable NoSQL technologies. For example, it is used in Facebook messaging, and handles about 135 billion messages per month [20]. HBase was selected for many reasons, including scalability and a simple consistency model [21, 22, 23]. In the following, HBase usage is described first, followed by a description of the techniques used by HBase to scale to cloud levels.

HBase usage: HBase is a key-value store that is an open source implementation of the ideas in Google's BigTable [24]. It is part of the Hadoop project, and as can be seen later in this chapter, is tightly integrated with Hadoop MapReduce (introduced in chapter 3 and described in detail later in this chapter). HBase can be considered as a datastore that keeps tables such that each row is indexed by a key. However, HBase is unlike relational databases, where the columns are the same for each row (and are specified by the database schema). In HBase, the columns in each row can vary. This is achieved as follows: when creating the row, the value of each column is specified as {*column name, value*} pairs. The column name consists of two parts – the *column family* and the *qualifier*. The column family is used for vertical partitioning of the database; recall the discussion in the section *Scaling Storage: Partitioning* about vertical partitioning being one of the partitioning methodologies that can increase scaling of databases. HBase stores different column families in different files. This is very valuable for performance tuning; multiple columns with the same column family are stored in the same file, and stored or retrieved together. Thus putting related columns in the same column family improves performance. Additionally, whenever a key is assigned a value, the old value is not overwritten. Instead, the new value is appended to the database with a timestamp. Periodically, a compaction process that deletes old timestamps is run. The number of old versions that should be retained can be specified.

Figure 5.6 illustrates these concepts. It can be seen that the table has 5 rows. There are two versions of the row with key value A at times *T1* and *T2*. Row A at *T1* had two columns – CF1:Q1 and CF1:Q3. These are in the same column family. However, it had only 1 column at time *T2*. Rows B and C have the same format as each other but different columns from row A. Row D has the same format as row A.

To make the concepts behind HBase use clearer, the following shows how HBase can be used to implement part of the Pustak Portal example given previously. The code samples in this section show how to insert transactions in the transaction table, and find transactions for a customer. It is assumed that a transaction table for holding the Pustak Portal transaction data (see section *Example: Pustak Portal Data*) has been created in HBase. The table is assumed to be named transTable, and it was created with a column family called transactionData for holding the transaction data. Note that the actual columns, which contain the transaction data values, have not been specified at the time of creation.

Row A	CF1:Q1=V1	CF1:Q3=V6	T1
Row A	CF1:Q1=V2		T2
Row B	CF2:Q2=V3		T3
Row C	CF2:Q2=V4		T4
Row D	CF1:Q1=V5	CF1:Q3=V7	T5

FIGURE 5.6

HBase data layout.

```
Connecting to HBase transaction table
    import org.apache.hadoop.hbase.HBaseConfiguration;
    import org.apache.hadoop.hbase.HTable;
    class transTableInterface {
        HBaseConfiguration HBaseConfig = new HBaseConfiguration(); // A
        HTable transTableConn = new HTable(HBaseConfig,"transTable");//B
    }
```

The code snippet shows how one can connect to the transaction table. It is assumed that class `transTableInterface` contains all the procedures for interacting with the transaction table. The variable `HBaseConfig` is automatically initialized in statement A with the connection parameters for HBase, which have to be stored in files `hbase-site.xml` or `hbase-default.xml` in the `CLASSPATH` [25]. Statement B stores the connection parameters to the transaction table in `transTableConn`.

```
Inserting a new transaction in HBase transaction table
import org.apache.hadoop.hbase.client.*;

class transTableInterface {
    public static insertRow (int transNum, int CustomerId, int BookId,
    float salePrice) {
        Put row = new Put (BytestoBytes (new Integer (CustomerId).
        toString() + "@" + new Integer (transId).toString())); // A
        row.add (Bytes.toBytes ("transactionData", Bytes.toBytes (new
        Integer (CustomerId).toString()));
    ...

        transTableConn.put (row); // C
}
```

The preceding sample code shows how to insert a new transaction into the transaction table. The method `insertRow` inserts a new transaction into the table. Statement A creates a new row object with the transaction id as a key. Since HBase is a key-value store, the transaction id has to be encoded into a single key. Here, the transaction id is encoded into a string of the form `<Customer_Id>@<Transaction_Num>`. Statement B adds the column `transactionData:BookId` to this row with the value given by `BookId`. Similar statements are needed to add the `salePrice`. These statements are omitted for brevity. Statement C finally inserts the row into the table. A default timestamp is provided, since there is no timestamp explicitly specified.

The rest of this section describes how to find all the transactions for a customer. Since HBase does not support secondary indexes, it is not possible to search the transaction table using the customer id. One possible method would be to maintain a table of customer ids and transaction ids, look up this table to find all the transaction ids for a customer, and then look up the transaction table to find the transactions. This is equivalent to maintaining a secondary index on customer ids in the application. However, this requires an extra query to lookup the transaction ids. The following is a method that finds the transactions directly from the transaction table. A modified version of this technique can be used to maintain and search a table of transaction ids and customer ids, if so desired.

```
FINDING ALL TRANSACTIONS FOR A CUSTOMER IN TRANSACTION TABLE
import org.apache.hadoop.hbase.client.*;
class transTableInterface {
    public static ResultScanner findCustTrans (int CustomerId) {
        Scan CustIdScan = new Scan(); // A
        RowFilter CustIdFilter = new RowFilter (CompareOp.EQUAL, new
        BinaryPrefixComparator (Bytes.toBytes (Integer (CustomerId).
        toString() + "@")); // B
        CustIdScan.setFilter(CustIdFilter)

        ...

        return (transTableConn.getScanner (CustIdScan); // C
}
```

The code snippet *Finding All Transactions for a Customer in Transaction Table* gives the sample code for finding all transactions for a customer. The key idea behind the code snippet is that since transaction ids are of the form <Customer_ Id>@<Transaction_Num>, to find all the transactions for a customer (say 38876), we merely need to look for transaction ids of the form 38876@xxxx. Additionally, the reason this query can be executed efficiently is that HBase keeps regions sorted on keys. Statement A creates a new scanner object. Statement B specifies that the scan condition is to look for transactions where the row key is equal to CustomerId@. This is specified by the RowFilter which has two parameters. The second parameter BinaryPrefixComparator specifies the comparison to be made (compare the initial part of the row key with the specified string). The first parameter (CompareOp.EQUAL) specifies that the comparison is to be for equality. Statement C executes the scan and returns the result. Though this technique is being used for finding transactions for a customer, a similar technique can be used if it is, for example, desired to keep a list of customers and books they have purchased or for maintaining a secondary index. This can be achieved by keeping a table with a key of the form <Customer_Id>@<Book_Id>.

HBase scaling: HBase provides auto scaling by horizontally partitioning tables based upon the key. A partition of a table is called a **region**, and an HBase server serving a region is called a **regionserver**. Therefore, HBase uses the range partitioning technique described earlier in the section *Row Partitioning or Sharding*. As the tables grow, they are automatically re-sharded under control of the **HMaster** server. HBase uses the **Zookeeper** clustering infrastructure to provide consistency and availability [26]. More details of Zookeeper can be found in chapter 6.

HBase also replicates the data based upon a user-specifiable parameter. Writes are written to all the replicas, and reads can be satisfied from any replica. Therefore, replication can be used to handle scaling for read-intensive workloads. It may be noted that since HBase uses sharding for scaling, the discussions in the section *Disadvantages of Sharding* are applicable.

HBase MapReduce: HBase is a key value store, and is a natural fit for processing by MapReduce. As MapReduce works on key-value pairs, splitting the input data among multiple nodes helps in scaling MapReduce applications [27].

> **NOTE**
>
> **Popular Key-Value Stores**
> - Amazon SimpleDB is described in Chapter 2 *Infrastructure as a Service*
> - Windows Azure Table Service is described in Chapter 3 *Platform as a Service*
> - *Cassandra : Described in this chapter.*

Cassandra

Cassandra [28] is a widely used key-value store with some interesting features both in terms of replication as well as data storage. The data storage features are described here; Cassandra's replication and consistency features are described in Chapter 6. Cassandra was originally an internal project at Facebook before it was released as an open source project. Since then, it is reportedly in use at both Twitter and Digg.

The basic key-value storage in Cassandra is similar to HBase and is influenced by Google's BigTable. The value is specified as in HBase, by a column family and column. The value is also time stamped; i.e., new values do not overwrite old values, but are appended with a timestamp.

There are two advanced features of Cassandra that are different from the basic functionality provided by HBase. They are:

1. Column names in Cassandra can be values, and not necessarily names of values. In this case, where a value is directly stored in the column name, the column value is left blank. For example, to store a phone number for users, it is not necessary to have a column called `PhNo` which stores values like 5555-5555. Instead, the value 5555-5555 can be directly stored as a column name, if so desired.

2. Columns can also be **super columns.** If a column in a column family is a super column, then all columns must be super columns; i.e., super columns and columns cannot be mixed in a column family. Super columns allow values to be lists of lists. Consider the example of Pustak Portal, where readers are to be allowed to store lists of their favorite books. This can be done by having a column called `favorites` and storing the names of the books as a list; e.g., "Hound of the Baskervilles, Maltese Falcon, Dr. Faustus, The Unbearable Lightness of Being". Suppose it is desired to categorize these as "Detective Fiction" with the value "Hound of the Baskervilles, Maltese Falcon", and "Literary Fiction" with the value "Dr. Faustus, The Unbearable Lightness of Being". In many key-value stores, it is possible to define columns `Detective Fiction` and `Literary Fiction` with appropriate values. In Cassandra, however, it is possible to define a super column called `favorites` with values "Detective Fiction", and "Literary Fiction" that are themselves columns with values "Hound of the Baskervilles, Maltese Falcon", and "Dr. Faustus, The Unbearable Lightness of Being", respectively.

NoSQL Systems: Object Databases

The other major type of NoSQL storage systems are object databases. These are databases that store objects, generally specified in XML notation. Object database systems thus allow the storage of more complex structures than key-value stores, which allow storage of values indexed by a single key. To some extent, the difference is not as great as it seems, since the value field in a key-value store is not interpreted by the store, and can encode a complex object. However, in the case of an object database, the database is aware of the structure of the object, and therefore, searches based on any field of the object are possible. In contrast, the only searches possible in key-value stores are those where the value is a simple value, such as an integer or string. Therefore, one important consequence of this difference is that the application programmer does not need to maintain secondary indexes, such as the mapping from customer ids to transaction numbers that are necessary in key-value stores.

MongoDB

MongoDB is a highly scalable storage system that stores structured objects (JSON objects). It is in use on Craigslist, a community forum to exchange local classifieds found at http://www.craigslist.org/, where MangoDB is being used to archive billions of records [29, 30].

    JSON: MongoDB stores objects that are specified in *Java Script Object Notation* (JSON) format [31]. JSON is a lightweight, text-based format that is simple for humans to read, as well as for machines to parse. It is a common way of serializing structured objects and can be used an alternative to XML. JSON objects are built from two fundamental constructs:

i. a list of name-value pairs enclosed in "{}" (which is treated like a structure)
ii. a list of values enclosed in "[]" that represents an array.

    These constructs can be compounded to create more complex objects that are supported by most programming languages; for example, arrays of structures or structures that contain sub-structures [32]. The transaction data for the Pustak Portal example from Table 5.3 in JSON format follows.

```
Pustak Portal Example transaction Data in JSON
{"Transaction_Num" : 6732,
"Customer_Id": 38876,
"Book_Id": 99420202,
"Sale_Price": 11.95 }
```

MongoDB concepts

The following is a brief overview of the programming concepts of MongoDB. First, every object in MongoDB must have an **object id** [33]. This is the first field of the object, and is named _id. If the id is not specified during creation of the object, a system-generated id named _id is inserted into the object. Objects in MongoDB are stored in **collections**, which correspond to tables in relational databases, in the sense that the objects in a collection are related to each other, and are stored together. Object ids should be unique in a collection.

Considering the Pustak Portal example, it can be seen that the transaction data can be represented by a collection, and similarly the customer data and inventory data can be collections as well. Using the transaction data described earlier, it can be seen that there is no single unique id for a transaction (since the key is composite). Therefore, no object id for the transaction will be specified. Therefore, the JSON encoding shown earlier can be used as a transaction object.

One of the powerful features of MongoDB is that objects can contain pointers to other objects (similar to foreign keys in relational databases). In the transaction data, it can be seen that both the `Customer_Id` and `Book_Id` fields can be pointers to other objects, since they could be object ids in their respective collections.

MongoDB programming

In the rest of this section, methods of programming MongoDB are considered [34]. The cases of inserting a transaction into the transaction table, and getting all transactions for a customer will be considered. The following code is a simple example of the set of statements needed to connect to a MongoDB database.

```
Connecting to a mongodb database
import com.mongodb.Mongo;
import com.mongodb.DB;
import com.mongodb.DBCollection;
import com.mongodb.BasicDBObject;
import com.mongodb.DBObject;
import com.mongodb.DBCursor;

Mongo connPool = new Mongo ("transDB", 27017); // A
DB dbConn = connPool.getDB ("db"); //B
```

Statement A connects to a MongoDB database server and statement B connects to a database on the server. Note that it is not necessary in MongoDB to explicitly create a database; the database is created the first time a client connects to it.

The next snippet shows the statements needed to insert a new transaction into the transaction data. It is assumed that the transaction data is in a collection called transactionData in the database db.

```
Inserting a new transaction
DBCollection transData = dbConn.getCollection("transactionData"); // A
BasicDBObject trans = new BasicDBObject(); // B
trans.put ("Transaction_Num", 6732); // C
trans.put ("Customer_Id", 38876);
trans.put ("Book_Id", 99420202);
trans.put ("Sale Price", 11.95);
transData.insert (trans); // D
```

It is not necessary in MongoDB to explicitly create the collection; the collection is created the first time an object is inserted into the collection (assuming that a connection to the database has already been initialized as in the previous example). Statement A gets a pointer to the transactionData collection if it already exists; otherwise it creates a pending pointer. Statement B creates an empty object, which is populated in statement C with the fields of the transaction shown earlier. This is then inserted into the transactionData collection by statement D. Statement D also creates the collection if it did not exist previously.

To find all transactions for a particular customer, it is necessary to be able to search by Customer_Id. This can be achieved by making it an index as follows.

```
transData.createIndex (new BasicDBObject ("Customer_Id", 1));
```

After Customer_Id has been defined as an index, it is possible to find all transactions for a customer as shown in the following code snippet. Note that in key-value stores, the store is indexed only by one key (Transaction_Id for the transaction table) so it becomes necessary in general for the application programmer to explicitly maintain a secondary index on Customer_Id. However, this may not be necessary for XML databases.

```
Finding all transactions for a customer
DBCursor results;
BasicDBObject query = new BasicDBObject(); // A

query.put ("Customer_Id", 38876); // B
results = transData.find (query);

while (results.hasNext()) {
    /* Process results */
}
```

In the preceding example code, statement A creates an empty query object. Statement B and the following statement create the query and execute it against the transaction data. The while loop iterates over the result set. Any desired processing can be inserted into the body of the loop. In the body of the loop, the variable results.next() points to the next item in the result set.

The previous sections looked at multiple techniques available to store scalable data. The developer can either choose to partition the relational database or use NoSQL datastores (either key-value pairs or object databases) to ensure that the central datastore can be used by different components of a cloud-hosted application. The next section provides in-depth guidance on developing cloud applications using the MapReduce paradigm.

MAPREDUCE REVISITED

As studied in Chapter 3, MapReduce is a popular paradigm of programming for the Cloud, which particularly works well for large-scale data processing. It is very effective for massively data-parallel applications that can be parallelized to crunch data on hundreds or thousands of CPUs. Traditional ways of writing parallel and distributed programs require the developer to explicitly split the tasks as multiple processes, deploy these processes on multiple CPUs and also manage the communication among the processes (through communication APIs) to exchange intermediate data values or final results. Writing such distributed applications is not very easy for a developer who has programmed for sequential machines. The MapReduce programming model makes development of such parallel applications very easy [35]. The programmer just specifies a map function and a reduce function for the application and the MapReduce framework does automatic parallelization and distribution of data to result in efficient parallel execution of the Cloud application. Furthermore, the platform ensures that the application is fault tolerant [36]. This section describes some advanced features of the MapReduce framework and provides some new insights and tips for application developers.

A Deeper Look at the Working of MapReduce Programs

As described earlier, in a MapReduce program, the programmer defines a Map function and a Reduce function. The Map function takes as input a key-value pair and generates a set of intermediate key-value pairs. The MapReduce platform then collates all the intermediate values from parallel Map function execution into groups that correspond to a single key and sends them to the Reduce function. The Reduce function, on the other hand, takes this intermediate key and the set of values corresponding to that key and combines these values to form a smaller number of key value pairs (typically one or zero values) as the overall result of the computation.

The processing flow for a MapReduce program is as follows:

- The input data is split into chunks, each of which is sent to different Mapper processes to execute in parallel. The parallel execution is achieved when the Map function just reads the relevant key-value pairs given to it.
- The result of the Mapper process is partitioned based on the Key and is sorted locally. The user can also provide the comparator operator here. This sorting is done by the MapReduce platform and is referred to as Shuffle.
- Result from the different Mappers that have the same key will be given as input to the same Reducer instance. The Reduce function (provided by the user) processes this sorted key-value data to generate the output.

In Chapter 3, a brief description of the data flow between the Map and Reduce tasks was described (Figure 3.25). Now, Figure 5.7 gives a more detailed view of the same data flow. As seen, the Shuffle performs a sorting of the keys and passes values belonging to the same key to the same Reduce task. As mentioned in Chapter 3, a simple distributed merge sort can be achieved if the map and reduce functions are identity functions. Within this processing flow, the user can define multiple functions to implement the required application, as well as optimize the

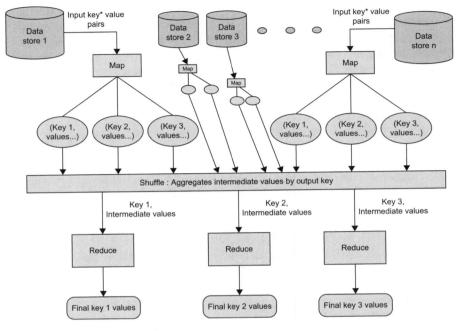

FIGURE 5.7

Detailed data flow in map.

execution of the application. In particular, the following functions can be defined by the user:

- `map(in_key, in_value)` : Process inputs and emit `((out_key, intermediate_value)list)`
  It may be noted that the key-value pair emitted by the map function can be (and it usually is) different from the inputs.
- `reduce(out_key, intermediate_value_list)` : Analyze and aggregate value list and emit `(out_key, aggregated_value_list)`
  The Reduce function processes the different values corresponding to the given key. So, the emitted value is for the same key.
- `combine(key2, value2_list)` : Analyze and aggregate value list and emit `(key2, combined_value2)`
- For efficient execution, the `combine` function can be defined to perform local aggregation of results corresponding to a single key. The `combine` function is called with the map results on the same processor, before sending it to a reduce instance executing elsewhere.
- `partition(key2)` : Determine a data partition and return the reducer number

The partition function is given the key with the number of reducers and returns the index of the desired reducer.

The `combine` and `partition` functions help in optimizing the execution of the parallel algorithm. The `combine` function reduces the unnecessary communication between the Mapper and Reducer functions by performing local consolidation of co-located data with same keys. The `partition` function can be used for efficient partitioning of the input data, for subsequent parallel execution. Typically, different records from data sources (could be different files or a set of lines from a given file or rows of a database) are used as the partitioning basis. Other sophisticated techniques such as horizontal partitioning in databases and data sharding, described in the earlier section, can also be implemented within this function. Sharding is most effective in a shared-nothing architecture such as the one in MapReduce and it can also use replication of shared data to achieve good performance.

Ideally, the communication between the Input data and the Mapper task can be minimized if we run the Mapper logic at the data split (without moving the data). However, this depends upon where the input data itself is stored and if it is possible to execute Mapper processes on the same node. For HDFS and Cassandra, it is possible to compute the Mapper task on the storage node itself and the Job Tracker takes the responsibility of co-locating the Mapper with the data split it processes, hence significantly reducing the data movement. On the other hand, pure data stores such as Amazon S3 do not allow execution of Mapper logic at the storage node. When running on Amazon Hadoop, it is necessary to create a Hadoop cluster in EC2, copy the data from S3 to EC2 (which is free), store intermediate results from MapReduce steps in HDFS on EC2, and write the final results back to S3 [37].

In general, the MapReduce APIs are very simple to use and allow specification of the parallelism in the application within the specific design paradigm of distributed merge-sort. The MapReduce platform (Hadoop for example) is expected to take care of automatic parallelization, fault tolerance load balancing, data distribution and network performance when implemented on a large network of clusters – as far as the specific application is concerned.

MapReduce Programming Model

From a programming model perspective, the MapReduce abstract model is based on the following simple concepts:

i. iteration over the input;
ii. computation of key/value pairs from each piece of input;
iii. grouping of all intermediate values by key;
iv. iteration over the resulting groups;
v. reduction of each group.

Though this programming model is somewhat restrictive, it can handle many problems encountered in the practice of processing large data sets. There are over 10,000 distinct MapReduce applications that use this new paradigm for cloud-hosted applications, just from Google. Further, any limitations in the expressiveness of the paradigm can be overcome by decomposing the problem into multiple MapReduce computations or solving the sub-problems in other ways.

The MapReduce paradigm provides a clean abstraction for programmers to easily develop data parallel applications. However, developers need to learn this new paradigm of programming that borrows a lot from functional programming concepts. The next subsection briefly introduces functional programming and its relation to the MapReduce programming model.

A formal definition of the MapReduce programming model is explained and analyzed in detail in a research paper from Stanford University and Yahoo! Research published in Symposium of Discrete Algorithms, SODA 2010 [38]. The definitions and the specifications of the model are quoted from that reference, with some minor notational modifications:

> "**Definition 2.1.** A mapper is a (possibly randomized) function that takes as input one ordered <key; value> pair of binary strings. As output the mapper produces a finite multiset of new <key; value> pairs. It is important that the mapper operates on one <key; value> pair at a time.
>
> **Definition 2.2.** A reducer is a (possibly randomized) function that takes as input a binary string k which is the key, and a sequence of values v_1; v_2; ... which are also binary strings. As output, the reducer produces a multiset of pairs of binary strings <k; $v_{k;1}$>; <k; $v_{k;2}$>; <k; $v_{k;3}$>; ... The key in the output tuples is identical to the key in the input tuple.
>
> A MapReduce program consists of a sequence <$M_1,R_1,M_2,R_2,M_3,R_3, ...$> of mappers and reducers. The input is a multiset of <key; value> pairs denoted by U_0. To execute the program on input U_0:
>
> For r = 1, 2, .. R, do:
>
> 1. Execute Map:
>   Feed each pair <k; v> in U_p-1 to mapper M_p , and run it. The mapper will generate a sequence of tuples, <k_1; v_1> ; <k_2; v_2>; ... Let U'_p be the multiset of <key; value> pairs output by M_p, that is,
>
> $$U'_p = \cup_{<kv> \in Up-1} M_p(<kv>)$$
>
> 2. Shuffle:
>   For each k, let $V_{k,p}$ be the multiset of values v_i such that $<k, v_i> \in U'_p$. The underlying MapReduce implementation constructs the multisets $V_{k,p}$ from U'_p
>
> 3. Execute Reduce:
>   For each k, feed k and some arbitrary permutation of $V_{k,p}$ to a separate instance of reducer M_r, and run it. The reducer will generate a sequence of tuples <k1; v1'> ; <k2;v2'>; ... Let U_p be the multiset of <key; value> pairs output by R_p , that is
>
> $$U_p = \cup_k R_p(<kV_{k,p}>)$$
>
> The computation halts after the last reducer, R_p, halts.

The author goes about defining a new class of problems called *MRC* and goes about to prove that the number of iterations needed to complete a MapReduce cycle is of O(log n). The SODA paper [38] offers more details of this rigorous evaluation of the MapReduce paradigm. Another workshop paper [39] also forms an interesting read for a reader interested in theoretical foundations.

Fundamental Concepts Underlying MapReduce Paradigm

The rest of this section describes the key concepts needed to understand the programming model – particularly the fundamentals of functional programming and data parallelism.

Functional Programming Paradigm

Quoting from the seminal ACM SIPOPS paper by Sanjay et al., which was the first paper to describe the MapReduce paradigm: "The MapReduce abstraction is inspired by the map and reduce primitives present in Lisp and many other functional languages" [40].

The functional programming paradigm treats computation as the evaluation of mathematical functions with zero (or minimal) maintenance of states or data updates. As opposed to procedural programming in languages such as C or Java, it emphasizes that the application be written completely as functions that do not save any state. Such functions are called **pure** functions. This is the first similarity with MapReduce abstraction. All input and output values are passed as parameters and the map and reduce functions are not expected to save state. However, the values can be input and output from a file system or a database to ensure persistence of the computed data. Programs written using pure functions eliminate side effects. So, the output of a pure function depends solely on the inputs provided to it. Calling a pure function twice with the same value for an argument will give the same result both times. Lisp is one such popular functional programming language where two powerful recursion schemes – called map and reduce – enable powerful decomposition and reuse of code. Similar combinators are available in Haskell, another functional programming language. Since Haskell has a simpler notation, the rest of the section uses Haskell's syntax in the examples.

Haskell's map combinatory computes the output list of values, by applying a common operation to the elements of an input list. The result of map is a sequence such that element j of the output list is the result of applying the function to element j of the argument list (or sequence). The resulting list is as long as the input sequences. The following example shows the map combinator used to double the values of the input list.

```
Haskell-prompt> map ((*) 2) [1,2,3]
[2,4,6]
```

The reduce function in Lisp combines all the elements of a sequence (or list) using a binary operator. For example, if the binary operator is "+", the result of reduce will be the sum of all the elements of input list. The equivalent of reduce in Haskell is called the `fold` operator. `foldl` is the left-associative fold operator and `foldr` is the right-associative one. In the following example to compute the sum of all numbers, the expression '(+)' denotes addition and the constant '0' is the default value.

```
Haskell-prompt> foldl (+) 0 [1,2,3]
6
```

As can be seen from the earlier described examples, the MapReduce programming paradigm also follows the functional programming model. The operators do not modify (overwrite) the data structures. They always create new ones while the original data is unmodified. The two functions operate on lists (much like Lisp and Haskell) and the data flow is implicit in the design of the program.

Though the high-level abstraction of map and reduce functional combinators hasmotivated the MapReduce framework, there are many differences. A detailed study of the similarities and differences between the MapReduce paradigm and the map-reduce combinators supported in functional languages is found in *Google's MapReduce Programming Model—Revisited* [41]. For example, the map function takes in a list of key-value pairs and generates new key-value pairs but the map function is expected to process the complete list (using an iterator or equivalent) using application-specific logic, as opposed to the map combinators in functional languages which define a simple operation that needs to be applied to each element of the list to generate the output list. Also, the length of the input and output lists for map combinator is the same, while that is not the case in the Map function of the MapReduce framework.

Parallel Architectures and Computing Models

MapReduce provides a parallel execution platform for data parallel applications. This and the next section describe core concepts involved in understanding such systems.

Flynn's Classification

Michael J. Flynn in 1966 created a taxonomy of computer architectures that support parallelism, based on the number of concurrent control and data streams the architecture can handle. This classification is used extensively to characterize parallel architectures. They are briefly described here:

- Single Instruction, Single Data stream (SISD): This is a sequential computer that exploits no parallelism, like a PC (single core).
- Single Instruction, Multiple Data Stream (SIMD): This architecture supports multiple data streams to be processed simultaneously by replicating the computing hardware. Single Instruction means that all the data streams are processed using the same compute logic. Examples of parallel architectures that support this model are array processors or Graphics Processing Unit (GPU).
- Multiple Instruction, Single Data Stream (MISD): This architecture operates on a single data stream but has multiple computing engines using the same data stream. This is not a very common architecture and is sometimes used to provide fault tolerance with heterogeneous systems operating on the same data to provide independent results that are compared with each other.

- Multiple Instruction, Multiple Data Stream (MIMD): This is the most generic parallel processing architecture where any type of distributed application can be programmed. Multiple autonomous processors executing in parallel work on independent streams of data. The application logic running on these processors can also be very different. All distributed systems are recognized to be MIMD architectures.

A variant of SIMD is called SPMD for Single Program, Multiple Data model, where the same program executes on multiple compute processes. While SIMD can achieve the same result as SPMD, SIMD systems typically execute in lock step with a central controlling authority for program execution.

As can be seen, when multiple instances of the Map function are executed in parallel, they work on different data streams using the same map function. In essence, though the underlying hardware can be a MIMD machine (a compute cluster), the MapReduce platform follows a SPMD model to reduce programming effort. Of course while this holds for simple use cases, a complex application may involve multiple phases, each of which is solved with MapReduce – in which case the platform will be a combination of SPMD and MIMD.

Data parallelism versus task parallelism

Data parallelism is a way of performing parallel execution of an application on multiple processors. It focuses on distributing data across different nodes in the parallel execution environment and enabling simultaneous sub-computations on these distributed data across the different compute nodes. This is typically achieved in SIMD mode (Single Instruction, Multiple Data mode) and can either have a single controller controlling the parallel data operations or multiple threads working in the same way on the individual compute nodes (SPMD).

In contrast, **task parallelism** focuses on distributing parallel execution threads across parallel computing nodes. These threads may execute the same or different threads. These threads exchange messages either through shared memory or explicit communication messages, as per the parallel algorithm. In the most general case, each of the threads of a Task-Parallel system can be doing completely different tasks but co-ordinating to solve a specific problem. In the most simplistic case, all threads can be executing the same program and differentiating based on their node-id's to perform any variation in task-responsibility. Most common Task-Parallel algorithms follow the Master-Worker model, where there is a single master and multiple workers. The master distributes the computation to different workers based on scheduling rules and other task-allocation strategies.

MapReduce falls under the category of data parallel SPMD architectures.

Inherent Data Parallelism in MapReduce Applications

Due to the functional programming paradigm used, the individual mapper processes processing the split data are not aware (or dependent) upon the results of the other mapper processes. Also, since the order of execution of the mapper function does not matter, one can reorder or parallelize the execution. Thus this inherent parallelism enables the mapper function to scale and execute on multiple nodes in parallel. Along the same lines, the reduce functions also run in parallel, each instance works on a different output key. All the values are processed independently, again facilitating implicit data parallelism.

The extent of parallel execution is determined by the number of map and reduce tasks that are configured at the time of job submission [42]. This number depends upon the inherent parallelism in the application and the number of nodes available in the MapReduce infrastructure. A general rule of thumb is to ensure that the number of map and reduce tasks is much larger than the available number of nodes. However, if the algorithm is not embarrassingly parallel, the maximum number of data splits should be chosen as the number of Map tasks; for example, if there are 100 nodes in a MapReduce cluster. The number of Map tasks can be set to larger than 1000 if the tasks have no dependencies at all. However, if, for example, the Map task is to each read from separate files and there are only a maximum of 10 files expected to be used, then the number of Map tasks should be set to 10. The number of reduce tasks should at least be the number of distinct keys expected in the intermediate results, as those are the computations that can be performed in parallel. Now if the map tasks are expected to generate diverse keys, one for each English alphabet, then the number of reduce tasks should be 26 or more. As described in the next paragraphs, there is a way of defining the partition function such that reduction tasks even for a single key can be parallelized by reducing in a hierarchical fashion. At the end of the day, the logic of the application or the algorithm used limits the amount of parallelism that can be exploited. Hence, choice of the right algorithm is important to make the best use of the platform capabilities. The next section gives some examples and tips for using the right algorithm.

Some Algorithms Using MapReduce

Clearly, there is a considerable amount of work needed from the developers to formulate the solution to their problem and design the application to suit the MapReduce paradigm. This section details a few example problems and an appropriate algorithm that can be used in a MapReduce context. The readers can use these as standard models and design their own applications along similar lines. Only key snippets or code fragments of the Map and Reduce functions are shown here for each example; complete Java code for one such sample was described in Chapter 3.

Word Count

The following is the most quoted simple example of counting word occurrences. The problem is to find the total number of word occurrences in a corpus of text documents. Each Map function is called with a key that is the document name and value has the document contents.

```
map(String key, String value):
for each word w in value:
    EmitIntermediate(w, "1");
```

```
reduce(String key, Iterator values):
int result = 0;
for each v in values:
result += ParseInt(v);
        Emit((key,AsString(result)));
```

The Map function just outputs the number '1' for each word. So, the intermediate key-value pairs are of the form {("this", "1"), ("is", "1"), ("a", "1"), ("nice", "1"), ("book", "1"), ..., ("a", "1"), ..., ("book", "1")...}. The Reduce function is called with common key values (a and book in the example). So, all that the Reduce function has to do is to just add the count (value) and emit the result for that particular word (key). Please note that not all the key-value pairs corresponding to a specific key may land at the same reducer. There may be hierarchical consolidation that can happen since the number of such key-value pairs can be much more than the number of reducers. So, the output of one Reduce function can go in as an input of another Reduce function along with the output of mappers, corresponding to the same key. So, we can define a combine function which is the same as the reduce function to enable local consolidation of index counts.

Sorting

Sorting is the simplest algorithm that MapReduce is most suited for. As described earlier, the MapReduce computation follows a distributed sorting pattern and hence having identity Map and Reduce functions automatically achieves sorting of its inputs.

For sorting, the inputs are a set of files that contain the elements to be sorted, one per line. The mapper key is the file name and line number and the mapper value will be the contents of the line.

```
// Sort Algorithm
map(String key, String value):
for each word w in value:
    EmitIntermediate(w, "");

reduce(String key, Iterator values):
int result = 0;
for each v in values:
        Emit((v,""));
```

This algorithm takes advantage of the reducer property that (key, value) pairs are processed in order by key and that the output from the reducers are themselves ordered. This approach will involve lots of communication during the shuffle as we assume a single reducer.

A major milestone in the development of MapReduce was the solution to the massive problem of sorting a terabyte of data using the TeraSort algorithm (proposed by Jim Gray in 1985) using Apache Hadoop. TeraSort absolutely fits the MapReduce programming model and works very well when a custom partitioner is used. This special partitioner should be such that all keys where sample[i - 1] ≤ key < sample[i] are sent to reduce i. This ensures that the output of reduce i are all less than the output of reduce $i+1$. We should also pick the hash function for the data such that $k1 < k2 \Rightarrow hash(k1) < hash(k2)$ and that will ensure that the sorting of the hash values automatically results in sorting of the keys.

The partition function used in this case of multiple reducers is given here:

```
partition(key) {
range = (KEY_MAX - KEY_MIN) / NUM_OF_REDUCERS
reducer_no = (key - KEY_MIN) / range
return reducer_no
}
```

TF-IDF

The Term Frequency – Inverse Document Frequency (TF-IDF) algorithm is the most common computation used in text processing and information retrieval applications. This is a statistical quantity used to measure the importance of a word with respect to a document corpus. The term frequency of term i in document j is given by the following equation, where $n_{1,j}$ is the number of occurrences of term t_i in document d_j

$$\text{tf}_{i,j} = \frac{n_{i,j}}{\sum_k n_{k,j}}$$

The summation in the denominator gives the number of occurrences of all terms in the document. The inverse document frequency measures the importance of the word, by comparing with its commonality of occurrence in other documents. Specifically, the Inverse Document Frequency is given by

$$\text{idf}_i = \log \frac{|D|}{|\{j : t_i \in d_j\}|}$$

Here $|D|$ gives the number of documents in the repository and the denominator gives the number of documents containing the term t_i. The problem is to compute `tf i,j * idfi`

In order to put this in MapReduce framework, the problem is broken into the following four jobs:

1. Compute word frequency within a document.
   - This is exactly the same as the first example in this section. The Mapper takes as input `(docname, contents)` and outputs `((term, docname), 1)`
   - The reducer sums the counts for each word in the document and outputs `((term, docname), n)`.
2. Compute the Word Counts for the documents.
   - Mapper takes as input `( (term,docname), n)` and outputs `(docname, (term, n))`.
   - Reducer sums the frequencies of the individual n's in the same document and also sends the original data from the mapper. It outputs `((term, docname), (n,N))` where n is the term frequency and N is the length of the document.

3. Find the Word Frequency in the corpus
   - For this the mapper takes as input `((term, docname), (n,N))` and outputs `(term, (docname, n, N, 1))` thus also passing the data that has already been computed.
   - The reducer sums the counts for the word in the corpus and outputs `((term, docname), (n,N,m))`.
4. The final job is to compute the TF-IDF value
   - For this the mapper takes as input `((term, docname), (n, N, m))` and calculates the TF-IDF as `(n/N)*log(D/m)` where D is the size of the document corpus. D can either be assumed or can be found in another simple MapReduce cycle. The mapper outputs `((term, docname), TF*IDF)`
   - The reducer in this case is an identity function

As can be seen from the earlier, more complex example, the short burst of data parallel activities in the algorithm are formulated as separate individual MapReduce jobs to result in the full execution of the algorithm.

Breadth-First Search

The last problem considered here is about graph-based algorithms [43]. Due to the functional programming nature of the application, the graph data structure cannot be stored in global memory and operated upon by different map and reduce nodes. Also, sending the entire graph to every map task will require a huge amount of memory. Therefore, the solution needs to carefully consider how the graph itself is represented.

A common way of representing graphs is to have the graph nodes in an array and maintain the edges or references to other nodes as a linked list. This representation requires that this common data structure be stored in a shared memory and protected with locks to avoid read-write collisions and inconsistencies. Another well-known approach is to store a graph as an **adjacency matrix**. Here, the graph is represented by a 2-d array (matrix) with the number of rows and columns equal to the number of nodes in the graph. The entry A[i, j] = 1 implies that there is an edge from node i to node j and a value 0 implies that there is no edge between i and j nodes. This representation nicely lends itself to data parallel operations on the matrix. Figure 5.8 shows an example graph and its adjacency matrix is shown in Table 5.5.

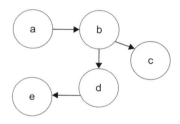

FIGURE 5.8

Representing a graph as an adjacency matrix.

Table 5.5 Adjacency Matrix

0	1	0	0	0
0	0	1	1	0
0	0	**0**	0	0
0	0	0	0	1
0	0	0	0	0

Table 5.6 Sparse Representation of Adjacency Matrix

1	2	2	3	2	4	4	5

While this is a simple way of representing the graph, most adjacency matrices for large graphs will be sparse with many 0's as can be seen even for this small graph in the example of Figure 5.8. Such sparse matrices are represented as arrays with only non-zero entries for every row (node). One sparse matrix representation for the previous example is shown in Table 5.6.

Table 5.6 shows how the adjacency matrix can be represented in an array. In the table, pairs of cells have been shaded in order to make the sparse representation clearer, and have no other significance. The first two array elements (1, 2) represents the fact that there is an edge from node 1 to node 2. It can be seen that the array contains a list of all the edges in the graph. This representation is very succinct and can be passed around among the map and reduce functions.

To take a concrete example of an algorithm that uses these concepts, a common graph search application of finding the Shortest Path from a source node to one or more destination nodes is described next. Readers who have done a basic data structure course would have learned about Dijkstra's algorithm and Breadth First Search (BFS). While Djikstra's algorithm is most efficient in terms of reducing the number of computations, the MapReduce version of the shortest path using the same concept will employ BFS to exploit maximum parallelism.

The overall idea is to find the solution to this problem inductively.

For `srcNode, lengthTo(srcNode) = 0`
For all nodes n directly reachable from `srcNode`:

`lengthTo(n) = 1`

For all nodes n reachable from some other group of nodes S:

`lengthTo(n) = 1 + min( lengthTo(m), m) where m is in S`

Now converting this algorithm to fit the MapReduce paradigm:

- The Mapper task receives a node n as the key with a value (D, reaches-to) where D is the distance of the node from the `srcNode` and `reaches-to` is the list of nodes reachable from n
- The Mapper advances the known frontier by one hop and performs the breadth-first-search to output (n,d,reaches-to) with new nodes added to the value.

- The algorithm stops when d stops changing.
- We need a non MapReduce task that handles the iteration and ensures termination of the processing when the length of the reaches-to stops changing.

More complex algorithms can be developed using MapReduce. The Apache Mahout project is a platform that implements multiple machine learning algorithms on Hadoop. The interested reader is encouraged to experiment with Mahout.

RICH INTERNET APPLICATIONS[2]

Since by definition cloud computing services have to be accessed over the internet, end user oriented applications need to have a pleasing interface that is both user friendly and rich in experience. Such applications are categorized as **Rich Internet Applications (RIA)**. The term richness is usually associated with the ability of the application to provide a very good user experience rather than just presenting the desired/information. An additional advantage is the ability to offload some processing to the rich clients.

Consider a simple example of an application showing sales data as a table of numbers for a series of years, and revenues for each of these years against different regions in a country. A traditional web application would get the data from the server and display it as a table. For any statistical computation on this data, the browser would need to go back to the server. Displaying a chart would need a further server interaction. With RIA, these all can be done right on the client side. Therefore, the web page looks "rich" in content and has lower delays during interaction – resulting overall in a much better user experience. This section describes platforms that enable development of such Rich Internet Applications.

Getting Started

Rich Internet Applications (RIA) can either run within a web browser with client-side scripts (JavaScript) and a browser plug-in or execute within a secure sandbox as desktop applications (e.g., Flash applications). For example, when registering at a web site, a simple validation of the username that it is an email can be done on the browser with a Javascript script, to give an interactive experience. Better still, users may remember search engines that support auto completion of search terms. Such experiences are possible with client-side scripting.

RIA platforms have their own runtime libraries, execution engines and rendering mechanisms. For example, Flex by Adobe [44] runs on the Flash runtime, and, for Microsoft Visual Studio (Expression Blend), the runtime would be Silverlight [45]. It may be noted that this runtime runs on the client side independent of the server. In fact the server may not even know the exact platform on which the

---

[2]Contributed by Dr. Prakash Raghavendra, Assisitant Professor, NITK-Suratkal, India.

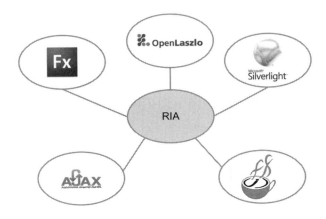

FIGURE 5.9

Illustration of some RIA technologies.

client application runs. This way the application development at the client and server side can go on independently. Additionally, the same security sandbox restrictions apply regardless of whether the application runs in the browser or in a desktop application. For some runtimes, such as Adobe, the runtime client source code for browser plug-ins can run on the desktop runtime as well. Figure 5.9 shows the logos of a few of the popular RIA technologies available today.

RIA Development Environment

The development of an RIA starts with an **Integrated Development Environment** (**IDE**) such as Flash Builder.[3] The developer uses this IDE to develop the application using two alternate views in the IDE. The first, called a **design view** is used to design the layout of the application, e.g., where buttons or text boxes should be placed. Most of the components needed by developers (e.g., various kinds of buttons and charts) are available in the (usually free) SDK. After completing the "look-and-feel" of the design, the **code view** is used to fill in source code for each component. For example, in a login screen, the developer would want to validate the user id and password entered in the text box provided, and if the validation fails, display an error message.

Generally, in IDEs, the code is written in some extension of XML. In the case of Flex, the markup language is known as **MXML**. However, as shown in Figure 5.10, the source code can contain **ActionScript** code as well. The ActionScript scripting language is an ECMA standard (like JavaScript). ActionScript methods are typically used for flow control and object manipulation features which are not available in MXML. Also, MXML is actually a higher-level abstraction built on top of

---

[3]Also sometimes referred to as Flex4.

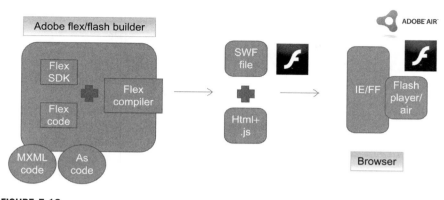

FIGURE 5.10

RIA development environment.

ActionScript. The SDK components, MXML code, and ActionScript code are input to the compiler (which is part of the SDK). The compiled output is an intermediate representation (SWF in the case of Flex). This SWF file in turn is embedded into an HTML wrapper, since browsers understand only HTML. The browser eventually calls the browser plug-in whenever it encounters SWF input (see Figure 5.10). It can also be seen that the same SWF code can be run in the Adobe AIR runtime on the desktop as well as a desktop application.

The following is an overview of the process for the well-known RIA technologies in Figure 5.9. The markup language for Visual Studio is called **XAML**. In the case of Microsoft Silverlight, the .NET SDK compiler converts XAML and SDK components into **CLR** intermediate code which is run on the .NET platform on the client side. Similarly, with the OpenLazslo platform, the markup language LZX can be compiled into either SWF or run directly on the Java Servlet Server with the same behavior and look-and-feel. In the case of **AJAX** (**Asynchronous JavaScript And XML**), the script is written in JavaScript, which is directly interpreted by the browser. So, no browser plug-in is needed in this case (in contrast to ActionScript or OpenLaszlo). However this may lead to browser dependencies and incompatibilities, and the same AJAX application may not run with the same behavior on all browsers. Finally, **JavaFX** has JRE as the runtime and JavaFX as the scripting language.

A Simple (Hello World) Example

The following is a simple example RIA application using Flex as an illustrative platform.

```
1 <?xml version="1.0" encoding="utf-8"?>
2 <mx:Application xmlns:mx="http://www.adobe.com/2006/mxml"
```

```
3 layout="absolute" creationComplete="init()">
4 <mx:Button id="mxmlButton" label="This one is done by MXML"    x="10"
y="10"    click="mxmlButton.label='MXML Button says Hello World!'"    />
5 <mx:Script>
6 <![CDATA[
7 import mx.controls.Button;
8 //Init Function is executed when the application boots

9 public var newButton:Button = new Button();

10 private function clickHandler(e:Event):void

        newButton.label='ActionScript Button - Hello World!';
11 }
12 private function init():void {

13 //Modify Properties
14 newButton.label = "This one is done by ActionScript";
15 newButton.x = 10;
16 newButton.y = 40;
17 newButton.addEventListener(MouseEvent.CLICK, clickHandler);
18 //Add the new button to the stage (Screen)
19 this.addChild(newButton);
20 }

21 ]]>
22 </mx:Script>
23 </mx:Application>
```

The previous code creates two buttons – one created by MXML code and the other by ActionScript in Flex3. As can be seen from the following, this example illustrates points. First, it provides an overview of the development process of a simple RIA application. Second, this application shows that all the MXML code is converted to ActionScript by the preprocessor.

The first line gives the XML version. Line number 2 gives the type of the application. There are two possibilities – mx:Application, which would be deployed and run on the browser or mx:WindowedApplication which would be deployed on the desktop runtime. These also give the XML namespaces from which the components should be picked up for the compilation and building the SWF binary. The same line also specifies how to layout the application. Here the layout is **absolute** which means that the layout offsets (like x=40 etc) are absolute. The other option is **relative**, which specifies offsets with respect to horizontal or vertical boxes within the main canvas. The creationComplete() statement tells the runtime to run the init() function when all the necessary initializations are complete. The runtime initializes many default objects and finally when it is ready to start the application it calls init() as declared.

> **NOTE**
>
> **Hello World example for RIA**
> - Shows that MXML and ActionScript can be mixed in the same script
> - MXML: XML declaration that creates button with attributes and mouse click action definition
> - ActionScript: define attributes, mouse click action as procedure

Line number 4 is the MXML declaration for creating the MXML button. The button has attributes such as the positioning (using x= and y=), the label, and specifying the action that should be taken when the button is clicked. The `init()` function creates an ActionScript version of the button. Lines 5 through 22 show how to create the same button in ActionScript with the same attribute. This is wrapped in the tag called `mx:Script` to distinguish between MXML code and the ActionScript code. As can be seen, these two can be mixed in the same application as shown.

The ActionScript code is as follows: first, the button is defined and created in line 9. The mouse click handler (which has to be executed when the ActionScript is clicked) is defined in line 10. Finally lines 12–20 invokes the main `init()` function which creates the button with attributes given. Now, when this simple application is compiled using the Flex IDE, it reports errors, if any. When the application is run in the Flex IDE, it opens up the browser and displays the page as shown in the Figure 5.11. Any difference in the screen can be seen when the application is launched and when one of the buttons is clicked, since the MXML is converted to ActionScript before execution.

FIGURE 5.11

Output of simple "Hello World" example.

Client-Server Example; RSS Feed Reader

As described earlier, Flex is a client-side technology. However, since the clients have to access a server, the Flash platform provides APIs for this purpose. The same is true with other client technologies listed before. It is not necessary for developers to write the code needed to connect to a server. Current RIA tools generate the client side code for any of the back ends supported if the developer provides some simple information such as the backend, the data structure being accessed, and how it has to be presented on the client side. In Flash4, these utilities are called the **data-centric** features of Flash4. Flash4 can automatically generate the client side code as well as the PHP (wrapper) code for the backend, for, say, updating the records, creation, deletion, etc. These facilities significantly reduce the amount of time taken to develop such applications.

Though each client technology may be connected to any backend (e.g., PHP, Java), a particular client technology may work better with some sets of back-ends. For example, though Flex supports many back ends such as Java, PHP, and Perl, its connectivity to PHP has better performance due to an open source library called AMFPHP, which is tuned to Flex/PHP.

The following example shows how to connect to a backend from Flex/Flash. Assume an RSS Feed Reader in Flex which reads the RSS feeds from a web site is to be written (here http://www.manfridayconsulting.it is considered for illustration). When the Flex application is started it reads the feed posted on this web site and displays it in a more user-friendly manner. Users can click on an item to get more information. The following code in Flex does this:

```
1. <?xml version="1.0" encoding="utf-8"?>
2. <mx:Application xmlns:mx="http://www.adobe.com/2006/mxml"
   layout="absolute" width="380" height="492">

3. <mx:Script>
4. <![CDATA[

5. import mx.rpc.http.HTTPService;
6. import mx.rpc.events.ResultEvent;
7. import mx.rpc.events.FaultEvent;

8. private var feed:HTTPService;

9. [Bindable]
10. public var feedresult:Object = null;

11. public function send_data():void {
12. feed = new HTTPService();
13. feed.method = "POST";
14. feed.addEventListener("result", httpResult);
15. feed.addEventListener("fault", httpFault);
16. feed.url = "http://www.manfridayconsulting.it/index.php?option=
    com_content&view=frontpage&Itemid=19&format=feed&type=atom";
17. feed.send(parameters);
```

```
18. }
19. public function httpResult(event:ResultEvent):void {
20. feedresult = event.result;

21. }
22. public function httpFault(event:FaultEvent):void {

23. }
24. ]]>
25. </mx:Script>

26. <mx:HBox y="10">
27. <mx:Button id="startbutton" click="send_data()" label="start"
    width="80"/>
28. <mx:VBox>
29. <!-The blog header->
30. <mx:Label text="{feedresult.feed==null?'':feedresult.feed.
    title}">
31. </mx:Label>
32. <mx:Label text="{feedresult.feed==null?'':feedresult.feed.
    subtitle}">
33. </mx:Label>
34.
35. <mx:DataGrid id="feedlist" dataProvider="{feedresult.
    feed==null?'':feedresult.feed.entry}"
    height="157"    selectedIndex="0">
36. <mx:columns>
37. <mx:DataGridColumn dataField="title" width="200" />
38. </mx:columns>
39. </mx:DataGrid>
40. </mx:VBox>
41. </mx:HBox>
42. <mx:ApplicationControlBar x="0" y="237" width="380" height="217">
43. <mx:TextArea height="180" width="354" borderStyle="solid"
    borderThickness="4" themeColor="#0E83E7" borderColor="#979DA1"
    cornerRadius="13" alpha="0.7" htmlText="{feedresult.feed==null?'':
    feedresult.feed.entry[feedlist.selectedIndex].content}"/>
44. </mx:ApplicationControlBar>
45. </mx:Application>
```

Some of the basic information in lines 1–4 has already been explained. There are three basic methods of getting information from the backend in Flex – **HTTPService, WebService** and **RemoteObject** service. HTTPService is used to get data from the backend using the HTTP protocol. WebService uses the SOAP messaging format over HTTP. It directly connects to the service end-point rather than talking to the PHP or Perl back-end. Finally RemoteObject Service uses native format to access business object data directly. This is possible only if the formatting is well agreed upon on both sides. For example, if Flex connects to Adobe's Cold Fusion backend, since both can talk to each other in native format,

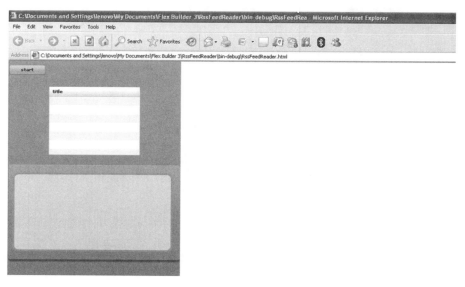

FIGURE 5.12

Output of the Feed Reader before clicking "start".

the Flex client can directly invoke methods on the server side and get the data in the native format. This gives much better performance since there is no need to send the data in XML format and parse the data at the client side.

The current example uses the HTTPService API in the Flex to get the RSS feeds in XML from the web site in lines 5–10. The method `send_data()` creates a new HTTPService object and fills in necessary details such as the URL, the event listeners, HTTP method to be invoked (`POST` or `GET`) and finally sends the request to the web site. These can be seen in lines 10–18. The event handlers (the result and faulty event handlers) are declared in lines 19–23. The actual UI components are declared from line 26. As can be seen in Figure 5.12, there are three UI components in this application – an HBox, a VBox and a text area to display the content of the feed. Once these are declared, the data has to be retrieved from the web site and **bound** to the respective UI component for displaying. These bindings are typically done through **id** fields. For example, we can see that the `feedResult` which is filled by the result event handler is used to fill in the `DataGrid` and then finally the details of these RSS feeds are passed, when clicked on, to the text area through the `feedlist` id of the DataGrid.

Advanced Platform Functionality

Before proceeding with a more complex example involving a web portal like Pustak Portal, this section presents some of the advanced functionality present in Flex4.

Event Handling: Event Handling is an important functionality present in every platform. RIA applications typically call methods asynchronously. For example, consider a Flex application which has two components – one to display the share prices of companies entered in a text box, and the other displaying the stock exchange index (live index). It is desirable that the index update in parallel with the share prices. Event handlers ensure that the entire Web application is not single-threaded, and that UI components of the same application can respond in parallel to user actions/inputs. This essentially gives the power of such applications.

At a high level, event handling works as follows. When an object needs to take an action based upon an event (e.g., in the example earlier, a stock market ticker updating itself in response to a change in the stock index) it registers a listener for the event. The event-handling subsystem invokes the listener when the event is complete, and the listener can take appropriate action. Examples of events include user actions, such as mouse clicks, as well as system events such as receipt of a reply from a remote server, or some change in the application such as creation or destruction of an object. The previous example contained a number of fault handlers (result and fault events).

RemoteObject invocation: As explained previously, RemoteObject service invokes methods on the backend by using a native and not necessarily standard protocol. Data is passed between the server and the application in a binary format called **Action Message Format (AMF)**. The example that follows shows a RemoteObject service and how to invoke a remote method on the ColdFusion backend. The package that is to be called is given by source and the methods and the corresponding event handlers are also shown.

```
<?xml version="1.0" encoding="utf-8"?>
<mx:Application>
...
    <mx:RemoteObject
        id="myRequest"
        destination="ColdFusion"
        source="flexapp.return">
        <mx:method name="returnRecords" result="returnHandler(event)"
            fault="mx.controls.Alert.show(event.fault.faultString)"/>
        <mx:method name="insertRecord" result="insertHandler()"
            fault="mx.controls.Alert.show(event.fault.faultString)"/>
    </mx:RemoteObject>
</mx:Application>
```

Advanced Example: Implementing Pustak Portal

Consider Pustak Portal to illustrate how we could develop a good client side using Flex and highlight the usage of the previously described features and utilities of the platform. It is assumed that there are two types of users for Pustak Portal. The first are the end-users who use platform services like documentation services (like document cleanup, image processing, etc), and the second are the component developers who would like to sell their components to Pustak Portal and get paid whenever their services are being used on the portal. The portal would need an application that displays the user's loaded images/documents. It also needs some way of allowing developers to publish their components for the customers to use for processing of images/documents. We can write one component to display such images and documents, and another component for processing these documents and displaying them (using item renderers).

The customized photo viewer can be written as an ActionScript component called myCollection.photoViewer. The application has created three components for simple illustrative purposes: ThumbNailView, CarouselView and SlideShow-View. These views are created as different components as shown in the following source code. Each of these have their own item renderers to view the photos stored in the gallery.

```
<mx:Application xmlns:mx="http://www.adobe.com/2006/mxml" xmlns="*"
    paddingBottom="0" paddingTop="0"
    paddingLeft="0" paddingRight="0"
    layout="vertical"
    pageTitle="Photo Viewer"
    creationComplete="init()" viewSourceURL="srcview/index.html">

    <mx:Script>
        <![CDATA[
            import mx.collections.ArrayCollection;
            import mx.rpc.events.*;

            import myCollection.photoViewer.Gallery;
            import myCollection.photoViewer.PhotoService;

            [Bindable]
            private var service:PhotoService;

            private function init():void
            {
                service = new PhotoService("data/galleries.xml");
            }
        ]]>
    </mx:Script>

    <mx:Style source="main.css" />

    <mx:Binding source="service.galleries.getItemAt(0) as
    Gallery"    destination="gallery" />

    <mx:ViewStack id="views" width="100%" height="100%">

        <ThumbnailView id="thumbnailView" gallery="{gallery}"
            ../>

        <CarouselView id="carouselView" gallery="{gallery}"
            ../>
```

```
        <SlideShowView id="slideshowView" gallery="{gallery}"
            ../>

    </mx:ViewStack>

</mx:Application>
```

Adding Video Playback to Pustak Portal

It's interesting to see how complex-looking applications such as a YouTube web site can be written in Flex relatively easily. This is due to its many advanced features. We will look at one such example in this section.

Consider how to write a Flex application which would play a given video. The video has to be a FLV video which can be played on Flash Player (since Flash Player is what runs the Flex application). Assume that the video is available in Pustak Portal and it can be accessed through HTML. The following code does this:

```
<?xml version="1.0" encoding="utf-8"?>
<mx:Application xmlns:mx="http://www.adobe.com/2006/mxml"
layout="vertical" horizontalAlign="center">

    <mx:Script>
        <![CDATA[
        import mx.events.VideoEvent;

        private var mute : Boolean = false;

        private function muteHandler(event:MouseEvent):void{
            if (!mute) {
                player.volume = 0;
                mute = true;
                muteButton.label = "Unmute";
            }
            else{
                player.volume = volSlider.value;
                mute = false;
                muteButton.label = "Mute";
            }
        }

        private function videoDisplay_playheadUpdate(event:VideoEvent):
        void{
            progressBar.setProgress(event.playheadTime, player.totalTime);
        }

        ]]>
    </mx:Script>

    <mx:Label text="Basic Video Player Example in Flex3"
    fontFamily="Georgia"
```

```
        fontSize="30" fontWeight="bold" color="#6D0A26"/>

    <mx:TextInput id="URLinput" x="10" y="10" width="500"/>

    <mx:VideoDisplay id="player" source="{URLinput.text}"
        maintainAspectRatio="true"
        width="450" height="350" autoPlay="false"
        playheadUpdate="videoDisplay_playheadUpdate(event);"/>
    <mx:ProgressBar id="progressBar" mode="manual" label=" "
    width="{player.width}"/>
    <mx:HBox width="450">
        <mx:Button label="Play" click="player.play()"/>
        <mx:Button label="Pause" click="player.pause()"/>
        <mx:Button label="Stop" click="player.stop()"/>
        <mx:Button id="muteButton" label="Mute" click="muteHandler
        (event)" width="70"/>
        <mx:HSlider id="volSlider"
            liveDragging="true"
            minimum="0.0"
                maximum="1.0"
                value="1.0"
                snapInterval="0.01"
                change="player.volume=volSlider.value"
                width="100"/>
        <mx:Label text="{int(player.playheadTime)} / {int(player.
        totalTime)}"
            color="#FFFFFF" width="73"/>
    </mx:HBox>

</mx:Application>
```

The main application starts with mx:TextInput which gets the URL that has the FLV file to be played in the video player. mx:VideoDisplay is a useful UI control in Flex SDK which can be used for playing a given FLV video. As can be easily seen, it takes source as a parameter, which should be set to the video location or the FLV file. playerUpdate is a method which would be called whenever there are some changes in the video at a regular interval specified. In our case, the times on the progress bar are updated whenever this method gets called. Next a progress bar is created that shows the length of the video played, and an HBox control which has player controls like Play, Stop, Mute and Pause for the video. A volume control slider is also available which sets the volume for the player. All these controls pass essential controls to the main controlling method VideoDisplay. The video player shown previously can be seen in Figure 5.13. This example can be extended to get other features such as playlists of the user or favorite videos. Various types of statistics about the videos played on the server can also be maintained (e.g., frequently played videos, last time the video was played).

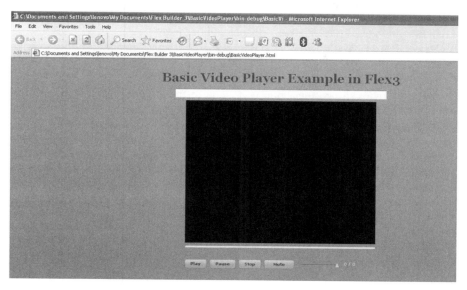

FIGURE 5.13

Output of the basic video player in Flex.

SUMMARY

In this chapter, multiple deep technical concepts that will aid in writing efficient cloud applications were discussed. The chapter started with techniques for developing efficient highly scalable applications with a particular focus on scaling storage and developing MapReduce applications. The basic principle of scale storage is to partition and three partitioning techniques were described. The first technique, functional decomposition, puts different databases on different servers. The second technique – vertical partitioning – puts different columns of a table on different servers. The third technique – sharding – is similar to horizontal partitioning in databases in that different rows are put in different database servers. However, the partitioning is not transparent to the application. Partitioning has disadvantages in that some features that are commonly possible in relational databases such as the ability to perform joins and guaranteed data integrity are made more complex. Though the partitioning techniques have been described in the context of relational databases, they are applicable to non-relational databases as well.

Next, NoSQL storage systems which have emerged as an alternative to relational databases have been described. The common characteristics of NoSQL systems are that, unlike relational databases, they have a flexible schema, and simpler interfaces for querying. Additionally, they commonly have built-in support for automatic scaling (typically via sharding and replication). However, as discussed in Chapter 6, many of them relax the strict consistency that relational databases provide, so that the performance is not hit.

Two types of NoSQL systems have been discussed. The first kind, key-value stores, typically store a value which can be retrieved using a key. The value can be a complex object; however, the key-value store treats the value as an opaque sequence of bytes. Since the value is opaque to the storage, records with different keys can have different formats. The second type, object/XML databases, store objects which can be retrieved based on a key, which can be part of the object. Additionally, indexes can be built on any attribute of the object. Object databases, therefore, typically allow more sophisticated queries compared to key-value stores. The detailed architecture of NoSQL systems is described in Chapter 6.

Next the emerging paradigm of developing cloud applications using the MapReduce technique was detailed. Basic concepts of data parallelism and functional programming were covered. Detailed dataflow within the MapReduce architecture was seen with an understanding of the parallization capability that MapReduce provides. It was realized that there is a need to develop new types of algorithms to leverage the data parallel computation platform enabled by MapReduce platforms. We looked at many advanced algorithms to solve typical subproblems (such as sorting, word count, TF-IDF) on MapReduce platforms. A formal specification of the MapReduce computation was also briefly described.

Rich Internet Technology relies on running the application either within the sandbox of the browser or as a desktop application. The development starts with writing the source in some extension of XML syntax like MXML (for Flex), XAML (Silverlight), LZL (for OpenLazslo) and so on. The application can have native ActionScript or JavaScript components in the same source file too. Tools like Flex/Visual Studio help the developer to use the design view when he designs the UI component layout and then switch to the source view for completing the interactions of the component and event handling. The source also can have embedded style sheets (CSS) for a standardized look and feel of the application. Once this is done, the whole application is compiled using the compiler given in the SDK and is ready to be rendered on the platform.

The current state of the technology is that there are only a few rendering engines which are popular. Currently, Flash (Adobe), which has captured the majority of the RIA applications, is the most popular to use due to the ease of building applications and the plethora of supported features. The other engines which are becoming popular are Silverlight (Microsoft) which is a .NET platform. OpenLaszlo is an open source effort to run this engine on either JSP server or on Flash. They claim the look and feel is identical on both these servers.

Adobe's Flash is much like a virtual machine that renders the graphics, multimedia and code pretty efficiently. Flash Player has a long history and the latest is FP version 10. Flash Player actually has both ActionScript Virtual machine (AVM) and a multimedia rendering engine. The current AVM interprets the AS3.0. It does sophisticated optimizations before running this on the runtime.

Similarly, Adobe has managed to keep the multimedia quality by bringing in the latest multimedia standards into Flash such as H.264 standards.

Silverlight is poised as a competitor to Flash from Adobe in this space. Though it may take some time for Silverlight to catch up with Flash as a market leader, Silverlight is impressive with its early versions. Silverlight uses XAML as its markup language. XAML can be embedded easily within the HTML and the JavaScript methods. One big advantage of Silverlight right now is that Silverlight objects are Search Engine Optimization (SEO) friendly, in the sense that these objects can be searched as with text pages, while Flash objects (which are compiled objects) cannot.

SUN's JavaFX is a new entrant into this space and can change the landscape with its huge Java adoption. Though Java is considered to be very heavy for client side virtual machines, still due to its vast adoption base, JavaFX can make a difference to the developer community.

Finally, it would be inappropriate to complete this technology overview without giving some insights into what is happening with HTML5 itself. With HTML5 video and audio rendering mechanisms, developers think that this may come close to replacing the runtimes like Flash and Silverlight. The biggest advantage is that it will not be necessary to download plug-ins to run the web application. Developers are looking forward to WebGL standards, which may define standards for Web application development in future. Only time can tell who will be the ultimate winner in this space.

References

[1] Vajgel P. Needle in a haystack: efficient storage of billions of photos. http://www.facebook.com/note.php?note_id=76191543919; [accessed 01.05.09].

[2] Persyn J. Database sharding, Brussels, Belgium: FOSDEM'09; 2009.

[3] By The Numbers: Twitter Vs. Facebook Vs. Google Buzz. http://searchengineland.com/by-the-numbers-twitter-vs-facebook-vs-google-buzz-36709; [accessed 08.10.11].

[4] Why does Wikipedia use MySQL as data store rather than a NoSQL database? Domas Mituzas. http://www.quora.com/Why-does-Wikipedia-use-MySQL-as-data-store-rather-than-a-NoSQL-database; [accessed 08.10.11].

[5] Gulliver I. A new generation of Google MySQL tools. http://flamingcow.dilian.org/2011/04/new-generation-of-google-mysql-tools.html; [accessed 08.10.11].

[6] Elliott-McCrea K. Using, Abusing and Scaling MySQL at Flickr. http://code.flickr.com/blog/2010/02/08/using-abusing-and-scaling-mysql-at-flickr/; [accessed 08.10.11].

[7] Very large databases. http://www.vldb.org/; [accessed 08.10.11].

[8] Ozsu M, Valduriez P. Principles of distributed database systems. Englewood Cliffs, NJ: Prentice-Hall; 1990.

[9] MySQL Reference Architectures for Massively Scalable Web Infrastructure, Oracle Corp., http://www.mysql.com/why-mysql/white-papers/mysql_wp_high-availability_webrefarchs.php; [accessed 08.10.11].

[10] Roy R. Shard - A Database Design. http://technology.blogspot.com/2008/07/shard-database-design.html; [accessed 28.07.08].

[11] Hu W. Better sharding with Oracle. Oracle Openworld 2008. http://www.oracle.com/technetwork/database/features/availability/300461-132370.pdf; 2008. [accessed 08.10.11].

[12] DeWitt, D, Gray, J. Parallel database systems: the future of high performance database systems. Commun ACM 1992;35(6):85–98.

[13] Obasanjo D. Building scalable databases: Pros and cons of various database sharding schemes. http://www.25hoursaday.com/weblog/2009/01/16/BuildingScalableDatabasesProsAndConsOfVariousDatabaseShardingSchemes.aspx; [accessed 08.10.11].

[14] Database sharding. http://www.codefutures.com/database-sharding; [accessed 08.10.11].

[15] Henderson C. Building Scalable Web Sites: Building, Scaling, and Optimizing the Next Generation of Web Applications. O'Reilly Media; 1st ed. (May 23, 2006), ISBN-13: 978-0596102357

[16] Scalebase Architecture. http://www.scalebase.com/resources/architecture/; [accessed 08.10.11].

[17] Spock Proxy – a proxy for MySQL horizontal partitioning. http://spockproxy.sourceforge.net/; [accessed 08.10.11].

[18] Hibernate Shards. http://www.hibernate.org/subprojects/shards.html; [accessed 08.10.11].

[19] DeCandia G, et al. Dynamo: Amazon's highly available key-value store. Stevenson, Washington, USA: SOSP'07; 2007.

[20] Facebook's New Real-Time Messaging System: HBase To Store 135+ Billion Messages A Month. http://highscalability.com/blog/2010/11/16/facebooks-new-real-time-messaging-system-hbase-to-store-135.html; [accessed 08.10.11].

[21] The Underlying Technology of Messages. http://www.facebook.com/note.php?note_id=454991608919#; [accessed 08.10.11].

[22] Borthakur D. Realtime hadoop usage at facebook – part 1. http://hadoopblog.blogspot.com/2011/05/realtime-hadoop-usage-at-facebook-part.html; [accessed 08.10.11].

[23] Borthakur D. Realtime hadoop usage at facebook – part 2 - workload types. http://hadoopblog.blogspot.com/2011/05/realtime-hadoop-usage-at-facebook-part_28.html; [accessed 08.10.11].

[24] Bigtable: A Distributed Storage System for Structured Data. OSDI 2006. http://labs.google.com/papers/bigtable-osdi06.pdf; [accessed 08.10.11].

[25] HBase 0.91.0-SNAPSHOT API. http://hbase.apache.org/docs/current/api/overview-summary.html; [accessed 08.10.11].

[26] George L. HBase Architecture 101 – Storage. http://www.larsgeorge.com/2009/10/hbase-architecture-101-storage.html; [accessed 08.10.11].

[27] Package org.apache.hadoop.hbase.mapreduce. http://hbase.apache.org/docs/current/api/org/apache/hadoop/hbase/mapreduce/package-summary.html#package_description; [accessed 08.10.11].

[28] Weaver E. Up and Running with Cassandra. http://blog.evanweaver.com/2009/07/06/up-and-running-with-cassandra/; [accessed 08.10.11].

[29] Zawodny J. Lessons Learned from Migrating 2+ Billion Documents at Craigslist. http://www.10gen.com/video/mongosf2011/craigslist; [accessed 08.10.11].

[30] Zawodny J. MongoDB live at Craigslist. http://blog.mongodb.org/post/5545198613/mongodb-live-at-craigslist; [accessed 08.10.11].

[31] Introducing JSON. http://www.json.org/; [accessed 08.10.11].

[32] JSON Example. http://json.org/example.html; [accessed 08.10.11].

[33] Object Ids. http://www.mongodb.org/display/DOCS/Object+IDs; [accessed 08.10.11].

[34] Mongo DB Java Tutorial. http://www.mongodb.org/display/DOCS/Java+Tutorial; [accessed 08.10.11].

[35] Introduction to Parallel Programming and MapReduce. http://code.google.com/edu/parallel/mapreduce-tutorial.html#MapReduce; [accessed 08.10.11].

[36] Dean J, Ghemawat S. MapReduce: A flexible data processing tool. CACM; 2010.

[37] Running Hadoop on Amazon EC2. http://wiki.apache.org/hadoop/AmazonEC2; [accessed 08.10.11].

[38] Karloff H, Suri S, Vassilvitskii S. A Model of Computation for MapReduce. Symposium on Discrete Algorithms (SODA); 2010.

[39] Google Cluster Computing, Faculty Training Workshop, Module IV: MapReduce Theory, Implementation, and Algorithms, Spinnaker Labs, Inc.

[40] Dean JJ, Ghemawat S. MapReduce: Simplified data processing on large clusters. In: OSDI'04, 6th Symposium on Operating Systems Design and Implementation, Sponsored by USENIX, in cooperation with ACM SIGOPS; 2004. p. 137–50.

[41] Lämmel R. Google's MapReduce programming model—revisited_. Redmond, WA, USA: Data Programmability Team Microsoft Corp.

[42] Ho R. Pragmatic programming techniques. Blog. http://horicky.blogspot.com/2010/08/designing-algorithmis-for-map-reduce.html; [accessed 08.10.11].

[43] Graph processing in MapReduce. http://horicky.blogspot.com/2010/07/graph-processing-in-map-reduce.html and http://horicky.blogspot.com/2010/07/google-pregel-graph-processing.html; [accessed 08.10.11].

[44] Programming Flex 3: The comprehensive guide to creating rich internet applications with Adobe Flex. O'Reilly Publications; 2008.

[45] Microsoft Silverlight 4: Step by Step. O'Reilly Publications; 2010.

Addressing the Cloud Challenges

INTRODUCTION

There are multiple key technical challenges that any cloud platform or application needs to address in order to truly provide a utility-like computing infrastructure. Some techniques used by current platforms to address the issue of scalability at the IaaS, PaaS and SaaS levels were discussed in Chapters 2, 3 and 4, respectively. Chapter 8 discusses the various features supported by current platforms to provide fine-grained monitoring of a cloud platform and infrastructure. This chapter describes in more detail, additional approaches that can be used to address the cloud challenges, and also provides some technical fundamentals needed to comprehend the limitations of the different approaches used. Three critical technical challenges posed by cloud computing are addressed here, namely:

1. Scalability: Ability to scale to millions of clients simultaneously accessing the cloud service,
2. Multi-Tenancy: Ability to provide the isolation as well as good performance to multiple tenants using the cloud infrastructure, and
3. Availability: An architecture that ensures that the infrastructure as well as applications are highly available regardless of hardware and software faults.

The scalability challenges needs to be addressed both at the computational as well as the storage access level. The first section details some architectures for linearly scaling the compute capacity by just adding more servers. Key theoretical concepts that help a developer to appreciate the performance bottlenecks that may arise in an application due to concurrent data access and solutions that one can employ to address them are discussed in the second section. The third section

255

deals with solutions and approaches to address the issue of enabling multi-tenancy and the fourth section describes architectures to ensure highly available cloud-hosted applications.

SCALING COMPUTATION

As discussed in earlier chapters, on-demand scaling of computation is one of the critical needs of any cloud computing platform. Compute scaling can be either done at the infrastructure level or platform level. At the infrastructure level, it is about increasing the capacity of the compute power, while at the platform level, the techniques are mainly to intelligently manage the different client requests in a manner that best utilizes the compute infrastructure without requiring the clients to do anything special during peaks in demand.

Scale Out versus Scale Up

There are fundamentally two main ways of scaling compute resources – known as scale up and scale out. **Scale up** or **vertical scaling** is about adding more resources to a single node or a single system to improve performance – such as addition of CPUs, use of multi-core systems instead of single-core or adding additional memory. The focus here is to make the underlying compute system more powerful. The more powerful compute resource can now be effectively used by a virtualization layer to support more processes or more virtual machines – enabling scaling to many more clients. In order to support on-demand scaling of the cloud infrastructure, the system should be able to increase its compute power dynamically without impacting the platform or application executing over it. Unless a system is virtualized, it is generally not possible to increase the capacity of a compute system dynamically without bringing down the system. Detailed information about virtualization technology and approaches used for virtualization is given in Chapter 9. Systems that are scaled up are shared memory systems such as symmetric multiprocessor systems. Examples of scale up machines are IBM POWER5 machine and HP Itanium Superdome servers. The advantage of scale up systems is that the programming paradigm is simpler, since it does not involve distributed programming, unlike scale-out systems.

   Scale out or horizontal scaling, on the other hand, is about expanding the compute resources by adding a new computer system or node to a distributed application. This distributed application is designed in such a way as to effectively use new compute resources added to the system. A web server (like Apache) is a typical example for such a system. In fact, given that most cloud applications are service-enabled, they need to be developed to expand on-demand using scaling-out techniques. The advantage of scale out systems is that commodity hardware, such as disk and memory, can be used for delivering high performance. A scale out system such as interconnected compute nodes forming a cluster can be more powerful than a traditional supercomputer, especially with faster interconnect technologies like

Myrinet and InfiniBand. Scale out systems will essentially be distributed systems with a shared high-performance disk storage used for common data. Unlike scale up systems, in order to leverage full power of scale out systems, there should be an effort from the programmer to design applications differently. Many design patterns exist for applications designed for scale out machines – examples include MapReduce, Master/Worker and TupleSpace, to name a few.

A study from Michael Maged, et al. [1] from IBM does a detailed comparison of scale out and scale up systems for search applications. They conclude that scale-out solutions have much better performance and price/performance over scale up systems. This is because a search application essentially consists of independent parallel searches, which can easily be deployed on multiple processors. Scale out techniques can be employed at application-level as well. For example, a typical web search service is scalable where two client query requests can be processed completely as parallel threads. The challenge in scale out systems, however, is the complex management of the infrastructure, especially when the infrastructure caters to dynamic scaling of resources. Additionally, as noted, applications that do not consist of independent computations are difficult to scale out.

Amdahl's Law

As noted in the earlier paragraph, it is not always possible to get better performance by just putting in more compute resources. Adding one more compute node does not necessarily double the performance of the application. The amount of speed up is limited by the extent to which the algorithm consists of parallel computations, or the inherent parallelism in the application. A well-known theory that explains this concept is Amdahl's Law. This law says that the maximum speedup that an application can achieve is limited by the portions of the application that need to execute sequentially. If α is the fraction of an application that needs sequential calculation, and $1 - \alpha$ can be parallelized, then the maximum speedup achieved by using P processors is given by:

$$\frac{1}{\alpha + \dfrac{1 - \alpha}{P}}$$

Even if 80% of the program can be run in parallel, but 20% needs to be executed sequentially (for example, to collect results of the parallel computation and display results), then the maximum speedup that one can achieve on 10 processors is only $1/0.28 = 3.6$ (check with $\alpha = 0.2$).

Given the limitation of performance shown by Amdahl's Law, cloud applications need to be carefully designed in order not to be hit by the previously mentioned constraint. One method of achieving parallelism is to use different processes or compute nodes for requests from different clients. So, essentially each request is processed in parallel and to completion. The parallelism is therefore coming in due to parallel requests. If client requests are independent of each other, α can be close to 0 and speedup = P, the full power of the compute resources can be used! If peak load is achieved, then the solution is to increase the physical resources (P) by just adding more compute resources. As noted previously, this model works well for applications such as search, where there is little interaction between client requests. Of course, it is not usually possible to make α equal to 0, as the requests will be served using shared data structures (say for web index). There again, techniques to enable multiple simultaneous reads (described in Chapter 5 under data partition) can be used. Cloud applications are therefore designed to use service-oriented architectures so that multiple client requests can be processed independently (as far as the service logic enables).

An additional approach could be to look for parallelism within a client request. Consider a Facebook-like application, where if a user updates his status, that could require updating the walls of all his friends. Part of the application (updating the user status and getting the friend list) is sequential, but the rest can be done in parallel. The scalability of a cloud application now is purely limited by the efficiency of request scheduling on the available compute hardware and efficient access to external resources (like storage, database) that the service may need to complete the request.

Scaling Cloud Applications with a Reverse Proxy

When we have a scale out architecture with a cloud application executing each client request on different compute nodes, one problem that needs to be addressed is that of service orchestration. Simplistically stated, the different nodes that the cloud application executes on should be transparent to the client and a single service end point needs to be published. This section describes a common way of accomplishing this using a reverse proxy.

A **reverse proxy** is basically an HTTP proxy server that retrieves content from one or more servers and behaves like an originating server for the client. This is unlike a **forward proxy** that enables multiple browsers to access external web servers. For example, hp.com can be accessed using multiple forward proxy servers that HP employees use in their browsers to access the Internet. However, hp.com will have a single reverse proxy server which receives requests from the Internet, and distributes them transparently to multiple web servers that will be serving the portal content. Since reverse proxies are frontends, they can be used for providing security through application firewall and data encryption, for optimizing the client-server communication, as well as balancing server load by efficient scheduling of the client requests on the servers.

A simple schematic of using a reverse proxy is shown in Figure 6.1. The browser accesses a web site, say http://xyz.com. The reverse proxy is hosted on the machine with the DNS name as xyz and is actually the front-facing server for the browsers. It, however, distributes the client request to different web application servers at the back-end (normally referred to as upstream servers) to get the request fulfilled. To scale to a larger number of clients, only a few more upstream servers need to be added behind the reverse proxy.

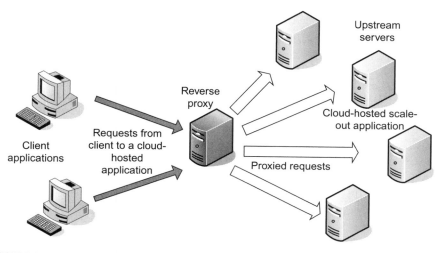

FIGURE 6.1

Schematic diagram showing the configuration with a reverse proxy.

The reverse proxy has to be really lightweight and should not become an overhead or bottleneck to server requests.

Nginx is one such reverse proxy which claims to be hosting more than 20 million web sites, at the time of writing of this book [2]. Nginx uses a simple round robin scheduler to forward client requests. There is also an option to use a hash-based scheduling to choose an upstream server based on hashing a configurable variable – that can be the request URL, incoming HTTP request headers or some combination of those.

A sample configuration for the Nginx server is shown in the code segment *NGINX Configuration.* The section called upstream lists the different virtual web servers that are configured at the backend. All one needs to do to scale the system is to add more servers and add those IP addresses in the upstream section. For detailed practical instructions to set up and use Nginx, the readers are referred to detailed cookbooks available on using Nginx for a practical configuration [3].

```
NGINX CONFIGURATION
user cloud-user;
worker_processes 1;
error_log /var/log/nginx/error.log;
pid        /var/run/nginx.pid;
events {
    worker_connections 1024;
}
http {
    include        /etc/nginx/mime.types;
```

```
default_type application/octet-stream;
access_log /var/log/nginx/access.log;
sendfile        on;
keepalive_timeout 65;
tcp_nodelay       on;
gzip on;
server {
    listen        80;
    server_name localhost;
    access_log /var/log/nginx/localhost.access.log;
    location / {
        proxy_pass http://one_loadbalancer;
    }
}
upstream sample_loadbalancer {
        server 10.1.1.3:80 ;
        server 10.1.1.4:80 ;
        server 10.1.1.5:80 ;
        server 10.1.1.6:80 ;
}
}
```

If the Nginx server is configured as a gateway with two network cards, it can also be used to scale out the servers to two different networks as well [4]. In fact, a very useful configuration is when one of those networks is inside an enterprise (private network) and the other is a public cloud – leading to a configuration that is one way of implementing a hybrid cloud. A detailed example of this is presented in the *OpenNebula* section.

Hybrid Cloud and Cloud Bursting: OpenNebula

Hybrid cloud is a combination of private and public clouds enabling expansion of local infrastructure to commercial infrastructure on a need basis. Using a hybrid cloud, an organization can leverage existing infrastructure available in-house and seamlessly include or supplement additional resources from public clouds based on demand. A hybrid cloud is most cost effective for the cloud user as it ensures good utilization of existing infrastructure. It enables **Cloud Bursting** of the private cloud by allowing the addition of extra capacity to a private infrastructure by borrowing from a public cloud (Figure 6.2).

This configuration can be extended to **Cloud Federation** to share infrastructure with collaborators and **Cloud Aggregation** to provide a much larger cloud infrastructure using multiple clouds. HP CloudSystem Enterprise is a commercial offering from Hewlett-Packard for hybrid clouds. Amazon's Virtual Private Cloud (VPC) also provides a hybrid cloud using a VPN connection between Amazon EC2 and a private cloud. OpenNebula is a popular open source cloud platform that is designed to support hybrid cloud and its internal details are described next.

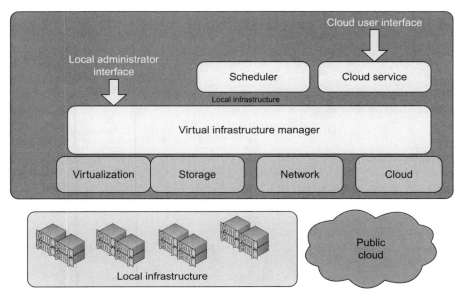

FIGURE 6.2

A hybrid cloud.

OpenNebula

OpenNebula is a distributed virtual machine manager that provides a virtualized infrastructure across multiple cloud platforms [5]. This open source project started in 2005 with the first release being made in March 2008, and has been seeing thousands of downloads per month ever since. The key design of OpenNebula is its modular system that integrates well with multiple heterogeneous cloud infrastructures and data centers, as shown in Figure 6.3. Figure 6.3 also shows the four basic layers that exist in the OpenNebula architecture. At the highest level are the EC2 and OCCI [6] layers. These are high-level APIs that allow OpenNebula to support applications that use Amazon EC2 and Open Cloud Computing Interface (OCCI) APIs, as well as interoperate with other clouds that support EC2 and OCCI. Below that is the core OpenNebula API, which provides the main OpenNebula functionality of virtualization. Below that are the resource management APIs and drivers, which abstract out the details of the resource management and allow OpenNebula to support heterogeneous virtualization, storage and networks. For example, the Virtualization Manager (VM) API has pluggable virtualization drivers to support different types of virtualization; the VMWare virtualization driver supports VMWare virtualization, and the Xen virtualization driver supports Xen virtualization. However, the VM APIs present a common abstraction to the core OpenNebula API, allowing it to support both types of virtualization. Similarly, the transfer manager (TM) API abstracts out the storage subsystem, which can support NFS,

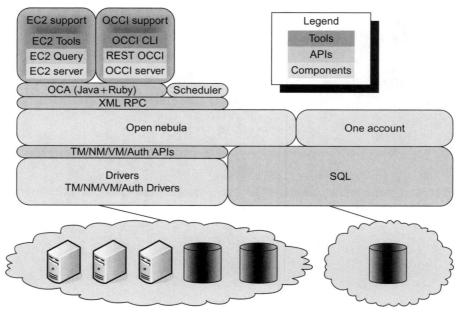

FIGURE 6.3

Different interfaces provided by OpenNebula.

MooseFS[1] and other storage protocols. The Auth API provides support for security and authentication, and the Network Manager API (NM API) allows for network management.

In terms of features, OpenNebula implements the EC2 Query API as well as the OCCI-OGF interface, enabling both custom and standard compliant cloud infrastructures to be integrated. For the on-premise infrastructure, it provides easy integration with any cluster schedulers (Local Resource Managers) such as SGE, LSF, and OpenPBS and Condor [7], enabling better use of local resources. The system has interfaces to allocate virtual machines and network elements, migrates virtual machines across processors, and has several user management and image management functionalities. It allows a physical cluster to dynamically execute multiple virtual clusters, enabling better on-demand resource provisioning, cluster consolidation and cluster partitioning. The allocation of physical resources to virtual nodes could also be dynamic dependent on its compute demands as migration functionality provided by existing VMMs can be used to move virtual machines to other processes, supporting heterogeneous workloads. Like any other IaaS infrastructure, a portal interface called **OpenNebula SunStone** is also available.

---

[1]MooseFS is a highly scalable centralized metadata distributed file system, described in detail at www.moosefs.org. Centralized metadata DFSes are described in Chapter 9.

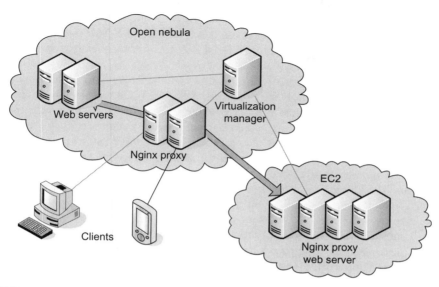

FIGURE 6.4

OpenNebula with reverse proxy for cloud bursting.

OpenNebula can be used in conjunction with a reverse proxy to form a cloud bursting hybrid cloud architecture with load balancing and virtualization support provided by OpenNebula (Figure 6.4) [8]. The OpenNebula VM controls server allocation in both the EC2 cloud as well as the OpenNebula cloud, while the Nginx proxy to which the clients are connected distributes load over the web servers both in EC2 as well as the OpenNebula cloud. In addition to web servers, the EC2 cloud also has its own Nginx load balancer.

Much research work has been developed around OpenNebula. For example, the University of Chicago has come up with an advance reservation system called Haizea Lease Manager. IBM Haifa has developed a policy-driven probabilistic admission control and dynamic placement optimization for site level management policies called the RESERVOIR Policy Engine [9], Nephele is an SLA-driven automatic service management tool developed by Telefonica and Virtual Cluster Tool for atomic cluster management with versioning with multiple transport protocols from CRS4 Distributed Computing Group.

Design of a Scalable Cloud Platform: Eucalyptus

In addition to OpenNebula, Eucalyptus is also an important open source cloud platform. The internal details and design of Eucalyptus are as follows. The description focuses on the use of virtualization technology to implement a complete cloud platform. **EUCALYPTUS** (for **Elastic Utility Computing Architecture Linking Your Programs To Useful Systems**) enables implementation of cloud systems over existing infrastructure for both private and hybrid clouds. A platform built using Eucalyptus supports Amazon AWS REST and SOAP interfaces, thus enabling clients that are intended for Amazon EC2 to work seamlessly over existing on-premise hardware.

Every machine that needs to become a part of the Eucalyptus cloud runs the **Node Controller** that controls the execution, monitoring and termination of virtual machines on the node (Figure 6.5). A **Cluster Controller (CC)** forms the front end for each cluster and manages and schedules the execution of the virtual machine on each node. There is also a **Storage Controller (SC)** called **Walrus** that provides block storage services with the same interface as Amazon EBS and S3 and can be used to store and retrieve virtual machine images and also application data. The key interface for users and administrators is the **Cloud Controller (CLC)**, which queries the different nodes and makes broad decisions about the virtualization setup, and executes those decisions through cluster controllers and node controllers. These modules are summarized later in this chapter. For more detail, please see the white papers from Eucalyptus, Inc. [10, 11].

A **Node Controller (NC)** executes on every node that is part of the cloud infrastructure and designated to host a virtual machine instance. The NC answers the queries from the Cluster Controller using the system APIs of the

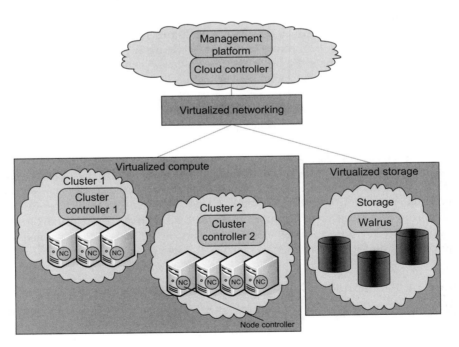

FIGURE 6.5

A schematic of key Eucalyptus modules.

operating system of the node and the hypervisor to get system information, such as number of cores, memory size, available disk space, state of the VM instance, etc. The APIs supported by an NC are `runInstance`, `terminateInstance`, `describeResource`, `describeInstance`, etc. Only authorized entities are allowed to make these API calls (using the standard mechanism of web services). To start a new VM instance, the NC makes a local copy of the image files, namely the kernel, the root file system and the ramdisk image from a remote image repository. It then creates a new end point in the virtual network overlay (described in the next paragraph) and requests the local hypervisor to boot from that instance. To stop an instance, the NC requests the hypervisor to stop the instance, tears down the virtual network end point and cleans up all the files in the root file system. So, the application has to use an external persistent storage to save the result of the execution.

The **Cluster Controller** runs on a system that is potentially on two networks – one network that connects it to the NCs forming the cluster and the other network to connect to the Cloud Controller. The functional APIs of CC are similar to NC, but they work on a set of nodes rather than specific nodes. The CC schedules incoming instance execution requests onto specific nodes, controls the instance virtual network overlay, and collects report information about a set of NCs. When a CC receives a set of instances to execute, it first checks the resource availability with each NC and schedules the instance on the first node that satisfies the resource criteria (such as CPU cores, memory, disk, etc) for executing the instance.

The CC is primarily responsible for the setup and tear down of the virtual network overlay that connects the different virtual machines. Since the application on each VM is potentially able to acquire MAC addresses, system IP addresses, and perform several supervisor privileged operations, it is mandatory to have another layer of virtualization to ensure security of other applications. While complete network level access will be provided for applications running on individual nodes, the CC should be able to fully manage and control the VM networks, providing VM traffic isolation, the definition of firewall rules between logical sets of VMs, and the dynamic assignment of public IP addresses to VMs at boot and run-time. The users will be allowed to boot-time attach their VMs to a logical network, which is assigned a unique VLAN (virtual LAN) tag and unique IP subnet (private IP range). This way, each set of nodes within a specific names network will be able to communicate among themselves, but are isolated from other sets of VMs. The CC can then be used as a router between VM subnets, and blocks traffic between VM networks (by default). The users will still have control of the firewall rules for their specific VM network. In order to make the network accessible from public IP addresses, users can request public IP addresses be assigned to certain VMs among their VM set. This access is managed using **Network Address Translation** (**NAT**) with dynamic destination NAT and source NAT address for public IP to private IP mapping, which can be defined either at boot-time or runtime. When VMs are distributed across clusters, the cluster front-ends are linked with a tunnel and all the VLAN tagged packets are tunneled from one cluster to another, either over TCP or UDP.

The data storage service of Eucalyptus is called **Walrus**. Walrus provides an interface compatible with Amazon S3 (described in Chapter 2) and is built using standard web services technologies (Axis2, Mule) and provides both REST and SOAP interfaces of S3. This module provides persistent data support for the instances that execute on the nodes – both for the VM image as well as storing/streaming of application data.

The role of Walrus is very critical to ensure scalability of the cloud application, since concurrent data access from multiple instances can potentially get blocked and delay one client request due to another. Walrus therefore does not provide locking for object writes. However, users are guaranteed consistency of write and read. If a write to an object is encountered while the previous write to the same object is in progress, the previous write is invalidated. Walrus authenticates and verifies a user by checking against the access control lists for the object that was requested and responds with a MD5 checksum of the object. Writes and reads are streamed over HTTP. Researchers can customize the authentication and streaming protocols of Walrus, as well.

The Cloud Controller is a set of web services that provides (a) system-wide arbitration of resource allocation, (b) governing of persistent user and system data, and (c) handling authentication and protocol translation for user-visible interfaces. A **System Resource State (SRS)** is maintained with data coming in from CC and NCs of the system. When a user's request arrives, the SRS is used to make an admission control decision for the request based on service-level expectation. To create a VM, the resources are first reserved in the SRS and the request is sent downstream to CC and NC. Once the request is satisfied, the resource is committed in the SRS, else rolled back on failure. A production rule system uses this information in the SRS and ensures that the SLAs are satisfied through an event-based design. Events such as timer events, network topology changes and memory allocations are used to modify the resource request and change system state as needed. The Data Services provided by CLC handle creation, modification, query and storage of stateful system and user data. Lastly, a set of web services provides entry points for user requests using a variety of interfaces (Amazon S3 and EC2), management and monitoring services for web console.

Eucalyptus is a very interesting work in cloud platforms as it enables researchers and technologists to get started not only in setting up new cloud platforms over existing infrastructures, but also to start researching and experimenting with new algorithms for scheduling resources, differing service level agreements and policies for allocation. It can be deployed just on a single laptop or on huge clusters of servers.

ZooKeeper: A Scalable Distributed Coordination System

Scale-out architectures work well if the client requests can be completed as independent processes and hence can be scheduled on different servers (or virtual machines). However, some applications may require multiple dependent processes to work together to solve a client request, using a messaging bus or database for co-ordination. Co-ordination of such distributed processes can be a very challenging task, as the different processes do not see the same shared data. This section describes a popular Open Source Apache project called **ZooKeeper**, which is a highly available and reliable coordination system [12, 13, 14].

ZooKeeper is a centralized coordination service that can be used by distributed applications to maintain configuration information, perform distributed synchronization, and enable group services. The ZooKeeper service implements efficient protocols for consensus and group management to give a simple abstraction for applications to perform leader election and group membership in a scalable manner. It can be used to just maintain a single configuration across the whole system – which turns out to be a very nontrivial functionality to achieve with linear scalability. ZooKeeper can also be used for event notification, locking and to implement a queuing system. An overview of ZooKeeper with an example usage of ZooKeeper API is next described.

Overview of ZooKeeper

ZooKeeper uses a shared hierarchical name space of data registers (called **znodes**) to coordinate distributed processes. Znodes give an abstraction of a shared file system but are more like a distributed, consistent shared memory that is hierarchically organized like a file system. ZooKeeper provides high throughput, low latency, highly available, strictly ordered access to the znodes. For reliability, three copies of the Zookeeper can be run so that it does not become a single point of failure. As it provides strict ordering, complex synchronization primitives can be implemented at the client.

ZooKeeper provides a name space very similar to a standard file system. Every znode is identified by a name, which is a sequence of path elements separated by a slash ("/"), and every znode has a parent except the root ("/"). A znode cannot be deleted if it has any children (like a folder cannot be deleted if it has files within it). Every znode can have data associated with it and is limited to the amount of data that it can have to kilobytes. This is because the ZooKeeper is designed to store just coordination data, such as status information, configuration, location information, and so on.

The ZooKeeper service maintains an in-memory image of the data tree that is replicated on all the servers on which the ZooKeeper service executes. Only transaction logs and snapshots are stored in a persistent store, enabling high throughput. As changes are made to the znodes (during application execution), they are appended to the transaction logs. When the transaction log grows big, a snapshot of the current state of all znodes is taken and is written to the persistent store (filesystem). Further, each client connects only to a single ZooKeeper server and maintains a TCP connection, through which it sends requests, gets responses, gets watch events, and sends heart beats. If the TCP connection to the server breaks, the client will connect to an alternate server. The client only needs to set up a session with the first ZooKeeper server; if it needs to connect to another server, this session will get reestablished automatically.

All updates made by ZooKeeper are totally ordered. It stamps each update with a sequence called **zxid (ZooKeeper Transaction Id)**. Each update will have a unique zxid. Reads and writes are only ordered with respect to updates; i.e., they are stamped with the last zxid processed by the server (last update). To achieve distributed synchronization, ZooKeeper implements a variant of the classic part time parliament or Synod protocol by Leslie Lamport called the **Zab (ZooKeeper Atomic Broadcast) protocol,** which is somewhat similar to Paxos Multi-Decree protocol [15] proposed by Butler Lampson, but is a two-phase commit protocol [16].

It is easy to understand the functionality of ZooKeeper if one thinks of it as a shared file system. The clients just read and write files (though of very small size). Read requests from a client are processed locally at the ZooKeeper server to which the client is connected, while write requests are forwarded to other ZooKeeper servers. Write requests need to go through a consensus protocol to ensure that the correct written copy is maintained. Sync requests are also forwarded to other servers but do not go through the consensus protocol. If the read request registers a watch on a znode, that watch is also tracked only locally at the ZooKeeper server. Thus, if the application has many read requests, then there is no impact on scalability, while write requests can reduce the performance for a large number of servers. Some details of the usage of ZooKeeper API is given next.

Using ZooKeeper API

To start a ZooKeeper server, do the following:

```
java -jar zookeeper-3.3.3-fatjar.jar server 2181 /tmp/zkdata
```

The previous command line starts the ZooKeeper server on port 2181 and instructs use of /tmp for storing its data. In production use, many instances of the ZooKeeper server are executed possibly in a cluster, and a more detailed configuration (which does not use a common /tmp folder) is as follows:

```
java -jar zookeeper-3.3.3-fatjar.jar server server1.cfg &
```

To study the APIs, an example from the ZooKeeper recipe [17] has been chosen. This example implements a barrier, which is a synchronization point in a parallel and distributed program. A **barrier** for a group of processes means that each process must stop at that point and cannot continue until the rest of the processes reach the same point. Distributed systems use barriers to block processing of a set of nodes until a condition is met, at which time all the nodes are allowed to proceed.

Barriers are implemented in ZooKeeper by designating a barrier node. If the barrier node exists (conceptually, if the file exists), then the barrier exists and the process needs to stop. The following are the sequence of calls that the application client needs to make.

1. Client calls the ZooKeeper API's `exists()` function on the barrier node, with `watch` set to true.
2. If `exists()` returns false, the barrier node has been removed and so the client proceeds.

3. Else, if `exists()` returns true, the clients wait for a `watch` event from ZooKeeper for the barrier node.

4. When the `watch` event is triggered, the client reissues the `exists( )` call, again waiting until the barrier node is removed.

The general idea of the implementation is to have a barrier node that serves the purpose of being a parent for individual process nodes. Suppose that we call the barrier node "/b1". Each process "p" then creates a node "/b1/p". Once enough processes have created their corresponding nodes, joined processes can start the computation. The barrier is in place if the barrier node exists.

The following is the Java code to implement a barrier using ZooKeeper API:

```java
import java.io.IOException;
import java.net.InetAddress;
import java.net.UnknownHostException;
import java.nio.ByteBuffer;
import java.util.List;
import java.util.Random;

import org.apache.zookeeper.CreateMode;
import org.apache.zookeeper.KeeperException;
import org.apache.zookeeper.WatchedEvent;
import org.apache.zookeeper.Watcher;
import org.apache.zookeeper.ZooKeeper;
import org.apache.zookeeper.ZooDefs.Ids;
import org.apache.zookeeper.data.Stat;

public class Barrier implements Watcher {

    static ZooKeeper zk = null;
    static Integer mutex;

    String root;

        /**
         * Barrier constructor
         *
         * @param address
         * @param root
         * @param size
         */
        Barrier(Zookeeper zk, String root, int size) {

            this.root = root;
            this.size = size;

            // Create barrier node
            if (zk != null) {
                try {
                    Stat s = zk.exists(root, false);
                    if (s == null) {
```

```
                    zk.create(root, new byte[0], Ids.OPEN_ACL_UNSAFE,
                            CreateMode.PERSISTENT);
                }
            } catch (KeeperException e) {
                System.out
                        .println("Keeper exception when instantiating
                        queue: "
                                + e.toString());
            } catch (InterruptedException e) {
                System.out.println("Interrupted exception");
            }
        }

        // My node name
        try {
            name = new String(InetAddress.getLocalHost()
            .getCanonicalHostName().toString());
        } catch (UnknownHostException e) {
            System.out.println(e.toString());
        }

    synchronized public void process(WatchedEvent event) {
        synchronized (mutex) {
            //System.out.println("Process: " + event.getType());
            mutex.notify();
        }
    }

    /**
     * Join barrier
     *
     * @return
     * @throws KeeperException
     * @throws InterruptedException
     */

    boolean enter() throws KeeperException, InterruptedException{
        zk.create(root + "/" + name, new byte[0],
        Ids.OPEN_ACL_UNSAFE,
                CreateMode.EPHEMERAL_SEQUENTIAL);
        while (true) {
            synchronized (mutex) {
                List<String> list = zk.getChildren(root, true);

                if (list.size() < size) {
                    mutex.wait();
                } else {
                    return true;
                }
            }
        }
    }
```

```
public static void main(String args[]) {
    // Create a ZooKeeper object
    try {
        System.out.println("Starting ZK:");
        zk = new ZooKeeper(address, 3000, this);
        mutex = new Integer(-1);
        System.out.println("Finished starting ZK: " + zk);
    } catch (IOException e) {
        System.out.println(e.toString());
        zk = null;
    }

    // Do some processing which is independent of other processes.

    // Now, client needs to synchronize
    Barrier b = new Barrier(zk, "/b1", new Integer(args[2]));
    try{
        boolean flag = b.enter();
        System.out.println("Entered barrier: " + args[2]);
        if(!flag) System.out.println("Error when entering the
        barrier");
    } catch (KeeperException e){

    } catch (InterruptedException e){

    }

    try{ // Cleanup
        zk.delete(root + "/" + name, 0);
    } catch (KeeperException e){

    } catch (InterruptedException e){

    }

    // Process rest of the distributed code

}
```

The main method creates an object of ZooKeeper class and keeps that in a static variable. When the application needs to enter a barrier, a Barrier object is created. The enter() method ensures that all the required number of processes come to this method in their respective processes and wait, using mutex.wait(). When the getChildren returns all the processes, then the mutex is released. The last process which comes to this barrier will release the barrier and only then will all the processes be released to continue activity.

ZooKeeper provides a very simple way to implement barrier synchronization, without which a lot of messages need to pass around to the processes. The reader should note that, although the semantics does look as if the distributed processes are synchronizing around creation and deletion of files in a common share, internally it is NOT happening that way. These files are NOT stored in any common file system but are maintained in in-memory data structures. The consensus algorithm implemented by ZooKeeper ensures that the synchronization is very efficient and scalable. This is exemplified by the fact that Apache uses ZooKeeper to coordinate distributed MapReduce processes in Hadoop.

SCALING STORAGE

This section provides some fundamental concepts needed to address the scalability challenge while using a common data store across application instances. In Chapter 5, various ways of partitioning and replicating the data have been discussed and those enabled one to scale beyond the throughput and capacity limitations of single storage systems. However, the chapter did not deal with the consistency problems of keeping the data in the various partitions [18]. In the Pustak Portal example, it was assumed that the Total_Bought, which represents the total value of books bought by a customer, can be kept consistent with the transactions in the Book Sales data. This is achieved by creating transactions that update the Total_Bought data whenever a new sale occurs. However, if data is at cloud scale, these two databases may be stored on separate storage systems. If a network partition occurs, it may not be possible to update the Total_Bought data each time a sale occurs.

Consistency and availability problems, such as those described earlier, are considered in more detail in this section. First, the section reviews the **CAP theorem**, which was first conjectured by Brewer in [19], and proved in Lynch and Gilbert [20]. The CAP theorem implies that consistency guarantees in large-scale distributed systems cannot be as strict as those in centralized systems. Specifically, it suggests that distributed systems may need to provide **BASE** guarantees instead of the **ACID** guarantees provided by traditional database systems [21]. Systems that are **eventually consistent** form an important subset of such systems [22]. Following this, we illustrate these principles by considering how this can be handled for the Pustak Portal example using different database and NoSQL storage systems. Finally, since this is an evolving area of research, we summarize some counter-views on the significance of the CAP theorem.

CAP Theorem

The CAP theorem states that no distributed system can provide more than two of the following three guarantees: **Consistency, Availability**, and **Partitioning-tolerance**. Here, **consistency** is defined as in databases; i.e., if multiple operations are performed on the same object (which is actually stored in a distributed system), the results of the operations appear as if the operations were carried out in some definite order on a single system. For example, if four operations O, P, Q, and R

are executed, it would never be the case that Q would see the results as if the first two operations were executed in the order *O-followed-by-P*, while R would see the results as if the first two operations were executed in the order *P-followed-by-O*. **Availability** is defined to be satisfied if each operation on the system (for example, a query) returns some result. The system provides **partitioning-tolerance** if the system is operational even when the network between two components of the system is down. This result has been formally proved by Lynch et al. [20].

Since distributed systems can satisfy only two of the three properties due to the CAP theorem, there are three types of distributed systems [19]. **CA (Consistent, Available)** systems provide consistency and availability, but cannot tolerate network partitions. An example of a CA system is a clustered database, where each node stores a subset of the data. Such a database cannot provide availability in the case of network partitioning, since queries to data in the partitioned nodes must fail. CA systems may not be useful for cloud computing, since partitions are likely to occur in medium to large networks. Note that partitioning may also include the case where the message latency is very high, so that the synchronization time becomes very high, effectively making it impossible to maintain consistency [23]. Hence, the other two types of systems are considered in the following sections.

CAP Theorem Example

To understand the constraints arising from large-scale distributed data, consider the following example, which parallels the usual method of proof. Assume that the Pustak Portal data from Chapter 5 is stored in the system illustrated in Figure 6.6, and that the customer data from Table 5.1 in Chapter 5 is partitioned among the four servers A, B, C, D. Further assume that the data in A, B, C are replicated in D for

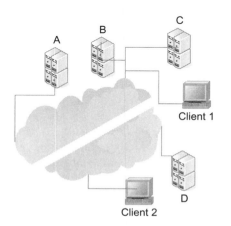

When not partitioned
▫ Client 1: Total_Bought=$5,665
▫ Client 2: Total_Bought=$5,665

When partitioned
CP system
▫ Client 1: Total_Bought=$5,665
▫ Client 2: Total_Bought=Unavailable
AP system
▫ Client 1: Total_Bought=$5,665
▫ Client 2: Total_Bought=$5,500

FIGURE 6.6

Behavior of CP and AP systems.

availability. Consider the case where both *Client 1* and *Client 2* want to find the value of Total_Bought for customer 38876.

If there is no network partitioning, all servers are consistent, and the value seen by both clients is the correct value (say $5,665). However, if the network is partitioned as shown in Figure 6.6, it is no longer possible to keep all the servers consistent in the face of updates. There are then two choices. One choice is to keep both servers up, and ignore the inconsistency. This leads to **AP (Available, Partition-tolerant)** systems where the system is always available, but may not return consistent results. In this case, the two clients could get differing values for Total_Bought; *Client 1* may see the correct value ($5,665) while *Client 2* may see a stale value (say $5,500). The other possible choice is to bring one of the servers down, to avoid inconsistent values. This leads to **CP (Consistent, Partition-tolerant)** systems where the system always returns consistent results, but may be unavailable under partitioning. If server *D* is brought down (which would typically happen, since the other partition has the majority of the servers) *Client 1* may get the correct value, but *Client 2* may not see any response. Recall again that partitioning may also include the case where the latency is very high.

Implications of CAP Theorem

Both of these choices have important implications for application design [22]. In CP systems, the application has to handle errors (since the query to unavailable data returns an error). While we have given the example of reads, the error could exist with writes as well, and could result in a transaction or business process being aborted. In AP systems, the client may get an incorrect result that may not reflect the most recent update (or *stale data*). There are two ways of dealing with this silent error. First, in some cases the inconsistency may not matter. For example, if we consider indexes maintained by search engines, it may not matter that a slightly outdated index is being searched, since only a small amount of data may have changed from the outdated index to the current index. Alternatively, the application may need to have logic to detect when it is reading incorrect data. For example, in Pustak Portal, it may not matter if a customer is querying the status of an order, and a stale value is displayed. Another example of this is the Internet *Domain Name System (DNS)*, where networking applications that query DNS are aware that they may get a stale IP address, and have logic to deal with this error.

An interesting question to consider is whether the CAP theorem holds only in cloud environments or in conventional (not geographically distributed) enterprise data centers as well. Theoretically, the CAP theorem holds in both situations. However, within an enterprise data center, there is generally sufficient redundancy in the networking that connects mission-critical servers to ensure that network partitioning does not occur. Failure of mission critical servers can occur, but techniques such as clustering are used to ensure that the failures are brief. Hence, for mission-critical applications, it can be assumed that the kinds of failures considered by the CAP theorem do not occur. For non-mission critical servers, failures can occur, but these failures can be tolerated by suspending the service temporarily. Therefore, though the CAP theorem applies within enterprise data centers as well, in practice its implications can be ignored.

The consequences of the CAP theorem seem to be well accepted, with eBay, for example, having decided to relax consistency in return for higher availability and scalability [24]. However, since this is still an area of active research, there exist views that the significance of the CAP theorem is overrated [25]. The objections can be summarized in four points:

1. The CAP theorem's view of the major data-related errors is idealized and incomplete. There are many other more important causes of database outage, including human or application error that corrupt the database, and outages for maintenance. It is necessary to plan for these as well.
2. There are many engineering trade-offs in distributed systems, and the choice of trade-offs must depend upon the system. For example, a mainframe is much more stable than Linux or Windows, and the trade-offs for mainframes should be different.
3. The CAP theorem is generally used to justify relaxing consistency. However, network partitions are rare compared to the other sources of outage listed earlier. Making a general decision based upon a rare occurrence is a bad decision.
4. Next-generation databases like VoltDB are orders of magnitude faster than present-day databases. By reducing the numbers of nodes needed, the CAP theorem becomes less important.

NOTE

AP (Available, Partition-tolerant) Systems
- Weak Consistency
- Eventual Consistency
- Read-your-writes Consistency
- Session Consistency
- Monotonic-write Consistency
- Variable Consistency

Implementing Weak Consistency

As noted previously, AP systems provide **weak consistency**. Hence, applications may need to recover or detect situations where the system returns incorrect data. The different types of weakly consistent systems are discussed later, together with a discussion of how these different systems can deal with data inconsistencies [22].

An important subclass of weakly consistent systems is those that provide **eventual consistency**. A system is defined as being **eventually consistent** if the system is guaranteed to reach a consistent state in a finite amount of time if there are no failures (e.g., network partitions) and no updates are made. The **inconsistency window** for such systems is the maximum amount of time that can elapse between the time that the update is made, and the time that the update is guaranteed to be visible to all clients. If the inconsistency window is small compared to the update rate, then one method of dealing with stale data is to wait for a period greater than the inconsistency window, and then re-try the query. Consider the case where a customer sends a large email using an email provider such as Yahoo! Mail. If the receiver is on a different email server, they may not see the email in their Inbox immediately (i.e., there is an inconsistency between the sender's Outbox and the receiver's Inbox). However, if the recipient waits for the inconsistency window (in this case, the email propagation time) the mail should be present in their Inbox.

Read-your-writes consistency is an important subset of eventual consistency, where the storage system guarantees that if a client updates a data item, it would never see an older version of the same data item. This kind of guarantee is useful, for example, for shopping applications such as Pustak Portal. If a customer is buying books, they would always see the latest version of their shopping cart, since it is likely that they would be the only person updating their shopping cart. A variation of this is **session consistency** where the client is guaranteed to see all made (by the client) in the same session with the storage system. **Monotonic-write-consistency** is a property whereby the system guarantees that writes occur in the storage system in the same order that they were initiated by the clients (i.e., that propagation delays do not affect the order of writes). This is an essential property to ensure simplicity of application programming.

Keeping Pustak Portal Data Consistent

The following subsection examines the consistency issues in more detail by considering the question of keeping Pustak Portal data consistent. It is assumed that the Pustak Portal data is as described in Chapter 5. Two scenarios (see Figure 6.7) are considered. The **replication scenario** is described in the section called *CAP Theorem*. It is assumed that for availability, customer data in servers *A,B,C* is replicated in *D*. The question to be considered is: when a customer completes a purchase, how can it be ensured that the value of `Total_Bought` is maintained consistently across the servers? It is also important to note that the same problem can arise if multiple values are to be updated, even in the presence of no replication. Therefore, in the **geographically distributed** scenario, it is assumed that after the customer purchase, the transaction data in server *C* as well as the value of `Total_Bought` in server *D* have to be updated consistently.

In the following sections, a general technique using **asynchronous replication** is described first. Subsequently, various cloud storage systems are considered that have specific mechanisms built in for weak consistency. In each case, the previous scenarios for keeping Pustak Portal data consistent are considered.

```
PART 1: PSEUDO-CODE FOR REPLICATION SCENARIO
Begin transaction /* on server C */
    result = SELECT * FROM custTable WHERE custID=Customer_Id; /*1*/
    New_Total_Bought = result.Total_Bought + Sale_Price;
```

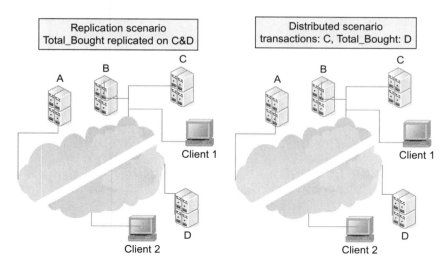

FIGURE 6.7

Consistency scenarios.

```
      result = UPDATE custRecord SET Total_Bought = New_Total_Bought WHERE
      custID=Customer_Id;
      Queue_message ("D", "Add", "custRecord", "Total_Bought", /*2*/
      Sale_Price.ToString());
    End transaction
```

Asynchronous Replication

As stated earlier, in the replicated scenario, it is necessary to keep servers C and D the same. In the geographically distributed scenario, servers C and D have to be updated such that the values in both servers are consistent. The basic idea is to update one of the servers, and create persistent messages to update the other servers [21]. A separate daemon process on the other servers is responsible for reading the update messages and performing the updates, ensuring **eventual consistency**. This technique is referred to as **asynchronous replication** or **log shipping**, since it essentially consists of replaying the update log for each server on the other servers. The server update and message creation is done inside a transaction, so that either both fail or both succeed. This technique is particularly popular with databases, such as MySQL, since databases always generate a transaction log. However, there may be many ways of performing the update, and it is necessary to carefully consider the sequence of actions that may take place in order to ensure consistency.

The code segment *Part 1: Pseudo-code for Replication Scenario* contains pseudo-code needed on server *C* for the first part of the process described earlier in the replication scenario. Statement 1 reads the value of Total_Bought for the customer. The next statement adds the `Sale_Price` of the book that has been bought to compute the new value of `Total_Bought` for the customer. The following statement updates the value of `Total_Bought` in server *C*. It is now necessary to update server *D* as well, to keep the two servers consistent. This is done in statement 2 by queuing a message to server *D* to update `Total_Bought` by adding the value of `Sale_Price` to the value of `Total_Bought` in server *D*. It is assumed that the message queuing service is transactional, so that either both the update of server *C* and the queuing of the message to server *D* succeed or both fail. This can be accomplished by, for example, the message service storing the messages in a database in the local server (*C* in this case), before sending it. Examples of transactional message services include *Java Messaging Service* (*JMS*) with the *Java Transaction API* (*JTA*) [26].

```
PART 2: PSEUDO-CODE FOR REPLICATION SCENARIO
read_without_dequeuing (message); /* 1 */
Begin transaction /* on server D */
    SELECT count (*) AS procFlag FROM msgTable WHERE message.msgId =
    msgId; /* 2 */
    if (procFlag) == 0 { /* 3 */
      process_message (message); /* Add Sale_Price to Total_Bought */
      INSERT INTO msgTable VALUES (message.msgId);
    }
End transaction
if (transaction successful) {dequeue (message)} /* 4 */
```

For the second part of the process, it is assumed that server *D* has a database (called `msgTable`) that keeps track of all the messages that have been processed. It is assumed that the message queuing system automatically adds a message id (called `msgId`) to each message, and that these message ids are stored in `msgTable`. The code segment *Part 2: Pseudo-code for Replication Scenario* shows the process, which executes on server *D*, in pseudo-code. Statement 1 reads the message at the head of the queue without removing it from the queue. Statement 2 looks up the message id of the message in the message table to see if it has been processed. The `if` statement in statement 3 is executed if the message id is not found, i.e., the message has not been processed. In that case, the message is processed, and `Total_Bought` is updated. Next, the message id is inserted into the message table. Both operations are performed in the same transaction, so that either both succeed or both fail. The final step, in statement 4, is to remove the message from the queue if the transaction completed successfully.

The geographically distributed scenario is similar to the previously mentioned. Here, it is desired to insert a new purchase into the transaction table on server *C*, and simultaneously update `Total_Bought` on server *D*. In this case, the three statements following statement 1 in code segment *Part 1: Pseudo-code for Replication Scenario* will be replaced by a single statement that inserts a new transaction into the transaction table on server *C*. The rest of the pseudo-code to queue a message to server *D*, as well as the code in code segment *Part 2: Pseudo-code for Replication Scenario* remain the same.

Complexities of Weak Consistency

From the description of the process mentioned previously, it is clear that servers C, D offer an eventual consistency model, since any update applied to C will eventually propagate to D and vice versa. However, it is important to note that to ensure consistency, it is necessary to study the operations as well as the cloud system carefully, and design the messages appropriately. The following is an example of how small changes in the operations performed on the server or the cloud system can lead to inconsistency [27].

Consider an alternate method for ensuring consistency – queuing a message to set `Total_Bought` to the value `New_Total_Bought` above. In other words, if `Total_Bought` is $2,000, and a purchase is made for $10, server C could generate a message to server D to set `Total_Bought` to $2,010. This may not work under the following scenario. Suppose the customer makes two purchases – the first one we mentioned earlier for $10 and the second one for, say, $15. Server C will then generate two messages under the alternate method – the first to set `Total_Bought` in server D to $2,010, and the second to set `Total_Bought` to $2,025. Suppose also that due to network delays or re-transmission errors, the first message to set `Total_Bought` to $2,010 is delivered after the second message to set `Total_Bought` to $2,025. In that case, `Total_Bought` in server D would be set to $2,010, and not $2,025 as desired. Therefore, the alternate method does not work in the case where message deliveries can be out of order. This example also illustrates that in designing such consistency protocols, it is dangerous to assume that messages will be delivered in order [27]. However, the error can be handled by discarding older messages. In the rest of this subsection, the modified algorithm which discards older messages will be referred to as **algorithm II**. The method of subsection *Persistent Messaging* will be referred to as **algorithm I**.

While algorithm II works under the previous scenario, there is an important scenario under which it may not work. Suppose the load-balancing algorithm, which decides which server to send any request to, randomly picks one of servers C and D to send a request to each time. Consider the scenario where the first purchase (for $10) is processed by server C, while the second purchase (for $15) is processed by server D. It can easily be seen that algorithm I would ensure eventual consistency, but that algorithm II would generate incorrect results. It is also to be noted that while algorithm I will lead to correct values for `Total_Bought` in C and D, at any given point in time, the value stored in either server may be incorrect. To ensure correct values for `Total_Bought`, the load balancing algorithm could be modified so that for each customer, there is a master server (C in this case) with the other server (D in the example) being used as a standby for failure or as a slave server for reads. The correct value of `Total_Bought` would then always be available on the master server under both algorithms I and II.

In summary, it can be seen that in order to work with weakly consistent cloud systems, to ensure consistency, it is necessary to consider the semantics of the operations being performed, as well as the details of the system, such as the load balancing algorithm used, and the order of delivery of messages. Maintaining consistency is simpler in master-slave replication systems. As discussed later, many popular databases, such as HBase, offer this kind of consistency for replication over a WAN, where network-partitioning may be more frequent.

Consistency in NoSQL Systems

The earlier discussion shows that it may not be feasible for highly scalable storage systems to support strong consistency. However, storage systems must support some sort of consistency guarantee (e.g., eventual consistency) that applications can use to detect and recover from inconsistent data. The rest of the section describes consistency in three well-known NoSQL systems: HBase, MongoDB and Dynamo/Cassandra. In each case, the architecture of the system is discussed, followed by a discussion of how to keep data consistent. Keeping data consistent consists of two steps: first, detecting that an inconsistency exists (conflict detection) and next, resolving the inconsistency. Both the steps may be done by the application or by the storage system. If the storage system has to resolve inconsistencies, it would generally use a simple rule such as the latest write wins.

HBase

HBase is part of the Apache Hadoop cloud project, an overview of which was given in Chapter 5 from a usage perspective. In this section, the HBase architecture is presented in such a way to understand the implementation of a cloud system before designing a method of keeping data consistent [28]. The HBase architecture is similar to the **BigTable** architecture developed by Google for its cloud services [29].

HBase Clusters: Figure 6.8 shows the HBase architecture. The left-hand side of the figure shows an individual HBase cluster. Each HBase cluster is intended to be in a single data center, so that network partitioning is not a concern within the cluster. The cluster consists of one or more **HMaster** servers (of which only one is active, and the others are on standby), together with multiple **HRegion** servers. Each HRegion server is responsible for serving a particular **region**. Recall from Chapter 5 that each HBase table consists of a set of key-value pairs. These are stored in sorted order of key by HBase. A region consists of a contiguous subset of keys (see Figure 6.8). The HMaster is responsible for dynamically dividing the table into regions, and allocating regions to HRegion servers so as to keep the load among HRegion servers balanced. It can be seen that HBase implements sharding, or horizontal partitioning, for scaling, where the partitioning is automatically performed by the system, and does not have to be explicitly performed by the user. For availability, data may be replicated within a cluster, but since network partitioning is not likely, these replicas will be consistent.

HBase Replication: HBase replication is also illustrated in Figure 6.8. An HBase table can be replicated over multiple HBase clusters (this is different from the within-cluster replication described previously). The clusters may be geographically distributed or used for different purposes (e.g., one cluster may be used for receiving real-time data while the other cluster may be used for doing offline analysis). One of the clusters is the **master** while the other clusters are **slaves**. All updates take place on the master cluster. The updates are batched and

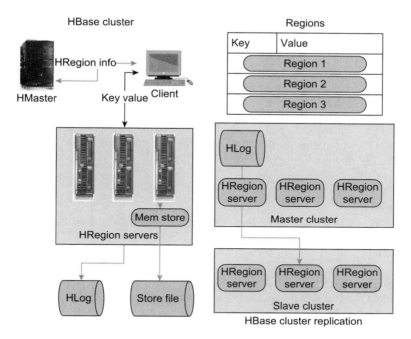

FIGURE 6.8

HBase architecture.

periodically pushed to the slave. To keep track of the updates that have taken place, the master uses the HLogs of the HRegion servers in the cluster. Updates are pushed to randomly selected HRegion servers in the slave cluster that are responsible for executing the update in the slave cluster. It can be seen that HBase replication follows the asynchronous replication method described earlier, and the slaves will be eventually consistent with the master, so HBase offers an eventual consistency model. However, the architecture of HBase is such that updates can take place only in the master cluster, so the replication is of the master-slave type described in Chapter 5. Thus, even if the clients are geographically distributed, they have to access the master cluster if they need to perform updates.

HBase operations are as follows. To operate on a particular key-value pair, the HBase client first contacts the HMaster to find the HRegion server storing that particular key. This value is cached, so the call is made only once. The client then transacts directly with the corresponding HRegion server. If the call is a **write**, a timestamp is appended to the write (see Chapter 5) and the new value is appended to the data without overwriting the old value. The update is written to all the replicas in the cluster, using a log to minimize latency. Actually, the update is first written to the log (**HLog**) and then stored in memory. Later, all the replicas are updated from the HLog. This technique reduces the latency needed to perform multiple writes. Reads can be performed from any replica, and by default return the value with the latest timestamp.

HBase Consistency: HBase has a simple model of consistency. Writes are directed to all replicas in a cluster, which is in a single data center. Therefore, consistency issues cannot arise within an HBase cluster. Reads will return the value with the highest timestamp, which implies that the latest write overwrites (by default) all earlier writes. However, HBase guarantees only eventual consistency across HBase clusters. Therefore, to be sure of getting the most recent version of the data, clients have to contact the master cluster, even if they are geographically distant. One method for getting around this limitation is to split each table into geographically contiguous tables, and have a separate master cluster for each table.

MongoDB

MongoDB is a document store for JSON objects and was introduced in Chapter 5. Since the replication architecture of MongoDB is similar to that of HBase, the MongoDB architecture is described only briefly here. The comments and techniques for keeping data consistent covered under the previous HBase section also apply to MongoDB.

The replication architecture of MongoDB is illustrated in Figure 6.9 [30, 31]. Multiple MongoDB nodes can be configured as a **replica set**, in which the data stored in MongoDB will be replicated. As in HBase, each individual node is actually a collection of MongoDB servers, among which the MongoDB table is sharded. MongoDB requires that the replica set contain an odd number of members (a null server called the **arbiter** can be added if it is desired to use two or some even number of actual replicas). After the configuration of the replica set, one of the nodes is elected as the **primary** (as shown in Figure 6.9) and the other nodes are **secondary** nodes [32].

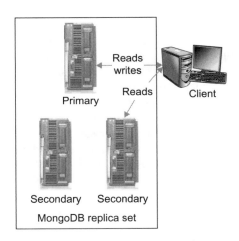

FIGURE 6.9

MongoDB architecture.

The primary receives (by default) all reads and writes. These are propagated to the secondary nodes using a log file called the **oplog** (which itself is a MongoDB document) [33]. To use the secondary nodes for reads (which may not be consistent with the primary at all times) the flag **slaveOkay** in the client configuration has to be set [34]. In case of a network partition, if the majority partition does not contain the primary, a new primary is elected. The minority partition can continue to service reads [35]. If there is no majority partition, both partitions continue to serve only reads.

It can be seen from the previous description that like HBase, MongoDB also offers an eventual consistency model for replication. Furthermore, as in HBase, replicas can be used only for reads, so the replication is again the master-slave type described in Chapter 5.

Dynamo/Cassandra

Dynamo is another highly available key-value store created as part of an experimental project at Amazon. Cassandra is a NoSQL system introduced in Chapter 5, which uses much of the Dynamo technology. These are described here because Dynamo has explicit support for detecting inconsistencies via an interesting technology called **vector clocks,** and they both have support for the innovative concept of **variable consistency** [36]. Additionally, **Riak**, another NoSQL storage system which is an open source re-implementation of Dynamo, has both these features as well.

Vector clocks: The principles behind Dynamo's vector clocks can be illustrated by a simple example. Assume that there are four processes A, B, C, D, which are updating a common variable x. If A sets x to 10, this is stored as ($x=10$; A:1) by the system. A:1 is the vector clock, which consists of the id of the process that did the write, together with the time (assumed to be 1). Suppose that B and C now read x simultaneously and both set it to 15. This is now stored as ($x=15$; A:1, B:2) and ($x=15$; A:1, C:3). The order of storage depends upon which of B and C completed first; recall that as in HBase, old values are not overwritten. The vector clock essentially maintains the history of all updates. The vector clock for B includes the id of A since B read the value updated by A, and similarly for C. If D now tries to read x, the system will detect an inconsistency from the two vector clocks for x. Examining the vector clocks A:1, B:2 and A:1, C:3, it is clear that x has been updated by B and C in parallel after the initial update from A (because C has seen only the A:1 update, and not the B:2 update). In general, if there are two vector clocks V and W, W is consistent with and later than V if every vector clock element in V is also found in W. D is now given both values and is expected to create a new consistent value for x. Note that the inconsistency could also have been detected at the time that C tried to write x. However, Dynamo emphasizes letting writes complete, so it chooses to detect inconsistencies during reads.

Variable consistency: It was seen that some NoSQL systems like HBase are AP systems, which are highly available, but offer eventual consistency. Relational databases, on the other hand, generally offer strict consistency. Dynamo had the explicit objective of allowing the degree of consistency to be chosen by the user. This method, which is also implemented in both Cassandra and Riak is as follows.

Suppose there are N replicas of a table. Dynamo allows specification of W, the number of replicas that must be written for any write operation to be considered a success. It also allows specification of R, the number of replicas that must be read for a read operation to be considered a success. Note that no matter what the value of R and N, Dynamo eventually writes to all replicas (including replicas that are presently down). The values of R and W only govern when the storage system notifies the application that a read or write is complete. Given an N, by proper choice of R and W, it is possible to have either strict consistency, like relational databases, or eventual consistency, like many NoSQL systems. If $R + W > N$, then the system enforces strict consistency. This can be seen from a simple example. Assume $N = 5$, $R = 3$, and $W = 3$. For any write, at least three replicas are written. Suppose replicas 1, 2, 4 are the replicas that are written by the latest write. The only way a read can return stale data is if it reads only replicas 3 and 5. However, since any read will read at least three replicas, any read will read at least one of replicas 1, 2, or 4, and return the latest value.

Conversely, if eventual consistency is sufficient, the user can set R, W such that $R+W < = N$. In this case, different reads may return different values; but eventually, the system will be consistent. In the previous example, if $R = 1$, $W = 1$, some reads may return the latest value, and some reads may not, depending upon which replicas are read and written. All replicas will eventually take the correct value, since Dynamo eventually will write to all replicas. The motivation for using $R = 1$, $W = 1$ is that the latency is lower than using a higher value. By default, Cassandra recommends using $R = W = $ Ceiling $((N+1)/2)$ where Ceiling rounds up $(N+1)/2$ to the next highest integer if it is a fraction. This value is called **QUORUM**, and it can be seen that it enforces strict consistency. The discussion on consistency in this section parallels the discussion in [27, 37, 38, 39, 40] which also discusses other issues, such as backup and restore.

MULTI-TENANCY

Earlier chapters have described relatively coarse-grained sharing of resources via virtualization. This chapter describes more fine-grained resource sharing, called **multi-tenancy**. In order to make the concept clear, consider an experiment conducted by Jacob et al. in the context of database. The experiment compares three methods of creating a database shared among multiple customers [41]. In the **shared machine** method, each customer was given their own database process and tables on a shared machine. In the **shared process** method, each customer had their own database tables, but there was only one database process which executed instructions on behalf of all customers. In the **shared table** method, in addition to the customers sharing the database process, the data was stored in shared tables (each row being prefixed with the customer id to indicate the customer to which the row belonged). Measurements showed that under the shared machine approach, PostGresQL used 55MB of main memory and 4 MB of disk memory for storing data for one customer. However, under the shared process approach, for 10,000 customers, PostGresQL used only 80 MB of main memory and 4,488 MB of disk memory. Clearly, the scalability of the system would be much better under the shared process method. Measurements were not presented for the shared table approach, but the scalability is expected to be even greater. In summary, the measurements show that the finer the granularity of sharing, the greater the scalability of the system.

However, the increased efficiency in scaling brings with it additional security requirements. For example, in the shared table approach, which is the most efficient from the resource sharing point of view, it is necessary to be able to specify access control for each row of the table [41]. Additionally, customization becomes difficult; in the shared table approach, how would it be possible for customers to add their own custom fields in the table? In the rest of the chapter, methods of implementing multi-tenancy with fine grained resource sharing while ensuring security and isolation between customers, and also allowing customers to customize the database, are described. First, security support for multi-tenancy is discussed. Next, techniques for resource sharing with security are described. Finally, support for customization is discussed.

NOTE

Multi-Tenancy Requirements

- Fine grain resource sharing
- Security and isolation between customers
- Customization of tables

Multi-Tenancy Levels

Implementing the highest degree of resource sharing for all resources may be prohibitively expensive in development effort and complexity of the system. A balanced approach, where there is fine grained sharing of resources only for important resources, may be the optimum approach. The four levels of multi-tenancy are described in the following list [42]; for any given resource in a cloud system, the appropriate level could be selected.

1. **Ad Hoc/Custom instances:** In this lowest level, each customer has their own custom version of the software. This represents the situation currently in most enterprise data centers where there are multiple instances and versions of the software. It was also typical of the earlier ASP model, which, as stated in Chapter 4, represented the first attempt to offer software for rent over the Internet. The ASP model was similar to the SaaS model in that ASP customers (normally businesses), upon logging in to the ASP portal, would be able to rent use of a software application like CRM. However each customer would typically have their own instance of the software being supported. This would imply that each customer would have their own binaries, as well as

their own dedicated processes for implementation of the application. This makes management extremely difficult, since each customer would need their own management support.

2. **Configurable Instances:** In this level, all customers share the same version of the program. However, customization is possible through configuration and other options. Customization could include the ability to put the customer's logo on the screen, tailoring of workflows to the customer's processes, and so on. In this level, there are significant manageability savings over the previous level, since there is only one copy of the software that needs to be maintained. Additionally, upgrades are seamless and simple.

3. **Configurable, multi-tenant efficient instances:** Cloud systems at this level in addition to sharing the same version of the program, also have only one instance of the program running which is shared among all the customers. This leads to additional efficiency since there is only one running instance of the program.

4. **Scalable, configurable, multi-tenant efficient instances:** In addition to the attributes of the previous level, the software is also hosted on a cluster of computers, allowing the capacity of the system to scale almost limitlessly. Thus the number of customers can scale from a small number to a very large number, and the capacity used by each customer can range from being small to very large. Performance bottlenecks and capacity limitations that may have been present in the earlier level are eliminated. For example, in a cloud email service like Gmail or Yahoo Mail, multiple users share the same physical email server as well as the same email server processes. Additionally, the emails from different users are stored in the same set of storage devices, and perhaps the same set of files. This results in management efficiencies; for example, if each user had to have a dedicated set of disks for storing email, the space allocation for each user would have to be managed separately. However, the drawback of shared storage devices is that security requirements are greater; if the email server has vulnerabilities and can be hacked, it is possible for one user to access the emails of another.

Tenants and Users

Before proceeding to discuss methods for implementing multi-tenancy, the reason behind the term multi-tenancy is described. In the case of a service like Salesforce.com, it is necessary to distinguish between the customers of a service (who are businesses) and the users of the services, who will be employees of the business. To avoid confusion, the customers of a SaaS or PaaS service are referred to as **tenants**, regardless of whether they are businesses or users (in the case of a service like Gmail). It is necessary for a cloud service to enforce strict isolation between tenants of the service. The term **user** continues to be used for the actual users of the service. Generally, the tenants of a service will specify the degree of isolation to be enforced between users.

Authentication

The key challenge in multi-tenancy is the secure sharing of resources. A very important technology to ensure this is authentication, which is the process by which a user signs on to the cloud system and accesses its resources. Clearly each business tenant would like to specify the users who can log in to the cloud system. Unlike traditional computer systems, the tenant would specify the valid users, but authentication still has to be done by the cloud service provider. Two basic approaches can be used: a **centralized authentication** system or a **decentralized authentication** system [42]. Either approach would allow incorporation of different authentication methods; e.g., 2 factor authentication or biometric authentication. In the centralized system, all authentication is performed using a centralized user data base. The cloud administrator gives the tenant's administrator rights to manage user accounts for that tenant. When the user signs in, they are authenticated against the centralized database. In the decentralized system, each tenant maintains their own user data base, and the tenant needs to deploy a **federation service** that interfaces between the tenant's authentication framework and the cloud system's authentication service.

Decentralized authentication is useful if **single sign-on** is important, since centralized authentication systems will require the user to sign on to the central authentication system in addition to signing on to the tenant's authentication system. However, decentralized authentication systems have the disadvantage that they need a trust relationship between the tenant's authentication system and the cloud provider's authentication system. Given the self-service nature of the cloud (i.e., it is unlikely that the cloud provider would have the resources to investigate each tenant, and ensure that their authentication infrastructure is secure), centralized authentication seems to be more generally applicable.

Implementing Multi-Tenancy: Resource Sharing

Another key technology to ensure secure resource sharing in a multi-tenant service is access control. Two forms of access control can be provided in a cloud service provider – **roles**, and **business rules** [42]. Roles consist of a set of permissions included in the role; for example, a storage administrator role may include the permissions to define storage devices. These permissions may not be included in a server administrator role. Generally, the cloud system should contain a set of default roles that are appropriate for the cloud system; e.g., a database administrator role for a PaaS system that includes a database. It should be possible for the tenant to use the default roles as templates, customize them for their usage, and assign them to users. The ability to specify roles for users, of course, is itself a permission that only certain roles can possess.

Business rules are policies that provide more fine-grained access control than roles provide, since they may depend upon the parameters of the operation. For example, in a banking application, it may be possible to specify a limit on the amount of money a particular role can transfer, or specify that transfers can occur only during business hours. Business rules are distinguished from roles in that whether an operation is permitted, or not, depends not just on the operation, but also upon the parameters (e.g., the amount of money to be transferred by the operation). Enforcement of business rules depends upon the application. These can be implemented using policy engines such as *Drools Expert* and *Drools Guvnor* [43].

There are broadly two types of access control models. One is based on access control lists (ACL) where each object is attached with a list of permissions for each role. The second approach is that of capability-based access control, which works just like a house-key. If a user holds a reference or capability to an object, he has access to the object. The key is like an unforgettable link to the object; just by virtue of the user having this key grants him access to the object [44].

Next, different methods of sharing resources for cloud applications using this access control are discussed. A case study of multi-tenancy in Salesforce.com and security aspects of Hadoop (MapReduce and HDFS) are also presented to illustrate these principles.

Resource Sharing

Two major resources that need to be shared are storage and servers. The basic principles for sharing of these resources are described first. This is followed by a deeper discussion that focuses on the question of how these resources can be shared at a fine granularity, while allowing the tenants to customize the data to their requirements [42, 45, 46, 47].

Sharing storage resources: In a multi-tenant system, many tenants share the same storage system. Cloud applications may use two kinds of storage systems: file systems and databases, where the term database is used to mean not only relational databases, but NoSQL databases as well. Since file systems already have well-known mechanisms for allocating files on shared storage, and restricting access to those files to specified users via ACLs and other mechanisms, they are not discussed further here. The discussion is focused on sharing data for different users in a database. The focus is also on multi-tenant efficient approaches where there is only one instance of the database which is shared among all the tenants.

There are two methods of sharing data in a single database – table sharing and **dedicated tables per tenant** [47]. In the dedicated table method, each tenant stores their data in a separate set of tables different from other tenants. This is illustrated in Figure 6.10, which shows the way auto repair stores may store data about their customers in a hypothetical portal called *MyGarage.com*. The figure shows three garages (*Best Garage, Friendly Garage,* and *Honest Garage*), each of which stores their customer data in their own table. Since most databases store each table in a separate set of files, access to these files can be restricted to the auto repair shop that owns the tables. This provides an additional layer of security. If the database is a relational database, the three garages can be registered as database users, and access rights can be set by the SQL statement `SQL GRANT SELECT, ..., ON FriendlyTable TO FriendlyGarage WITH GRANT OPTION`. This statement gives access rights to the table `FriendlyTable` to the database user `FriendlyGarage`. The `WITH GRANT OPTION` clause allows the tenant to further give access rights to other database users.

The other alternative, the **shared table** approach, is illustrated in Figure 6.11 for the same set of data. In this case, the data for all tenants is stored in the same

Best garage

Car license	Service	Cost

Friendly garage

Car license	Service	Cost

Honest garage

Car license	Service	Cost

FIGURE 6.10

Dedicated tables.

Data table 1

Tenant Id	Car license	Repair	Cost
1			
2			
2			
1			
3			
2			

Metadata table 1

Tenant Id	Data
1	Best garage
2	Friendly garage
3	Honest garage

FIGURE 6.11

Shared tables.

table in different rows. One of the columns, **Tenant Id**, identifies the tenant to which this row belongs. The shared table method is clearly more space-efficient than the dedicated table method. When the application performs an operation on behalf of a tenant, it can use a view to select only those rows that belong to the tenant. Hence, the shared table method may use more computing resources than the dedicated table method. For additional security, the data for each tenant can be encrypted using a key for the tenant. An auxiliary table, called a **metadata table**, stores information about the tenants.

Sharing compute resources: Different approaches to sharing compute resources are possible for the previous two storage sharing approaches [47]. In the dedicated table method, each tenant has their own set of files. Therefore, operating system features for security can be used to ensure that one tenant cannot read the tables of another tenant. Consider the case in Linux where the application is a multi-threaded application, with each thread serving a request for some tenant. In this case, a thread can set its FSUID to the userid of the tenant that it is executing requests for. The thread would then be allowed to access only the files for which the tenant has access rights. However, in the shared table case, the cloud system clearly relies upon the application to ensure security of the data.

Customization: It is important for the cloud infrastructure to support customization of the stored data, since it is likely that different tenants may want to store different data in their tables. For example, in the automobile repair shop examples given earlier, different shops may want to store different details about the repairs carried out. Three methods for doing this are described in the following paragraphs. It is to be noted that difficulties for customization occur only in the shared table method. In the dedicated table method, each tenant has their own table, and therefore can have different schema.

Figure 6.12 illustrates the **pre-allocated columns** method [45, 46, 47]. In this method, space is reserved in the tables for **custom columns**, which can be used by tenants for defining new columns. In the figure, two custom columns, called Custom1 and Custom2, are shown. A real implementation would have more (e.g., Salesforce. com, described later, has 500). In the data table, the type of the custom columns is defined as string. The actual type is stored in the metadata table. As can be seen from the metadata table in the figure, *Best Garage,* which focuses on excellence in service, has stored the Service Rating, which is an integer, in Custom1, whereas *Friendly Garage* stores the name of the Service Manager for each service call, which is a string, in the same field. The tenant *Honest Garage* is not using this column. To actually use the field, it has to be cast to the type shown in the metadata table.

The major problem with the pre-allocated columns technique is that there could be a lot of wasted space. If the number of columns is too low, then users will feel constrained in their customizations. However, if the number is too big, there will be a lot of space wastage. The **name-value pair** method does not suffer from these deficiencies and is shown in Figure 6.13. In this method, Data Table 1 (which has the standard pre-defined columns provided by the application) has an extra column which is a pointer to a table of name-value pairs (Data Table 2 in

Data table 1

Tenant Id	Car license	Service	Cost	Custom1	Custom2
1					
2					
2					
1					
3					
2					

Metadata table 1

Tenant Id	Tenant name	Custom1 name	Custom1 type
1	Best garage	Service rating	int
2	Friendly garage	Service manager	string
3	Honest garage		

FIGURE 6.12

Pre-allocated columns.

the figure) which indicates additional custom fields for this record. In the example shown, the first data record (which belongs to tenant 1 – *Best Garage*) has a custom field, which is indicated by a pointer into Data Table 2, which is called a **pivot table** [48]. The pivot table record shows that this custom field contains the Service Rating which is of type int (name with NameID 15 in metadata table 1). In case there are additional custom fields associated with this record, there can be additional records in Data Table 2 with the same id of 275.

While the name-value pair method is space efficient, unlike the custom column method, it is necessary to re-construct the data before it is used by *joins*. In the **XML method**, the final column of the standard database is an XML document, where records of any arbitrary structure can be stored. This is somewhat similar to the pureXML storage system described in Chapter 2. This method is therefore not discussed further.

Case Study: Multi-Tenancy in Salesforce.com

Since Force.com and Salesforce.com are major platforms that implement multi-tenancy, the principles are illustrated by describing resource sharing and access control in the Force.com platform, which is the PaaS platform on which the Salesforce.com service is built. The tables used by Force.com are described first, followed by an example.

For achieving multi-tenancy in Force.com, two metadata tables are important [49, 50]. The first table, called the **Objects** table, describes the objects in the

Data table 1

Tenant Id	Car license	Service	Cost	Name-value pair rec
1				275
2				
2				
1				
3				
2				

Data table 2 (name-value pairs)

Name-value pair rec	NameID	Value
275	15	5.5

Metadata table 1

Name Id	Name	Type
15	Service rating	int
	Service manager	string

Metadata table 2

Tenant Id	Data
1	Best garage
2	Friendly garage
3	Honest garage

FIGURE 6.13

Name-value pairs.

system. Objects are similar to tables in database terminology, and the Objects table contains a GUID (globally unique id), the ObjID (object id), OrgID (the tenant who owns the object), and the object name ObjName. The second table is the **Fields** metadata table, which contains a description of the fields (similar to columns). The Fields metadata table contains the FieldID, owning OrgID, ObjID to which this field belongs, the FieldName, and type of the field, together with a Boolean value IsIndexed, which indicates whether it is necessary to index this field, and the FieldNum which indicates the field number of the field in the record, which will be described later. The **Data** table uses the pre-allocated table method to share a table among the various tenants. The data table contains a GUID, OrgID, and ObjName as the first three fields. This is followed by fields Value0, Value1, …, Value500 which store the actual data values (as described earlier for pre-allocated tables). `Value0` corresponds to `FieldNum` 0, `Value1` to `FieldNum` 1, and so on. The names of the fields and type of values can be found in the Fields table.

Figure 6.14 illustrates this design with an example. It is assumed that a tenant with `OrgID` 77 owns a table called `SalesTab`. The Objects table contains an entry for this table, which has an `ObjID` of 134. From the Fields table, it can be seen that this object has three fields — `CustomerID`, which is an integer, `CustAddr`, which is a string, and `LastSaleDt`, which is a date. `CustomerID` and `LastSaleDt` have associated indexes (which is described next). The Data table contains an entry (row) for this object in which the `CustomerID` is 93, the `CustAddr` is New Delhi, and the `LastSaleDt` is 06-Aug-2010. The `ObjID` for this row is 134 (indicating that it belongs to the `SalesTab`) and the `OrgID` is 77.

Indexes are maintained in Salesforce.com using a variant of the pivot table method described earlier in this section. It is not possible to index the Data table directly, since different rows in the same column may have different fields. For example, while `Value0` contains `CustomerID` if the row belongs to `SalesTab`, it may contain some other field with a different datatype if the row belongs to a different object. Force.com therefore uses an auxiliary table called **Indexes** for the purpose of indexing. The Indexes table contains a column for each datatype supported in Force.com; Figure 6.14 shows three of these columns — one each for strings, numerical values, and dates. Force.com creates one row for each indexed field in an object. In the example, there are two indexed fields — `CustomerID` and `LastSaleDt`. As can be seen, the Indexes table has one entry for each field; the entry for `CustomerID` is in the `NumValue` column (since `CustomerID` is an integer), and the entry for `LastSaleDt` is in the `DateValue` column. The `GUID` and `FieldNum` fields identify the record and field number, respectively. A query to find all transactions for the customer with `CustomerID` equal to 93 will translate into a query to the Indexes table to find all the rows where `ObjID=134` (indicating that the row belongs to

Data table

GUID	OrgID	ObjID	Value0	Value1	Value2	Value3
5757	77	134	93	New Delhi	06-Aug-2010	

Objects table

GUID	ObjID	OrgID	ObjName
1445	134	77	SalesTab

Fields table

FieldID	OrgID	ObjID	FileName	Datatype	IsIndexed	FieldNum
56	77	134	CustomerID	Integer	1	0
62	77	134	CustAddr	String	0	1
83	77	134	LastSaleDt	Date	1	2

Indexes

OrgID	ObjID	FieldNum	GUID	StringValue	NumValue	DateValue
77	134	0	5757		93	
77	134	2	5757			06-Aug-2010

FIGURE 6.14

Force.com multi-tenancy.

`SalesTab`) and `FieldNum=0` (indicating the row is for `CustomerID`) and `NumValue=93`. Subsequently, the `GUID`s can be used to find other fields in the same rows.

Multi-Tenancy and Security in Hadoop[2]

Hadoop is used by many enterprises and some of the installations store sensitive, business critical data in HDFS. Many of these installations are set up in a way that multiple users, possibly from different groups, share them. Authenticated access to the business critical data is therefore important in such a multi-tenant setup. Strong authentication based on Kerberos protocol was introduced in Hadoop-0.21 [51]. Kerberos [52] based authentication was chosen over public key operations (SSL) as it is faster and provides better user management. For example, to revoke access permission to a user, just deleting the user from the centrally managed Kerberos distribution center (KDC) is sufficient, unlike in SSL where a new certificate revocation certificate has to be generated and propagated to all the servers. Before getting into the security aspects of HDFS, a brief description of HDFS architecture is given.

HDFS Architecture

The Hadoop Distributed File System (HDFS) is a distributed file system optimized to store large files and provides high throughput access to data. HDFS was introduced from a usage and programming perspective in Chapter 3 and its architectural details are covered here. In HDFS, files are divided into blocks and distributed across the cluster. The blocks are replicated to handle hardware failure, and checksums are added for each block for corruption detection and recovery. Figure 6.15 gives the high-level architecture of HDFS and a brief description of the architectural components follows. From the architectural description, it can be seen that HDFS is a centralized metadata distributed file system.

NameNode: The NameNode is the central point of contact for the HDFS. It manages the file system's metadata. The metadata, at a high level, is a list of all the files in the file system, the mapping from each file to the list of blocks the file has. This metadata is persisted on disk. As in other file systems, one of the significant attributes of the metadata that is built at runtime is the mapping from the file blocks to the physical locations of the blocks. The NameNode also controls the read/write accesses to the files from clients. The NameNode keeps track of the nodes in the cluster, the disk space the nodes have, and whether any node is dead. This information is used to schedule block replications for newly created files, and also to maintain a sufficient number of replicas of existing files.

DataNodes : The DataNodes are the slaves in the HDFS cluster. When a client makes a request to create a file and write data to it, the NameNode assigns certain DataNodes to write the data to. If the replica of the file under construction is, for example, 3, a write pipeline would be set up between the three DataNodes. The blocks would be written to the first DataNode in the pipeline, and that

---

[2]Content contributed by Mr. Devaraj Das, Yahoo! Inc., United States.

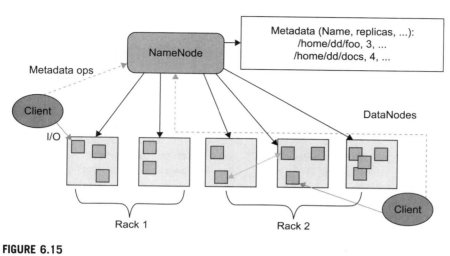

FIGURE 6.15

High-level architecture of the HDFS.

DataNode would write the blocks to the next DataNode in the pipeline, and so on until the last DataNode. A write is considered successful when all the replicas have been successfully written. This guarantees data consistency. The DataNodes also serve up blocks when clients request them to do so. They remain in touch with the NameNode, periodically send disk utilization reports, and periodically send block reports. The block reports are used by the NameNode to map the blocks of a file to its locations.

The Secondary NameNode: The edits in the file system's namespace are stored in an edits log file akin to the transaction log file traditionally seen in the database world. The secondary NameNode periodically polls the NameNode and downloads the file system image file. It also gets the edits log file, and merges the two. The new file system image file is then uploaded to the NameNode. This is done so that the file system image stays close to the in-memory representation of the filesystem in the NameNode. If the NameNode ever crashes, a new Name-Node can be brought up quickly with the image that was last successfully merged.

The HDFS Client: The client talks to the NameNode first for any file access. For file creations, the NameNode updates its metadata for the newly created file. It also chooses DataNodes that the client should write the file blocks to. For file open requests, the NameNode responds back with the set of locations that the client could read the data blocks from. If there are multiple DataNodes from where a given block could be read, the client chooses the one that is closest to it. This reduces the amount of data sent over the network.

HDFS utilizes rack-awareness and replication for high availability. In a real-world deployment, a cluster is composed of many racks. The machines within a rack are connected together on a high bandwidth network. A switch interconnects the racks. Typically, the inter-rack bandwidth is much lower, and that bandwidth is shared between many hosts, ultimately. In order to minimize the chances of data loss, the blocks are replicated on at least one off-rack machine (assuming the file has a replica count greater than one).

HDFS Security

Figure 6.16 shows the interactions for a user trying to access some file from the HDFS [53, 54]. It is standard Kerberos authentication [52] between the User and the NameNode. Briefly, the User, NameNode and DataNode are known to the KDC. First, the user requests the KDC for a ticket and the Kerberos server returns an encrypted ticket (TGT). The TGT is decrypted and presented again to the authentication service of the Kerberos server requesting for a service ticket. The returned service ticket is used to access the NameNode service. Similar interaction happens between the DataNode and the NameNode.

The DataNode typically stores lots of data blocks, and they could belong to different files owned by different users. When a request for reading a data block comes from a user, the DataNode needs to ensure that the user is authorized to read the block in question. Hadoop defines tokens for authorizing such accesses. That token is called **Block Access Token**. NameNode generates the Block Access Tokens when a client makes a request for accessing a file's blocks for reading or for writing.

Data accesses can be made from MapReduce tasks as well and those accesses need to be authenticated too. In other words, tasks need to talk to the NameNode and DataNodes. This is where there is a shift from the regular Kerberos authentication.

Delegation tokens: In a large cluster comprised of thousands of machines, at any point in time there could be tens of thousands of tasks, all trying to access the NameNode for file accesses. Multiple waves of thousands of these tasks may be trying to authenticate themselves at around the same time. The KDC could end up becoming a bottleneck in a large secure Hadoop cluster.

To avoid this problem, Hadoop defines a token for the authentication between the tasks and the NameNode. That token is called the **Delegation Token**.

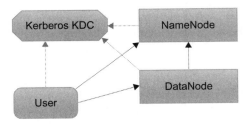

FIGURE 6.16

Secure interactions to access a file in HDFS.

The delegation token is issued by the NameNode upon a client request and has the same semantics for expiration and renewal as a TGT granted by a Kerberos KDC. Needless to say, the client authenticates itself using Kerberos to make that request.

The Delegation Token consists of a TokenIdentifier and a Password. Clients get these tokens from the NameNode, and use them to establish a secure communication channel via the *SASL-Digest* protocol.

MapReduce security

A high-level overview of the architectural components of MapReduce was explained in Chapter 3 and Figure 3.31. Now, the security issues in MapReduce are to do with authentication of users trying to talk to the JobTracker for submission of jobs, getting jobs' statuses, etc., and authentication of tasks that run as part of jobs. The other issue is about authorizing users for actions such as "kill-job", "kill-task", etc. Standard Kerberos authentication is used for the communication between the user and the JobTracker. Authorization of users for performing actions on jobs is based on *Access Control Lists* that the job submitter provides during job submissions.

During job submission, the client part of the Hadoop framework implementation makes a request for a Delegation Token (as outlined in the previous section, tasks require a Delegation Token to talk to the HDFS). The other token is the **Job Token**, and the client generates this. These tokens are sent to the JobTracker as part of the job submission request (Figure 6.17).

The TaskTrackers that run the tasks of a job make a copy of the tokens on the disk in a private location visible to only the TaskTracker user and the job owner user. The tasks read that file upon startup and load the tokens in memory. The tasks do mutual authentication with the TaskTracker using the Job Token. This is true for both the RPC and the shuffle communication paths.

Tasks run as the job owner user on the compute nodes. The TaskTracker creates a sandboxed environment for the tasks. Tasks outputs on the local disk (Map outputs, for example) are not accessible by other users.

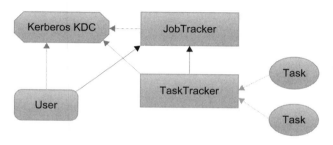

FIGURE 6.17

MapReduce security.

AVAILABILITY

Cloud services also need special techniques to reach high levels of availability. Mission-critical enterprise services generally have availability in the 99.999% range. This corresponds to a downtime of 5 minutes in an entire year! Clearly, sophisticated techniques are needed to reach such high levels of reliability. Even for non-mission critical applications, downtime implies loss of revenue. It is therefore extremely important to ensure high availability for both mission-critical as well as non-mission-critical cloud services.

There are basically two approaches to ensuring availability [55]. The first approach is to ensure high availability for the underlying application upon which the cloud service is built. This generally involves one of three techniques. **Infrastructure availability** is ensuring redundancy in infrastructure, such as servers, so that new servers are always ready to replace failed servers. Similarly, **middleware availability** deals with middleware redundancy, and **application availability** is achieved via application redundancy. The other approach, which is the focus of this section, is to build support for high availability into the cloud infrastructure.

Two types of support can be built into the cloud infrastructure for high availability. Recall that in a cloud service, for scalability, generally multiple instances of an application will be running. The first technique is **failure detection,** where the cloud infrastructure detects failed application instances, and avoids routing requests to such instances. The second technique is **application recovery,** where failed instances of application are restarted.

Failure Detection

Many cloud providers, such as Amazon Web Services' Elastic Beanstalk, detect when an application instance fails, and avoid sending new requests to the failed instance. In order to detect failures, one needs to monitor for failures.

Failure Monitoring: There are two techniques of failure monitoring [55]. The first method is **heartbeats,** where each application instance periodically sends a signal (called a heartbeat) to a monitoring service in the cloud. If the monitoring service does not receive a specified number of consecutive heartbeats, it may declare the application instance as failed. The second is the method of **probes**. Here, the monitoring service periodically sends a probe, which is a lightweight service request, to the application instance. If the instance does not respond to a specified number of probes, it may be considered failed.

There is a trade-off between speed and accuracy of detecting failures. To detect failures rapidly, it may be desirable to set a low value for the number of missed heartbeats or probes. However, this could lead to an increase in the number of false failures. An application instance may not respond due to a momentary overload or some other transient condition. Since the consequences of falsely declaring an application instance failed are severe, generally a high threshold is set for the number of missed heartbeats or probes to virtually eliminate the likelihood of falsely declaring an instance failed.

Redirection: After identifying failed instances, it is necessary to avoid routing new requests to these instances. A common mechanism used for this in HTTP-based protocols is HTTP-redirection. Here, the Web server may return a 3xx return together with a new URL to be visited. For example, if a user types "http://www.pustakportal.com/" into their browser, the request may first be sent to a load-balancing service at Pustak Portal, which may return a return code of 302 with a URL "http://pps5.pustakportal.com". Here, pp5.pustakportal.com is the address of a server that is currently known to be up, so that the user is always directed to a server that is up.

Application Recovery

In addition to directing new requests to a server that is up, it is necessary to recover old requests. An application independent method of doing this is **checkpoint/restart**. Here, the cloud infrastructure periodically saves the state of the application. If the application is determined to have failed, the most recent checkpoint can be activated, and the application can resume from that state.

Checkpoint/Restart: Checkpoint/restart can give rise to a number of complexities. First, the infrastructure should checkpoint all resources, such as system memory, otherwise the memory of the restarted application may not be consistent with the rest of the restarted application. Checkpointing storage will normally require support from the storage or file system, since any updates that were performed have to be rolled back. This could be complex in a distributed application, since updates by a failed instance could be intermingled with updates from running instances. Also, it is difficult to capture and reproduce activity on the network between distributed processes.

In a **distributed checkpoint/restart**, all processes of distributed application instances are checkpointed, and all instances are restarted from a common checkpoint if any instance fails. This has obvious scalability limitations and also suffers from correctness issues if any interprocess communication data is in-transit at the time of failure.

Ubuntu Linux, for example, has support for checkpoint /restart of distributed programs [56]. Even sequential applications can be transparently checkpointed if linked with the right libraries, using the Berkeley Lab Checkpoint/Restart Library [57]. It can also invoke application-specific code (that may send out a message to the users, or write something in a log file, etc.) during check pointing and restart. A commercial offering that uses a different approach is described next.

Librato Availability Services

Librato Availability Services is an application-independent restart mechanism [58]. Librato runs applications over an **OS Abstraction Layer,** which is interposed between the applications and the OS. This user space layer keeps track of the application state, and is responsible for periodically checkpointing the application. There is no recompilation or relinking of the application needed.

Figure 6.18 shows an abstract view of Librato services. It sits in between the application libraries and OS to virtualize OS API calls that carry state. These availability services capture periodic checkpoints for the application's state – including terminal I/O, network sockets, process state, IPC state as well as time functions. It does only an incremental checkpointing, saving time and space for checkpoint images. Upon a failure, Librato Availability Services restore the application from its last checkpoint, either on the same node or a different node. Librato checkpoints even parallel programs that use message passing interface.

Use of Web Services Model

Hadoop MapReduce framework uses a special case of checkpoint/restart where failed jobs are restarted from the beginning on some other node (the number of retries are configurable). TaskTrackers are *blacklisted*, and they are not given new tasks (unless the cluster has too few healthy TaskTrackers). If TaskTrackers fail too often to run tasks, they are deemed unhealthy by the monitoring framework.

In general, if the application is completely based on service-oriented architecture, just restarting the individual services may be sufficient to recover from the error. This method will lose any service requests that were in the process of being served. However, the service user would have got an error and hence will retry to get the service response. If the application is not built in a pure-service model, additional effort to ensure that the application state is consistent and that the service is ready to start serving the next batch of user requests is needed. Here, checkpoint/restart techniques become very necessary.

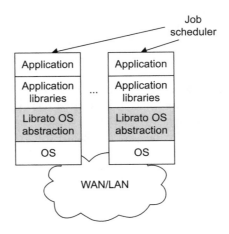

FIGURE 6.18

OS abstraction layer provided by Librato Availability Services.

An other alternative to the checkpoint/restart method is for the applications to work in a **transactional paradigm**. When an application instance fails, some signal (e.g., closing of network connections) is sent to the other instances, which abort all work in progress for the failed instance. When the failed instance restarts, it restarts all transactions in progress. Additionally, other instances restart any requests they made to the failed instance. For applications designed purely using a web services model, even subcomponents fall in this second category. Web Services Transaction Specifications [59] (WS_Coordination, WS_Atomic, WS_Transactions) define mechanisms and protocols to be used by web services in order to be interoperable and execute on any vendors web services platform.

SUMMARY

In this chapter, first, approaches to attack the cloud scalability challenge were described both for compute as well as storage systems. For compute scalability, if the application instances are independently scheduled on independent processors, then just adding more servers can scale to a large number of clients. However, it is not very common to find applications that are totally independent and have only one process. Amdahl's Law puts bounds on the amount by which an application can be scaled. For 3-tier applications, there are two ways of scaling, by either adding compute power to each of the tiers of the application or by breaking down the application components in such a way that the individual components (application nodes) are self-sufficient with adequate amounts of database and messaging bus. More sophisticated coordination among distributed processes can be supported using a specialized middleware such as ZooKeeper. Another approach that has been looked at to avoid making the database as a bottleneck is to use noSQL or key-value pairs to store the data and hence allow much more concurrency in data access.

The problems of scaling storage were also discussed. It was shown that the CAP theorem implies that in any system with network partitioning, either consistency or availability has to be given up. In many cases (e.g., where a financial balance has to be looked up) it may not be possible to give up consistency. In those cases, the system may not be available during network partitions. If it is possible to relax consistency requirements, various forms of *weak consistency* can be guaranteed. One technique that can generally be used with any partitioned storage system is asynchronous updates, where any partition that is updated propagates its changes asynchronously to other partitions. However, to guarantee correctness, it is necessary to carefully analyze the storage system and the operations being performed. Additionally, the storage system itself may provide guarantees, such as read after write consistency, which guarantees that any read made after a write will reflect the change due to the write. In these cases, the guarantees provided by the storage system can be used to ensure correctness. To illustrate these principles, the usage of three storage systems that offer weak consistency – HBase, MongoDB, and Dynamo/Cassandra – were described.

Subsequently, the problem of multi-tenancy, or fine-grained resource sharing, was considered. Multi-Tenancy is the major difference between the earlier technologies of ASPs (application service providers) and cloud SaaS systems, and the efficiencies due to multi-tenancy are a major reason for the success of SaaS systems. Multiple levels of multi-tenancy were discussed. However, it is not necessary for all components of a cloud system to be at the highest and most efficient level of multi-tenancy; it is only necessary that the most important components be at a high level of multi-tenancy. Three methods of providing multi-tenancy – pre-allocated columns, pivot tables, and XML columns – were considered. While pre-allocated columns are not space-efficient, they are easy to work with and are efficient in computation. The other two techniques, pivot tables and XML columns, are more space efficient but less easy to work with. A detailed description of multi-tenancy in Salesforce.com was presented to illustrate how these design trade-offs have been made in a production-quality deployed system.

Finally, approaches taken to ensure high availability of cloud applications were discussed. Availability can be at infrastructure level, platform level or application level. Since this is a developer-oriented book, approaches to provide application-level availability were discussed. Service-oriented applications can adhere to the web services transaction specification to work in a transaction-oriented manner, in which case, simply starting the applications from the beginning will be sufficient for correct execution. In more complex cases, sophisticated checkpoint-restart mechanisms need to be employed. Two methods of checkpoint-restart were described: first, where the applications had to be recompiled/relinked in order to achieve transparent checkpointing, and second, a commercial offering from Librato, which provided an OS abstraction for application-independent checkpointing.

Some approaches to tackle the technical challenges posed by cloud computing have been tried at the client side as well. In order to deliver good interactive applications, use of client-side scripts (Javascript) that can perform asynchronous operations to back-end services using AJAX (Asynchronous Javascript and XML) is becoming more common. Here, the application running within a browser need not necessarily refresh or submit a web page in order for the application to contact the back-end cloud service, but can be performed instead by the client-side application using a background thread. More recently, techniques used in Javascript programming are being used even at the server end to create faster services. An example of this is Node.JS technology [60] that is an open source server-side event-driven Javascript environment that can handle parallel requests very well. Due to its event-based model, all actions are non-blocking potentially enabling maximum resource utilization. Event-driven models are also very good for high availability due to the transaction semantics. Though a young project, Node.JS is a promising technology that may address some of the key technical challenges of the Cloud if the runtime is well implemented.

References

[1] Michael M, Moreira JE, Shiloach D, Wisniewski RW. Scale-up x Scale-out: A Case Study using Nutch/Lucene. IBM Thomas J. Watson Research Center, IEEE 2007.

[2] Nginx Home page. http://nginx.org/; [accessed 08.10.11].

[3] Nginx Books. http://nginx.org/en/books.html; [accessed 08.10.11].

[4] Scaling out Web Servers to Amazon EC2 using OpenNebula. https://support.opennebula.pro/entries/366704-scaling-out-web-servers-to-amazon-ec2; [accessed 08.10.11].

[5] OpenNebula HomePage. http://www.opennebula.org/; [accessed 08.10.11].

[6] Open Cloud Computing Interface. http://occi-wg.org/; [accessed 08.10.11].

[7] Tannenbaum T, Litzkow M. The Condor distributed processing system. Dr. Dobbs Journal. http://drdobbs.com/high-performance-computing/184409496; 1995 [accessed October 2011].

[8] Integrating Public Clouds with OpenNebula for Cloudbursting. https://support.opennebula.pro/entries/338165-integrating-public-clouds-with-opennebula-for-cloud-bursting; [accessed 08.10.11].

[9] Rochwerger B, Caceres J, Montero RS, Breitgand D, Elmroth E, Galis, A et al. The RESERVOIR model and architecture for open federated cloud computing. Wolfsthal IBM J Res Dev 2009;53(4):1–11.

[10] Nurmi D, Wolski R, Grzegorczyk, C, et al. The Eucalyptus Open-source Cloud-computing System. 9th IEEE/ACM International Symposium on Cluster Computing and the Grid, CCGRID 2009.

[11] Eucalyptus Open-Source Cloud Computing Infrastructure - An Overview, August 2009, A White Paper, Eucalyptus Systems, Inc.

[12] Zookeeper: A Reliable, Scalable Distributed Coordination System. http://highscalability.com/blog/2008/7/15/zookeeper-a-reliable-scalable-distributed-coordination-syste.html; [accessed 08.10.11].

[13] Deploying Zookeeper Ensemble. http://sanjivblogs.blogspot.com/2011/04/deploying-zookeeper-ensemble.html; [accessed 08.10.11].

[14] Zookeeper Wiki. https://cwiki.apache.org/confluence/display/ZOOKEEPER/Index; [accessed 08.10.11].

[15] PaxosRun. https://cwiki.apache.org/confluence/display/ZOOKEEPER/PaxosRun; [accessed 08.10.11].

[16] The Two-Phase Commit protocol. http://msdn.microsoft.com/en-us/library/cc941904(v=prot.10).aspx; [accessed 0810.11].

[17] Zookeeper Home page. http://zookeeper.apache.org/; [accessed 08.10.11].

[18] Lindsay BG. Notes on Distributed Databases, http://ip.com/IPCOM/000149869; 1979 [accessed 08.10.11].

[19] Brewer, E. A. Towards robust distributed systems (Invited Talk), Principles of Distributed Computing, Portland, Oregon. Also http://www.eecs.berkeley.edu/~brewer/cs262b-2004/PODC-keynote.pdf; 2000 [accessed 08.10.11].

[20] Lynch N, Gilbert S. Brewer's conjecture and the feasibility of consistent, available, partition-tolerant web services. ACM SIGACT News 2002;33(2):51–59.

[21] Pritchett D. BASE: An Acid Alternative. ACM Queue 2008;6(3)May/June.

[22] Vogels W. Eventually consistent. Commun ACM 2009;52(1):40–44.

[23] Abadi D. Problems with CAP, and Yahoo's little known NoSQL system. http://dbmsmusings.blogspot.com/2010/04/problems-with-cap-and-yahoos-little.html; [accessed 08.10.11].

[24] Trading Consistency for Scalability in Distributed Architectures, Floyd Marinescu & Charles Humble. http://www.infoq.com/news/2008/03/ebaybase;jsessionid=A7D8F82180 426608EE396765D73B1A5C; [accessed 08.10.11].

[25] Stonebraker M. Clarifications on the CAP Theorem and Data-Related Errors. http://voltdb.com/company/blog/clarifications-cap-theorem-and-data-related-errors; [accessed 08.10.11].

[26] Java Transaction API. http://www.oracle.com/technetwork/java/javaee/jta/index.html; [accessed 08.10.11]

[27] Comparing NoSQL Availability Models, Adrian Cockcroft. http://perfcap.blogspot.com/2010/10/comparing-nosql-availability-models.html; 2010 [accessed 08.10.11].

[28] The Apache HBase Book, Chapter 10: Architecture. http://hbase.apache.org/book.html#architecture; [accessed 08.10.11].

[29] Chang F, Dean J, Ghemawat S, Hsieh WC, Wallach DA, Burrows, M et al. Bigtable: A distributed storage system for structured data. ACM Trans Comput Syst 2008;26(2).

[30] MongoDB Replication, Dwight Merriman. http://www.slideshare.net/mongosf/mongodb-replication-dwight-merriman; [accessed 08.10.11].

[31] Replica Sets – Basics. http://www.mongodb.org/display/DOCS/Replica+Sets+-+Basics; [accessed 08.10.11].

[32] Replica Sets – Voting. http://www.mongodb.org/display/DOCS/Replica+Sets+-+Voting; [accessed 08.10.11].

[33] Replica Sets – Oplog. http://www.mongodb.org/display/DOCS/Replica+Sets+-+Oplog; [accessed 08.10.11].

[34] Why Replica Sets. http://www.mongodb.org/display/DOCS/Why+Replica+Sets; [accessed 08.10.11].

[35] Replica Set FAQ. http://www.mongodb.org/display/DOCS/Replica+Set+FAQ; [accessed 08.10.11].

[36] DeCandia G, Hastorun D, Jampani M, Kakulapati G, Lakshman A, Pilchin, A et al. Dynamo: Amazon's highly available keyvalue store. Proceedings of twenty-first ACM SIGOPS Symposium on Operating systems principles, New York, NY; 2007.

[37] NoSQL Netflix Use Case Comparison for Cassandra. http://perfcap.blogspot.com/2010/10/nosql-netflix-use-case-comparison-for.html; 2010 [accessed 08.10.11].

[38] NoSQL Netflix Use Case Comparison for MongoDB. http://perfcap.blogspot.com/2010/10/nosql-netflix-use-case-comparison-for_31.html; 2010 [accessed 08.10.11].

[39] NoSQL Netflix Use Case Comparison for Riak. http://perfcap.blogspot.com/2010/11/nosql-netflix-use-case-comparison-for.html; 2010 [accessed 08.10.11].

[40] NoSQL Netflix Use Case Comparison for Translattice. http://perfcap.blogspot.com/2010/11/nosql-netflix-use-case-comparison-for_17.html; 2010 [accessed 08.10.11].

[41] Jacobs D, Aulbach S. Marz 2007. Ruminations on Multi-Tenant Databases. 12.GI-Fachtagung fur Datenbanksysteme in Business, Technologie und Web (BTW 2007), 5 bis 9, Aachen, Germany.

[42] Chong F, Carraro G. Architecture strategies for caching the long tail. http://msdn2.microsoft.com/en-us/library/aaa479060(printer).aspx; [accessed 08.10.11].

[43] Drools - The Business Logic integration Platform. http://www.drools.org; [accessed 08.10.11].

[44] Linden TA. December 1976. Capability-based addressing.

[45] Aulbach S, Grust T, Jacobs D, Kemper A, Rittinger J, 2008. Multi-Tenant Databases for Software as a Service: Schema-Mapping Techniques. ACM SIGMOD'08, June 9–12. Vancouver, BC: Canada; 2008.

[46] Aulbach S, Jacobs D, Kemper A, Seibold M. A Comparison of Flexible Schemas for Software as a Service. ACM SIGMOD'09: Providence, Rhode Island, USA; 2009.

[47] Chong F, Carraro G, Nolter R. Multi-tenant data architecture. http://msdn.microsoft.com/en-us/library/aa479086.aspx; [accessed 08.10.11].

[48] Agrawal R, Somani A, Xu Y. Storage and Querying of E-Commerce Data. Proceedings of the 27th VLDB Conference, Roma, Italy; 2001. p. 149–158.

[49] Salesforce.com: The Force.com Multitenant Architecture. http://www.apexdevnet.com/media/ForcedotcomBookLibrary/Force.com_Multitenancy_WP_101508.pdf; [accessed 08.10.11].

[50] Weissman CD, Bobrowski S. The design of the force.com multitenant internet application development platform. ACM SIGMOD'09: Providence, Rhode Island, USA.

[51] O'Malley O, Zhang K, Radia S, Marti Ram, Harrell C, 2009. Hadoop Security Design. Yahoo! Inc. https://issues.apache.org/jira/secure/attachment/12428537/security-design.pdf; 2009 [accessed 08.10.11].

[52] Walla M. Kerberos Explained. Microsoft TechNet. http://technet.microsoft.com/en-us/library/bb742516.aspx; [accessed 08.10.11].

[53] Becherer A. Hadoop Security Design. iSec Partners, Black Hat USA 2010, Las Vegas, July 28-29. https://media.blackhat.com/bh-us-10/whitepapers/Becherer/BlackHat-USA-2010-Becherer-Andrew-Hadoop-Security-wp.pdf; [accessed 08.10.11].

[54] O'Malley O, Zhang K, Radia S, Marti R, Harrell C. Yahoo!. Hadoop Security Design. https://issues.apache.org/jira/secure/attachment/12428537/security-design.pdf; 2009 [accessed 08.10.11].

[55] Abraham S, Thomas M, Thomas J. Enhancing Web Services Availability. IEEE International Conference on e-Business Engineering (ICEBE'05).

[56] LAN SSI Checkpoint, Ubuntu manual. http://manpages.ubuntu.com/manpages/hardy/man7/lamssi_cr.7.html; [accessed 08.10.11].

[57] Berkeley Lab Checkpoint/Restart (BLCR) User's Guide. https://upc-bugs.lbl.gov/blcr/doc/html/BLCR_Users_Guide.html; [accessed 08.10.11].

[58] Librato Availability Services. http://www.hp.com/techservers/hpccn/hpccollaboration/ADCatalyst/downloads/Librato_AvS_ds.pdf; [accessed 08.10.11].

[59] Web Services Transactions Specifications, IBM, BEA Systems, Microsoft, Arjuna, Hitachi, IONA. http://www.ibm.com/developerworks/library/specification/ws-tx/; [accessed 08.10.11].

[60] NodeJS Home page. http://nodejs.org/; [accessed 08.10.11].

Designing Cloud Security

INFORMATION IN THIS CHAPTER:

- Cloud Security Requirements and Best Practices
- Risk Management
- Security Design Patterns
- Security Architecture Standards
- Legal and Regulatory Issues
- Selecting a Cloud Service Provider
- Cloud Security Evaluation Frameworks

INTRODUCTION[1]

Cloud security has unique challenges arising from the use of a shared infrastructure, and rapid movement of servers and workload in the infrastructure. If Tom Hacker has an account on a cloud service provider, the security of all the data stored in the cloud would depend upon the ability of the cloud provider to withstand the attacks from Tom Hacker. An example is the attack on Twitter [1] where a hacker broke into support tools used by Twitter support, and used the tools to compromise the accounts of many celebrities. Clearly, if the celebrities had not used a shared infrastructure, the attack would not have been successful.

The security of a cloud infrastructure depends upon both the technology as well as the processes and practices in place. For example, not writing down passwords is a strongly recommended security practice. But the most advanced security technologies are useless if system administrators do not follow this practice, and leave written passwords in easily accessible places! Some aspects of Cloud security at a technology level has been covered in the earlier chapters. For example, Chapter 2 describes how cryptographic keys are used for security in Amazon, Chapter 3 describes the security features of Azure, Chapter 4 describes how OAuth can be used to grant permission to access personal information on Facebook and Chapter 6 describes the security controls available in MapReduce. The focus of this chapter is on the non-technological aspects of security; i.e., on

---

[1]This chapter is abridged from the book "Securing the Cloud" by Vic (J.R.) Winkler.

processes and practices. The practices also include good design principles to follow when designing a cloud infrastructure (e.g., on the necessity of having a security server for monitoring).

This chapter first looks at the requirements for cloud security and the design of a secure infrastructure for a cloud. Subsequently, the topic of risk management, which consists of assessing the various threats and designing security measures to handle them, is discussed. Next, some useful design patterns that can be used to ensure cloud security are examined. An example of security design for a PaaS system using these design patterns is included. A number of standard cloud security architectures that can be leveraged for implementing cloud security are then discussed.

The next part of the chapter discusses security issues involved in public clouds, since this is an area of great interest to all skeptics as of this writing. First, legal and regulatory issues in using public clouds are discussed. This is followed by a section on the criteria that can be used for selecting a cloud service provider based on security. This is followed by procedures for evaluating cloud service provider security developed by standards bodies, which can be used to supplement the security criteria discussed earlier.

CLOUD SECURITY REQUIREMENTS AND BEST PRACTICES

The cloud consists of a shared infrastructure that can be rapidly configured on demand to meet business needs. At a high level, the cloud infrastructure can be partitioned into a **physical** infrastructure, and a **virtual** infrastructure. The security requirements and best practices can also similarly be divided into the requirements for physical security and those for virtual security.

The basic objectives of cloud security are to ensure the confidentiality, integrity and availability of the cloud system. **Confidentiality** implies that there is no unauthorized access to functions of the cloud system. **Integrity** requires that the cloud system be protected against tampering (e.g., against implanting of viruses that steal passwords or corruption of data). The **availability** requirement is that the system should not be made unavailable by, for example, a denial of service attack that puts a great deal of load on the system, preventing legitimate users from using the system. In addition, the above objectives may also be impacted by legal requirements. For example, if the system stores health-related data, certain levels of confidentiality may be legally mandated. Therefore, the cloud system should be able to support the required legal constraints.

From a pragmatic view, there are a number of additional objectives that also need to be taken into account when designing cloud security. These include:

i. Cost-effectiveness: Security implementation should not greatly increase the cost of a cloud solution.
ii. Reliability and performance: Also should not be greatly impacted by cloud security.

Physical Security

Physical security implies that the data center the cloud is hosted in should be secure against physical threats. This includes not only attempts at penetration by intruders, but also protection against natural hazards and disasters such as floods, and human error such as switching off the air conditioning. It is important to note that security is only as strong as its weakest link. An interesting example of this is provided in *Securing the Cloud* [2], which describes a public grid computing data center built in London on the site of an old brewery, which had very thick walls. However, the street entrance to the facility was faced with un-reinforced glass that could easily be broken, and an unsecured window to a restroom within the facility was within easy reach of a ladder.

To ensure physical security, a multi-layered system is required. This includes:

i. A central monitoring and control center with dedicated staff
ii. Monitoring for each possible physical threat, such as intrusion, or natural hazards such as floods
iii. Training of the staff in response to threat situations
iv. Manual or automated back-up systems to help contain threats (e.g., pumps to help contain the damage from floods)
v. Secure access to the facility. This requires that the various threats to the data center be identified, and appropriate procedures derived for handling these threats.

Virtual Security

The following best practices have been found to be very useful in ensuring cloud security.

Cloud Time Service

If all systems in the datacenter are synchronized to the same clock, this is helpful both to ensure correct operation of the systems, as well as to facilitate later analysis of system logs. It is particularly important in correlating events occurring across geographically distributed systems. A common way to do this is by use of the **Network Time Protocol** (**NTP**). NTP is a protocol that synchronizes the clock on a computer to a reference source on the Internet [1]. To protect against false reference sources, the protocol messages can be encrypted. Due to the importance of having a common timeline, there should be at least two paths to reliable time sources (such as WWV and GPS), and the time sources should be verifiable.

Identity Management

Identity management is a foundation for achieving confidentiality, integrity and availability. Some of the requirements for identity management are that:

i. It should scale to the number of users typically found in a cloud system
ii. Due to possible heterogeneity in cloud systems, a federated identity management system that allows establishing a single identity and single sign-on across multiple different types of systems may be needed.

iii. The identity management system should satisfy applicable legal and policy requirements (for example, allow deleting of users across the system within a specified time period)

iv. Maintain historical records for possible future investigation.

Access Management

The core function of access management is to allow accesses to cloud facilities only to authorized users. However, additional requirements are to:

i. Not allow unrestricted access to cloud management personnel

ii. Allow implementation of multi-factor authentication (e.g., use of a password together with a digital key) for very sensitive operations.

It is also good practice to:

i. Disallow shared accounts, such as admin

ii. Implement white-listing of IP addresses for remote administrative actions.

Break-Glass Procedures

It is desirable for the access management system to allow alarmed **break-glass procedures**, which bypass normal security controls in emergency situations. The analogy is with breaking the glass to set off a fire alarm. Clearly, it is important to ensure that the break-glass procedure can be executed only in emergencies under controlled situations, and that the procedure triggers an alarm.

Key Management

In a cloud, with shared storage, encryption is a key technology to ensure isolation of access. The cloud infrastructure needs to provide secure facilities for the generation, assignment, revocation, and archiving of keys. It is also necessary to generate procedures for recovering from compromised keys.

Auditing

Auditing is needed for all system and network components. The audit should capture all security-related events, together with data needed to analyze the event such as the time, system on which the event occurred, and userid that initiated the event. The audit log should be centrally maintained and secure. It should be possible to **sanitize** or produce a stripped-down version of the audit log for sharing with cloud customers, in case their assistance is needed to analyze the logs.

Security Monitoring

This includes an infrastructure to generate alerts when a critical security event has occurred, including a cloud-wide intrusion and anomaly detection system. The intrusion detection systems may be installed both on the network as well as the host nodes. It may also be necessary to allow cloud users to implement their own intrusion and anomaly detection systems.

Security Testing

It is important to test all software for security before deployment in an isolated test bed. Patches to software should also be tested in this environment before being released into production. Additionally, security testing should be carried out on an ongoing basis to identify vulnerabilities in the cloud system. Depending upon the risk assessment, some of these tests may be carried out by third parties. There should also be a remediation process to fix identified vulnerabilities.

RISK MANAGEMENT

Risk management is the process for evaluating risks, deciding how they are to be controlled, and monitoring their operation. Since risk management is important in identifying the important security threats to the system, it is discussed before describing how to implement security for a cloud.

When managing risk, a number of factors need to be kept in mind. First, the suitable approaches in different domains (e.g., finance and healthcare) may be different. As a result, the appropriate security measures may also vary significantly. Second, in attempting to provide the best security, it is not effective to implement every possible security measure, as this could result in making the system very difficult to use. Rather, there should be a careful trade-off between the impact of the risks involved, and the cost of the security measure, measured both in terms of impact to usage of the system as well as the actual cost of security. For a system which is already secure to a great extent, increasing security measures produces increasingly lower returns. Therefore, risk management is a business decision that balances the benefits of increased security against the cost.

Risk Management Concepts

The following is an overview of some of the important concepts used in risk management. Central to the risk management process is the idea of deploying security controls in information systems depending upon the security requirement of the system. A **security control** is a safeguard (process or system function) to prevent, detect or respond to a security risk. NIST divides security controls into three broad categories – **Technical, Operational,** and **Management** [3]. The controls in each category are further sub-divided into 18 families. As an example, **Audit and Accountability** is one of the families, and **Response to Audit Processing Failures** (which, as the name implies, is how the appropriate organization will respond to an audit processing failure) is one of the security controls in this family.

The other key concept is the security requirement of the system, defined in the FIPS 200 standard [4]. FIPS 200 defines the security requirement of the system as **low-impact, moderate impact,** or **high-impact** depending upon the impact of a security breach in the system. The motivation behind this definition is that high-impact systems have the greatest requirement in terms of security controls.

A system is defined to be a **low-impact system** if the result of a security breach is that there is a limited degradation in capability, but the system is able to perform its primary functions. **Moderate impact systems** are those where the system is able to perform its primary functions, but there is a significant degradation in the functions; while **high impact systems** are those where the system is incapable of performing some of its primary functions. More details regarding both security controls and security requirements can be found in *Securing the Cloud* [2].

Risk Management Process

The following is a risk management process detailed in the chapter titled "Cloud Security Architecture Standards" in the book *Securing the Cloud* [2]. This process is based upon work in NIST 800-53 [3] and the ISO 27000 standards.

1. **Information Resource Categorization:** The first step is to evaluate each information resource in the organization from the perspectives of:
   a. Criticality – the impact to the business of a security failure
   b. Sensitivity – the confidentiality of the resource
   This evaluation will determine the level of security to be provided for each resource. Consider a cloud infrastructure where there is a separate management network for managing the cloud, and a user network for the use of the cloud applications and users. In this scenario, the management network is more critical than the user network accessed by users, since a successful attack on the management network would allow an intruder to take over the entire cloud infrastructure.
2. **Select Security Controls:** Next, security controls appropriate to the criticality and sensitivity of the information resources need to be selected. In the example given earlier, the management network may be protected by whitelisting IP addresses (i.e., allowing only machines with certain pre-registered IP addresses to be on the management network; these IP addresses will generally be for machines physically inside the work premises). Here, whitelisting IP addresses is a security control, and forces administrators to work only from within office premises, which may be an acceptable security measure. This control may not be appropriate for the user network. If the user network is also protected by whitelisting IP addresses, the user would have to register a new IP address for whitelisting each time they go to a new location and try to access the corporate network.
3. **Risk Assessment:** After deciding upon the security controls to be implemented, it is necessary to determine if the controls provide adequate protection against the anticipated threats, and to augment the controls if more protection is needed.
4. **Implement Security Controls:** Next, the security controls decided upon would need to be implemented. These security controls may be administrative, technical or physical. The example presented earlier is an example of a technical security control.

5. **Operational Monitoring:** Once the security controls are implemented, their effectiveness in operation should be continuously monitored.
6. **Periodic Review:** The security controls in place should be periodically reviewed to determine if they continue to be effective. The need for review comes from the fact that:
   a. New threats may appear
   b. Operational changes (e.g., new software) may result in requiring a change in security design.

SECURITY DESIGN PATTERNS

After the discussion of cloud security requirements, and the discussion of risk management, the following are several design patterns that can be leveraged for constructing a secure cloud. A design pattern is a class or category of designs that can be customized to fit a particular situation.

Defense in Depth

This is a well-known design principle that has been in use for many years, for example, in the design of castles and fortresses. It states that defenses should be layered, so that an attacker has to overcome multiple defenses before gaining access to important resources. Medieval castles, for example, were typically guarded by a moat in addition to a drawbridge. After crossing the drawbridge, the entrance to the castle would be through a narrow entrance guarded by a heavy gate. In a similar way, remote administrative access to a cloud system could be allowed only through a VPN. For further protection, this access could be allowed only from white-listed IP addresses. Furthermore, an administrator may be required to provide a one-time password for additional security.

Honeypots

A **honeypot** is a decoy computer system that appears attractive to an attacker. While the attacker is attacking the honeypot under the impression that it is a worthwhile system to control, they can be observed by security personnel who can then attempt to trap and control the attack. Honeypots are widely used in network security. In the cloud context, a honeypot virtual machine can be deployed, which would monitor any suspicious attempt to break into the virtual machine. Honeypots can be deployed both by the cloud service provider as well as cloud customers.

Sandboxes

Sandboxing refers to a technique in which software is executed in a restricted environment inside the operating system in which it is running. Since the software is being executed in a restricted environment, an attacker who breaks into the software does not have unrestricted access to the facilities provided by the operating system. This limits the amount of damage an attacker who has gained control of the software can do; additionally, the attacker has to overcome the sandbox if they have to gain full control over the operating system. Sandboxes thus provide defense in depth as well. As described in Chapter 3, many PaaS systems come with a runtime environment the core of which is an application sandbox, such as in Azure and Google App Engine.

Network Patterns

In addition to ensuring isolation in the computing elements and storage, it is also necessary to ensure isolation in the network.

VM Isolation

New techniques have to be used to isolate traffic between VMs that share the same physical hardware, since this traffic does not enter the switching network. The solution in this case depends upon the security features offered by the VM, and could include:

i. Encryption of traffic between VMs
ii. Tightened security controls on VMs, such as the ports that will accept traffic.

Subnet Isolation

It is good practice to have physically separate traffic for administrative network traffic, customer network elements, and storage networks. Physically separate networks are preferred due to the possibility of mis-configuration in virtual LANs (VLAN) that are not physically separate. However, this is likely to drive up costs, so a trade-off may be needed. Routing between the networks can be handled by firewalls.

Common Management Database

A **Common Management Database (CMDB)** is a database that contains information regarding the components of an IT system. The information includes an inventory of the components, as well as their present configuration and status. The presence of a CMDB simplifies implementation and management of an infrastructure, including security, since it ensures that all administrative components have a single consistent view of all the components. A CMDB is even more essential in a cloud infrastructure, due to the extreme dynamism of cloud computing, where applications may migrate from one server to another, and the actual physical resources used by an application may change very rapidly.

Example: Security Design for a PaaS System

The following is an example of the security design for a PaaS system consisting of a DBMS and an Identity Management server (see Figure 7.1). The scenario

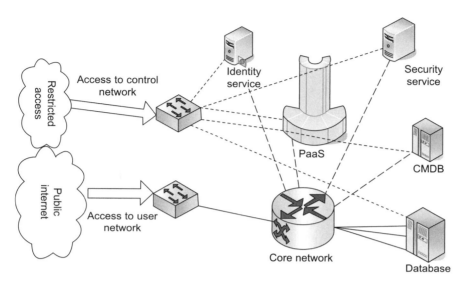

FIGURE 7.1

PaaS security design.

being considered is that of a cloud service provider who wants to expose a DBMS via the cloud as a PaaS (and DaaS) offering. The design satisfies the cloud security requirements discussed earlier, and leverages the design patterns presented.

External Network Access

Figure 7.1 shows that there are two entry points into the cloud network. The first is the access to the control network for administration. The second is the interface used for public access to the cloud services. For the purposes of security, these two access points are distinct, and lead to separate physical networks. To provide defense in depth, the control network access can be limited to whitelisted IP addresses (as described earlier, these are pre-registered addresses that are generally from the subnet reserved for machines on the office premises). Multi-factor authentication can be made mandatory for increasing secure access to administrative functions. The access to the public network is via two switches, to increase availability via redundancy.

Internal Network Access

As seen in Figure 7.1, the management network is physically separated from the public (or user) network, in order to reduce the risk of an attacker accessing the cloud via the public network and attempting to access the management network. The DBMS is connected to the public network via an aggregated set of links to provide increased bandwidth as well as availability. The DBMS server may be accessed from the internal PaaS service as well. Similarly, the PaaS service may also be accessed from both the internal network as well as the external network. However, the security server, which performs audit and other security functions, need not be accessible from the external network.

Server Security

Since the example system is a PaaS system, the database server is managed by the cloud provider, and the database is offered as a service to the customers. Access to the cloud services can be managed via the identity server shown together with access control. Hence, the security of the database is managed by the cloud service provider. Database isolation can be obtained by using some of the approaches to multi-tenancy described in Chapter 6, *Addressing the Cloud Challenges*. The database itself can be secured by disallowing access to unneeded ports in the server, and by implementing an intrusion detection system on the server hosting the database. An additional security layer can be implemented by checking the ODBC connections to the database.

Security Server

The diagram also includes a security server to perform security services, including auditing, monitoring, hosting a security operations center, and security scanning of the cloud infrastructure.

SECURITY ARCHITECTURE STANDARDS

As stated previously, to secure a cloud it is necessary to systematically build security into processes and components of a cloud. The following are a variety of standard and well-known security architectures for cloud computing that can be leveraged for this purpose. For greater detail, please see *Securing the Cloud* [2].

SSE-CMM

The **System Security Engineering Capability Maturity Model** is an adaption of the well-known **Capability Maturity Model** (**CMM**) for software engineering by Carnegie Mellon University [5]. It is the basis of the **ISO/IEC 21827** standard. Similarly to CMM, it defines five capability levels for any organization, and allows organizations to assess themselves, and put in place processes to improve their levels. The SSE-CMM model is not specific to cloud security.

ISO/IEC 27001-27006

This is a set of related standards under the ISO/IEC 27000 family that provides an Information Security Management System. It is fundamentally different from SSE-CMM, which is a maturity model. While SSE-CMM allows each organization to evaluate how secure their processes are, it does not specify what that process is.

In contrast, the ISO/IEC 27000 family of standards specifies a set of requirements that organizations must satisfy (e.g., there should be a process to systematically evaluate information security risks). The ISO/IEC 27000 family of standards is not specific to cloud security.

European Network and Information Security Agency (ENISA)

The **Cloud Computing Information Assurance Framework** from ENISA is a set of assurance criteria designed to assess the risk of adopting cloud services, compare different Cloud Provider offers, obtain assurance from the selected cloud providers, and reduce the assurance burden on cloud providers [6]. It is based upon applying ISO/IEC 27001-27006 to cloud computing. There is a larger number of assurance criteria defined under the report *Cloud Computing Benefits, Risks, and Recommendations for Information Security* [7] which, in addition to assurance criteria, offers an assessment of the benefits and risks of cloud computing.

ITIL Security Management

ITIL (the **Information Technology Infrastructure Library**) is a well-known and comprehensive set of standards for IT service management. It was originally a set of recommendations developed by the U.K. government's Central Computer and Telecommunications Agency. The section on security management is based upon ISO/IEC 27002. An advantage of using ITIL Security Management is that ITIL itself is very common in many data centers, hence the use of ITIL-SM will have a smaller learning curve and result in an integrated security solution.

COBIT

ISACA,[2] an international organization devoted to the development of IT governance standards [8], has developed the *Control Objectives for Information and Related Technology* [9]. This is a set of processes and best practices for linking business goals to IT goals, together with metrics and a maturity model. COBIT is broader in scope than ISO/IEC 27000, since it relates to IT governance.

NIST

The US National Institute of Standards and Technology has a number of whitepapers and other resources in its Security Management & Assurance working group [10]. These are targeted at U.S. federal agencies; however, many of the recommendations will apply to other organizations as well. The reader may recall that NIST has been very heavily referenced in this book starting from Chapter 1.

---

[2]The original expansion of the acronym ISACA is no longer used, and ISACA is simply known by its acronym.

LEGAL AND REGULATORY ISSUES

Cloud computing may involve additional legal and regulatory issues due to the possible involvement of a third party – the cloud service provider. It is important to note that the law may not apply in the same way to a cloud service provider as it does to an enterprise. For example, considering health data collected by a business to which HIPAA is applicable, the business that collects the data is responsible for ensuring that HIPAA is followed even if part of the business' IT infrastructure is in the cloud of a private cloud provider. Therefore, it is important to understand how the laws apply to different parties under various scenarios. Of particular importance are laws around any data that may be collected. Since local, national, and international laws may apply (due to the geographical distribution of the cloud infrastructure) it is important to consider the impact of these laws as well in detail.

NOTE

Legal Issues
- Covering third-party risks
- Data-handling issues
- Litigation-related issues

COBIT and Safe Harbor are examples of laws that apply if the enterprise has operations in the USA, Canada or the EU. These laws apply to the storage and transfer of data, as well as its protection. Other applicable laws, such as the Health Insurance Portability and Accountability Act (HIPAA), apply mainly in specific domains such as the health care industry. However, since enterprises sometimes store employee health information, some of the enterprise data may be subject to HIPAA even though the enterprise itself may not be in the health care industry.

The laws and regulations will typically specify who is responsible for the accuracy and security of the data. HIPAA requires that there be a particular official who is responsible for ensuring compliance. The Sarbanes-Oxley act, on the other hand, jointly designates the CFO and CEO of the enterprise. Failure to comply with the appropriate laws could, of course, lead to the imposition of penalties and fines by regulatory bodies, as well as prosecution of officials held responsible for complying with the laws. Legal penalties can be substantial in themselves, particularly for small and medium business. For example, the Payment Card Industry Security Standards Council can impose fines up to $100,000 per month.

The rest of this section examines typical issues that arise from the applications of these laws. The focus is on US and EU laws, but laws in other countries are frequently similar. First, covering the risks arising from the presence of a third party (the cloud service provider) is considered. The second set of issues arises from the need for ensuring data security. The third set of issues deals with the obligation of the cloud service provider during litigation. These are described in more detail in *Securing the Cloud* [2].

Third-party Issues

Third-party issues arise when obtaining service from a public cloud service provider. Legally, it is an enterprise's responsibility to ensure that all subcontractors obey the appropriate laws; i.e., if a subcontractor is found to be guilty of violating a law such as HIPAA, the enterprise cannot plead ignorance. The primary method for ensuring this is the contract with the subcontractor and its implementation. The contract with the subcontractor must specify that the subcontractor will comply with all applicable laws, and that these obligations will be imposed on subsequent subcontractors (i.e., if the subcontractor, in turn, subcontracts parts of their contract to another party). However, mere signing of a contract is not sufficient; adequate monitoring of the implementation is also needed. These are considered in more detail below, in the order in which they would arise.

NOTE

Third-party Issues

- Due diligence
- Contract negotiation
- Implementation
- Termination

Contractual Issues

Due diligence

The enterprise should define the scope of the cloud services needed (e.g., would it include any health-related data to which HIPAA is applicable), and then specify the regulations and compliance standards that need to be adhered to (HIPAA if any health-related data is to be stored in the cloud). The process of due diligence may rule out a cloud service provider (because they are not able to satisfy the applicable laws) or limit the scope of the cloud service that can be utilized (because no cloud service provider is able to provide the appropriate level of security and control).

While the focus in this section is on due diligence to handle legal risks arising out of the presence of a third party, it should be clear that the due diligence process should also consider risks arising from the stability and reliability of the cloud service provider (e.g., are they likely to exit the cloud service market) and the criticality of the business function being outsourced. More details can be found in *Securing the Cloud* [2].

Contract negotiation

The next phase after the due diligence process is to negotiate a contract with the cloud service provider. Unlike traditional outsourcing contracts, it is possible that cloud service providers may have a standard online click-through agreement that is not customizable. This is at least partly due to the economics of cloud computing, which favor standardization. In many cases, where the risk is low, a standardized agreement may be acceptable.

One way cloud service providers can avoid having to negotiate custom agreements with each customer is through external accreditation. For example, the American Institute of Certified Public Accountants [11] provides a certification known as the **Statement on Auditing Standards** or **SAS 70** for service organizations. This certifies that the service organization has been audited by an external auditor and that the organization follows adequate controls and safeguards when handling data from multiple customers. Therefore businesses can examine the security certifications obtained by the cloud service provider in order to determine compliance with applicable laws.

Implementation

Next, the enterprise has to ensure that the safeguards laid out in the contract are actually being followed. For example, if sensitive data is to be handled differently, then it is important to check that the appropriate procedure is actually followed. Additionally, it is important to continuously re-evaluate the system to check for changed circumstances (e.g., the sensitivity of the data being outsourced has increased, or an external accreditation has been revoked).

Termination

Contract terminations (normal or otherwise) are the times when compliance is most at risk, since the service provider may be reluctant to take adequate security precautions. Therefore, it is important to identify an alternative service provider and ensure timely and secure transfer of the services. Needless to say, it is also extremely important to ensure that sensitive data is deleted from the original service provider's system.

Data Handling

In addition to the general problem of ensuring that cloud service providers comply with appropriate regulations, there are a number of concerns that specifically center around their handling of data.

Data Privacy

Organizations have to protect the privacy of the data that they have collected, and use the collected data only for the purpose for which it was collected. Organizational data cannot generally be sold to third parties. These restrictions have to be followed by subcontractors, including cloud service providers.

Privacy laws often state that individuals can access their own data and modify or delete it. It is necessary to ensure that a cloud service provider makes the same facilities available in a timely manner.

> **NOTE**
>
> **Handling Issues**
>
> - Data privacy
> - Data location
> - Secondary use of data
> - Disaster recovery
> - Security breaches

Data Location

Laws on the handling of data differ from country to country. Therefore, transferring confidential data between countries may be problematic. In a cloud context, the location of the data centers and backups needs to be known in advance, to ensure that legal problems do not arise. This is one of the reasons that Amazon allows specification of a region for its storage services[3] that governs the location of the data center where the data is to be stored. Note that data location considerations may arise in private clouds as well.

As an example of the diversity in laws, consider the following: European Union (EU) member countries have extremely complex data protection laws with very stringent requirements. For example, EU countries require that in order to transfer data outside the EU, enterprises must inform individuals that their data will be transferred to a country outside the EU, and also obtain a clearance from the Data Protection Authority. The difficulty in obtaining the clearance depends upon the country; for example, under a reciprocal agreement between the EU and the USA, a US cloud service provider only has to self-certify by registering with the U.S. Department of Commerce. In contrast, certain countries such as China have laws that allow local governments unlimited access to data, and encryption of data is prohibited unless local governments can decrypt it when they require.

The large difference between laws in different countries implies that if data is stored in multiple countries, then the enterprise has to abide by the most stringent set of data storage laws. Consider the case of a company that maintains two replicas of its internal data, one in the US and one in the EU, it is likely that the company would have to abide by EU laws, since these laws apply to the replica.

Secondary Use of Data

In addition to disallowing unauthorized access to data, enterprises need to ensure that cloud service providers do not use the data for data mining or other secondary usage. To ensure this, it is necessary to carefully read the service agreements exhibited by cloud service providers before clicking on the *I Agree* button. Unfortunately, it is rare for users to carefully read the agreements, as shown by the case of the online gaming store GameStation [2]. On April 1st, GameStation changed

---

[3]More details about regions are specified in Chapter 2, *Infrastructure as a Service*.

its service agreement to state that it owned the souls of its users. It is reported that only 12% of the users even noticed the change.

Business Continuity Planning and Disaster Recovery

Most organizations would have implemented **Business Continuity Planning (BCP)** to ensure continued operation in the face of any catastrophic and unforeseen disaster, such as a terrorist attack or earthquake. BCP typically involves identifying the possible catastrophes, carrying out **Business Impact Analysis,** and using the results of the analysis to formulate a recovery plan. **Disaster Recovery (DR)** is the part of the BCP that involves the recovery of IT operations. Since IT operations have become increasingly critical, DR is a very important part of a BCP.

When using a public cloud provider, it is important that the BCP and DR be expanded to include catastrophes that impact the public cloud provider. In the case of a natural disaster or other calamity, a cloud service provider's datacenters may become unavailable. Examples of these include:

i. an explosion that took place in 2008 in "The Plant" datacenter in Houston that took nearly 9,000 people offline.
ii. Google's "rolling blackout" in February 2009, caused by a software upgrade error, which resulted in the loss of mail service to many customers.

In this eventuality, it is necessary that there be a well-thought out disaster recovery plan. The disaster recovery plan should be formulated before deploying applications to the cloud, and implemented during deployment (e.g., by performing regular backups of data). Additionally, the cloud service provider's DR plans should be studied. It is important to use features that the cloud service provider may provide for DR, such as the use of multiple data locations.

Security Breaches

In the eventuality of a security breach, it is necessary to be informed of the breach as quickly as possible so that corrective action can be taken. For example, in the United States, there are laws that require individuals to be notified if their data is stolen. It is therefore necessary to understand the cloud service provider's disclosure policy, and understand how quickly they would notify their customers. To avoid ambiguity, the service agreement should specify the actions to be taken during a breach.

In some cases, a business may discover the security breach before their cloud service provider. In this case, the business should notify the cloud service provider, since the breach may have affected other customers of the cloud service provider as well. Here also, the contract should specify the obligations of the business that discovers the security breach, in order to avoid possible ambiguity about the responsibilities of the business and the cloud service provider.

Litigation Related Issues

Another set of issues arise from the obligations of the cloud service provider during litigation. The litigation may involve either the business that is using the cloud or the cloud service provider itself. If the business is involved in litigation, and is asked to make available certain data as part of the court proceedings, it is important to know if the cloud service provider can satisfactorily respond to the request. This is important since the courts will hold the business, and not the cloud service provider, responsible for responding to the request.

It is also possible that the cloud service provider may be asked directly to provide some data as part of litigation involving the business. In this case, it is important that the cloud service provider notify the business in a timely manner, to allow the business to contest the request if needed.

SELECTING A CLOUD SERVICE PROVIDER

Security is one of the major concerns for people who are going to select a public cloud service provider. The following are criteria for evaluating the security of a cloud service provider. There are two steps to this process – the first step is to enumerate the risks present. The next step is to evaluate how well the cloud service handles the risk. These steps are as below.

Before describing the steps, it is to be noted that in practice, the evaluation is not as straightforward as it may seem. The economics of cloud computing do not allow cloud service providers to engage in detailed negotiation with customers. Frequently, it may be necessary to rely on published material to evaluate the level of security provided. Information about security may be available in the standard contract, which could be evaluated by a security expert to provide information on the strength of the security infrastructure. However, it is possible that the published material is inaccurate or out of date. One method out of this impasse is for the cloud service provider to be certified by a third party in accordance with some security standard. However, this has not yet become a common practice.

Heroku (http://heroku.com) is an exception to the generalization that it is difficult, if not impossible to assess the security infrastructure of a cloud service provider. The architecture of Heroku (including the security architecture) is described very clearly making heavy use of graphics.

Listing the Risks

A checklist of potential risks (derived from work by ENISA) is presented in Chapter 8 of the book titled *Securing the Cloud* [2]. This table can be used as a starting point for deriving the potential risks in the cloud system. An excerpt from the table is given in Table 7.1.

The first three columns in Table 7.1 list the risk, and its probability of occurrence and impact, respectively. The column labeled **Affected Assets** lists the assets that could be compromised if the risk in column 1 occurs. The last column lists the factors that could cause the risk. The first risk listed, **Subpoena and e-discovery**, is a legal risk. The second risk, **Multi-tenancy**, is partly a technical

Table 7.1 List of Risks for Cloud Systems

Risk	Probability	Impact	Affected Assets	Factors
Subpoena and e-discovery	High	Medium	Reputation and customer trust; personal and sensitive data; service delivery.	Lack of resource isolation; data stored in multiple jurisdictions; lack of transparency.
Multi-Tenancy	Low	High	Reputation; data exposure; service delivery; IP address blacklisting.	Isolation failure (technology or procedural); indirect: other tenant fails in their security responsibility in which unfairly taints reputation of CSP and by transference other tenants; multi-tenancy complicates intervention and remediation.
CSP outsourcing	Low	Medium	Reputation and customer trust; personal and sensitive data; service delivery.	Hidden dependencies on 3rd party services; lack of transparency.

risk, since one of the factors listed – isolation failure – could be technical. The final risk listed, **CSP outsourcing**, is a business risk.

Security Criteria for Selecting a Cloud Service Provider

The criteria for selecting a cloud service provider can be based on multiple aspects, namely security processes, system management, and technology.

Security Processes

The cloud service provider should have a comprehensive set of security policies that cover all aspects of security. It is also desirable that the security staff not report to the same person as the operational staff to ensure independence of operation. However, there should be close co-operation between the two groups, similar to the functioning of testing groups and development groups in software organizations. There should be a practice of conducting periodic vulnerability scans to identify weak spots in the cloud infrastructure. There should be a comprehensive set of logs which are retained long enough to meet regulatory requirements. In case of a security incident, there should be quick response and transparent reporting to the customers. There should be a Security Operations Center that continually monitors security parameters and that can serve as a central control point during security incidents.

System Management

System management is important since if secure system management processes are not in place, it is easy for an attacker to use the management infrastructure in order to gain control of key systems. The following are some key components of secure system management processes. First, there should be a formal change management procedure with documentation and approval for changes to the infrastructure. There should be an upgrade and patch management process that ensures that security patches are applied in a timely manner to reduce the window of opportunity for any known vulnerabilities in the system to be exploited. Data should be periodically backed up to ensure business continuity. The provider should have strong Service Level Agreements (SLAs) in place and have processes to back these up.

Technology

The cloud service provider should have invested in system components that provide state of the art security. These include hardened routers (since routers are exposed to the external Internet), firewalls, security monitoring systems, including host and network intrusion detection systems. Implementation of multi-tenancy is an extremely important topic. A good example is the description by Ristenpart et al. [12] on how a group of security researchers were able to circumvent the restrictions imposed by virtualization in Amazon EC2, allowing the researchers' virtual machine to gather information about other virtual machines on the same physical server.

CLOUD SECURITY EVALUATION FRAMEWORKS

The previous section considered criteria for selecting a cloud service provider. However, various industry organizations have developed standard frameworks for evaluating the security of a cloud. This section describes some of these already existing frameworks that can be used for evaluating cloud security. More details can be found in *Securing the Cloud* [2].

Cloud Security Alliance

The **Cloud Security Alliance (CSA)** has a number of frameworks that are useful for evaluating various aspects of cloud security. A few are described next.

1. The **Cloud Controls Matrix (CCM)** assists cloud customers in assessing the overall risk of a cloud provider [13].

2. The **Consensus Assessments Initiative Questionnaire** documents security controls that exist in cloud (IaaS, SaaS, PaaS) systems, with the objective of providing security control transparency.
3. The **Security Guidance for Critical Areas of Focus in Cloud Computing** whitepaper provides security guidance for a number of key areas in cloud computing, including architecture and governance.
4. **Domain 12: Guidance for Identity and Access Management** published in April 2010 is an analysis of identity management for the cloud.
5. The objectives of **CloudAudit** are to provide the means to measure and compare the security of cloud services. The method used to accomplish this is to define a standard set of APIs for measuring the performance and security that are to be implemented by all cloud service providers.

European Network and Information Security Agency (ENISA)

The European Network and Information Security Agency (ENISA) has a number of efforts for cloud security, notably *Cloud Computing Information Assurance Framework* [6] and *Cloud Computing Benefits, Risks and Recommendations for Information Security* [3]. These have been discussed in detail earlier in this chapter in the *Security Architecture Standards* section.

Trusted Computing Group

The **Trusted Multi-Tenant Infrastructure Workgroup** of the TCG is intending to develop a security framework for cloud computing. The focus of this workgroup is end-to-end cloud security. The approach taken by this group is to leverage existing standards and integrate them to define an end-to-end security framework. This framework can then be used as a basis for compliance and auditing.

SUMMARY

This chapter has focused on processes and practices to be followed in order to ensure a robust security architecture. First, the requirements for the cloud security infrastructure were considered. This can be divided into two parts – ensuring the security of the physical infrastructure, and best practices for security processes and technology. Subsequently, the concept of risk management was described. Risk management is the process of evaluating the possible security threats to the system, identifying the major risks, and putting in place security controls to handle them. The FIPS 200 standard for identifying the impact of a risk and the NIST 80053 standard for security controls were described. Subsequently, security design patterns and principles (e.g., that more security-critical parts of the cloud infrastructure should have greater security protection) that should be followed to design the security infrastructure for a cloud were described. A high-level security design for a PaaS system based upon these design patterns was discussed next. The PaaS security design illustrates how the design patterns discussed earlier can be put into practice. Finally, various security architectures which can be leveraged to implement cloud security were discussed (e.g., ITIL-SM, which is the Security Management section of the well known ITIL IT service management standard.

The second part of the chapter focused on security concerns arising out of the use of public clouds. First, legal and regulatory issues were considered. The first set of issues arises from the fact that, legally, a cloud service provider is a subcontractor, and it is the responsibility of the business to ensure that they are in compliance with all legal and regulatory issues. Then, issues arising out of the fact that a cloud service provider is a "third party" in any litigation were discussed. In a cloud (public or private), there can also be legal issues arising from the geographic location in which data is stored, since the data is then subject to the jurisdiction of that country. A checklist for evaluating the security of a cloud service provider was described. Finally, a high-level review of methods for evaluating the level of security of a cloud service that are being evolved by various standards bodies was described.

References

[1] Raphael J. R. Twitter Hack: How It Happened and What's Being, PC World, http://www.pcworld.com/article/156359/twitter_hack_how_it_happened_and_whats_being_done.html; 2009 [accessed 13.10.11].

[2] Winkler JR. Securing the Cloud, Syngress, 29 April 2011, ISBN 978-1597495929.

[3] NIST Special Publication 800-53 Revision 3. Recommended Security Controls for Federal Information Systems and Organizations, http://csrc.nist.gov/publications/nistpubs/800-53-Rev3/sp800-53-rev3-final.pdf; 2009 [accessed 08.10.11].

[4] Minimum Security Requirements for Federal Information and Information Systems. http://csrc.nist.gov/publications/PubsFIPS.html [accessed 13.10.11]

[5] System Security Engineering Capability Maturity Model. http://www.sse-cmm.org/index.html [accessed 13.10.11].

[6] Cloud Computing Information Assurance Framework. http://www.enisa.europa.eu/act/rm/files/deliverables/cloud-computing-information-assurance-framework [accessed 13.10.11]

[7] Cloud Computing Benefits, Risks and Recommendations for Information Security. http://www.enisa.europa.eu/act/rm/files/deliverables/cloud-computing-risk-assessment/at_download/fullReport [accessed 13.10.11].

[8] ISACA. http://www.isaca.org/About-ISACA/History/Pages/default.aspx [accessed 13.10.11].

[9] COBIT Framework for IT Governance and Control. http://www.isaca.org/Knowledge-Center/COBIT/Pages/Overview.aspx?utm_source=homepage [accessed 13.10.11].

[10] Computer Security Division Security Resource Center. http://csrc.nist.gov/groups/SMA/index.html [accessed 13.10.11].

[11] American Institute of Certified Public Accountants. http://www.aicpa.org [accessed 13.10.11].

[12] Ristenpart T, et al. Hey, You, Get Off My Cloud: Exploring Information Leakage in Third-Party Compute Clouds. In: Proceedings of the 16th ACM Conference on Computer and Communications Security, New York, NY; 2009. Also http://citeseerx.ist.psu.edu/viewdoc/download?doi=10.1.1.150.681&rep=rep1&type=pdf; [accessed 08.10.11].

[13] Controls Matrix (CM). Cloud security alliance V1.2. https://cloudsecurityalliance.org/research/initiatives/cloud-controls-matrix/; 20010 [accessed 08.10.11].

Managing the Cloud

INTRODUCTION

Ease of managing a cloud infrastructure forms a critical part of any cloud solution, since simplicity of usage and freedom from IT management are two important values provided by cloud models. As introduced in previous chapters, the cloud architecture consists of technologies at IaaS, PaaS, and SaaS layers. Therefore, a key requirement for the cloud architecture is efficient management of resources at all three layers of the stack. Specifically, the questions to be addressed include how to monitor performance and health of resources, how to perform fault diagnostics and recovery, and how to enforce SLAs during operation of the resources. While these are issues faced in any IT management system, these problems become harder for cloud management. The larger scale of the systems being managed, support for multi-tenancy, need for better precision of monitoring to support the pay-per-use model, and elasticity in the resources make the problem much harder. Automation is needed to replace manual operations and reduce overall costs. The overall objective is to maintain SLAs specified by the user, which have to be translated and ensured across the IaaS, PaaS, and SaaS layers.

This chapter first looks at the approaches used for IaaS monitoring and management using two IaaS solution case studies described in Chapter 2, *Infrastructure as a Service*. These are CloudSystem Matrix and Amazon EC2 (using Amazon CloudWatch). To study the approaches used for managing PaaS systems, the example of Microsoft Azure is revisited and the management tools used for the same are detailed. Finally, tools to manage SaaS systems are studied using NetCharts and Nimsoft as case studies.

MANAGING IAAS[1]

A fully automated solution for provisioning multiple resources requires creation of automated workflows, coordination across multiple resource types, and automated configuration of systems, middleware, and applications. Runtime maintenance requires monitoring of highly dynamic distributed infrastructure, monitoring dynamic partitioning, allocation, and de-allocation of infrastructure. Distributed Management Task Force (DMTF) is an industry consortium that develops, maintains and promotes standards for systems management in enterprise IT environment. DMTF proposed architecture and other standardization efforts are described in Chapter 10. In this section, two IaaS Systems introduced in Chapter 2, namely CloudSystem Matrix and Amazon EC2, are used as examples to explain the management of IaaS with a specific focus on their runtime management aspects.

Management of CloudSystem Matrix

HP CloudSystem Matrix provides a self-service interface that consumers and administrators can use to perform on-going operations over the lifetime of the service [1]. These could be simple activities such as re-boot or just getting console access to the environment, or more advanced activities such as adjusting the resources assigned to the service – expanding to meeting demand growth, as well as reducing resources during low utilization periods. These and other such operations are available from the CloudSystem Matrix **administrator portal** as well as via Web Service APIs.

Figure 8.1 shows the functional block diagram of the Matrix environment with components that enable runtime management capabilities. The administrator portal enables site maintenance as well as operations management capabilities. It also includes the assignment of resources to **resource pools** and enablement of groups of users to draw from these pools. As described in Chapter 2, the resource pools contain resources associated with virtual machines, physical servers, networks and IP addresses, storage capacity and deployable software. Each of these resources has an internal manager that interacts with the corresponding data center resources. When a request is initiated via the portal or API to create a new service instance or allocate additional resources to an existing service, the allocation and scheduling engine evaluates the available resources in the resource pool, picks an appropriate resource, and then allocates it to run the workload. Administrator tools also support capacity planning associated both with demand growth as well as the impacts of maintenance schedules. A combination of these built-in and optional add-on tools/components enables the ongoing administration of the Matrix environment. The following are some tools that are tailored towards particular administrative roles.

---

[1]Contributed by Dr. Vanish Talwar and Mr. Nigel Cook, Hewlett-Packard Labs.

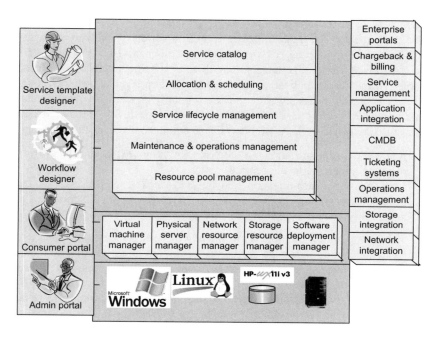

FIGURE 8.1

A high-level block diagram of CloudSystem Matrix.

IaaS Administrator of CloudSystem Matrix

This role is concerned with managing the on-going administration of the IaaS infrastructure. Particular concerns are around the monitoring of on-going self-service requests, the available capacity of IaaS resource pools, replacement of failed infrastructure components, and routine patching and upgrade of server, network and switch firmware components. CloudSystem Matrix provides an integrated console to perform these operations. Some of the available administrative capabilities include:

a. Realtime dashboard summarizing the overall state of CloudSystem Matrix
b. Assignment or migration of server resources to self-service user resource pools
c. Historical capacity trending of CPU, memory, I/O and power on nominated groups of resources
d. Ability to simulate the effects of workload growth or resource addition/removal on the capacity trends in (c)
e. Realtime status monitoring and reporting for all matrix infrastructure components
f. Workload migration tools allowing physical or virtual workloads to be manually migrated by the administrator
g. Integrated firmware patching tools

Self-Service Monitoring

The consumers of HP IaaS offerings can use a variety of built-in tools, as well as add-on tools provided by HP, open source or other third-party sources to monitor their deployed services. Notable among these is HP SiteScope [2], which provides a variety of metrics at application level and transaction level as well as resource level. These consumers of the infrastructure are primarily concerned with the state of their infrastructure components, as well as the service levels delivered from their infrastructure services. Some of the available administrative capabilities include:

a. Real-time dashboard showing their service components and the corresponding resource allocation to the service
b. Service component utilization statistics and calendar views
c. Service-level monitoring tools such as HP Software's SiteScope and Business availability center.

This combination of tools allows synthetic user transactions, such as a shopping cart request or web page access, to be applied to a particular service, and the response time measured and monitored over time. This gives a view of not just whether the components of a service are running, but an indication of the level of service that an end consumer would experience. As an example, if the measured service level was too high, it might be an indication that resources could be removed from the service, reducing costs. Similarly, should the measured resource time be too slow, this could again be an indication that additional resources need to be applied to the service to increase performance.

As mentioned earlier, runtime maintenance can be performed using the administrator portal or through Matrix APIs. The APIs are exposed as Web Service interfaces and client access is available in a large variety of languages (C++/Java/Python/Ruby/Actionscript to name just a few) based on built-in or widely used open source libraries. The Matrix environment can be queried to provide a definition of these exposed services. For example, for a Matrix system installed with IP address 192.168.0.25, to access the WSDL (Web Service Description Language), type into the web browser:

```
https://192.168.0.25:51443/hpio/controller/soap/v1?wsdl
```

Matrix also distributes a command line interface that invokes the same web service interfaces and allows a similar implementation in the user's favorite shell.

A Programming Example to Control Elasticity

This section illustrates how these APIs can be used to adjust the resources associated with the Pustak Portal service introduced in Chapter 1. Referring back to the Pustak Portal Matrix templates from Chapter 2, the number of servers in the web tier were initially specified to be 6 servers. From the self-service portal the consumer has the ability to request additional servers to be added, up to the maximum of 12 servers. The consumer also has the ability to quiesce and reactivate

Table 8.1 Sample System Scaling for the Pustak Portal

Load	Concurrent Users	Web Tier	App Tier	Database Tier
Small	1,000	2	2	2
Medium	5,000	6	4	2
Large	10,000	8	5	2
X Large	50,000	12	6	3

servers in a tier. For example, in a tier that has 6 provisioned servers, the consumer can request 3 servers be quiesced, which will cause those servers to be shut down and the associated server resource released. However, a quiesced server disk image and IP address allocation is retained, so that the subsequent re-activate operations can occur quickly, without requiring a server software re-provisioning operation.

In order to maintain service levels and contain costs, the owner can dynamically scale the resources in the environment to make sure that the service has just enough server and storage resources to meet the current demand, without the need to be pre-allocated and have a lot of idle resources. The service scaling can be performed depending on the number of concurrent users accessing the system, shown in Table 8.1. The owner may also want to ensure that there is just enough storage capacity for the service, such as wanting to maintain a minimum 25 GB of storage capacity headroom. To facilitate this, it is assumed that a simple CGI or REST based web service interface exists that returns the number of concurrent users on the site, as well as unused capacity in the database.

In the following example Java code, the open source *cxf* library will be used to scale the service resources based on the number of concurrent users using the web services API.

```
package com.hp.matrix.client;

import java.io.IOException;
import java.util.HashMap;
import java.util.Map;

import javax.security.auth.callback.Callback;
import javax.security.auth.callback.CallbackHandler;
import javax.security.auth.callback.UnsupportedCallbackException;

import org.apache.cxf.endpoint.Client;
import org.apache.cxf.endpoint.Endpoint;
import org.apache.cxf.frontend.ClientProxy;
import org.apache.cxf.jaxws.JaxWsProxyFactoryBean;
import org.apache.cxf.ws.security.wss4j.WSS4JOutInterceptor;
import org.apache.ws.security.WSConstants;
import org.apache.ws.security.WSPasswordCallback;
```

```java
import org.apache.ws.security.handler.WSHandlerConstants;

import com.hp.io.soap.v1.IO;
import com.hp.io.soap.v1.RequestInfo;
import com.hp.io.soap.v1.RequestStatusEnum;

public class Adjust {
    final static long GB = 1000*1000000L;
    protected IO endpoint;
    protected String serviceName;

    public Adjust(String url, String username, String password,
    String serviceName)    {
        endpoint = newWebServiceEndpoint(url, username, password);
    }

    public Boolean adjustServers(long concurrentUsers) throws
    Exception {
        Boolean adjustmentMade = false;
        int webSize,    appSize, dbSize;

        if (concurrentUsers <= 1000) {
            webSize = 2; appSize = 2;        dbSize = 2;
        } else if (concurrentUsers <= 5000) {
            webSize = 6; appSize = 4;        dbSize = 2;
        } else if (concurrentUsers <= 10000) {
            webSize = 8; appSize = 5;        dbSize = 2;
        } else {
            webSize = 12; appSize = 6; dbSize = 3;
        }


        String requestId;
        requestId = endpoint.setLogicalServerGroupActiveServerCount
        (serviceName, "DB Cluster", dbSize, true, null);

        if(requestId != null) {

            Wait.For(endpoint, requestId);

            adjustmentMade = true;
        }
        requestId = endpoint.setLogicalServerGroupActiveServerCount
        (serviceName, "App Server", appSize, true, null);
        if(requestId != null) {
            Wait.For(endpoint, requestId);
            adjustmentMade = true;
        }
        requestId = endpoint.setLogicalServerGroupActiveServerCount
        (serviceName, "Web", webSize, true, null);
        if(requestId != null) {
```

```
            Wait.For(endpoint, requestId);
            adjustmentMade = true;
        }
        return adjustmentMade;
    }
    public Boolean adjustStorage(long free) throws Exception {
        if(free < 25*GB) {

            String requestId = endpoint.addDiskToLogicalServer
            Group(serviceName, "DB Cluster", "db");
            Wait.For(endpoint, requestId);

            return true;
        }
        return false;
    }

    private static class Wait {
        static Boolean For(IO service, String requestId) {
            try {
                while(true) {

                    RequestInfo info = service.getRequestInfo
                    (requestId);

                    RequestStatusEnum status =
                    info.getStatus().getEnumValue();
                    if(status == RequestStatusEnum.COMPLETE ||
                        status == RequestStatusEnum.FAILED) {
                        if(status == RequestStatusEnum.COMPLETE)
                            return true;
                        else
                            return false;
                    }
                    Thread.sleep(15*1000);
                }
            } catch (Exception e) {
                return false;
            }
        }
    }

    public static void main(String[] args) {
        Adjust a = new Adjust(" https://1.1.1.1:51443/hpio/
        controller/soap/v1",
                    "automation", "password", "myService" );
        while (true) {
            long concurrentUsers = getConcurrentUsers();
            long diskFree = getFreeSpace();
            a.adjustServers(concurrentUsers);
```

```
                a.adjustStorage(diskFree);
                Thread.sleep(5*60*1000);
        }
}
```

The sample code main method illustrates the conceptual steps for maintaining the appropriate level of resources in the Pustak Portal environment. The main routine commences by creating a new instance of an `Adjust` object that will enable the on-going adjustment of the resources associated with a service called `myService` that is being managed by a CSA Matrix with an IP address 1.1.1.1 (fictitious IP address). The Matrix service will now be accessible by an account with username `automation` and a password of `password`.

The sample control loop uses web services calls `getConcurrentUsers` and `getFreeSpace` to query information from the service. These calls are assumed to be specific to the Pustak Portal implemented through a CGI process or some other method. The `adjustServers` and `adjustStorage` methods are then invoked to make adjustments as necessary to the resources on `myService` and it then sleeps for 5 minutes.

The majority of the processing is contained within the `Action` class. The instantiation method invokes a method `newWebServiceEndpoint` to create a web services endpoint to Matrix with the appropriate credentials.

The `adjustServers` method has one argument specifying the current number of concurrent users. The code commences by mapping from this number of users to the appropriate size of web, application and database servers as specified in Table 8.1. The code then uses successive calls to the `setLogicalServerGroupActiveServerCount` web service call to request adjustment of the number of servers in the database, application and web service tiers. This web service call will initiate an adjustment of the number of servers in a particular tier, or return null if the tier size currently matches the specified count. Where an adjustment is required, the web service call returns a request identifier which can be used to track the progress of the request. In the sample code the method `Wait.For` is invoked passing the `requestId`. The `For` method polls to check the status of the request using the web service call `getRequestInfo`, and finally returns when the request either successfully completes, or ends in failure.

The `adjustStorage` method has one argument specifying the current free storage in the environment. When the amount of free storage is less than 25GB, the web service call `addDiskToLogicalServerGroup` is used to create and attach additional shared storage to the servers in the database tier `DB Cluster`. The existing disk `DB` is used as a stereotype for the new storage. The web server call returns a `request Id`, and the `Wait.For` method is used to monitor the progress until the operation completes.

EC2 Management: Amazon CloudWatch

In Chapter 2, there was a detailed description of the features of Amazon EC2 and related products. This section briefly describes the monitoring support provided by

Amazon CloudWatch [3]. CloudWatch provides monitoring for Amazon EC2 instances, Amazon EBS Volumes, Elastic Load Balancers, and RDS database instances. It provides access to a wide range of metrics such as CPU utilization, disk reads and writes, network traffic, latency, and client-request count. It also provides statistics such as minimum, maximum, sum, and average of various parameters. Use of Amazon CloudWatch provides customers with a visibility into resource utilization, operational performance, and overall demand patterns for their instances.

It can be invoked both as a web service and through the command line. The monitoring information obtained from Amazon CloudWatch can enable various management functions. For example, it enables **Auto Scaling**, which allows the dynamic addition or removal of Amazon EC2 instances based on Amazon Cloud-Watch metrics. The monitoring data collected by Amazon CloudWatch can be accessed using the AWS Management Console, web service APIs or Command Line Tools.

End-users can use Amazon CloudWatch to monitor their instances on Amazon EC2 by either using AWS Management Console or by using command line tools. For example, the following command line can be used to enable monitoring when launching an instance. The `gsg-keypair` is the secret key described in the section titled *Getting Started* in Chapter 2.

```
geetham$> ec2-run-instances ami-2bb65342 -k gsg-keypair - monitored
```

Once CloudWatch has been enabled to monitor the instance, the data can be obtained by either using the Amazon CloudWatch API or the AWS Management Console. Figure 8.2 [4] and Figure 8.3 [5] show some screenshots of the AWS CloudWatch for a sample of gathered data.

When using programmatically, the `GetMetricStatistics` API can be used to return data for one or more statistics of a given metric. The API `ListMetrics` lists the set of metrics for which recorded data is available. As of writing of this book, the following metrics were available for EC2 instances.

CPUUtilization	The percentage of the allocated compute units currently used by the instance
DiskReadOps	Completed read operations from all disks available to the instances.
DiskWriteOps	Completed write operations to all hard disks available to the instance.
DiskReadBytes	Bytes read from all disks available to the instance.
DiskWriteBytes	Bytes written to all disks available to the instance.
NetworkIn	The number of incoming bytes received on all network interfaces by the instance.
NetworkOut	The number of outgoing bytes sent on all network interfaces by the instance.

Additionally, useful statistical information based on these metrics are also supported by Amazon CloudWatch, such as minimum, maximum, sum, average,

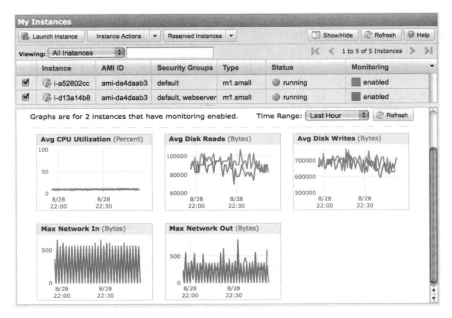

FIGURE 8.2

Screenshot of Amazon Cloudwatch.

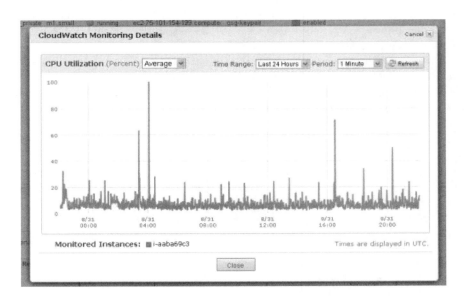

FIGURE 8.3

A more detailed view of Amazon Cloudwatch.

samples and so on. More information on other metrics available for Amazon EBS (Elastic Load Balancing) and Amazon RDS are available in the metrics page of the developer manual [6]. Amazon CloudWatch is basically a metrics repository; an Amazon tool (EC2, EBS or RDS) just puts its metrics into it and can retrieve statistics based on those metrics, set alarm points for notifications or provide appropriate auto scaling functionality.

In summary, techniques for IaaS cloud management not only relate to fine-grain monitoring of various compute or storage metrics (detailed using Cloud-Watch as an example) but also includes methods of maintaining SLAs, especially to ensure elasticity of resources (detailed using Matrix API as an example). The next section now gives some details of managing a PaaS system.

MANAGING PAAS[2]

Similarly to an IaaS system, a PaaS system needs to maintain SLAs and to provide appropriate runtime administration features. In this section, Windows Azure [7] will be used as an example to explain the management of a typical PaaS system.

Management of Windows Azure

In Chapter 3, Windows Azure, the .Net-based popular Cloud platform was described. In this section, the management aspects of Azure will be studied. First, the section provides an overview of the Windows Azure SLAs followed by a discussion of the management capabilities with Windows Azure.

Service Level Agreements (SLAs)

Windows Azure has separate SLAs for the storage, compute, CDN and App Fabric components. The reader is referred to Chapter 3 of this book for more details of these components. For compute, Microsoft guarantees that when customers deploy two or more role instances in different fault and upgrade domains, the web roles will have external connectivity at least 99.95% of the time. Additionally, Microsoft guarantees that 99.9% of the time corrective action will be initiated when the fabric controller detects that a role instance is down. Similarly on the storage front, Microsoft guarantees that at least 99.9% of the time correctly formatted requests to Windows storage for adding, updating, reading and deleting data will be processed correctly. Requests that are throttled because the application does not obey back-off principles and requests that fail because of application logic (like creating a container that already exists) are not considered to be failures of the service.

---

[2]Contributed by Mr. Gopal R. Srinivasa, Microsoft Research, India.

For SQL Azure, Microsoft guarantees a **Monthly Availability** of 99.9% during a calendar month. **Monthly Availability Percentage** for a specific customer database is the ratio of the time the database was available to customers to the total time in a month. Time is measured in 5-minute intervals in a 30-day monthly cycle. Availability is always calculated for a full month. An interval is marked as unavailable if the customer's attempts to connect to a database are rejected by the SQL Azure gateway.

Uptime percentage commitments and SLA credits for Service Bus and Access Control are similar to those specified previously in the Windows Azure SLA. Due to inherent differences between the technologies, underlying SLA definitions and terms differ for the Service Bus and Access Control services. Details are available in the App Fabric SLA [8]. The latest versions of the list of committed Windows Azure SLAs are maintained at [9].

Managing Applications in Azure

Availability: Two key aspects of ensuring availability of applications are the concepts of **upgrade domains** and **fault domains**. As mentioned in earlier chapters, running multiple role instances in multiple fault domains ensures that a single hardware fault will not bring down all the instances. Upgrade domains are units of upgrade – they ensure that at least one instance of a role is running when other instances are being upgraded, either by the fabric controller or by the customer. Allocation of roles to different upgrade or fault domains is completely controlled by the Fabric controller. However, customers are allowed to configure the number of upgrade domains for their applications through the Service configuration (*.cscfg) file.

For high availability, it is necessary that many instances of a role be created. System administrators must judiciously select the number of instances of the roles they need and the number of upgrade domains based on the service load, the number of versions of the application supported in parallel, and the cost of running multiple instances of their roles.

Monitoring: The primary mechanism to monitor the uptime of a cloud application is through the Diagnostics API, described in the *Windows Azure* section of Chapter 3. Both Web and Worker roles can raise Windows events when errors are encountered. In addition, the IIS diagnostics module logs failed HTTP requests. Roles can also log performance data based on which administrators can choose to increase or decrease the size of the VMs allocated to each roles. Each role has an instance of the Diagnostics Manager class running as a separate process on the same VM. The Diagnostics manager processes events, performance data and trace messages raised by the role and stores the data generated on the local system.

Administrators can either choose to configure the manager to upload the logs to Azure storage periodically or to do it on-demand. Administrators can use the DeploymentDiagnosticsManager class to create their own application that monitors service logs, or alternatively, use third-party applications like Cerebrata's Azure Diagnostics Manager to monitor the roles of their Azure applications.

Microsoft's System Center and Microsoft Management Console (MMC) can also be used to monitor Azure applications. However, uploading logs to the Azure store is time consuming, and there is additional time needed for downloading the logs onto the administrator's machine. So, using this mechanism is not a practical option for real-time monitoring of Azure applications.

TIP

A Useful Class for Monitoring

`TraceSource`: A class in the .NET diagnostics API that allows applications to trace the execution of code. Among other features, the class allows applications to log messages agnostic of the target to which the messages are directed.

For real-time monitoring and notification, roles must write events to a message queue which is monitored by a diagnostic application (or a notifying application). Alternatively, the developer can direct the App Fabric to log messages to an on-premise logging service which can raise notifications as appropriate. The App Fabric SDK contains an example of using the .NET `TraceSource` API with the App Fabric to create a real-time notification system for Windows Azure. A brief description follows. Essentially, the method is to create a `TraceListener` object that writes to an on-premise message-logging web service that processes the messages. Communication between the `TraceListener` and the on-premise message-logging service is through the `ServiceBus` (described in Chapter 2).

While using the mechanism, care should be taken to only log actionable error messages to the service, to both limit network load and limit the cost of the service. In addition, even though access to the on-premise logging service is through a secure channel, care should be taken not to expose PII and confidential data. Best practices for monitoring Azure-hosted applications can be found in *Monitoring and Diagnostic Guidance for Windows Azure Hosted Applications* [10].

Common Administrative Functions: The Azure portal provides single point access to all management and administrative functions. In addition, the Azure Management API provides REST-based APIs for common service administration functions. In order to automate builds and deployment, this API can be used – note though that the API is only available over a secure HTTP connection. Therefore, the account owner should upload appropriate certificates and share public keys with the service administrators to enable automated management.

The management API provides functions to publish new versions of the application, increase/decrease the number of roles, change storage keys, and so on. In addition, to change role-related settings, like tracing options or other configuration settings for a role, clients can use the `DeploymentDiagnosticsManager` class to publish new configurations to a role or a set of roles. In fact, tools such as Microsoft Management Console (MMC) can also be used.

The Windows Azure platform management plug-in for MMC is available at *Windows Azure MMC* [11]. The plug-in offers many features including the ability to upload diagnostics logs from the VMs, download and view the logs, and perform service administration functions. Using the App fabric for real-time application monitoring is described in the free e-book, *Azure from the Trenches* [12].

As seen in this section, in addition to routine resource monitoring and management functionality, PaaS solutions need to provide platform-specific monitoring capabilities.

MANAGING SAAS

The monitoring of Salesforce.com (described in Chapter 4) is used as an example of how SaaS environments are managed. Two example solutions follow – those provided by Netcharts and Nimsoft, respectively. These solutions help to identify when Salesforce encounters slowdowns or outages and allows businesses to react on time.

Monitoring Force.com: Netcharts

NetCharts [13] is an application that provides useful performance information in a well-integrated manner for Salesforce.com. It provides an up-to-date dashboard view of the **key performance indicators** (**KPIs**). Dashboards can be shared across Salesforce users within an organization. The dashboard provides powerful analytics, helping users make optimal decisions and increase operational efficiency. Key relationships and anomalies can be identified, and business trends can be predicted as well. Figure 8.4 [13] shows the Netcharts dashboard.

Monitoring Force.com: Nimsoft

Nimsoft [14] provides monitoring solutions that apply to the IaaS, PaaS, and SaaS stack. In particular, the solution for the SaaS stack can be used to monitor Salesforce.com applications providing detailed quality of service metrics and alarms, thus delivering insights to minimize the business impact of Salesforce downtime or performance problems. Metrics monitored include average transaction time, number of transactions, and instance status, as well as an organization's Salesforce implementation, including file and data storage, login timing, API calls, query execute time, and more. Figure 8.5 shows the Nimsoft monitoring dashboard for Salesforce.com [15].

The Nimsoft product architecture is built around a scalable, highly reliable message bus, with a lightweight "publish and subscribe" communications model. It also has hundreds of modular probes for both agent-less and agent-based monitoring. One unique capability is zero-touch setup – the capability to automatically configure and distribute probes to new physical or virtual systems. This capability can be integrated with a CMDB as well as with a change management or provisioning system.

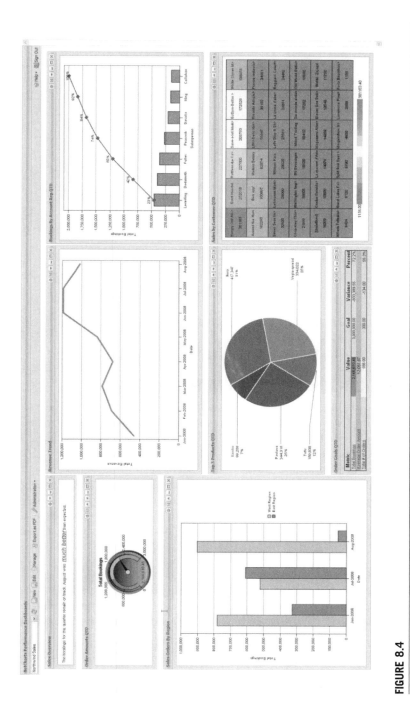

FIGURE 8.4

Netcharts application monitoring Salesforce.com.

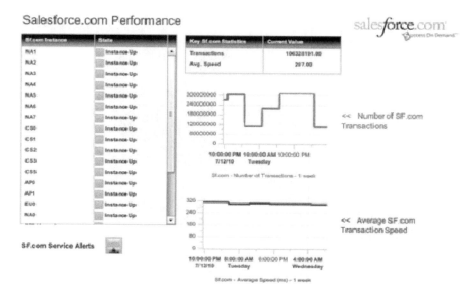

FIGURE 8.5

Nimsoft application monitoring Salesforce.com.

OTHER CLOUD-SCALE MANAGEMENT SYSTEMS

The separation of functionality across IaaS, PaaS, and SaaS layers provides a good abstraction for cloud systems. However, having separate management systems for each of these layers results in inefficient operations and necessitates coordination and exchange of information across the layers. Additionally, broader aspects of ensuring the health of the cloud system such as energy management, decentralized control, failure resilience and tools for infrastructure assessment are needed to provide a more holistic solution. The remainder of this section presents some existing efforts to address a few of these challenges in the context of two systems that provide cloud assessment and multi-cloud management capabilities.

HP Cloud Assure

HP Cloud Assure [16] is a cloud management offering delivered via HP Software-as-a-Service, and is a suite of solutions for assessing security, performance, and availability of cloud services. It is a turnkey solution applicable to IaaS, PaaS, and SaaS.

- **Security** is assessed by performing security risk assessment, common security policy definitions, automated security tests, centralized permissions control, and web access to security information. Further assessment is done by scanning networks, operating systems and web applications and performing automated penetration testing.

- **Performance** is assessed by testing for bandwidth, connectivity, scalability, and end-user experience. HP Cloud Assure offers a comprehensive performance testing service to make sure the cloud providers meet end-user bandwidth and connectivity requirements and that the cloud applications scale to support peak usage.
- **Availability** is assessed by testing and monitoring web-based application business processes and identifying and analyzing performance issues and trends. HP Cloud Assure monitors the cloud-based applications, isolates problems, and identifies root causes with ability to drill-down into specific application components.

RightScale

RightScale [17] provides automated solutions for cloud management, and has support for managing interactions with multiple cloud infrastructures. Figure 8.6 gives the key modules of RightScale, which are briefly described here:

- **Cloud Management Environment** provides the Management Dashboard similar to the one provided by Amazon CloudWatch and Matrix. It is also a place where the administrator can get access to the server templates and other deployment information,
- **Cloud-Ready ServerTemplates** provide pre-packaged solutions based on best practices for common application scenarios to speed up deployments on the cloud. Multiple groups of servers can be architected to work together.

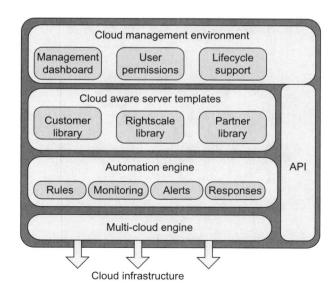

FIGURE 8.6

RightScale Cloud management platform.

- **Adaptable Automation Engine** adapts resource allocation as required by system demand, system failures or other events based on active monitoring. Tools are provided for managing multi-server deployments over the entire lifecycle.
- **Multi-Cloud Engine** interacts with the cloud infrastructure APIs of multiple cloud providers. This eliminates lock-in to any single cloud vendor and allows deployment across multiple clouds, including ability to move applications from one cloud to another.

Compuware

Compuware [18] offers a cloud monitoring suite of products that directly measure the performance experienced by end users and customers. It allows for detecting and diagnosing performance problems experienced by a cloud application, prioritizing the problems in terms of business impact, and helping resolution of the problem.

For detecting performance problems, Compuware offers the following methods:

- Real-user monitoring: data can be collected from access devices of actual users to detect performance problems in the cloud application

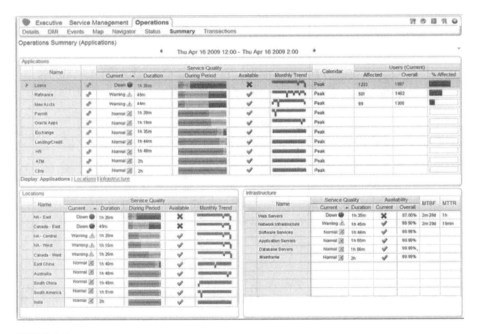

FIGURE 8.7

Compuware Gomez Cloud monitoring platform [19].

- Synthetic monitoring: The cloud application can also be monitored but by listening posts on the following networks:
    * Compuserve's own network of servers that reside on local networks worldwide
    * Compuserve's network of servers that reside on the Internet backbone
    * Any office or data center of the enterprise

By correlating the data from all the sources, the cause of the problem (e.g., the cloud provider, or network congestion) can be determined.

Figure 8.7 shows a screenshot of the Compuware monitoring platform [20]. As can be seen from the sample dashboard, data about the performance of applications as well as the infrastructure are shown. Further, the overall performance of machines at various locations is shown to identify potential network issues. More details of such cloud scale monitoring can be found at [20], which is a virtual community setup to foster a collaboration between organizations interested in exchanging strategies, best practices and resources for deploying and managing applications in the cloud.

SUMMARY

The shift of IT systems to the cloud represents a paradigm change in the development of computing and storage systems. This poses several new challenges for the design of effective management technologies. Traditional monitoring and management technologies were developed for enterprise environments typically catering to single customer environments deployed in the range of thousands of servers. Cloud systems represent multi-tenant environments providing computing systems and applications as a service to consumers as a utility. These systems are in the range of tens of thousands of servers, and are growing fast to several tens of thousands of servers serving millions of users. Existing cloud deployments mostly rely on traditional monitoring and management systems that do not cater to all of the cloud needs. While efforts are being made to address these gaps (as illustrated by example systems presented earlier in this chapter), several open research challenges remain to designing fully automated, closed-loop management solutions for meeting customer service level agreements (SLAs) and cloud provider cost metrics. Some of these key challenges are as follows.

Cross-layer optimization across IaaS, PaaS, SaaS layers: The separation of functionality across IaaS, PaaS, SaaS layers provides a good abstraction for cloud systems, however, having separate management systems for these layers results in silo-ed operations and subsystem-level solutions. Much can be done to improve efficiency through coordination and exchange of information across these layers. Higher-layer SLAs need to be effectively translated to lower layers to make management decisions at those layers (e.g., at IaaS) SLA-aware. Similarly, lower-layer abstractions can be exposed as appropriate to higher layers in the stack to make them more effective for the cloud operation.

Scale for monitoring and management: Traditional monitoring and management systems are typically centralized. These approaches won't scale to the several tens of thousands (and potentially millions) of management objects in cloud systems. Approaches that are more distributed, and have scalability properties that allow easy scale-up and scale-down of the monitoring and management systems, are yet to be designed. Furthermore, scale goes beyond raw system size in that one also has to take into account the multiple time and length scales at which different system components and levels of abstraction operate – for example, queries for entire data center health vs. a specific disk subsystem, or managing high rate web requests vs. lower rate virtual machine migrations.

Sustainability and energy management: Given the scale and scope of cloud data centers, energy efficiency is a critical requirement to meet cost, regulations, and environmental constraints. Power and cooling systems are a growing fraction of the costs in data centers, and techniques that minimize power consumption and use intelligent mechanisms for cooling are needed. In addition, the problem needs an end-to-end perspective wherein sustainability needs to be the driving factor during the manufacturing of cloud server systems, as well as day-to-day operations of cloud data centers.

In addition, future research can enable better accounting and billing techniques to more accurately leverage monitoring information from clouds. Federation of management systems across multiple clouds, both public and private is another area of future improvements.

This chapter studied many commercial solutions for cloud management. It first looked at management support at each of the cloud layers – IaaS, PaaS and SaaS. The features provided by CloudSystem Matrix to control elasticity or on-demand provisioning of resources were studied. A detailed look at the runtime monitoring features of Amazon CloudWatch was presented next. To understand the roles and responsibilities of managing a PaaS system, the SLA management and monitoring aspects of Azure were studied. Two monitoring systems for Salesforce were studied to appreciate the techniques that can be used for SaaS management. Finally, the chapter examined products that try to cross-layer monitoring needs and help improve the performance of the end-to-end cloud application irrespective. Chapter 10, *Future Trends and Research Directions*, describes a more advanced large-scale management and monitoring system called Open Cirrus that addresses some of the concerns around sustainability and energy management.

References

[1] HP CloudSystem Matrix. http://www.hp.com/go/matrix; [accessed 09.10.11].

[2] HP SiteScope software. http://www8.hp.com/us/en/software/software-product.html?compURI=tcm:245-937086; [accessed 09.10.11].

[3] Amazon CloudWatch. http://aws.amazon.com/cloudwatch/; [accessed 09.10.11].

[4] CloudWatch DashBoard. http://d36cz9buwru1tt.cloudfront.net/console_thumb_cw_1.png. Accessed from http://aws.amazon.com/console/ on 14 Oct 2011; [accessed 09.10.11].

[5] CloudWatch Graph Metrics. http://d36cz9buwru1tt.cloudfront.net/console_thumb_cw_2.png. Accessed on 13 Oct 2011 from http://aws.amazon.com/console/; [accessed 09.10.11].

[6] Metrics, http://docs.amazonwebservices.com/AmazonCloudWatch/latest/DeveloperGuide/; [accessed 09.10.11].

[7] Windows Azure. http://www.microsoft.com/windowsazure/; [accessed 09.10.11].

[8] Windows Azure AppFabric Service Bus. Access control and caching SLAs. http://www.microsoft.com/download/en/details.aspx?displaylang=en&id=4767; [accessed 09.10.11].

[9] Windows Azure Service Level Agreements. https://www.microsoft.com/windowsazure/sla/; [accessed 09.10.11].

[10] Monitoring and Diagnostic Guidance for Windows Azure hosted applications. http://download.microsoft.com/download/4/C/B/4CB0167F-B6D9-4B46-8DF1-69CCCA66FDDE/SystemCenterOperationsManagerMonitoringforAzureHostedAppsatMicrosoft.pdf; [accessed 09.10.11].

[11] Windows Azure MMC. http://code.msdn.microsoft.com/windowsazuremmc; [accessed 09.10.11].

[12] Azure from the trenches, vol 1. http://bit.ly/downloadazurebookvol1; [accessed 09.10.11].

[13] NetCharts. http://sites.force.com/appexchange/listingDetail?listingId=a0330000000gujqAAA; [accessed 09.10.11].

[14] Nimsoft. http://www.nimsoft.com/solutions/; [accessed 09.10.11].

[15] Nimsoft for Salesforce CRM. http://v4.nimsoft.com/solutions/images/cloud_salesforce_cloud.png; [accessed 09.10.11].

[16] HP CloudAssure. http://www.hp.com/go/cloudassure/; [accessed 09.10.11].

[17] RightScale Cloud Computing Management Platform. http://www.rightscale.com/; [accessed 09.10.11].

[18] Application Performance Management. Driven by End-User Experience, Compuware. http://www.gomez.com/wp-content/downloads/19560_APM_Overview_Br.pdf; [accessed 09.10.11].

[19] Web Performance Monitoring. http://www.gomez.com/wp-content/downloads/19779_Web_Perf_Monitoring_Br.pdf; [accessed 09.10.11].

[20] CloudSleuth. Decoding the mysteries of the cloud. http://www.cloudsleuth.net; [accessed 09.10.11].

Related Technologies

INFORMATION IN THIS CHAPTER:

- Server Virtualization
- Two Popular Hypervisors
- Storage Virtualization
- Grid Computing
- Other Cloud-Related Technologies

INTRODUCTION

This chapter reviews multiple technologies that are often confused with cloud computing, such as Grid computing, Utility computing, Distributed computing, and Virtualization. Each such technology is briefly described and the similarities, differences and ways of leveraging it within a cloud infrastructure are discussed. Additionally, wherever the technology is more relevant to cloud computing (virtualization) the different design and architectural aspects of the technology are discussed in detail. Server and storage virtualization is key to cloud computing, and these key technologies are presented first. Grid computing is considered next where its similarities and differences with respect to cloud computing are studied. The final section briefly covers other cloud-related terminologies.

SERVER VIRTUALIZATION

Server virtualization is a key technology that enables Infrastructure as a Service (IaaS). It abstracts away the physical hardware that the software (application as well as OS) is running on, and makes it appear as if the software is running in a **virtual machine** (or virtual hardware). As a result, server virtualization is used to provide the following important features of cloud computing. Since the software appears to be running in a virtual machine, applications can be moved from one physical machine to another by recreating the virtual machine on the target physical hardware. This is used for load balancing, as well as for consolidating multiple virtual machines on the same physical hardware, leading to more efficient use of the hardware and improved availability. Furthermore, since each application is running in its own virtual machine, it cannot interfere with applications running in other virtual machines. This aspect is important for implementing multi-tenancy and is similar to the way a process can only access its own virtual address space, and is prevented from accessing the virtual address space of other processes.

The following gives an overview of how server virtualization is accomplished, after which a detailed description of hypervisor-based virtualization that is used in IaaS implementations is presented. Finally, two important virtualization solutions – Xen and VMWare – are studied to illustrate how these virtualization techniques are used.

There are broadly two main categories of software virtualization, namely **system virtualization** and **process virtualization** [1]. In process virtualization, the virtualization software runs above the OS and hardware combination and only provides user-level instructions (ABI) or OS library (API) compatibility (typically called runtime support). Examples of process virtualization include Sun's Java Virtual Machine, Microsoft's .Net, or even binary translators like HP ARIES and Transmeta Crusoe. On the other hand, in system virtualization, the virtualization software is in between the host hardware machine and the guest software and its primary role is to provide virtualized hardware resources as depicted in Figure 9.1. System virtualization enables elasticity in hardware without affecting the guest software – a primary requirement for cloud computing. We therefore, focus mainly on system virtualization in this section.

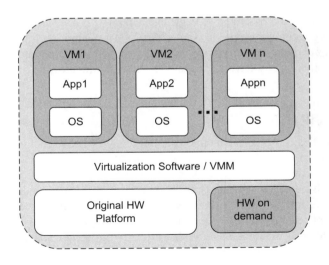

FIGURE 9.1

System virtualization.

Hypervisor-based Virtualization

The software responsible for system virtualization is called the **Virtual Machine Monitor (VMM)** or **hypervisor**. The combination of OS and application that runs on top of the virtualization software is called a **guest** or **Virtual Machine (VM).** A hypervisor allows multiple operating systems to run concurrently on the host hardware (Figure 9.1). These instances can potentially be used by different users and hence hypervisors also provide the isolation between the different guest processes, which is key to supporting multi-tenancy. Further, the hypervisor handles any changes to the processor the application is running on without affecting the user's OS or application, providing the most needed agility for a cloud infrastructure.

Virtualization as such is not a new technology, having been first implemented in IBM mainframes. In 1967, CMS single-user OS running on top of the CP-40 hypervisor was one of the earlier time-sharing systems [2]. The benefits of virtualization, such as server consolidation and isolation between applications, quickly became apparent and virtualization became a standard feature on mainframes [3]. Interest in virtualization spread beyond mainframes with the Disco project at Stanford [4] which showed that by the use of hypervisors, it was possible to efficiently run multiple instances of Silicon Graphics IRIX OS on a NUMA multiprocessor without rewriting IRIX. This led to the development of hypervisors for Unix systems to enable server consolidation. We discuss details of hypervisor based virtualization next.

Types of Hypervisors

Hypervisors are classified into two categories: Native hypervisors and hosted hypervisors [3]. **Bare metal** or **native hypervisors** run directly on the hardware, providing all the features (e.g., I/O) needed by the guests (Figure 9.1). **Hosted hypervisors** run on top of an existing OS and leverage the features of the underlying OS. Virtual machines run on top of the hosted hypervisor, which runs on top of an existing OS. This is inefficient, so the inefficiencies of hosted architectures have led to the development of **hybrid hypervisors** [5] where the hypervisors run directly on the hardware, but leverage the features of an existing OS running as a guest (Figure 9.2). Bare metal hypervisors include the early mainframe hypervisors as well as VMWare ESX server, and kvm, a hypervisor for Linux. Hosted hypervisors include VMWare GSX server. Xen and Microsoft's Hyper-V are examples of hybrid hypervisors.

> **NOTE**
>
> **Types of Hypervisors:**
> * Native Hypervisor
> * Hosted Hypervisor
> * Hybrid Hypervisor

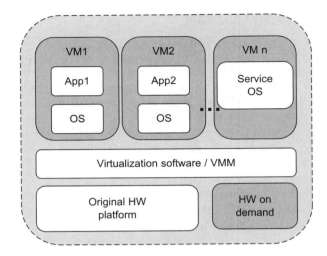

FIGURE 9.2

Hybrid hypervisor.

Techniques for Hypervisors

There are different techniques used for hypervisor-based virtualization. **Trap and emulate virtualization** is a basic technique used from the days of the earliest hypervisors. This technique, however, has some limitations and multiple approaches to overcome those have been developed, such as binary emulation and paravirtualization. More details follow.

Trap and Emulate Virtualization

At a very high level, all three types of hypervisors described earlier operate in a similar manner. In each case, the guests continue execution until they try to access a shared physical resource of the hardware (such as an I/O device), or an interrupt is received. When this happens, the hypervisor regains control and mediates access to the hardware, or handles the interrupt.

To accomplish this functionality, hypervisors rely on a feature of modern processors known as the **privilege level** or **protection ring**. The basic idea behind privilege levels is that all instructions that modify the physical hardware configuration are permitted at the highest level, At lower levels, only restricted sets of instructions can be executed. Figure 9.3 shows the protection rings in the Intel x86 architecture [6], as an example. Other hardware architectures have similar concepts. There are four rings, numbered from 0 to 3. Programs executing in Ring 0 have the highest privileges, and are allowed to execute any instructions or access any physical resources such as memory pages or I/O devices. Guests are typically made to execute in ring 3. This is accomplished by setting the **Current Privilege Level** (**CPL**) register of the processor to 3 before starting execution of the guest.

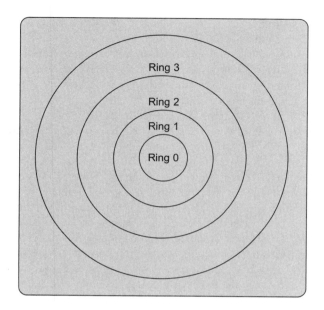

FIGURE 9.3

X86 protection rings.

If the guest tries to access a protected resource, such as an I/O device, an interrupt takes place, and the hypervisor regains control. The hypervisor then emulates the I/O operation for the guest. The exact details depend upon the particular hypervisor (e.g., Xen or Hyper-V) and are described in detail later. Note that in order to emulate the I/O operation, it is necessary for the hypervisor to have maintained the state of the guest and its virtual resources.

Limitations of Trap and Emulate Virtualization

The trap and emulate technique has two major limitations. First, as in any other emulation technique, there is some amount of performance overhead incurred due to this technique. Second, and more importantly, not all architectures are suitable for implementing trap and emulate virtualization. A formal specification of the properties a computer architecture must have to be virtualizable is discussed by Popek et al. [7]. In order to be virtualizable, the set of **sensitive** instructions must be a subset of the **privileged** instructions. Sensitive instructions are defined as those that are either **behavior sensitive** or **control sensitive**. Behavior sensitive instructions are those whose behavior depends on the processor privilege level. If behavior sensitive instructions are executed by a guest running under a hypervisor, the results obtained could be different from executing these with the guest running directly on the hardware at a higher privilege level, since the results depend upon the privilege level. This could lead to potential errors in the execution of the guest. Control sensitive instructions are those that change the processor privilege level, and therefore should be privileged instructions.

An example may clarify this information. On the x86 architecture the `popf` instruction can change system flags that control interrupt delivery. If the `popf` instruction is executed by a guest in non-privileged mode, there is no trap. Rather, the attempt to change the system flags fails silently. The x86 architecture, therefore, cannot be virtualized using the classical trap and emulate technique [8], since the hypervisor cannot detect that the guest is executing the `popf` instruction and emulate it. The `popf` instruction is an example of a sensitive instruction that is not privileged; i.e., does not cause a trap if executed in non-privileged mode. Clearly, if all sensitive instructions were a subset of the privileged instructions, the x86 architecture could be virtualized using trap and emulate virtualization.

The other limitation of trap and emulate virtualization is the potential performance overhead. As described earlier, the guest generates a trap whenever it tries to directly access the physical resources of the system, such as I/O. A straightforward and general method for dealing with this is to emulate the access. Thus, if the guest OS sets up a I/O request consisting of a SCSI request block which is then queued for execution, the hypervisor can emulate the execution of the request on the virtual disk that is exposed to the guest. This can lead to a great deal of performance overhead, since emulation is necessarily slower than direct execution in the hardware. Additionally, there is the context switch overhead from the guest to the hypervisor.

Software Extensions to Trap and Emulate Virtualization

Two major software techniques can be used to overcome the limitations of trap and emulate virtualization. One technique is **binary translation**. Here the hypervisor includes a binary translator which replaces the sensitive instructions by equivalent non-sensitive instructions at run-time, and leaves non-sensitive instructions unchanged [8]. The technique is similar to just-in-time translation in JVMs, and yields similar overheads.

The other software technique is **paravirtualization**, where the guest is modified (re-written) not to use the sensitive instruction, but to directly invoke hypervisor APIs which would provide an equivalent service. Paravirtualization is widely used for reducing the overheads associated with I/O virtualization. In the context of the I/O request example earlier, the guest OS would execute a hypervisor API that would perform the I/O. The disadvantage with this technique is that it is not hypervisor-independent; i.e., the modifications have to be carried out for every hypervisor under which the guest could run. So, paravirtualization requires rewriting of the guest OS.

Hardware Support for Virtualization

To provide more efficient support for virtualization, Intel and AMD created new processor extensions to support virtualization in the hardware. In the following subsections, we first describe **VT-x**, an Intel technology that helps virtualize Intel x86 processors. Next, we provide an overview of a technique called **Extended Page Tables (EPT)** which helps virtualize memory, followed by **VT-d**, a technology to assist in the virtualization of I/O. Similar hardware assists are available for AMD processors. As an example, the Intel i3-2100 processor supports VT-d and AMD-V is supported by AMD Athlon 64 X2 family of processors.

Hardware Support for Processor Virtualization

VT-x, earlier called **VanderPool**, represents Intel's technology for virtualization on x86 processors. VT-x provides hardware assists for virtualization by defining two modes for processor execution: **VMX root operation** and **VMX non-root operation** [9]. Hypervisors are intended to execute in VMX root operation, which is almost identical to normal execution in earlier x86 processors without VT-x. Guests execute in VMX non-root operation, which has been defined to help support virtualization. In each mode of operation, there are four privilege levels. Thus, the hypervisor can operate at ring 0 in VMX root operation, and guests can operate at ring 0 in VMX non-root operation (see Figure 9.4).

Recall from the earlier discussion that two major responsibilities of hypervisors are, first, the necessity of ensuring that sensitive instructions execute correctly, and second, keeping track of the state of the guest. VT-x provides assistance for both of these features. To implement its functionality, VT-x makes use of a new data structure called the **Virtual Machine Control Structure (VMCS)**. VMCS provides facilities for controlling the execution of sensitive operations as well as saving the state of guests. Additionally, VMCS also provides facilities for storing the state of the hypervisor. Full details of the operation of VT-x are beyond the scope of this book and can be found in an interesting article by Rich Uhlig et al. [9].

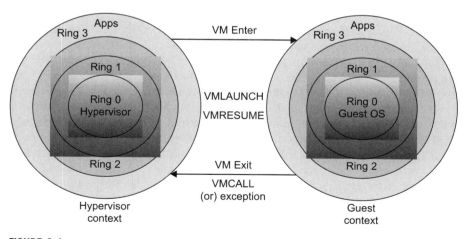

FIGURE 9.4

VT-x provides clean privilege separation.

How does VT-x save the guest state? Conceptually, the method by which the processor state of the guest is saved under VT-x is simple. When a guest ceases execution and exits to the hypervisor (called **VM exit**), the state of the guest (including all processor state registers and control registers) is saved in the VMCS and the state of the hypervisor restored in the VMCS. The reverse process is followed when a guest is dispatched for execution by the hypervisor (a process called **VM entry**).

How does VT-x assist in correct execution of sensitive instructions? Consider the case where a guest OS (which is executing in VMX non-root operation) wishes to execute instructions to mask all interrupts. This is controlled by two controls in the VMCS. If the **external interrupt exiting control** is set, then all external interrupts will cause control to transfer to the hypervisor. If the **interrupt-window exiting control** is set, then the guest will not be interrupted until it enables interrupts. When the guest attempts to execute instructions to mask interrupts, the hypervisor can set the two controls appropriately. Then, when an interrupt occurs, the hypervisor can check the settings of the controls to decide whether to keep the interrupts pending or reflect them to the guest.

The hypervisor can also decide how to handle privileged instructions. Certain instructions that would unsafely change processor state (e.g., CPUID, RDMSR) always cause traps to the hypervisor. However, the action taken with certain other instructions (e.g., HLT, INVLPG) can be configured appropriately.

Hardware Support for Memory Virtualization

Before discussing hardware assists for memory virtualization, one should understand the performance overheads associated with the trap and emulate technique. Virtual memory is generally implemented by page tables in the hardware that map virtual addresses to physical addresses. Additionally, to speed up processor execution, translations of frequently used addresses are cached in TLBs, so that these translations need not be computed from the page tables.

In a virtualization scenario, guests can no longer be allowed to directly manage the page tables and TLBs. Instead, the hypervisor has to trap all attempts by the guest OS to modify the page tables and TLBs and set up the appropriate mappings. Specifically, the guest OS would attempt to create a mapping between **guest virtual addresses** and **guest physical addresses** (addresses that the guest thinks are physical addresses). For example, the guest may try to create a page table entry stating that page p is mapped to physical address x. However, since the guest does not have access to the physical memory, this page may actually refer to physical page y. x is referred to as a **guest physical address**. For correct operation of the system, the hypervisor has to load the map between the guest virtual addresses and actual physical addresses into the page table (in the previous instance, between p and y). The hypervisor maintains this mapping in **shadow page tables** with the help of an auxiliary mapping from guest physical addresses to actual physical addresses.

> **NOTE**
>
> **Reduce overheads of memory virtualization using**
> * Extended Page Tables (EPT)
> * Virtual Processor ID (VPID)

In the previous scenarios, trapping the guest when it tries to modify the page tables is a source of performance overhead. Also, maintenance of shadow page tables is complex and prone to error. An additional source of performance overhead is the necessity of purging the TLB each time a new guest executes, since translations valid for one guest would not be valid for another guest.

In order to overcome the previously described performance overheads, there are two hardware assists for memory virtualization in Intel x86 processors [10]. The first consists of the **Extended Page Tables (EPT)**. EPT support is enabled by setting the appropriate fields in the VMCS control structure. Figure 9.5 illustrates the operation of EPT. The guest stores the mapping from the guest virtual page to the guest physical page in the page tables. The hypervisor stores the mapping from the guest physical page to the actual physical page. During operation, the processor looks up both tables in sequence to compute the translation. In the example earlier, to translate page p, the processor first looks up the page tables to get the guest physical page x. Subsequently, it looks up x in the EPT to find the actual physical page y.

EPT allows the guest full control over the processor page tables, enhancing performance by removing the need to trap the guest each time it tries to access the page tables. The hypervisor may trap the guest only the first time it tries to access guest physical page x in order to map x in the EPT; or it may have allocated physical pages to the guest in advance, so the trap is not needed in general. In either case, performance is enhanced.

The other assist for memory virtualization is the **Virtual Processor ID (VPID)**. This is also enabled in the VMCS structure. VPID eliminates the need for the hypervisor to flush the TLB upon the exit of a VM. This is because the processor tags each translation stored in the TLB with the VPID associated with

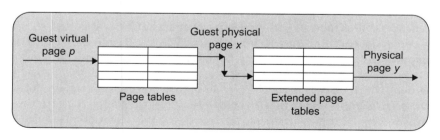

FIGURE 9.5

Extended page tables.

the VM. The VPID is associated with the VM by the hypervisor in the VMCS structure.

Hardware Support for IO Virtualization

Trap and emulate virtualization introduces overheads in I/O functionality as well. The overheads occur in two phases:

1. During VM initialization while the VM discovers the I/O (network and storage) adapters and devices attached;
2. During VM operation when each I/O request is trapped and emulated by the hypervisor (since the VM cannot be allowed to access the physical devices).

More detail on these overheads follows. After the system boots up, the hypervisor will be ready to present (to any VM) a number of I/O adapters in PCI/PCIe slots, as well as a number of virtual devices (virtual network switches and disks) to which these virtual adapters appear to be connected. Then, traps will occur during VM initialization when the guest accesses the virtual adapters to initialize them, as well as discover the virtual network switches and virtual disks the VM is connected to. In the case of virtual disks, the guest will attempt to initialize the virtual disks, which will typically map to a disk partition, a logical volume or a file.

During guest operation, the guest may attempt to send messages over its network adapter. The hypervisor would have to trap these messages, and route them, either to another VM in the system, or to a remote system. In the case of I/O requests to a storage device, the hypervisor would have to emulate the I/O to the disk partition, logical volume, or file. I/O emulation would require the hypervisor to receive interrupts, and then reflect them to the appropriate guest. It may also involve the additional overhead of doing the I/O to hypervisor address space, and then copying the data to the VM address space.

> **NOTE**
>
> **Reduce overheads of I/O virtualization using**
> - Interrupt Remapping
> - DMA Remapping

Intel's VT-d technology can reduce the overhead of I/O virtualization. It has two components, **Interrupt Remapping** and **DMA Remapping** [5]. **DMA remapping** is targeted at eliminating the need for hypervisors to translate guest virtual addresses in I/O commands. It allows hypervisors to define **protection domains** (which correspond to VMs) and define, for each protection domain, address translation tables that translate guest virtual addresses to physical addresses. This also provides isolation between the different guests, since one guest would not be able to do I/O to the address space of another guest. Additionally, it also eliminates the overhead of copying the data from hypervisor address space to guest address space (after the I/O transfers data to hypervisor address space). **Interrupt remapping** is a technology that allows the hypervisor to ensure that interrupts from I/O devices can be delivered directly to the appropriate guest. By removing the need for the hypervisor to intervene when a guest tries to access I/O devices and adapters, it can be seen that VT-d reduces the overhead of I/O virtualization.

Note that VT-d technology may not be appropriate in all circumstances. For example, VMWare provides the option of using a file to emulate a disk storage device. VT-d cannot be used to support this kind of virtualization, since I/O to the file has to be carried out by some file system, and not directly by the CPU. In general, VT-d can be used for virtualization of I/O to devices that are emulated in the hardware.

TWO POPULAR HYPERVISORS

As described earlier, virtualization is a complex technology involving techniques for virtualizing CPU, memory and I/O. In the following subsection, two well-known hypervisors – VMWare and XenServer – are studied to illustrate how they use the techniques described earlier.

VMware Virtualization Software

VMware Inc. is a popular provider of virtualization software for desktops and enterprise servers. The VMware hypervisor makes use of all the virtualization technologies previously described [11]. Figure 9.6 shows the architecture of the VMware ESX 3i server [12]. Each virtual machine runs on top of a **Virtual Machine Monitor** (**VMM**), which is a process running under the vmkernel. The **vmkernel** which contains OS functions, such as scheduling and networking, runs

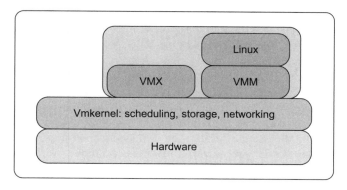

FIGURE 9.6

High-level architecture of VMware ESX 3i server.

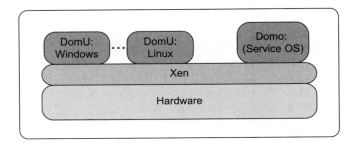

FIGURE 9.7

XenServer architecture.

on top of the hardware. Each VM also has a helper process called **VMX** associated with it.

For CPU virtualization, the VMM uses a combination of binary translation and VT-x. The VMware VMM uses paravirtualization for I/O virtualization. For Windows, where the source code is not available, the VMWare VMM uses the Windows **filter driver framework** [13]. This allows code to be installed above the Windows I/O drivers that will make hypervisor calls to vmkernel for I/O.

XenServer Virtual Machine Monitor

XenServer[1] is a widely used open source hypervisor available under GNU GPL v2. The architecture of XenServer is shown in Figure 9.7. In XenServer, the guest VMs are called **domains**. Domain 0 is a specially privileged VM which has access to the physical hardware. XenServer makes use of paravirtualization for I/O virtualization; I/O requests from any other non-domain 0 VM (called **domU**) are sent to dom0. In Linux, the paravirtualization is accomplished by rewriting the Linux code. Since Windows source code is not available, XenServer does not officially support Windows. Support for Windows using the various hardware assists (called **HVM mode** in Xen terminology) is in an experimental mode at this time. Similarly to VMware, Xen also leverages the VT-x, VT-d, EPT and VPID hardware assists. Xen does not use binary translation.

The architecture of Xen differs from VMware in that in Xen, the support for virtualization is split between the Xen hypervisor and Dom0. This allows Xen to leverage an already existing OS for Dom0; in fact, Dom0 is a version of Linux, allowing Xen to leverage the evolving capabilities of Linux for managing hardware, and focusing the energies of the Xen developers upon hypervisor support.

To summarize, server virtualization involves techniques for virtualizing the CPU, memory, and I/O. The classic technique for virtualization is trap and

---

[1]Before acquisition by Citrix, XenServer was known simply as Xen. These two terms are used interchangeably here.

emulate, but it has some high overheads and in some cases (x86 architecture) may not be feasible. In this case, binary rewriting or Intel's VT-x technology can be used. For memory virtualization, paravirtualization or Intel's EPT and VPID techniques can reduce virtualization overhead. However, the disadvantage of paravirtualization is that it requires rewriting of the guest OS. Paravirtualization can also reduce the overheads associated with I/O virtualization. In some circumstances, Intel's VT-d technology can also reduce I/O virtualization overheads. As described in Chapter 6, server virtualization helps in realizing some of the critical characteristics of a cloud infrastructure (IaaS), such as multi-tenancy, elasticity, availability and also in dramatically increasing the utilization levels of the cloud infrastructure.

STORAGE VIRTUALIZATION

In addition to scaling CPU resources (described in the previous section), cloud environments for IaaS have to scale storage resources as well. Similarly to CPU virtualization, there exist techniques for virtualizing storage resources to enable on-demand addition and deletion of storage.

Storage Virtualization can be defined as a means through which physical storage subsystems are abstracted from the user's application and presented as logical entities, hiding the underlying complexity of the storage subsystems and nature of access, network or direct, to the physical devices. As in server virtualization, this abstraction helps applications to perform normally despite changes to the storage hardware. Storage virtualization also enables higher resource utilization by aggregating the capacity of multiple heterogeneous storage devices into storage pools, enables easy provisioning of the right storage for performance or cost, as well as provides ability to centrally manage pools of storage and associated services.

Broadly, there are two categories of storage virtualizations: **file level** and **block level**. A file system virtualization provides an abstraction of a file system to the application (with a standard file-serving protocol interface such as NFS or CIFS) and manages changes to distributed storage hardware underneath the file system implementation. Block-level virtualization, on the other hand, virtualizes multiple physical disks and presents the same as a single logical disk. The data blocks of this logical disk may be internally mapped to one or more physical disks or may reside on multiple storage subsystems. Different techniques are used to handle the complexity and optimized usage of these two types of storage virtualizations.

File Virtualization

File virtualization creates an abstraction layer between file servers and their clients. This virtualization layer manages files, directories or file systems across multiple servers and allows administrators to present users with a single logical file system. A typical implementation of a virtualized file system is as a network file system that supports sharing of files over a standard protocol with multiple file servers enabling access to individual files. File-serving protocols that are typically employed are NFS, CIFS and Web interfaces such as HTTP/WebDAV.

Simple implementations of network file systems and virtualized file systems that provide a single name space are covered in traditional textbooks [14]. The focus here will be on techniques to implement scalable file virtualization such as distributed file systems, which is of relevance to cloud computing.

A **distributed file system (DFS)** is a network file system wherein the file system is distributed across multiple servers. DFS enables location transparency and file directory replication as well as tolerance to faults. Some implementations may also cache recently accessed disk blocks for improved performance. Though distribution of file content increases performance considerably, efficient management of metadata is crucial for overall file system performance. It has been shown that 75% of all file system calls access file metadata [15] and distributing metadata load is important for scalability. Scaling metadata performance is more complex than scaling raw I/O performance since even a small inconsistency in metadata can lead to data corruption. There are two important techniques for managing metadata for highly scalable file virtualization:

a. Separate data from metadata with a centralized metadata server (used in Lustre, Panasas [16–18])
b. Distribute data and metadata on multiple servers (used in Gluster, Ibrix [19, 20] Nirvanix)

Distributed File Systems with Centralized Metadata

A centralized metadata management scheme achieves scalable DFS with a dedicated metadata server to which all metadata operations performed by clients are directed. Lock-based synchronization is used in every read or write operation from the clients. The detailed working of such a system can be studied using the popular open source file system called **Lustre**. In centralized metadata systems, the metadata server can become a bottleneck if there are too many metadata operations. However, for workloads with large files, centralized metadata systems perform and scale very well.

Lustre

Lustre is a massively parallel, scalable distributed file system for Linux which employs a cluster-based architecture with centralized metadata. This is a software solution with an ability to scale over thousands of clients for a storage capacity of petabytes with high performance I/O throughput. Lustre is available for free download under GNU GPL license and was used by half of the top 30 supercomputers at the time of writing of this book.

The architecture of Lustre (Figure 9.8) includes the following three main functional components, which can either be on the same nodes or distributed on separate nodes communicating over a network [21]:

1. **Object storage servers** (OSSes), which store file data on object storage targets (OSTs).

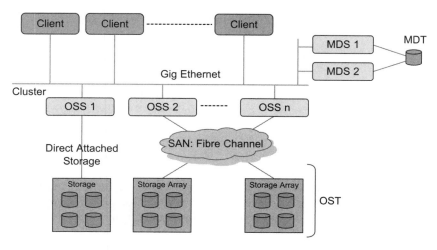

FIGURE 9.8

Architecture of Lustre file system.

2. A single metadata target (MDT) that stores metadata on one or more **Metadata servers** (MDS), and
3. **Lustre Clients** that access the data over the network using a POSIX interface.

When a client wishes to perform an operation on a file, it consults the MDT, a dedicated file system, to discover which objects constitute a file. These objects are stored on one or more OSTs. An OST is also a dedicated file system that exposes read/write operations to data objects. Disk storage attached to the servers can be directly partitioned and formatted as file systems. Optionally, they can be organized as LVs (logical volumes) using the Logical Volume Manager. The OSS and MDS servers store data using a modified version of the EXT3 file system.

Lustre can stripe files over multiple OSTs for better file I/O speeds. When multiple objects are associated with a file (MDS inode), data in the file is striped across all the objects. Hence, capacity and bandwidth scaling is achieved depending on the number of OSTs a file is striped over. With striping, the first chunk of the file is placed on the first disk, the second chunk on the second disk, and so on, until all the OSTs have been used up, at which point the file wraps around to the first disk. The number of bytes in a chunk is user-specifiable. To use striping, a Lustre client must use the Lustre Logical (Object) Volume manager (LOV).

A brief overview of the end-to-end operation of Lustre follows. When a client accesses a file, it does a filename lookup on a MDS. Then, MDS creates a metadata file on behalf of the client or returns the layout of an existing file. The client then passes the layout to a logical object volume (LOV) for read or write operations. The LOV maps the offset and size to one or more objects, each residing on a separate OST. The client then locks the file range being operated on and executes one or more parallel read or write operations directly to the OSTs. With this approach, bottlenecks for client-to-OST communications are eliminated, so the total bandwidth available for the clients to read and write data scales almost linearly with the number of OSTs in the file system.

Lustre uses read-only caching of data in the OSS that enhances performance when multiple clients access the same data set. It also provides other optimization features such as read-ahead and write-back caching for performance improvements. Striping support described earlier is also a very good way of improving I/O performance for all files, since reading and writing simultaneously increases the available I/O bandwidth. Lustre also supports an innovative file-joining feature that joins files in place, when the file is striped.

Lustre has a very good failover feature which adds to the availability of the solution [22]. As in other cluster configurations, failover support in a cluster is provided by configuring duplicate servers to perform the functionality; typically they are configured in pairs. In most clusters, there are two types of failovers configured – they are active/active or active/passive. In an active/passive configuration, the active node provides resources and serves data while the passive node stands by in idle state. When the active (primary) node fails, the passive (secondary) node comes in and takes over the functionality. In an active/active functionality, both the nodes are active and each provides a subset of resources. If one of the nodes fails, the second node takes over the resources from the fail node.

The active/active configuration is recommended for an OSS. Though multiple OSSes are configured to serve an OST, at any point, the OST is partitioned between the OSSes. For MDT failover, on the other hand, an active/passive configuration is required; i.e., two MDSes are configured for every MDT, and only one is active at any point in time.

Let us look at a failover scenario. When a client attempts to do I/O to a failed Lustre target, it continues to try until it receives an answer from any of the configured failover nodes for the Lustre target. A user-space application does not detect anything unusual, except that the I/O may take longer than usual to complete. Therefore, high availability in the Lustre File System is completely application transparent.

More information, including detailed working of Lustre, is available in a joint technical report from Sun Microsystems and the National Center for Computational Sciences [23]. The Lustre Center of Excellence at Oak Ridge [24] and the Lustre community [25] also contain much detailed information.

Distributed File Systems with Distributed Metadata

The complementary approach to Lustre is distributed metadata management, such as GlusterFS, where metadata is distributed across all nodes in the system, rather than using centralized metadata servers. Such systems have greater complexity than centralized metadata systems, since the metadata management is spread over all the nodes in the system.

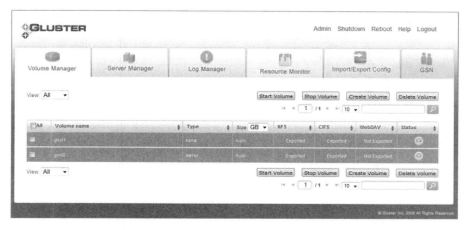

FIGURE 9.9

Gluster management console.

GlusterFS

GlusterFS is an open-source, distributed cluster file system without a centralized metadata server [26]. It is also capable of scaling to thousands of clients, Petabytes of capacity and is optimized for high performance. It is accompanied by a web-based management interface and installer that makes it more suitable for cloud computing even from a user interface perspective (Figure 9.9).

GlusterFS employs a modular architecture with a stackable user-space design. It aggregates multiple storage bricks on a network (over Infiniband RDMA or TCP/IP interconnects) and delivers as a network file system with a global name space. Unlike Lustre, it does not employ a separate index of metadata. Instead it employs a new technique called Elastic Hash Algorithm, which avoids metadata lookup, adding to better performance [27]. It is also different in its failover architecture, where every cluster is configured to be active and any file in the entire file system can be accessed from any server simultaneously.

It consists of just two major components: a Client and a Server. The Gluster server clusters all the physical storage servers and exports the combined diskspace of all servers as a Gluster File System. The Gluster client is actually optional and can be used to implement highly available, massively parallel access to every storage node and handles failure of any single node transparently.

The GlusterFS server exports storage volumes to remote clients and the GlusterFS client accesses remote storage volumes using POSIX interfaces. They can also mount the file system locally using FUSE (a popular Linux file system software that helps in mounting file systems, for more details see fuse.sourceforge.net). Alternatively, for client systems that do not support FUSE, a user space client called Booster is available as a shared object.

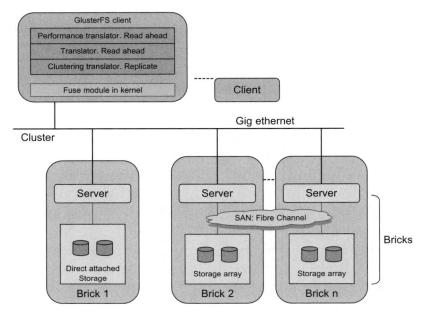

FIGURE 9.10

Architecture of Gluster.

Figure 9.10 shows an overview of the architecture of Gluster. GlusterFS uses the concept of a storage brick consisting of a server that is attached to storage directly (DAS) or through a SAN. Local file systems (ext3, ext4) are created on this storage.

Gluster employs a mechanism called **translators** to implement the file system capabilities. Translators are programs (like filters) inserted between the actual content of a file and the user accessing the file as a basic file system interface [28, 29]. Each translator implements a particular feature of GlusterFS. Translators can be loaded both in client and server side appropriately to improve or achieve new functionalities. Examples of translators that are deployed in Gluster are Symbolic Links (which implements symbolic links), performance translators, clustering translators and scheduling translators. In a symbolic link translator, an access to the symbolic link starts the translator, which would forward the request to the file-system that contains the file the link points to.

Translators also allow optimization control at a much finer level as well. A **Read Ahead** translator, for example, employs caching logic, which performs data read pre-fetches enabling read performance. A **Write Behind** translator delays the write operation and allows the client to process the next operation. Subsequently, it aggregates multiple smaller write operations into fewer large write operations and hence improves write performance. Clustering translators support GlusterFS to effectively use multiple servers for clustered storage. **A unify** translator aggregates sub-volumes from the storage and presents them as a single volume [30]. It allows a particular file to reside on one of the sub-volumes in the storage cluster and employs a "scheduler" to determine where a file resides.

Gluster performs very good load balancing of operations using the I/O Scheduler translators [31]. Adaptive Least Usage (ALU) is one such translator wherein the GlusterFS balances load across volumes. Further, the optimized load is defined by the following "sub-balancers" and that enables one to fine-tune the load balancing feature as per the application-need:

- Disk-usage: Free and used disk space on the volume
- Read-usage: Quantum of read operations performed from this volume
- Write-usage: Quantum of write operations performed done from this volume
- Open-files-usage: Number of open files from this volume
- Disk-speed-usage: The disk's spinning speed

GlusterFS also supports file replication with the **Automatic File Replication (AFR)** translator, which keeps identical copies of a file/directory on all its sub-volumes [32, 33]. Here, all file system operations (I/O and control) are performed on all its sub-volumes. Operations that do not perform file or directory modifications are sent to all the sub-volumes and the first successful reply is passed back to the application. However, read operations accessing data from a file AFR are handled by routing all reads from a particular file to a specific server. Consistency across sub-volumes is achieved by a lock whenever a modification is being made to file/directory or directory. A change log is maintained that keeps track of the data or metadata changes performed.

Self healing is another important feature supported by Gluster. In situations of data inconsistency across different copies of a file, the change log mentioned earlier is used to determine the correct copy version. The self-healing feature works as follows. On a directory access, the correct version is replicated on all sub-volumes, by deleting/creating necessary entries. On a file access, if the file is missing, it is created on all sub-volumes, and metadata is changed if different from the correct version. Data updates are performed periodically if the change log indicates mismatch.

Gluster is therefore a potential technology that can be used to provide scalable, available and highly performing storage hardware for a cloud storage infrastructure. So, it is usually referred to as a cloud file system and has been used with RackSpace cloud-hosting solution. Further information about Gluster can be found in the Gluster community page [34].

Block Virtualization

The other type of storage in data centers is block storage such as that found in a Fibre Channel, iSCSI or direct-attached storage. Block storage has very good performance, and is used widely for database transaction processes, while having worse manageability [35]. However, the performance of file level and block level storage is close enough that many enterprise customers use file storage for many of their needs. Providing virtualized block storage is critical for IaaS cloud vendors.

Block-level virtualization technique virtualizes multiple physical disks and presents the same as a single logical disk. The data blocks are mapped to one or more physical disks sub-systems. These block addresses may reside on multiple storage sub-systems, appearing however as a single storage (logical) storage device.

Block level storage virtualization can be performed at three levels:

a. Host-Based
b. Storage Level
c. Network level

A well-known traditional technique for host-based storage virtualization is the use of a **Logical Volume Manager** (**LVM**), a virtualization layer that supports allocation and management of disk space for file systems or raw data with capabilities to dynamically shrink or increase physical volumes, or combine small chunks of unused space from multiple disks or create a logical volume that is greater than the size of the physical disk, all these transparently.

Storage-device level virtualization creates **Virtual Volumes** over the physical storage space of the specific storage subsystem. Storage disk arrays provide this form of virtualization using RAID techniques. Array controllers create **Logical UNits** (**LUNs**) spanning across multiple disks in the array in RAID Groups. Some disk arrays also virtualize third-party external storage devices attached to the array. This technique is generally host-agnostic and has low latency since the virtualization is a part of the storage device itself and in the firmware of the device.

As the two techniques are well covered in traditional text books, the focus in the following is the newer area of network-based virtualizations.

Network-Based Virtualization

This is the most commonly implemented form of scalable virtualization. In this approach, the virtualization functionality is implemented within the network connecting hosts and storage, say a Fibre Channel Storage Area Network (SAN). There are broadly two categories based on where the virtualization functions are implemented: either in switches (routers) or in appliances (servers). In a **switch-based** network virtualization, the actual virtualization occurs in an intelligent switch in the fabric and the functionality is achieved when it works in conjunction with a metadata manager in the network. On the other hand, in an **appliance-based** approach, the I/O flows through an appliance that controls the virtualization layer.

Both switch-based and appliance-based models can provide the same services: disk management, metadata lookup, data migration and replication. In appliance-based implementation, the appliance, a dedicated hardware device, sits in between the host and the storage, and I/O requests are targeted at the appliance. In the switch-based model, intelligent switches also sit in between the host and the storage, but try to perform their function transparently using techniques to snoop on incoming I/O requests and performing I/O redirection. Services requiring fast updates of data and metadata may not perform well in a switch-based solution, as it is difficult to ensure atomic updates to metadata.

Further, there are broadly two variations of an appliance-based implementation. The appliance can either be **in-band** or **out-of-band**. In in-band, all I/O requests and their data pass through the virtualization device and the clients do not interact with the storage device at all. All I/O is performed by the appliance on behalf of the clients. In out-of-band usage, the appliance only comes in between for metadata management (control path), while the data (I/O) path is directly from the client to each host (with agents on each host/client). This mode is somewhat similar to Lustre's mode of having separate metadata servers (but for block). The following describes one example of each of these different virtualization techniques.

HP SAN Virtualization Services Platform

HP StorageWorks SAN Virtualization Services Platform **(HP SVSP)** is a switch-based storage virtualization solution wherein an intelligent FC **switch** runs virtualization functionality using specialized ASICs (Application Specific Integrated Circuits). Translation of logical to physical addresses and the redirection of I/O is performed in these switches. An **out of band** metadata manager (an **appliance**) manages the control operations. This is called a split-path architecture.

In this split-path architecture, the intelligent switch splits the data and the control operations in the network. The intelligent switch manages the I/O data path while the metadata control operations are routed to the out of band manager, which could be an **appliance**. The need for host agents which direct virtual I/O requests to the correct physical storage is thereby eliminated, since this is done transparently in the switch. The appliance performing metadata management has the physical storage visibility and allocates virtual volume mapping. Virtual volumes are presented to hosts as disk drives. On a host I/O to the virtual volume, the virtual volume's logical address is mapped to a physical address, and I/O is sent directly to the storage devices.

Figure 9.11 shows the high-level architecture of HP SVSP. It mainly includes Data Path Modules (or DPMs), which are intelligent switches, and Virtualization Server Managers (or VSMs), which are appliances. The virtualization functionality is performed both by the DPMs and VSMs. The DPM performs real-time parsing of FC frames by examining packets. The DPM gets its virtual-to-physical storage mappings from the VSM. VSM performs data management operations including functionality such as replication and backup. The VSM and DPM coordinate for all management and control path operations without interference in the data path between servers and storage arrays, hence supporting high I/O throughput to storage arrays.

The solution includes replication support as well as snapshots, mirroring and non-disruptive data migration. Also, since I/O traffic flows directly through the ASIC, the latency problem can be made imperceptible to applications without the need to resort to caching.

IBM SAN Volume Controller

IBM SAN Volume Controller **(SVC)** is a storage virtualization appliance-based solution in a Fibre Channel storage area network. The appliance is positioned in-band in the I/O path of the network, thereby separating the fabric in two sections.

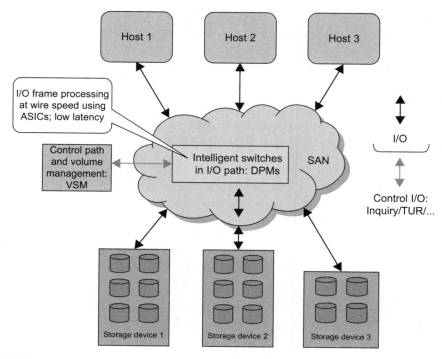

FIGURE 9.11

HP SAN virtualization platform architecture.

One is the section of the appliance facing the host on one side of the network where it appears as a storage device. Second is the section of the appliance facing the storage arrays where it appears as an Initiator (Host). Such an appliance implementation in a network has to examine every data packet, resulting in additional I/O packet processing and hence additional latency. This overhead is overcome by using a cache in the appliance. Cache usage enables write-back acknowledgements to be sent to the host even prior to the data actually having been written to the physical storage. The appliance manages cache synchronization with physical storage consistency and cache coherency.

The virtualization layer of SVC supports block-level aggregation for storage devices in the SAN and volume management by mapping physical storage into logical volumes presented to servers in the SAN. The back-end physical storage is hidden from direct visibility to servers through zoning in the SAN.

Figure 9.12 shows the high-level architecture of this IBM solution. A **node** is the virtualization layer appliance supporting caching and replication services. These nodes in pairs are called **I/O groups.** Multiple I/O groups form a cluster. A **virtual volume** or a **VDisk** is presented to a host server by one I/O Group of this cluster. All I/O to a VDisk from a server are routed to one specific I/O Group in

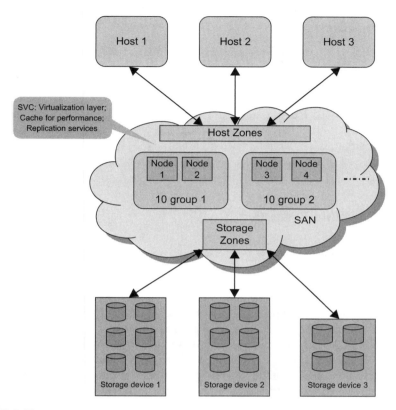

FIGURE 9.12

Architecture of IBM SVC.

the cluster and processed by the same node of the I/O Group, called a preferred node. On a node failure, the surviving node takes over the preferred node tasks, thereby facilitating high availability.

Servers can be mapped to more than one I/O Group of an SVC cluster for accessing VDisks from separate I/O Groups. VDisks can be moved between I/O Groups for load distribution. The physical storage seen by the clusters is referred to as **managed disks** or **MDisks**. A **Managed Disk Group** (**MDG**) is a collection of MDisks. A VDisk seen by a server is capacity provisioned out of one or more MDGs. An MDisk comprises a number of extents wherein the size of the extent is user controllable. So, unlike IBM SVC, HP SVSN is a purely appliance-based solution.

So far in this chapter, technologies were described that can be used by an IaaS vendor to set up scalable, elastic hardware resources used to serve a cloud user. The remaining sections give a concise description of related technologies that are sometimes confused with cloud computing and explain the similarities and differences between cloud computing and the specific technology.

GRID COMPUTING

Cloud computing is frequently compared to grid computing. Grid computing also has the same intent of abstracting out computing resources to enable utility models and was proposed at least a decade earlier than cloud computing, and there are many aspects of grid computing that have formed the basis of the requirements placed on a cloud. Having said that, there are also very specific differences between a grid computing infrastructure and the features one should expect from a cloud computing infrastructure. This can be seen by first describing some fundamental aspects of grid computing and then comparing them with those of cloud computing.

Overview of Grid Computing

The vision of grid computing is to enable computing to be delivered as a utility. This vision is most often presented with an analogy to electrical power grids, from which it derives the name "grid". So, grid computing was meant to be used by individual users who gain access to computing devices without knowing where the resource is located or what hardware it is running, and so on. In this sense, it is pretty similar to cloud computing. However, just as electrical power grids can derive power from multiple power generators and deliver the power as needed by the consumer, the key emphasis of grid computing was to enable sharing of computing resources or forming a pool of shared resources that can then be delivered to users. So, most of the initial technological focus of grid computing was limited to enabling shared use of resources with common protocols for access, Also, since the key takers of this fascinating vision were educational institutions, a particular emphasis was given to handle heterogeneous infrastructure, which was typical of a university datacenter. From a technical perspective, a software-only solution was proposed (Globus) and implemented on this heterogeneous infrastructure to enable use of these resources for higher computing needs. Once reasonably successful within universities, grid computing faced a serious issue when it came to sharing resources across commercial institutions. Establishing trust and security models between infrastructure resources pooled from two different administrative domains became even more important.

Three Fundamental Characteristics of a Grid

In 2002, Ian Foster from Argonne National Laboratories proposed a three-point checklist for determining whether a system is a grid or not. Ian Foster along with Steve Tucker in the popular article "Anatomy of Grid" defined grid computing as *"coordinated resource sharing and problem solving in dynamic, multi-institutional virtual organizations."*

So, the key concept emphasized was the ability to negotiate resource sharing agreements among a set of participating parties – where sharing did not really mean "exchange" but direct access to computing resources either in a collaborative resource sharing or negotiated resource brokering strategies. Further, this sharing was highly controlled with resource providers and consumers grouped into virtual organizations primarily based on sharing conditions.

The following is the precise simple checklist that was proposed: A **grid** is a system that

1. Co-ordinates resources that are not subject to centralized control
2. Using standard, open, general purpose protocols and interfaces
3. To deliver nontrivial quality of service

The first criterion states that a grid should integrate computing resources from different control domains (say servers from computer centers of different universities, each center having a different system administrator in each university). Technologically, this requirement addresses the issues of cross-domain security, policy management, and membership. Use of a common standard for authentication, authorization, resource discovery and resource access becomes a necessity in such cases and hence the second criterion. Finally, in an effort towards commercializing the usage of shared resources, it is important to support various quality-of-service parameters such as response time, throughput, availability or even co-allocation of resources to meet user demands.

A Closer Look at Grid Technologies

First of all, grid computing defines a notion of a virtual organization to enable flexible, co-ordinated, secure resource sharing among participating entities. A **virtual organization (VO)** is basically a dynamic collection of individuals or institutions from multiple administrative domains. A VO forms a basic unit for enabling access to shared resources with specific resource-sharing policies applicable for users from a particular VO (Figure 9.13). The key technical problem addressed by grid technologies is to enable resource sharing among mutually distrustful participants of a VO who may have varying degrees of prior relationship (perhaps none at all) and enable them to solve a common task.

An extensible and open **Grid Architecture** shown in Figure 9.14 was defined by Ian Forster in *The Anatomy of the Grid* [36] in which protocols, services, APIs, and SDKs are categorized according to their roles in enabling resource sharing. The **Grid Fabric** layer provides the resources to which shared access is mediated by grid protocols. These can be computational resources, storage systems, catalogs, network resources or even a logical entity, such as a distributed file system, computer cluster, or distributed computer pool. A well-known toolkit for the fabric layer is the **Globus Toolkit** that provides local resource specific operations on existing computing elements [37]. The **Connectivity** layer includes the core protocols for communication and authentication for inter-node communication. The key aspects of these protocols include single sign on, delegation, user-based

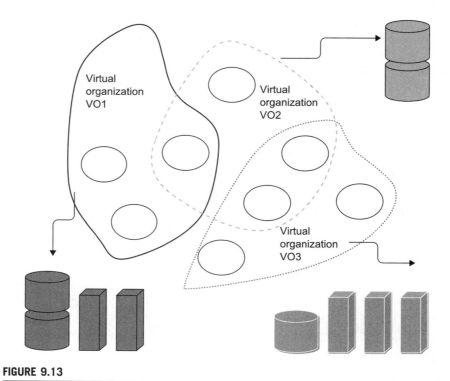

FIGURE 9.13

Virtual organizations.

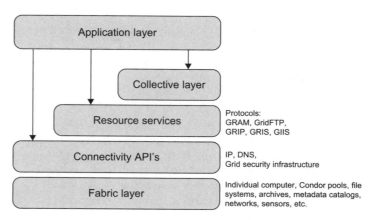

FIGURE 9.14

Layered grid architecture.

trust relationships and integration with local security solutions. One important protocol whose reference implementation is available in Globus is the public key based **GSI protocol (Grid Security Infrastructure)**, which extends TLS (Transport Layer Security) to address these issues. The resource layer includes APIs and SDKs for secure negotiation, monitoring, control, accounting, and payment for operations on a single shared resource. An example protocol at this layer is the **GRAM (Grid Resource Access and Management)** protocol used for allocation, monitoring and control of computational resources; and the **GRIP (Grid Resource Information Protocol)** and **GridFTP (File Transfer Protocol),** which are extensions of LDAP and FTP protocols. The **Collective** Layer implements a variety of sharing behaviors with directory services, brokering services, programming systems community accounting and authorization services and even collaborative services. One such service is the **GIIS (Grid Information Index Servers)** that supports arbitrary views on resource subsets, which can be used with LDAP and the DUROC library that supports resource co-allocation. More details of these services can be found at the Globus Technical Papers web site [38].

Current implementations of Open Grid architecture follow a Web Services-based interface enabling interoperability between different implementations of the protocols. Since web services by definition are stateless, the Grid community (Globus alliance) introduced a set of enhanced specifications called **Web Services Resource Framework (WSRF)** that web services could implement to become stateful. **Open Grid Services Architecture** now defines a service-oriented grid computing environment, which not only provides standardized interfaces, but also removes the need for layering in the architecture and defines a concept of virtual domains, allowing dynamic grouping of resources as well. Interested readers can look up the complete OGSA specification at http://www.ogf.org/documents/GFD.80.pdf

The standard bodies involved in evolving the grid protocols were (a) The Global Grid Forum, (GGF); (b) Organization for the Advancement of Structured Information Standards (OASIS); (c) World Wide Web Consortium (W3C); (d) Distributed Management Task Force (DMTF); and (e) Web Services Interoperability Organization (WS-I).

A reference implementation of these protocols is available in a popular open source software toolkit called **Globus** toolkit (GT), which was developed by the Globus alliance, a community of organizations and individuals developing fundamental technologies behind the grid [39–41]. The nice thing about this software is that it enables existing resources to easily join a grid pool by enabling the required protocols locally. Figure 9.15 shows a high-level block diagram of the components provided in GT5. To get started on setting up a grid, one just needs to download and install GT on any of the supported platforms. To create a resource pool, it is a good idea to install a resource scheduler such as the Condor cluster scheduler and configure that as a grid gateway for resource allocation. After some initial security configurations (obtaining signed certificates and setting up access rights), the grid can be up and running!

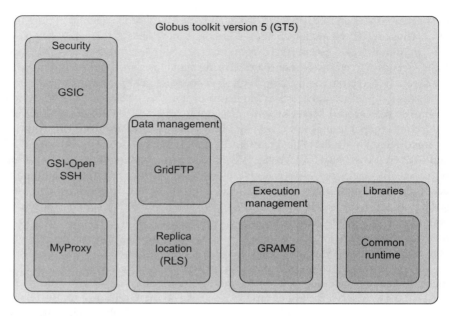

FIGURE 9.15

Globus toolkit.

> **NOTE**
>
> **Some popular grid projects**
> - Grid Physics Network GriPhyN driven by University of Chicago,
> - Particle Physics Data Grid (PPDG), a collaboration project now merged with iVDGL,
> - EU DataGrid now part of EGEE (Enabling Grids For E-sciencE),
> - NASA's Information Power Grid,
> - DOE Science Grid and DISCOM Grid that link systems at DOE laboratories, and
> - TeraGrid that links major U.S. academic sites.

Comparing Grid and Cloud

From the earlier description of grid computing, it can be seen that it has many similarities with cloud computing. However, there are differences as well, notably the fact that grid computing emphasizes the pooling of resources from multiple organizations, and that it mostly targets high-performance computing (HPC) applications. This section compares the two technologies in more detail using different parameters. Readers are referred to studies made in 2008 [42, 43] for a detailed comparison of grid and cloud computing from a practical implementation perspective.

Similarities between Grid and Cloud

The key similarity between cloud computing and grid computing is the intent of providing resources that can scale and go beyond what a user personally owns. In grid computing, the scalability is provided by increasing the utilization of resources and is achieved by load balancing across shared resources. On the other hand, scalability in a cloud service is achieved by using sophisticated auto-re-provisioning techniques or simply by provisioning more than what the user asked for (always catering to peak loads).

The need for multitasking and multi-tenancy is also common between the two. Multiple users can simultaneously access the same resources and run multiple instances of applications. However, since cloud computing typically involves a more commercial agreement between the vendor and the user, the system has a more rigorous need for multi-tenancy at every aspect of the stack – infrastructure, platform as well as application.

Since both the forms of computing require use of resources from someone else, either the cloud vendor or collaborator in the grid case, strict service-level agreements need to be in place to ensure fair play, especially when the resource usage comes with certain commercial agreements. Similarly, many grid systems provide support for application failover (Condor) and this is particularly useful for long running HPC applications to restart from the nearest failure point. Fault tolerance of applications on a cloud system is, in fact, critical and the vendor needs to ensure service availability through appropriate failover mechanisms.

Differences between Grid and Cloud

Given the detailed discussion of cloud computing in the earlier chapters and the short introduction to grid computing, it will be clear that there are differences between the computing models. A grid basically links disparate resources from multiple organizations to form one large infrastructure pool. Grid computing allocates compute and storage resources to a user from a **shared pool of assets** that can even have a contribution from the user's own organization! The key focus is in harnessing unused resources and typically these resources are heterogeneous in nature. On the other hand, cloud infrastructure will usually consist of homogeneous resources and is provided by a single vendor to a consumer or user (different from the vendor).

The typical way of using a large number of resources on a grid is through **advance reservation**. In fact, there were many advance reservation algorithms (Grid-ARS) and APIs (GridEngine) [44] proposed around 2005, to enable optimal resource utilization in grid systems. On the contrary, no reservation is needed in a cloud infrastructure. On-demand resource provisioning is one of the key benefits of cloud computing. The resources are supposed to magically expand when the demand increases. Some of the techniques and APIs provided to enable this elasticity in computing have been described earlier, and massive scale up of resources on demand is a key aspect of cloud computing, which removes the need for advance resource reservations.

Another aspect that is different between the two models is the ownership of resources. Since resources from multiple organizations are pooled, the machines in a grid pool will typically come from different **administrative domains**. So, protocols to manage authenticated access in such a virtual organization become important. Resources on a cloud, however, are owned by a single cloud vendor and any joint partnerships are handled at a business level and no technology components for the same are used.

Further, in a cloud environment, consumers use what they need and **pay** only for what they used (even in a private cloud, different departments in a business may pay for their resource usage) – while payment is not an aspect studied in the grid context. Users may also pay implicitly by contributing their resources to a shared pool for other's use. So, while fine-grained usage monitoring becomes important on a cloud, it is not of much value in a grid system. There are also differences in the target user segment that the two computing models address. The target segment for cloud computing is established industry, academia and also startups or new ventures. And they are hosted by commercial companies like Amazon and HP, who charge users for what they use. On the other hand, the target population for a grid are primarily researchers and technology collaborators (groups of institutions) that are interested in sharing their individually owned resources among each other.

Grid computing is a software-only solution, with tools (Globus toolkit) deployed to enable grid protocols over existing systems. A cloud-based solution, on the other hand, involves technologies at multiple layers of the stack, leading to different cloud models (IaaS, PaaS and SaaS). Also, grid applications are parallel, distributed, message-passing applications that either execute certain modules on specialized computing resources located in a different geography, or execute a data parallel application loosely coupled and distributed on a number of similar compute and storage resources. Grids are therefore suited for HPC applications for large-scale computation where large data sets are crunched by parallelizable compute intensive applications. A cloud application, on the other hand, need not be a distributed application. It needs to be architected in a way to scale based on demand. So apart from using distributed machines, it can also use a scale-out technique on clusters or parallel threads on multiple compute nodes with a shared memory, for example. Cloud computing is also used to host web services that tend to be long-serving daemon-like services that run for a long time, as opposed to grid applications that tend to be more compute intensive and batch-like, needing a lot of resources for a limited amount of time (and this estimated completion time is used for prior reservation of the resources). Similarly, the unit of storage used by a cloud consumer can vary from 1 byte to petabytes, where a data grid is particularly useful for large-scale data storage and manipulation.

Since cloud applications execute on a web browser, they are much easier to use without any client software installed; whereas grid applications tend to be distributed and need specific types of heterogeneous resources requiring appropriate grid schedulers for installation. Though the consumers here too can use a simple browser-like interface, the results of grid applications tend to large amounts of data that require sophisticated visualization tools to consume. The key aspect of cloud is abstraction of complex technologies – be it hardware, software or applications – and delivering it in the most simplistic fashion. The main advantage of clouds over grid is **simplicity of usage** and that of grids over cloud is efficient use of resources.

NOTE

Comparing Grid and Cloud Computing

A very nice table comparing the similarities and differences between grid and cloud has been published by The Israeli Association of Grid Technologies (IGT) and is available at http://www.grid.org.il/_Uploads/dbsAttachedFiles/Comparing-Cloud-Grid.pdf

---

Combining Grid Computing with Cloud Computing

Can we combine the two technologies? Though in principle, it is possible to deliver cloud computing services over a resource pool of a grid system, the business viability of harnessing such resources from different organizations to collectively deliver as a joint cloud infrastructure vendor seems less likely. Similarly, it is possible to think of a cloud infrastructure participating as one of the nodes in a resource pool enabling shared access to cloud-hosted paid infrastructure. Again, linking up the pay-per-use model with sharing is tricky. While the technologies underlying both grid computing and cloud computing may converge or become interoperable in the future, differences in the commercial aspects will remain, specifically around type of usage and access patterns.

OTHER CLOUD-RELATED TECHNOLOGIES

The following are other technologies that are similar to cloud computing but, like grid computing, are distinct technologies.

Distributed Computing

Distributed computing is a much broader technology that has been around for more than three decades now. Simply stated, distributed computing is computing over distributed autonomous computers that communicate only over a network (Figure 9.16). Distributed computing systems are usually treated differently from parallel computing systems or shared-memory systems, where multiple computers share a common memory pool that is used for communication between the processors. Distributed memory systems use multiple computers to solve a common problem, with computation distributed among the connected computers (nodes) and using message-passing to communicate between the nodes. For example, grid computing, studied in the previous section, is a form of distributed computing where the nodes may belong to different administrative domains. Another example is the network-based storage virtualization solution described in an earlier section

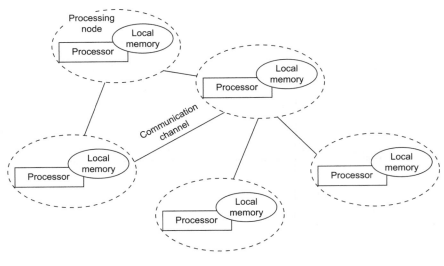

FIGURE 9.16

A distributed computing system.

in this chapter, which used distributed computing between data and metadata servers.

Developing applications for distributed memory machines is much more involved than traditional sequential machines. Sometimes new algorithms need to be developed to solve even a well-known problem (sorting huge sequences of numbers). In order to ease the burden on programmers, parallelizing compilers that convert sequential programs written for traditional computers to distributed message programs exist, particularly for distributed SMP (symmetric multiprocessor) clusters. Distributed computing, however, can include heterogeneous computations where some nodes may perform a lot more computation, some perform very little computation and a few others may perform specialized functionality (like processing visual graphics). One of the main advantages of using distributed computing (versus supercomputers like Cray where thousands of processors are housed in a rack and communicate through shared memory) is that efficient scalable programs can be designed so that independent processes are scheduled on different nodes and they communicate only occasionally to exchange results – as opposed to working out of a shared memory with multiple simultaneous accesses to a common memory.

With that description, it is probably obvious that cloud computing is also a specialized form of distributed computing, where distributed SaaS applications utilize thin clients (such as browsers) which offload computation to cloud-hosted servers (and services). Additionally, cloud-computing vendors providing (IaaS and PaaS) solutions may internally use distributed computing to provide highly scalable cost-effective infrastructure and platform.

Utility Computing

Utility computing has been a vision of many for a long time. John McCarthy, referring to *computers of the future*, said that computing will be organized as a public utility like the telephone system, and that was way back in the 1960s [45]! By definition, utility computing is packaging of computing resources (computation, storage, applications) as a metered service similar to a traditional public utility (such as electricity, water, natural gas, or the telephone network). The primary advantage of this model was low or no initial cost to acquire computer resources; instead, computational resources are essentially rented. Early efforts towards delivering utility computing was from HP, where it launched InsynQ to provide on-demand desktop hosting services, and later on launched a product called Utility Data Center (UDC), which enabled a user to carve out required infrastructure from a fixed set of resource pools and create isolated personal virtual data centers. Similarly, in the 1990s Sun Cloud and Polyserve Clustered File System were efforts to offer storage as a service.

It can be seen that cloud computing has attempted to make the complete computing stack – the infrastructure, platform and applications – as a service, delivering each of them as a metered computing resource with a pay per use model. Cloud computing is the most recent technology innovation which has made utility computing a reality!

Autonomic Computing

Autonomic computing, proposed by Paul Horn of IBM in 2001, shared the vision of making all computing systems manage themselves automatically. It refers to self-managing characteristics of distributed computing resources, which recognize and understand changes in the system, take appropriate corrective actions completely automatically, with close to zero human intervention. The key benefit is drastic reduction in the intrinsic complexity of computing systems and making computing more intuitive and easy to use by operators and users. The vision is to make computing systems self-configuring, self-optimizing, and self-protecting – as well as self-healing.

Independently, several similar efforts arose towards simplified IT management, such as ITIL (IT Infrastructure library) methodologies and ITSM (IT service management) technologies, WSDM (Web Services distributed management), and the like. Several research groups are still working on self-healing systems and policy management systems that can handle sophisticated service level agreements to enable better automated decision making. We have seen some good success with many products now also focusing on easy manageability as one of the important goals.

Given that the objective of cloud computing is to simplify computing systems, provide elasticity in computing and high availability of systems, any new innovation towards making machines more autonomic will directly feed into cloud infrastructures. Virtualization technologies, described earlier, provide the right level of abstractions to dynamically handle changes to the hardware resources and cater to on-demand elasticity. Simplified manageability solutions that are currently provided by cloud vendors were described in Chapter 8 with specific case studies. So, it may not be wrong to say that cloud computing shares the vision of autonomic computing and more.

Application Service Providers

The trend of hosting applications as a service for others to use started as early as the 1990s. The vendors who would host such applications accessible by their clients using just web browsers were called application service providers. With this definition, it does look very similar to SaaS, and SaaS vendors could be called ASPs. However, there were several limitations when any off-the-shelf application with a browser-based interface was hosted as a service [46]. Many of these applications did not have the capability to handle multi-tenancy, customized usage for every user, and also did not have automated deployment and elasticity to scale on demand. Nevertheless, it is safe to say that the ASP model was probably a forerunner of the SaaS model of cloud computing.

SUMMARY

This chapter has looked at some important technologies that have influenced the development of cloud computing. Some of the techniques used for storage and server virtualization were studied in detail. How CPU, memory and I/O virtualization can be performed using the trap and emulate method, together with its limitations and approaches to overcome the same with software extensions and hardware assists were described. These described techniques were studied in the context of two popular virtualization software packages, namely VMware and Xen. The different techniques used to virtualize storage were studied, where physical storage sub-systems were abstracted from the user's application and presented as logical entities, hiding the underlying complexity of the storage subsystems. Techniques and architectures used to provide both file-level as well as block-level virtualized access were discussed through appropriate case studies. It could be seen that in order to provide scalable storage, sophisticated techniques to efficiently manage file system metadata become critical, with case studies of Lustre and Gluster. The chapter also looked at architectures for network-based block virtualization where the abstraction could be provided either by having smart routers or on specialized appliances, through case studies from popular SAN solutions from HP and IBM. Virtualization is a very important and fundamental technology that enables hardware resources to expand or contract in an application transparent manner – and as seen in Chapter 6, virtualization enables some of the key characteristics of a cloud infrastructure. Understanding and appreciating the complexities in implementing these techniques enables a developer to look at cloud infrastructure as a holistic solution.

Other related technologies that are often mistaken to be equivalent to cloud computing were discussed – particularly grid computing which shares the same broad vision of cloud computing – that is, to enable computing as a utility. However, as seen from the description, grid computing is more focused on enabling resource sharing among a group of collaborating institutions, which may or may not have a financial agreement (forming a virtual organization), which is a clear contrast with the business models of the cloud. From a technology standpoint, grid computing also provides a form of virtualization of resources, but not at the level of usage of physical resources, rather only to virtualize or normalize the protocol to access and manage resources. The heterogeneity in the resources is visible to the user and, in fact, leveraging these heterogeneous computing resources without owning it all is one of the benefits of grid computing. Finally, we observed and related some additional terminologies like utility computing, autonomic computing, distributed computing, etc., to cloud computing. By this chapter, you should now be able to clearly articulate the key values of cloud computing and compare and contrast those with the other related technologies.

References

[1] Smith JE, Nair R. The architecture of virtual machines. IEEE Comput 2005; 38(5): 32–38.

[2] Meyer RA, Seawright LH. A virtual machine time-sharing system. IBM Syst J 1970; 9(3):199–218.

[3] Goldberg RP. Survey of virtual machine research. IEEE Comput 7(6):34–45.

[4] Bugnion E, Devine S, Govil K, Rosenblum M. Disco: running commodity operating systems on scalable multiprocessors. ACM Trans Comput Syst 1997; 15(4):412–447.

[5] Abramson D, Jackson J, Muthrasanallur S, et al. Intel virtualization technology for directed I/O. Intel Technol J 2006; 10(3):179–192.

[6] Intel Architecture Software Developer's Manual Volume 3: System Programming.

[7] Popek GJ, Goldberg RP. Formal requirements for virtualizable third generation architectures. ACM Commun 1974; 17(7):412–421.

[8] Adams K, Agesen O. A comparison of software and hardware techniques for x86 virtualization, ASPLOS'06, October 21–25, San Jose, CA.

[9] Uhlig R, Neiger G, Rodgers D, Santoni A.L., Martins F.C.M., Anderson A.V., et al. Intel Virtualization Technology. IEEE Comput 2005, 38(5):48–56.

[10] Intel® 64, IA-32 Architectures Software Developer's Manual, Volume 3B: System Programming Guide, Part 2.

[11] Understanding Full Virtualization, Paravirtualization, and Hardware Assist, WP-028-PRO-01-01, VMware Inc. http://www.vmware.com/files/pdf/VMware_paravirtualization.pdf; 2007 [accessed 13.10.11]

[12] The Architecture of VMware ESX Server 3i, Charu Chaubal, Revision: 20071113 WP-030-PRD-01-01, VMware Inc. http://www.vmware.com/files/pdf/ESXServer3i_architecture.pdf; 2007 [accessed 13.10.11]

[13] Filter Driver Development Guide, download.microsoft.com/download/e/b/../filterdriver developerguide.doc [accessed 13.10.11]

[14] Bach, M. The Design of the UNIX Operating System, Prentice Hall, June 6, 1986, 978–0132017992

[15] Jacob DR, Lorch JR, Anderson TE. A comparison of file system workloads. In: Proceedings of the USENIX annual technical conference; 2000, Usenix Association, Berkeley, CA. p. 41–54.

[16] Panasas Architecture. http://www.panasas.com/products/architecture.php [accessed 13.10.11].

[17] Panasas® Storage for Petascale Systems. http://performance.panasas.com/wp-panasas storageforpetascalesystems-jan10.html [accessed 13.10.11].

[18] Scalable Performance of the Panasas Parallel File System. http://performance.panasas. com/wp-scalableperformanceofthepanasasparallelfilesystem-2008.html [accessed 13.10.11].

[19] HP Ibrix reference: HP and HPC Storage. http://www.hpcadvisorycouncil.com/events/ switzerland_workshop/pdf/Presentations/Day%203/3_HP.pdf [accessed 13.10.11].

[20] HP Ibrix reference: HP StorageWorks X9000 File Serving Software User Guide

[21] Lustre architecture. http://wiki.lustre.org/lid/subsystem-map/subsystem-map.html; 2010 [accessed 13.10.11]

[22] A Deep Dive into Lustre Recovery Mechanisms. https://docs.google.com/viewer? url=http://wiki.lustre.org/images/0/00/A_Deep_Dive_into_Lustre_Recovery_Mechanisms. pdf, 2011 [accessed 13.10.11]

[23] Wang F, Oral S, Shipman G, Drokin O, Wang T, Huang I. Understanding Lustre file-system internals. Oak Ridge National Laboratory; 2009.

[24] Lustre Center of Excellence at Oak Ridge National Laboratory. http://wiki.lustre.org/index. php/Lustre_Center_of_Excellence_at_Oak_Ridge_National_Laboratory#Lustre_Scal ability_Workshop_-_Feb_10_.26_11.2C_2009.2C_ORNL [accessed 13.10.11]

[25] Lustre Community Events, Conferences and Meetings. http://wiki.lustre.org/index.php/ Lustre_Community_Events,_Conferences_and_Meetings [accessed 13.10.11].

[26] GlusterFS 2.0.6. http://www.gluster.com/community/documentation/index.php/Gluster FS_2.0.6 [accessed 13.10.11].

[27] Elastic Hash Algorithm. http://ftp.gluster.com/pub/gluster/documentation/Gluster_ Architecture.pdf [accessed 13.10.11].

[28] GNU Hurd translator. http://www.gnu.org/software/hurd/hurd/translator.html [accessed 13.10.11].

[29] Gluster translators. http://www.gluster.com/community/documentation/index.php/ Translators_v2.0 [accessed 13.10.11].

[30] Understanding Unify Translator. http://www.gluster.com/community/documentation/ index.php/Understanding_Unify_Translator [accessed 13.10.11].

[31] GlusterFS Schedulers. http://www.gluster.com/community/documentation/index.php/ Translators/cluster/unify [accessed 13.10.11].

[32] Understanding AFR Translator. http://www.gluster.com/community/documentation/ index.php/Understanding_AFR_Translator [accessed 13.10.11].

[33] Internals of Replicate. http://www.gluster.com/community/documentation/index.php/ Internals_of_Replicate [accessed 13.10.11].

[34] Gluster Community Homepage. http://www.gluster.com/community/documentation/ index.php/Main_Page [accessed 13.10.11].

[35] Future of Block Storage in the Cloud. Said Syed, Cloud Computing Journal. http:// cloudcomputing.sys-con.com/node/909540 [accessed 13.10.11].

[36] Foster I, Kesselman C, Tuecke S. The Anatomy of the Grid - Enabling Scalable Virtual Organizations; 2001.

[37] Globus Homepage. http://globus.org [accessed 13.10.11].

[38] Globus Technical Papers. http://www.globus.org/alliance/publications/papers.php [accessed 13.10.11].

[39] Foster I. Globus Toolkit Version 4: Software for Service-Oriented Systems. IFIP international conference on network and parallel computing, Springer-Verlag LNCS 3779; 2005. p. 2–13.

[40] Foster I. A Globus Primer, Describing Globus Toolkit Version 4.

[41] Foster I. Globus Toolkit Version 4: Software for Service Oriented Systems. Comput Sci Technol, July 2006.

[42] An EGEE comparative study: grids and clouds evolution or revolution, June 2008. http://www.informatik.hs-mannheim.de/~baun/SEM0910/Quellen/EGEE-Grid-Cloud-v1_2.pdf; 2008 [accessed 13.10.11].

[43] Myerson J. Cloud Computing versus Grid Computing, IBM, Mar 2009.

[44] Managing Advance Reservations in Sun Grid Engine, Sun Grid Engine Information Center, 2010.

[45] Ganek A. Overview of Autonomic Computing: Origins, Evolution, Direction. http://www.maiuscentral.com/w/images/7/76/Garek.pdf [accessed 13.10.11].

[46] Differences between ASP model and SaaS model. www.luitinfotech.com/kc/saas-asp-difference.pdf [accessed 13.10.11].

Future Trends and Research Directions

INFORMATION IN THIS CHAPTER:

- Emerging Standards
- Cloud Benchmarks
- End-user Programming
- Open Cirrus
- Open Research Problems In Cloud Computing

INTRODUCTION

Since cloud computing is a rapidly evolving technology, this chapter describes some future developments that are likely to become important. A Gartner survey has shown that one of the major inhibitors to cloud computing is the lack of standardization leading to vendor lock-in [1]. Of course, this is partly due to the fact that cloud computing is rapidly evolving, making standardization difficult. The first section in this chapter, titled *Emerging Standards,* surveys new standards that have the potential to address this concern. Another problem with vendor lock-in is that even if standards were to emerge, currently there is no accepted method for a cloud user to compare different cloud vendors and select the best for a particular application. This is in contrast to the situation in, say, databases, where there are benchmarks such as TPC-C that allow different database vendors to be compared. The second section, called *Benchmarks,* therefore, describes efforts underway to develop benchmarks that can help in assessing the suitability of a particular cloud system for an application. The third section describes Open Cirrus, a large research testbed for research in cloud-computing technology, which may be very useful for readers interested in experimenting with novel cloud solutions or algorithms. The last section of the chapter, titled *End User Programming,* describes research efforts that would make it possible for users who are not programmers to develop personal applications with simple scripts and programs.

EMERGING STANDARDS

Lack of standards leading to vendor lock-in has been found to be a major customer concern for Cloud Computing [1]. This problem increases when we go higher up in the cloud computing stack. SaaS customers have a greater lock-in than PaaS customers, since they have to migrate from one application platform to another; similarly PaaS customers have a greater lock-in than IaaS customers, since they have to migrate from one cloud platform to another. The migration is made more difficult because cloud computing is a rapidly evolving technology; hence different clouds may offer differing functionality.

In spite of this rapid evolution, standards are emerging in multiple areas related to cloud computing. Since cloud computing is based on **Service Oriented Architecture (SOA)**,[1] standardization efforts have focused on standardizing the services and interfaces provided by clouds. Different standards bodies are focused on standardizing different type of cloud services.

Storage Networking Industry Association (SNIA)

The Storage Networking Industry Association (SNIA), a well-known standards development organization for the storage and database world, has recently proposed a standard way of using cloud storage called the **Cloud Data Management Interface (CDMI)** [2]. The standard enables the users to develop cloud applications without being locked into a specific vendor for storage services. This standard is endorsed by many key organizations working on the development of cloud technologies, such as **ITU-T** (the **International Telecommunication Union**), the **TeleManagement Forum**, **SIENA** (the **European Standards and Interoperability for Infrastructure Implementation Initiative**), and **NIST** (the **U.S. National Institute of Standards and Technology**). CDMI is targeted at a set of specific use cases. Each use case is supported by some CDMI APIs. For unsupported use cases and functionality, vendors can define their own CDMI extensions.

NOTE

CDMI Use Case Summary

- Elastic provisioning
- Cloud backup
- Cloud archiving
- Cloud storage

CDMI use cases: The CDMI standard addresses a number of use cases of cloud storage, namely, (a) catering to elastic on-demand access to storage – increasing or decreasing storage provisioning to be able to handle the load on a specific data object; (b) outsourcing regular backup of data; (c) retaining data for a certain number of years for audit compliance and other legislative needs; (d) storage for cloud-computing applications, which is the use case that has been extensively described in this book. In all of the previous use cases, there are a set of service

---

[1]SOA refers to a software architecture designed with a set of principles and methodologies in the form of interoperable (web) services.

APIs specified. The cloud user just uses a URL to access the cloud storage, and the vendor can perform any needed optimizations at the backend to ensure that the access is efficient and satisfies the quality of service that has been agreed upon. So, these standards are useful both to the vendor as well as the consumer of storage. Figure 10.1 depicts the cloud storage model proposed by SNIA [3]. First of all, multiple standard storage access protocols are supported for data access in the form of block access (iSCSI), file access (POSIX) or database table access. Additionally, once a cloud storage provider has hosted a customer's data in the cloud, the customer can use CDMI to tell the cloud storage provider the list of data services needed for a specific data object.

The standard prescribes special metadata called **data-system metadata** that is used to tag data. These tags specify the non-functional requirements for handling of the data, such as, whether the data needs archiving, backup, or encryption. The data-system metadata allows for detailed specification of the requirements; for example for backup, it is possible to specify if the backup is to be done daily instead of weekly, the number of copies that are needed for this data object, and the retention period. Once vendors have implemented the CDMI interface, the

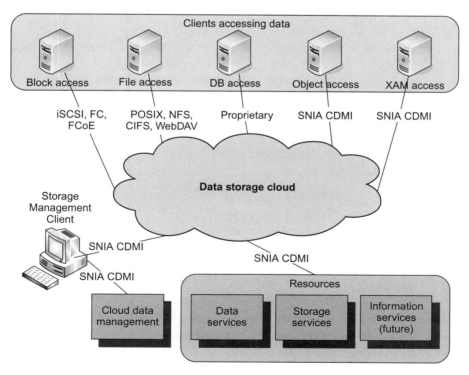

FIGURE 10.1

CDMI cloud storage reference model.

customers can move their data from one cloud vendor to another without any change in the application.

CDMI APIs: The CDMI APIs are specified in terms of **containers** and **objects** (resource). The user creates a container, puts the relevant data objects in it and specifies the data services needed for the container. This allows the user to group data according to their storage requirements. Every resource is addressable with a **unique identifier**, enabling a scale-out architecture at the backend. The standard supports five types of resources:

1. Container
2. Data object
3. Capabilities
4. Domain mime type
5. Queue mime type

Container and Data Object mime types are self explanatory. The **Domain** mime type is to access billing and activity information and the **Queue** mine type gives access to audit trails and access logs. The **Capability** mime type provides the information about security and access control data for a specific object. All this information can be obtained programmatically and not only through a user interface.

The following shows an example API to request (GET method) the capabilities of a storage resource.

```
GET /cdmi_capabilities/ HTTP/1.1
Host: cloud.example.com
Content-Type: application/vnd.org.snia.cdmi.capabilitiesobject+json
X-CDMI-Specification-Version: 1.
```

A typical response to the request as prescribed by CDMI SNIA technical position [4] should be:

```
HTTP/1.1 200 OK
Content-Type: application/vnd.org.snia.cdmi.capabilities+json
X-CDMI-Specification-Version: 1.0
{
    "objectURI" : "/cdmi_capabilities/",
    "objectID" : "AABwbQAQWTYZDTZq2T2aEw==",
    "parentURI" : "/",
    "capabilities" : {
        "cdmi_domains" : "true",
        "cdmi_export_nfs" : "true",
        "cdmi_export_webdav" : "true",
        "cdmi_export_iscsi" : "true",
        "cdmi_queues" : "true",
        "cdmi_notification" : "true",
        "cdmi_query" : "true",
        "cdmi_metadata_maxsize" : "4096",
```

```
        "cdmi_metadata_maxitems" : "1024",
        "cdmi_size" : "true",
        "cdmi_list_children" : "true",
        "cdmi_read_metadata" : "true",
        "cdmi_modify_metadata" : "true",
        "cdmi_create_container" : "true",
        "cdmi_delete_container" : "true"
    },
    "childrenrange" : "0-3",
    "children" : [
        "domain/",
        "container/",
        "dataobject/",
        "queue/"
    ]
}
```

The APIs prescribed by the standard use the RESTful protocol, i.e., they consist of **CRUD** operations (**Create, Read, Update** and **Delete**). The messages that encode the parameters and results of the operations consist of key-value pairs in JSON[2] format. The interface is therefore similar to other NoSQL applications. Standard HTTP verbs (PUTs and GETs) are used in the API and all other semantics of the data are passed in the body of the message payload. Different mime types are used for different types of resources, as described earlier. A new RFC to define special mime types to be used by CDMI has been defined. There are also search APIs for metadata search, so that it is easy for the stored data to be searched through a query. In the background, the storage system metadata such as access control list, access time and others can be used by the cloud vendor to optimize the storage.

CDMI extensions: CDMI also has a change control process under SNIA. One can extend CDMI for proprietary vendor functions, and still maintain core compatibility with all the other vendors. If many vendors implement a new feature, then that feature will be added to the standard.

All of these aspects of CDMI are depicted in Figure 10.2. These standards are developed as a part of the SNIA **Cloud Storage Initiative** (**CSI**). This is predominantly a marketing initiative that fosters adoption of cloud storage and the model of delivering on-demand storage as an elastic, pay-as-use service. SNIA has also announced the formation of a **Cloud Backup and Recovery Special Interest Group** (**Cloud BUR SIG**) to foster the backup and recovery industry by educating potential users, and hence creating demand for such services.

---

[2]See Chapter 5, *Paradigms for Developing Cloud Applications*.

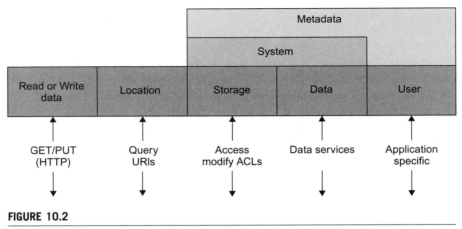

FIGURE 10.2

CDMI APIs and resource domain model.

DMTF Reference Architecture[3]

The **Distributed Management Task Force** (**DMTF**) is an industry consortium that develops, maintains and promotes standards for systems management in an enterprise IT environment. A subgroup of this organization called the DMTF **Cloud Incubator Standards** group defined the first cloud management architecture in July 2010 [5] shown in Figure 10.3. This architecture and the accompanying use cases documents describe standardized interfaces and data formats that can be used to manage cloud environments, mainly IaaS platforms. At a high level, the key concept is that a cloud service provider abstracts the resources at the IaaS layer (servers, storage, network, etc.) and provides them as a service to a cloud consumer. The provider not only exposes multiple services for the functionality of the platform (functional interfaces) but also provides access to artifacts such as Service-Level Agreements (SLA), OS images, any service templates for customization and so on.

The DMTF architecture defines six lifecycle states for this cloud service, and Figure 10.4 depicts these states in a conceptual overview of cloud management activities. The first state involves defining a service **template** wherein the consumer provides a description of and interfaces to the desired cloud service, including the desired configuration. This is submitted by the consumer to the cloud provider. An **offering** is then created by the cloud service provider which adds constraints, costs, billing information, and policies to the template, and is then offered to the consumer. The consumer and provider then enter into a **contract**, with agreements for costs, SLAs and so on. The provider then **provisions** a service instance as per the contract with the consumer. Multiple resources may be provisioned during this step. Subsequently, the cloud provider does **runtime maintenance** and manages the deployed service, such as monitoring resource usage, raising alarms on

---

[3]Contributed by Dr. Vanish Talwar, Hewlett-Packard Labs, USA.

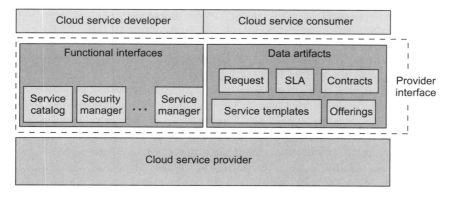

FIGURE 10.3

Data reference architecture for cloud management.

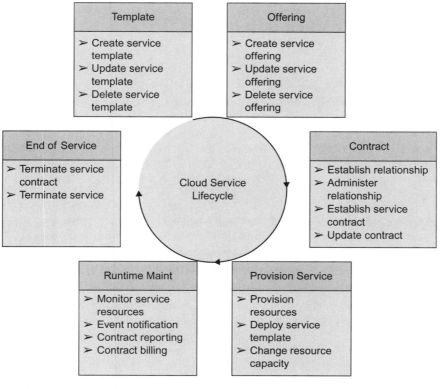

FIGURE 10.4

DMTF cloud service lifecycle.

abnormal behavior, and adjusting resource allocations. Finally, the provider **halts a service instance**, and reclaims resources given to that service.

With the complexity and scale in cloud systems, several of these management tasks become non-trivial in computation, design, and in the number of execution steps performed. Automation is needed to replace manual operations and reduce overall costs. However, there are several challenges to achieve a fully automated solution. Provisioning multiple resources requires creation of automated work-flows, coordination across multiple resource types, and automated configuration of systems, middleware, and applications. Runtime maintenance requires monitoring of highly dynamic distributed infrastructure, monitoring dynamic partitioning, allocation, and de-allocation of infrastructure. Overall objectives are to maintain SLAs specified by the user, which have to be translated across the IaaS, PaaS, and SaaS layers, as well as to maintain data center metrics such as energy efficiency and sustainability. All of these need to take place under the constraints and challenges of silo-ed IT infrastructures, scale, multiple management protocols, and multiple control loops.

The current solutions address these management challenges to some extent, but several open questions remain to achieve fully automated, self-managing solutions that can scale to the future cloud systems.

NIST

Another organization that has played an important role in standardization efforts around cloud computing is **NIST (National Institute of Standards and Technology**, US Department of Commerce). The work of NIST in defining cloud terminology was extensively discussed in Chapter 1 and standards around cloud security were described in detail in Chapter 7. Just to recall, NIST defined the standard terminologies used by the cloud community today, such as IaaS, PaaS, SaaS, private cloud, public cloud, etc. In fact, this is the standards body that came up with the most accepted definition of the term "cloud computing" as follows:

> *Cloud computing is a model for enabling ubiquitous, convenient, on-demand network access to a shared pool of configurable computing resources (e.g., networks, servers, storage, applications, and services) that can be rapidly provisioned and released with minimal management effort or service provider interaction.*

NIST also defined the four deployment models for the cloud: public cloud, private cloud, community cloud and hybrid cloud. As described earlier, private clouds are operated just for an organization, and public clouds (e.g., Amazon) are available for use by the general public. Community cloud is an infrastructure that is shared by multiple institutions with shared concerns. Hybrid cloud infrastructure is a combination of private, public and community clouds which are interoperable using standardized or proprietary technology and provides sharing of data and application across the clouds. Chapter 6 described some of the tools used to create Hybrid Clouds (such as Eucalyptus and OpenNebula).

IEEE

As part of its cloud push, IEEE started two working groups in April 2011. These are IEEE P2301, the *Draft Guide for Cloud Portability and Interoperability Profiles,* and IEEE P2302, the *Draft Standard for Intercloud Interoperability and Federation*, which will together look at a wide variety of areas that need standardization for the cloud computing community. The P2301 workgroup will work on standardizing cloud portability and management, using a number of file formats and interfaces. The P2302 workgroup will focus on cloud-to-cloud interoperability and federation. It will, for example, work on standardizing gateways that can handle data exchange between clouds. Since this effort was newly initiated at the writing of the book, the reader should refer to the latest drafts at http://standards.ieee.org [6, 7].

Open Grid Forum (OGF)

Another open community-led specification is spearheaded by the OGF, a standards development organization for grid computing and other distributed computing systems. OGF has started a working group called **Open Cloud Computing Interface (OCCI)** to focus on vendor-independent access to resources. OCCI also provides service APIs for remote management of cloud infrastructure.

Figure 10.5 describes the role of OCCI with the provider's environment. As seen, the key benefit of OCCI is to enable an OCCI client to connect to an OCCI implementation over a vendor's infrastructure without having any prior knowledge of the resources. OCCI makes these resources discoverable and accessible through the simple concept of resource types. There are three fundamental categories underlying OCCI – resources, actions, and links. Any component available through OCCI is a **resource** – be it a virtual machine, a user or a simple job. One resource

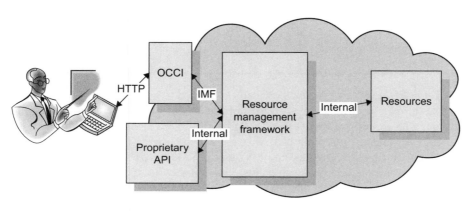

FIGURE 10.5

OCCI's place in a provider's architecture.

is associated with another using a **link** type. An **action** represents an operation that can be performed on the resource instance. There are other types that represent the schema or classification type hierarchy for the resources.

CLOUD BENCHMARKS

Cloud standards enable a cloud user to develop services in a manner in which they can be reused on a different vendor's platform. In contrast, cloud benchmarks help customers compare various cloud systems and choose the right one for final deployment. A benchmark consists of a **workload** that is run against a computer system to produce a standard set of measurements that can be used to analyze the system. The workload consists of a series of commands that load the computer system. For example, the **Transaction Processing Performance Council-C** benchmark (**TPC-C**) defines a standard database workload (e.g., queries, updates) that can be run against a database. Using the data produced by the TPC-C run, it is possible to measure the cost per query of the system.

Benchmarks are useful for many purposes. First, benchmarks can be used to compare different systems. In the TPC-C example, the measurements can be used to select the least expensive system from many alternatives. Benchmarks can also be used to tune or configure systems. For example, multiple TPC-C runs can be made against differently configured databases with the same database software (such as varying the amount of memory in the CPUs) to find the best configuration. Finally, benchmarks can be used for capacity planning; when installing a new database, the TPC-C measurements of a system can be used to estimate the number of CPUs, amount of memory, and other resources that are needed for the database.

> **NOTE**
>
> **Uses of Benchmarks**
> - System comparison
> - Tuning and configuration
> - Capacity planning

The usefulness of a benchmark, clearly, is related to how closely the benchmark workload matches the actual workload on the system. For this reason, the well-known web server workloads (e.g., *httpperf* [8], *SPECWeb2005* [9]) may not be useful for measuring clouds [10]. The reasons are that the earlier web server benchmarks were designed to study systems where the workload predominantly consisted of users accessing web pages. This will not be relevant for many cloud applications, such as social computing applications where users upload photos and other documents that are accessed by other users. Another difference is that many cloud applications run within a web browser and leverage rich clients (e.g., Flash) to perform some processing in the client. This processing can lead to "light-weight" (e.g., AJAX) requests being sent to the server (e.g., when signing up for a new userid on a web site, the client may make a background request to see if the userid is available before the registration is complete). This changes the nature of the workload. Finally, the pay-as-you-go economics of cloud computing imply that benchmarks should try to exercise the system from the point of view of easy scalability and growth.

In the rest of this section, various benchmarks are discussed. First, **Cloudstone**, a well-known **system benchmark** (benchmark that measures all the components of a cloud) is described. This is followed by a description of **Yahoo Cloud Serving Benchmark (YCSB)**, a **storage benchmark** (i.e., that benchmarks cloud storage systems). Finally, **CloudCMP**, a research collaboration between Duke University and Microsoft Research that aims to compare the performance and cost of various cloud service providers, is described. The benchmarks will be described in a standard format: first, the setup (computer systems and programs used) will be described, followed by important components, such as the workload generator. Then, the measurements produced by the benchmark will be discussed, followed by example results.

Cloudstone

Cloudstone is a benchmark from the University of California, Berkeley, and Sun Microsystems. It is intended to measure the performance of social-computing applications on a cloud, thus providing insight into the performance characteristics of the cloud system. Figure 10.6 shows the components of Cloudstone. They consist of **Olio**, a social-event calendar application, which can be deployed as shown on the cloud system to be benchmarked. Olio has a three-tier architecture where the web server tier runs Apache, and the database tier runs MySQL. The middle tier can be either Ruby or PHP, resulting in two different implementations, either of which can be deployed. **Faban** is a workload generator that runs on the clients and simulates large numbers (thousands) of users simultaneously accessing Olio. Finally, the **Tools** shown perform management tasks, such as deploying Olio, and measuring the performance of the cloud system. The results of the Cloudstone benchmark are the cost of running Olio on the cloud system in **dollars per user per month**.

NOTE

Cloudstone Components
- Olio: calendar application
- Faban: workload generator
- Measuring and management tools.

All the previously described Cloudstone software is available both in the form of regular source code and binaries, as well as Amazon AMIs that can be run on EC2. To run Cloudstone on other cloud systems, it is necessary to convert the source code or binaries to the form deployable on the other cloud system.

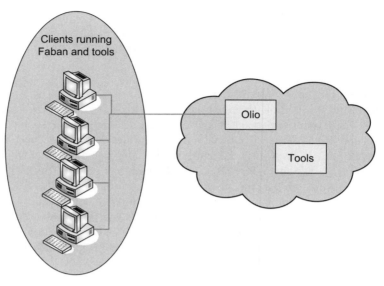

FIGURE 10.6

Cloudstone components.

Faban Workload Generator

Faban is a **Markov chain based workload generator**, i.e., it assumes that each client is in a particular state at any time. The client then issues a series of commands, which is characteristic of that state. It could then transition to another state based upon certain probabilities (the **Markov chain state transition probabilities**) where it could issue another series of commands. For example, from the `initial` state, the client may transition with probability 1 to the `login` state, where the client issues the commands to login to Olio. From the login state, it may transition with a certain probability to a `daily calendar` state where (after a random delay) it issues the HTTP commands to display the daily calendar, with another probability to a `weekly calendar` state, and so on. Such workload generators have been found to be very general and model the activity of users well. For example, it is not necessary that all the users of the system submit identical transactions; it is possible to model different types of users who submit different types of transactions [11]. Faban has a description of the state transition probabilities, as well as the commands issued in each state. By running many independent copies of Faban on the clients, workloads consisting of thousands of users may be simulated.

Cloudstone Measurements and Results

As stated earlier, Cloudstone reports the **dollars (or cost) per user per month** for the cloud system being benchmarked (assuming the cloud system is a typical public cloud where the CSP charges based on usage). This is accomplished by dividing C, the cost of the system per month, by M, the maximum number of users that can be supported by the system.

To find M, Faban is run with a specified number of users during a measurement interval (5 minutes), and the Cloudstone tools are used to check whether the benchmark **Service Level Agreement** (**SLA**) is violated. The SLA is described in more detail later in this section. If the SLA is not violated, the number of users is increased. M is defined as the maximum number of users that can be run without violating the SLA.

Cloudstone defines two SLAs called SLA-1 and SLA-2. SLA-1 states that 90% of response times to requests made by the simulated users is less than the specified value. This value depends upon the type of request from the simulated user (e.g., login) and varies from 1 to 4 seconds. Similarly, SLA-2 states that 99% of the response times are less than the specified value. Faban measures the response time of each request to Olio, and Cloudstone provides tools to compute the 90th percentile and 99th percentile of response time. From this, it can easily be determined if the SLAs are violated.

Example Cloudstone Results

The Cloudstone benchmark was used in *Cloudstone* [10] to study various configurations to find the most cost-effective configuration for hosting Olio on EC2. To generate the configurations, three factors were varied:

- The first was the type of EC2 instance used.[4] Two different types were used; type *C1.XL* had 7 GB RAM and 20 compute units (8 cores of speed 2.5 compute units each). The second type *M1.XL* is a large memory instance that had 15 GB RAM but only 8 compute units of CPU (4 cores of speed 2 compute units each). These two instance types were considered as their cost (at the time of the experiment) was the same at $0.80 per hour.
- The second factor varied was the implementation. Three different implementations: Ruby, Ruby with caching enabled,[5] and PHP with caching enabled were considered.
- The third factor was the number of application servers.

After running the Cloudstone benchmark, it was found that the cost per user per month varied from $1.40 per user per hour to $8.50 per user per hour, depending upon the configuration and the implementation. The lowest cost implementation used Ruby+caching on C1.XL servers with 2 application servers. It was seen that the difference between the highest and lowest cost is more than a factor of 6. Therefore, Cloudstone was quite useful to find the best system design for optimizing the architecture of the Olio deployment. Furthermore, additional

---

[4]For a detailed description of the various types of Amazon EC2 instances, please see Chapter 2, *Infrastructure as a Service*.
[5]For more details of the caching, please see [10].

interesting conclusions could be drawn from the runs; for example it was found that logging caused significant performance degradation, reducing the maximum request rate by approximately 20%; and that the **nginx** load balancer significantly increased the throughput compared to the **mod_proxy** load balancer. A detailed discussion of the difference between nginx and mod_proxy, including workloads where each web server is superior, can be found in *Nginx Primer 2* [12].

Yahoo! Cloud Serving Benchmark

Yahoo! Cloud Serving Benchmark (YCSB) is a benchmark that measures the performance of a cloud storage system (such as HBase) against standard workloads, such as a threaded conversation application where users scan conversations and append their own posts [13]. The workload can also be customized to simulate the storage requests from any application. Figure 10.7 shows the components of the benchmark. The **YCSB Client** is a multi-threaded Java program whose components are shown in Figure 10.7. The **workload generator** generates requests to load the database, as well as the storage requests made by the application. The **statistics** module collects important statistics, such as the maximum number of I/O requests per second the storage cloud can provide. The **database plug-ins** make the actual I/O requests to the storage; plug-ins are provided for important storage systems such as HBase. YCSB provides mechanisms to create plug-ins to any other storage system. The workload generator and statistics modules are discussed in greater detail next.

YCSB Workload Generator

The YCSB workload generator can generate a number of standard workloads, as well as custom workloads. The reason for this is that the performance of the storage system may vary, depending upon the workload, due to the different design decisions made while implementing the storage system. As a result, different storage systems may be optimal for different workloads. The standard workload is implemented by a class called `CoreWorkload`. To define a new workload, this class should be replaced by a new class that extends the `Workload` class. This class

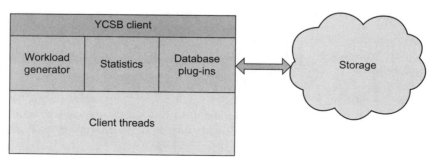

FIGURE 10.7

Yahoo! Cloud Serving Benchmark architecture.

should have two methods – `doInsert` to initialize the database, and `doTransaction` to execute a storage operation.

The workload generator operates in two phases. The first phase loads the database (which could take hours); the second phase performs operations on the database. Measurements are conducted in the second phase (typically 30 minutes).

There are three major parameters that control the operation of the workload generator. These are the parameters that generally have been found to be important in other (non-cloud) storage benchmarks as well, such as IOZone [14]. The first is the **operation mix**, e.g., the number of read requests versus the number of write requests. The operations performed by the workload generator are **insert, delete, read, update** (**write**), and **scan** (search the entire database looking for a key, then read a specified number of records). The second is the **record size** of the records being read. The third parameter is the **popularity distribution**; i.e., the probability that a particular record may be read or written.

YCSB provides three popularity distributions. The first is the **Zipf** distribution, which is characteristic of access probabilities in a large number of areas such as the popularity of words in a language, the distribution of sizes of US firms, the popularity of web sites, and the distribution of incomes [15]. The Zipf distribution is given by the following formula:

$$p(k) = K(1/k)^\alpha$$

The equation finds the probability that the `kth` item would be selected, and K and α are parameters of the distribution. Under the Zipf distribution, the first few items are very popular, and the popularity declines very rapidly for later items, depending upon the value of α. However, the Zipf distribution is not appropriate for simulating situations where new items are more popular than older items, such as blog posts. For this, YCSB provides the **Latest** distribution. This is the same as the Zipf distribution, except that newly inserted items are moved to the top of the list. The final distribution is the **Uniform** distribution, where all records have equal probability of being accessed. This could be characteristic of databases, where all records have equal probability of being accessed.

Table 10.1 summarizes the standard workloads provided by YCSB, together with example applications they are intended to be representative of. They are largely self-explanatory. In workload C, it is assumed that the actual user profile is stored separately; hence the workload is read-only. In workload E, the Zipf distribution is used to select the conversation and thread to be read; the Uniform distribution is then used to select a number of records to read.[6]

YCSB Measurements and Results

YCSB currently performs two sets of measurements (called tiers) for measuring the performance and scalability of cloud storage systems. An additional two sets

---

[6]In this instance, the Uniform distribution is not being used as a popularity distribution to select a particular item.

Table 10.1 YCSB Standard Workloads

No.	Workload Description	Operation Mix	Popularity Distribution	Example Application
A	Update heavy	Read: 50%, Update: 50%	Zipf	Recording user session actions
B	Read heavy	Read: 95%, Update: 5%	Zipf	Photo site; mostly view photo, but also update tag
C	Read only	Read: 100%	Zipf	User profile cache
D	Read latest	Read: 95%, Insert 5%	Latest	User status update; mostly read status
E	Short ranges	Scan: 95%, Insert: 5%	Zipf & Uniform	Threaded conversations clustered by thread

of measurements for measuring the impact of availability and replication are proposed, but not yet implemented as of this writing. These sets of measurements are described in the rest of this section.

Tier 1 – Performance: In this set of measurements, multiple runs are performed, for different values of load on the storage system. The load on the storage system is measured in terms of throughput (operations/sec). For each value of load, the response time latency per operation is measured. The increase in latency as the load on the storage systems increases (until saturation) is studied.

Tier 2 – Scalability: Two different aspects of scalability are studied. In the scale-up measurements, after each benchmark run is complete, the data on the storage system is deleted, additional servers are added to the storage system, the storage system is loaded with proportionately more data, and the benchmark is re-run to find the saturation throughput of the new system. Ideally, the maximum throughput per server should remain constant. In the elastic speedup measurements, after the measurements with the existing servers are completed, the new server(s) are added without deleting any data, the storage system is re-configured to use the new server, and a new set of measurements is made. The maximum throughput per server should remain constant here as well.

Tier 3 – Availability: It is proposed that to measure the impact of availability, faults (e.g., failure of a server) should be injected into the storage system, and the resulting degradation in performance be measured. Issues that need to be dealt with are the mechanism to inject faults into heterogeneous storage systems in a uniform manner. As of this writing, this has not yet been implemented.

Tier 4 – Replication: Replication increases the availability of a storage system by providing for multiple replicas of the data. However, it also results in additional overhead of replication, as well as complexity in keeping the replicas consistent. A detailed discussion of replication in cloud systems can be found in

Chapter 6, *Addressing the Cloud Challenges*. It is proposed to measure these trade-offs for a particular system by suitable modification of YCSB.

Example YCSB Results

In this section, example results from the YCSB runs are described. Four storage systems – Cassandra, HBase, sharded MySQL, and PNUTS – were studied. These systems are described in detail in Chapter 5 *Application Development Paradigms*. For the **Update Heavy** workload, Cassandra had the best throughput (11798 operations/sec), followed in order by HBase, PNUTS, and sharded MySQL (7283 operations/sec). However, for the **Short Ranges** workload, with ranges of 100 records, HBase and PNUTS are roughly equivalent (1519 and 1440 operations/sec, respectively) while Cassandra is much worse (<100 operations/sec). This is because Cassandra is optimized for writes (leading to better performance on the Update Heavy workload), while the scan support was relatively new at the time of measurement. More details can be found in *Benchmarking Cloud Serving Systems with YCSB* [16].

The scalability measurements also yielded interesting results, showing that Cassandra and MySQL had good scaleup, while HBase tended to be unstable in performance for small (<3) clusters. The elastic speedup results showed that re-partitioning overhead in the version of Cassandra that was studied is high, resulting in the system taking a long time (of the order of hours) to stabilize after adding new servers.

CloudCMP

This section describes CloudCMP, a research project between Duke University and Microsoft Research [17, 18, 19, 20]. CloudCMP is aimed at enabling comparison shopping of cloud service providers by predicting the performance and cost of running an application on a cloud service provider. The papers contain measurements of four well-known cloud platforms: Amazon AWS, Microsoft Azure, Google AppEngine, and Rackspace CloudServers.

One of the challenges of such a project is the fact that different cloud providers differ significantly, and coming up with a common methodology may be difficult. For example, cloud providers could have different cloud models (IaaS, PaaS, SaaS), and offer different services as well. Additionally, the cloud providers also have different pricing methods. To overcome this difficulty, CloudCMP uses a four-step process.

1. CloudCMP characterizes all cloud providers in terms of a set of standard services (such as an *Elastic compute cluster*).
2. Next, CloudCMP attempts to characterize the pricing and performance of the standard services available from each service provider (e.g., the price/performance of computing available from the service provider).
3. The service requirements of each application are derived (e.g., the compute power per transaction).
4. Finally, the price and performance of each application on each service provider is derived.

CloudCmp Architecture

CloudCmp models a cloud as a combination of four standard services that measure compute, storage, internal networking, and WAN. These services, and their characterization, are given later in this section, following which the section describes how to model a typical 3-tier web service in CloudCmp. Details of the tools used to measure these metrics can be found in *CloudCmp* [20].

Elastic Compute Cluster: These services model the compute services of a cloud. CloudCMP measures three metrics associated with the compute services. The first is the **benchmark finishing time**, which is the time to run a standard benchmark. The benchmark is similar to conventional CPU benchmarks. The second metric is the **benchmark cost**. These two metrics together provide insight into cost-performance trade-offs of various clouds; for example, comparing the costs of various Amazon EC2 instance types with their costs. The third metric is the **scaling latency**, which is the time taken to allocate a new compute instance. This is an important metric, since it determines how quickly a system can scale, and is typically in the 100s of seconds as of this writing.

Persistent Storage Service: as seen in Chapters 2 through 4, various cloud providers offer different types of storage services. These are characterized by CloudCmp into three types: table, blob and queue storage. Table storage consists of relational as well as NoSQL storage which operates on structured data. CloudCmp models three types of operations on table storage: **get, put**, and **query**. **Blob** storage consists of storage that can **download** or **upload** a binary file (for example, a file storage service like Amazon S3). Finally, queue storage (as in Windows Azure) can be used for messaging and is modeled using **send** and **receive** operations. For each operation, CloudCmp measures the operation response time and the cost. Additionally, for replicated storage, the time taken to reach a consistent state is measured (this is the same as the **inconsistency window** described in Chapter 6, *Addressing the Cloud Challenges*).

Intra-cloud Network: This measures the internal network that connects the various cloud components. It is characterized by two metrics: **TCP throughput** and **TCP response time**. TCP throughput is used since it is assumed that the cloud traffic is predominantly TCP.

WAN: The **optimal WAN latency** measures the latency experienced by an application from *PlanetLab* nodes to the closest data center of the cloud. Planet-Lab is a distributed network of computers that is intended to be used as a research testbed. It has over 1000 nodes and 500 sites as of June 2010. The computers in the network belong to the research institutions and universities that are members of PlanetLab. So, the benchmark considers PlanetLab as a typical WAN and takes measurements from there.

Figure 10.8 shows how to model a typical 3-tier service running on Amazon EC2 in CloudCMP. The optimal WAN latency is used to estimate the latency from the point of access to the nearest Amazon data center. The intra-cloud network statistics are next used to estimate the latency to reach the application server. Then, the elastic compute cluster statistics are used, together with the application's

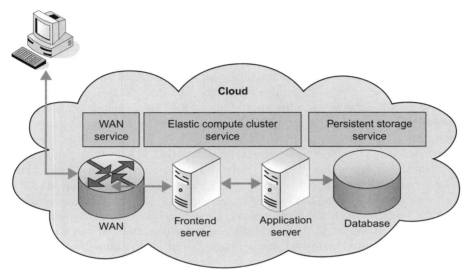

FIGURE 10.8

CloudCmp architecture.

CPU requirements, to estimate the performance in the frontend server tier. Similarly, the performance metrics in the application server tier can be estimated. Finally, the persistence storage service statistics can be used to estimate the storage requirements.

CloudCmp Results

CloudCmp [20] presents the result of a comparison between AWS, Windows Azure, Google App Engine, and CloudServers in an anonymized fashion, where the 4 providers are listed as C_1 through C_4 instead of being named. The following are some of the results presented in the paper.

Elastic Compute Cluster: *CloudCmp* [20] lists the instance types provided by each provider, their cost per hour, as well as their benchmark finishing time. The conclusion is that the price performance of the different providers varies greatly. For example, $C_4.1$ (the first instance type offered by vendor C_4) is reported to be 30% more expensive than $C_1.1$ but twice as fast). When comparing the cost to run each benchmark, it was found that the smallest instance of the cloud providers was the most cost-effective. Additionally, it was found that scaling latency was below 10 minutes for all providers, with some providers achieving latency less than 100 seconds. Linux instances were found to be created faster than Windows instances.

Persistent Storage: Table storage was tested with both a small table (1K entries) and a large table (100K entries) for all the providers other than C_2, which did not have a table service. All table services were found to have large variations in response time. As an example, across all the providers, the median of the response time was 50 ms, while the 95th percentile was twice as large at 100 ms. In terms of scaling, all the providers were found to scale well (no degradation in response time) with up to 32 parallel threads. In terms of the inconsistency time, all providers other than C_1 were found to not have any inconsistency. C_1 provided an API option to force strong consistency which was found not to have much impact on latency. However, without the strong consistency option, C_1 was found to have an inconsistency window of 500 ms (if the 99th percentile of inconsistency times is taken). Cost per operation was found to be comparable across all providers.

Blob download times were measured with small (1KB) blobs and large (10MB) blobs. Again, only three of the service providers were considered, since C_3 did not offer a blob service. With small blobs, all providers other than C_2 were found to show good scaling performance (up to 32 concurrent downloads), with C_4 being the best. With large blobs, C_4 and C_1 were found to continue to scale better; however, C_1 had the best performance. Study of the maximum throughput suggested that in the case of both C_1 and C_2, the intra-cloud network was the performance bottleneck, since the maximum achievable throughput was close to the intra-cloud network bandwidth.

E-Commerce web site: *CloudCmp* [20] presents a projection of the performance of TPC-W, a benchmark for transactional web services that uses an e-commerce site to generate the workload. The benchmark was modified to remove `JOIN` and `GROUP` operations, since these are not in the table service. The projection, based on CloudCmp, predicted that C_1 should offer the lowest response time. This was verified by actually running the benchmark, which confirmed that cloud provider C_1 had the lowest response time.

Other results comparing the intra-network latency and WAN latency of the service providers, as well as projections of their performance for various applications such as Blast, can be found in *CloudCmp* [20].

END-USER PROGRAMMING

This section looks at the future of Cloud Application development – that of an end user becoming a developer of applications! In Chapter 3, it was stated that the value of the Web to end-users would be greatly increased if end-users could integrate the data and services found on the Web to create new, more meaningful services. Examples of this include a user planning a vacation, who may want information on available flights and hotels [21]. Furthermore, the user may want to monitor the Web for changes in flight timings and prices in order to take advantage of favorable changes.

If end-users are to be able to develop their own programs for utilizing Web data, the programming systems must be easy to understand, learn, use and teach [22]. *End-User Development* [22] categorizes end-user programming (EUP) systems into two categories.

- The first category is the parametrization or customization category – into this fall systems that allow users to choose among alternate behaviors that are built into the application, such as setting email filters.
- The second category consists of systems that allow program creation and modification. This category includes programming by example, visual programming, and macros.

Since both parametrization and macros (such as in Microsoft Excel) are well known, in the rest of this section, the other two sub-categories – programming by example, and visual programming – are discussed.

Visual Programming

Visual programming refers to development tools that allow the development of programs by visual means, typically by connecting boxes that represent pre-defined programming functionality. Such tools facilitate the development of programs by non-programmers. In Chapter 5, *Paradigms for Developing Cloud Applications,* mashups and Yahoo Pipes, which are typical examples of visual programming, were described in detail.

Programming by Example

Programming by example is a very popular technique in EUP. Under programming by example, a user provides examples of the type of search or procedure desired, and the system generates a procedure to perform this type of computation [22]. Two research projects are described in the rest of this section which illustrate this approach. First, the HP Labs TaskLets project [23] uses programming by example to help users generate widgets that can perform complex tasks on mobile devices with limited computing functionality. Koala, the second project, uses a combination of programming by example and natural language processing to enable non-programmers to write computer scripts that capture business workflows.

TaskLets

Widgets have become a very popular way to access the Internet from mobile phones. A mobile widget generally is designed to run on smart phones that have limited display and input capabilities. The widget accepts simple text input, accesses information available on the Internet, and displays the desired result. A typical widget may input a bank account number, access the bank's web site, navigate to the account balance, and display it as simple text. The advantage of mobile widgets is that it is not necessary to maintain a parallel web site for mobile devices, and the web pages already developed for PCs can be leveraged.

Geetha et al. [23] define a concept called **TaskLet** to represent a user's personal web interaction pattern. To create a new TaskLet, all the user needs to do is to demonstrate the task (Web interaction) once using her web browser by giving some sample inputs on all the relevant web sites. This sequence of Web interactions needed to perform the Web task is modeled within a TaskLet. A TaskLet captures a user's preferred way of accomplishing a Web task – compressing the sequence of Web actions needed to perform a specific task in a user-specified way. These TaskLets can be user-created, shared, customized and composed with other TaskLets and web services (such as language translator, text summarizer).

So the TaskLets provide a framework to allow end-users to create the desired widget, so that end-users with mobile phones can create widgets to access any desired web site, and also widgets that may synthesize information from multiple web sites. A number of challenges need to be addressed for achieving this objective. The first challenge, of course, is **program synthesis**, or the method by which a user can create a personal widget. The second is that the synthesis method must be **resilient to change**, since web pages may change (e.g., by the addition of new security methods, or by reformatting). In that case, it is desirable that the widget not perform erroneously, and for the user to not have to rewrite the widget. Additionally, users who create a widget may wish to share it with others, and it is necessary to ensure privacy for any personal data (e.g., userids) stored in the widget. Finally, mobile connections are also prone to disruption, so it is necessary for the framework to provide robust disconnection management support. Description of the solution proposed in *End User Programming of Task-based Mobile Widgets* [24] follows.

Figure 10.9 illustrates the various phases of the lifecycle of a TaskLet. Consider the case of a user who wants to develop a TaskLet that will display their bank balance on their mobile phone. This can be accomplished using the TaskLet authoring tool (browser plug-in) as follows:

First, the user hits the "record" button in the TaskLet authoring tool and then performs the web action for checking the bank balance, i.e., the user can logon to the web site of his bank, go to the web page that contains the bank balance, and indicate to the TaskLet system that the bank balance is the quantity of interest. The TaskLet system then creates a TaskLet for performing the same actions, which is stored in the TaskLet Repository. At a later time, when the user does not have access to a PC, the user can invoke the previously created TaskLet from their mobile phone. The invocation can be via SMS, the Internet, or even via voice. After the TaskLet is invoked, it will display the bank balance on the mobile phone. The task need not be a simple task like the previous task; it may be a complex task such as booking a 2-day trip from Bangalore to Delhi by a favorite airline, and then reserving a room at a favorite hotel using a credit card. The internal details of these steps are described in more detail in the following paragraphs.

TaskLet creation overview: The first step in the TaskLet lifecycle is TaskLet creation. As stated previously, the user performs the desired task on the Web using a browser on a PC. The TaskLet system records the user actions, and analyzes them together with the web pages on which the actions were performed. The analysis generates the semantics of the user actions in the form of a script, called a TaskLet Template Script (TTS). The TaskLet is then parametrized and

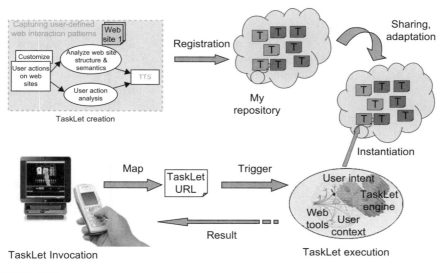

FIGURE 10.9

TaskLet life cycle.

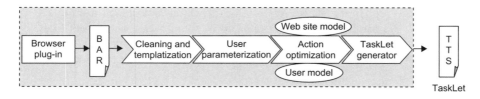

FIGURE 10.10

TaskLet authoring.

stored in the TaskLet repository hosted as an SaaS. It can then be invoked from the mobile device, to perform the desired action.

User action recording: The details of the TaskLet creation process are shown in Figure 10.10. As shown, the first step is to record the user's actions. This is done by a browser plug-in, which has a record button to start and stop recording. After the final page containing the content of interest is reached, the user selects the contents to be displayed after TaskLet execution by double clicking. Consider the case where the user wants to develop a TaskLet to look up his bank balance. After logging on, and reaching the web page containing the bank balance, the user can double click on the bank balance. When the TaskLet is finally executed on the mobile device, the TaskLet will log on to the bank, navigate to the page with the bank balance, extract the bank balance, and display it on the mobile device. If other results are desired (for example, details of the last transaction) it is possible to double click on this as well; both the bank balance and last transaction will then be displayed after TaskLet execution.

It is also possible to select and display information on multiple web pages. In the more complex travel reservation example given earlier, the information of interest may be the confirmation number for the airline reservation (available on the airline reservation page) as well as the hotel confirmation number. If the user selects both these numbers on the appropriate web pages, they will both be displayed when the user executes the TaskLet from his mobile device.

TaskLet generation: The recorded user actions are stored in a **Browse-Action-Recording (BAR)** file. The BAR file also contains details of the fields to be extracted. The TaskLet authoring service parses and analyzes the BAR file to create a recording template. The template script contains browser actions with variables replacing the inputs used during recording. In addition to form inputs, the variables may also be hyperlink selections. During this process, the user is asked to specify the properties of the variables, and also which variables are input parameters. For example, in the travel scenario, the user will be asked do you want to change the flight 'date', 'destination' in every run? An answer of yes will result in the appropriate variable being classified as an input parameter (and asked for as input during TaskLet execution). The privacy settings of each of the variables (e.g., credit card number) are also input.

After the TaskLet is created, it is stored in the **TaskLet Repository (TLR)**, a cloud hosted repository of web tasks. Each TaskLet is assigned a unique URI with which the user task can be repeated. It is, therefore, a web object like any other, and can be shared, annotated or "invoked" from any device. The TLR also allows TaskLets to be shared with other users needing the same functionality.

```
EXAMPLE TaskLet Template Script with Authentication
1. GOTO URL=http://lib.hpl.hp.com/
2. HYPERLINK POS=1 TYPE=A ATTR=TXT:ACMDigitalLibrary
3. INPUT POS=1 TYPE=TEXT FORM=NAME:emp ATTR=NAME:UID CONTENT={{EMP_ID}}
4. SUBMIT POS=1 FORM=NAME:emp ATTR=NAME:ACTION
5. INPUT POS=1 TYPE=TEXT FORM=NAME:qiksearch ATTR=NAME:query CONTENT=
{{TITLE}}
6. SUBMIT POS=1 TYPE=IMAGE FORM=NAME:qiksearch ATTR=NAME:Go
7. EXTRACT HREF POS=1 TYPE=A ATTR=TXT:*Pdf*
```

TaskLet templates: The previous code snippet shows an example of the TTS for a TaskLet that accesses the HP Labs Research Library (not a public web site) to accept as input the title of a paper, and return the URL of the paper after authentication with the HP employee id. Each line in the script consists of an **opcode** followed by a number of **operands**. The opcode represents the action to be performed (e.g., GOTO a URL), while the operands are the parameters. The variables {EMP_ID} and {TITLE} represent the employee id (which is used for authentication), and the title of the paper being searched for, respectively. Since the title is the only input in this TaskLet (the employee id being fixed) it is asked for on every TaskLet invocation, while the employee id is constant. A similar script for accessing the text directions from Google Maps is shown next. It may be noted that these code snippets are not written by developers but are automatically generated by the authoring tool, when the user does programming by just browsing.

```
EXAMPLE TaskLet Template Script for Google Maps
1. GOTO URL=http://maps.google.com/
2. HYPERLINK POS=1 TYPE=A ATTR=TXT:GetDirections
3. INPUT POS=1 TYPE=TEXT ATTR=Id:d_d CONTENT={{SRC_VAR}}
4. INPUT POS=1 TYPE=TEXT ATTR=Id:d_daddr CONTENT={{DEST_VAR}}
5. SUBMIT POS=1 FORM=ACTION:/maps ATTR=ID:d_sub
6. EXTRACT TXT POS=1 ATTR=CLASS:altroute_info&&TXT:*
```

TaskLet execution: Details of TaskLet execution are shown in Figure 10.11. The TaskLet, which is stored in the TLR (owned by the mobile service provider, for example) is first invoked by the user from his mobile device. This happens over SMS, the Internet, or potentially even via voice. Next, the **TaskLet Execution Engine** (**TEE**) creates a new instance of the TaskLet and executes it. As part of the execution, the TaskLet asks for any user input needed. The TEE also attempts to compensate for changes to web sites. Recall that the TTS script contains opcodes. These opcodes may be syntactic or semantic. In the case of a syntactic opcode, the operands are used exactly as is. For example, in the case of the syntactic opcode GOTO, the TEE accesses the URL as specified by the operand. However, in the case of a semantic opcode, such as HYPERLINK, if the attempt to access the specified URL fails, the TEE will attempt to find a semantically equivalent URL (such as substituting the word "astrology" for horoscopes). Semantic equivalence is applied to extracted fields from web pages as well. Details can be found in *End User Programming of Task-based Mobile Widgets* [24].

CLOUD AT THE CENTER OF THE SOLUTION

- Web tasks in the Cloud
- Browser-based authoring
- Pay-per-use
- No infrastructure setup needed
- End-User App Repository
- Multi-device access
- Works on existing web portals and cloud services

Use of Cloud in TaskLet solution

Though not explicitly mentioned in the description, cloud computing forms the core of the TaskLet solution. First of all the TaskLet repository resides completely in the Cloud. The TaskLet authoring tool also runs as a cloud service and is accessible from a browser. Since TaskLet execution also happens in the cloud, it is possible to create a business model around TaskLet execution that caters to a pay-per-use pricing. Further, different types of thin clients (diverse mobile phones) can be used to invoke TaskLet in the Cloud and access the short TaskLet results after executing a complex web task.

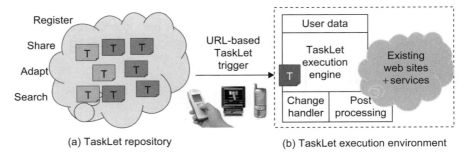

(a) TaskLet repository (b) TaskLet execution environment

FIGURE 10.11

TaskLet execution.

CoScriptor

CoScriptor [25, 26] is a system that is intended to allow users to capture details of business processes in an enterprise as scripts that can be edited and customized by users. CoScriptor relies upon an approach called **sloppy programming**. Under this approach, users write scripts in a human-understandable language to perform tasks of interest. By not requiring the scripts to be written in a programming language with rigid syntax, CoScriptor attempts to enable non-programmers to write and edit scripts as well. The CoScriptor interpreter attempts to analyze the script as a sequence of expressions composed of keywords that specify an action, and attempts to perform the corresponding actions. CoScriptor also allows users to record the actions to be performed, instead of writing it down. These ideas are described in more detail using an example from *Koala* [26].

CoScriptor use case: In this example, an employee called Tina wanted to use the company's online ordering system to order a pen that was not listed in the online catalog. In order to help her, a colleague had emailed her instructions on how to order video cassettes, which also were not in the catalog. The code snippet for the same is shown next.

```
Example CoScriptor Script
1. go to https://www.buyondemand.com
2. scroll down to the "Shop by commodity" section, click "View
commodities"
3. from the list of commodities, select "MRO/SUPPLIES"
4. …
5. the resulting screen is entitled "Full Buyer Item". For "Item
Description" enter "MiniDV digital videotape cassette, 60 minutes at SP
mode". For "Estimated Unit Price" enter "3.25". For "quantity" enter how
many you want.
6. …
```

In fact, CoScriptor also uses programming by demonstration as a supplementary method for editing – when the CoScriptor engine encounters an error command, it opens a browser for the user to show how to execute a natural language command in the script.

First CoScriptor goes to the web site. CoScriptor then attempts to execute the second step starting `scroll down`. It ignores the phrase starting `scroll down`, finds a link labeled "View commodities", and attempts to follow it. While executing this step, both the corresponding step in the script as well as the link "View commodities" are highlighted in order to let the user (Tina in this case) know the step that is about to be executed. When step 5 is reached, CoScriptor halts, since it assumes that any instruction with the word `you` indicates that a user action is needed.

The prior example demonstrates the key feature of how CoScriptor uses concepts from programming by demonstration to enable end user programming. Though the TaskLet approach is much simpler for the user to use, the script language used by CoScriptor is in natural language and may appeal to a good fraction of the user community as well.

OPEN CIRRUS[7]

Open Cirrus is a testbed for research and innovation in cloud computing. The goal of Open Cirrus is to foster system research around cloud computing, expose the research community to enterprise/industry level requirements, provide realistic traces of cloud workloads, and more importantly, to provide vendor-neutral open-source stack and APIs for cloud research, and provide an overall ecosystem for cloud services modeling.

The Open Cirrus community initiative grew out of a discussion between HP, Intel, and Yahoo! in early 2008. At the time of the writing of this book, the community consisted of 14 geographically distributed sites (see Figure 10.12), each donating at least 1,000 cores and accompanying memory and storage [27]. Each site is managed independently and the overall testbed is therefore a federation of heterogeneous sites. This was a design choice made initially to enable more comprehensive research in cloud services and, in particular, management.

Open Cirrus envisions that, just like Internet today, the future of cloud computing will consist of multiple cloud providers contributing to a seemingly single ubiquitous cloud from which users can get computation and storage, as well as many services. From today's state of the art to this vision, there are numerous research questions that need to be addressed and technologies developed. Open Cirrus was created to help with this kind of research.

Process of Getting onto Open Cirrus

The process for using Open Cirrus is simple and automated. Nodes can be obtained from a self-service tool that can allocate nodes on an hourly basis. The tool also allows selection of the operating system, specific machines and has a

---

[7]Contributed by Dr. Dejan Milojicic, Hewlett-Packard Labs, USA.

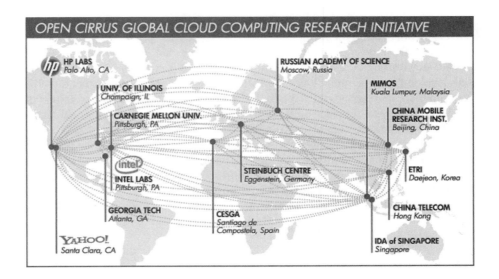

FIGURE 10.12

Distribution of Open Cirrus nodes and partners.

more sophisticated user interface for searching for machines with consecutive static IP addresses, types of machines, system administrator views, etc. The ultimate goal of the hourly allocation is to enable increased sharing. A typical use case is a request for a large number of cores (up to a thousand) for a short amount of time, during which scalability, performance, reliability, and functional testing can be conducted and then machines passed to other users.

The process for becoming an Open Cirrus site entails ensuring that the site will have at least 1,000 cores available for conducting Cloud computing research and that it will make a fraction thereof available for other sites and other users. In addition, an agreement is signed with Open Cirrus sponsors to address legal situations in case attacks are staged from any of the sites. Export and privacy rules are also addressed. Beside the process for obtaining Open Cirrus nodes, there is also community building, which involves conducting monthly meetings (replicated for two regions) and bi-annual summits. Summits became IEEE sponsored and usually feature a plethora of research from many areas of cloud computing and from researchers across many continents. The second summit in 2011, in Atlanta, Georgia, will emphasize cross Open Cirrus site services. For example, the BookPrep service will be showcased, running across the sites in Palo Alto, Georgia Tech, KIT, CMU, MIMOS, and ETRI.

Management of Large Scale Cloud Research Tests

Several research projects in areas such as networking, sustainability, exascale computing, storage, service composition, and security are using Open Cirrus. Some of these projects require access to the hardware or the systems software of the underlying machines and therefore they would need to expose physical machines to the users. This is in contrast to typical cloud computing, where virtual machines are made available to users. Several administrative tools/services are needed to support the maintenance of the resources at the physical level. The remainder of this section will address some of these services, in particular the **Cloud Sustainability Dashboard** and **Node Reservation System** as examples of the requirements for a novel management framework for a Research Cloud Computing Testbed.

Figure 10.13 describes architectural components of an Open Cirrus site (Open Cirrus Cloud Computing Stack and global services), as well as the kinds of research it is currently being used for at HP Labs. Open Cirrus enables a consolidated infrastructure of credible scale for conducting experiments, as well as consolidated users. At the bottom of the stack, the networking research can get traces from the testbed, followed by hardware designers who can understand requirements and behavior of cloud services, followed by management research, which can better understand typical processing, memory, storage stack, followed by services research, etc.

This type of testbed needs to change and allow interposition at different levels of the stack, such as making changes to the wiring (networking), operating system (hardware research), default monitoring configurations and scheduling. This consequently requires provisioning of both virtual machines and physical nodes for the user. The former is the usual case in cloud computing, while the latter is typical of systems research, such as Emulab. The second requirement for heterogeneity support is catered from the cross-regional, global testbeds. However, these regions (America, EU, Asia-Pacific) have different privacy and export rules as noted in Chapter 7, so there is a need for human verification of the users prior to being allocated resources. The third requirement derives from the previous one, which is the need for federation. Federation is accomplished at multiple levels, first at the

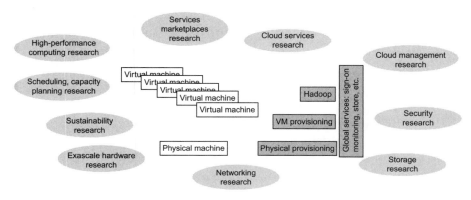

FIGURE 10.13

Open Cirrus node architecture.

security level, through the global sign on (as well as other services, such as global monitoring); next at the physical provisioning level (by extending the node reservation system), the virtual provisioning level (by federating Eucalyptus and eventually Tashi), and finally at the individual services level. A few key tools developed for Open Cirrus for resource allocation (Node Reservation System), scalable monitoring of different metrics, and a sustainability dashboard for energy and other resource usage are described next.

Node Reservation System

While cloud computing promises unlimited resources, in practice every cloud provider has a limited stock of hardware, which it shares among the users. In the case of a research testbed, the limits are obvious. A typical Open Cirrus site has at minimum 1,000 cores, so overall the testbed has slightly above 15,000 cores. Many research experiments require a significant number of cores to conduct experiments. **The node reservation system** provides users with reserved (guaranteed) access to a requested hardware configuration of desired configuration (via a built-in search for specific resources) and at a requested time. Furthermore, this is a tool (Figure 10.14) that

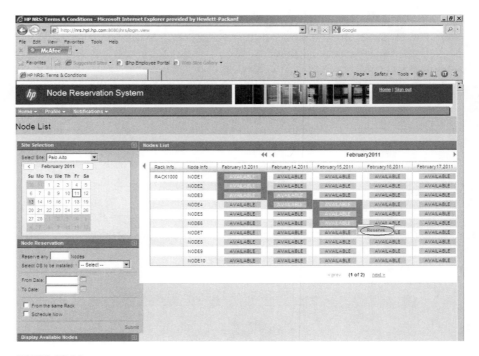

FIGURE 10.14

Node reservation system GUI.

enables federation at the physical node level, by enabling users to request machines from other Open Cirrus sites. This node reservation service meets all requirements (physical provisioning, heterogeneity, and federation).

Scalable Monitoring System

Monitoring is another key service needed to gain insights into the cloud infrastructure. The monitoring infrastructure needs to be continuous and on-demand to quickly detect, correlate, and analyze data for a fast reaction to anomalous behavior in the cloud. A key challenge is to deal with the huge volume of monitoring data that would be produced across multiple nodes and virtual instances. In addition, the monitoring data is collected at multiple levels of the stack – physical platform, virtualization, OS, and application layers – and thus the analysis needs to perform correlation of multiple metrics. Traditional approaches using centralized and reactive data collection, aggregation and analysis across datacenter subsystems and machines will not be able to scale to millions of cores. A scalable monitoring infrastructure is being experimented on at HP Labs Open Cirrus site that does analysis in a distributed manner (see Figure 10.15) using a computation graph structure. The architecture scales up and down and is configurable based on local optimizations. One example of analysis performed is anomaly detection. Considering the online nature of the service, the anomaly detectors execute lightweight statistical methods that raise alarms based on metric distributions [28].

Cloud Sustainability Dashboard

The Cloud Sustainability Dashboard is another global service that exemplifies the needs of systems research (see Table 10.2). It collects various information about the resources used, aggregates the information at the individual site level as well as across sites and reports to the site managers/owners and potentially to users who want to be sustainability aware about the underlying cloud where their services execute. Again, this service meets the requirements for the physical and virtualized access, for heterogeneity (different sites have different interfaces for integration) and federation.

OPEN RESEARCH PROBLEMS IN CLOUD COMPUTING

This section details the author's views of some of the major research challenges that are yet to be addressed in Cloud Computing.

At the IaaS and PaaS layers, enabling configuration, build and deployment in a complete self-service mode while supporting multiple tenants and providing a view of elastic and scalable infrastructure is not a trivial task. Novel middleware architectures and policy management algorithms to ensure satisfaction of SLAs are still needed. Appropriate resource modeling with reflection (self-awareness)

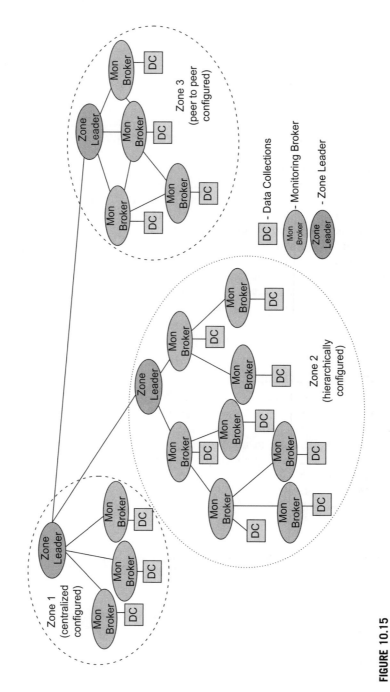

FIGURE 10.15

Scalable monitoring and analysis system.

Table 10.2 Cloud Sustainability Dashboard

| Open Cirrus Site | Economical ($) | | | | | Ecological | | | | | Social | | | |
	IT	Cooling	Ntwk	Support	Econo. Overall	CO2 (tonnes-eq)	water (mill. Gal)	Resource Use (GJ-eq)	Ecolog. Overall	State of Devt.	Risk of Instability	Social Overall
Site 1	$0.72	$0.35	$0.16	$0.43	Good	6.0	2.6	83	Good	High	Low	Poor
Site 2	$1.27	$0.59	$0.21	$1.11	Poor	6.8	3.3	96	Fair	High	Very Low	Fair
Site 3	$1.05	$0.47	$0.12	$1.07	Poor	5.9	2.3	81	Good	High	Low	Poor
Site 4	$0.75	$0.35	$0.12	$0.61	Good	6.1	2.7	85	Good	High	Very Low	Fair
Site 5	$0.27	$0.13	$0.05	$0.09	Good	4.3	2.4	59	Good	Low	High	Poor
Site 6	$1.82	$0.77	$0.11	$1.17	Poor	10.2	4.3	142	Poor	High	Low	Poor
Site 7	$1.23	$0.54	$0.11	$0.98	Fair	15.0	4.4	192	Poor	High	Low	Poor
Site 8	$0.55	$0.26	$0.10	$0.16	Good	6.9	2.6	95	Fair	Med.	Low	Fair
Site 9	$1.01	$0.44	$0.10	$0.83	Fair	5.3	2.5	74	Good	High	Very Low	Fair

capabilities to support self-scaling and self-management is needed. Scalable management and orchestration of server, storage and network resources without affecting the cloud user are really a challenge.

For example, the concept of application containers, though prescribed in some standards (CDMI) and used in some research efforts [29], enables a cloud user to use the system without bothering about hardware failures and software upgrades. Optimization algorithms for intelligent placement of these containers on the vendor's Cloud infrastructure are also attractive research question.

It is also not easy to build efficient cloud-enabled applications that take advantage of the scalability, reliability and agility provided by the cloud platform. There is also a scope to develop application frameworks that enable rapid creation of efficient cloud applications. Novel applications of Cloud Computing leveraging the always-connected nature of the infrastructure, as well as potential usage in mobile environments, promise to be very interesting. Context awareness of mobile applications is very critical to deliver a good personalized user experience. So, a standard means of communicating the user context to the cloud vendor becomes important as well.

As seen in the Sustainability Dashboard of Open Cirrus, cloud platforms in future are likely to start billing the usage based on power consumption! This opens up research opportunities not just in the cloud platform but also in cloud applications to build power-efficient applications, algorithms and platforms. Models, tools and metrics for ensuring energy efficiency at the platform level as well as the overall application level are needed.

Again as exemplified by Open Cirrus, many cloud platforms will need to be created in collaboration and partnerships and hence the challenges of resource aggregation from multiple diverse cloud providers creates some interesting problems, not just for management but also for resource provisioning. Novel architecture models to support this aggregation, brokering algorithms for performance, proximal scheduling, high availability and energy efficiency are possible.

Privacy, security and trust management at IaaS, PaaS and SaaS are yet to be solved completely. This becomes even more challenging when the security and privacy needs to be provided not just between a cloud vendor and cloud user, but also across multiple cloud providers that have aggregated resources for a common vendorship.

From a programming perspective, since MapReduce and Hadoop have gained a lot of popularity, converting a traditional algorithm or application into the MapReduce paradigm is suitable for an intern project. In fact, there is still no formal method to determine *MapReducibility* of algorithms and applications [30]. Very little work has been done on the theoretical foundations for MapReduce as well.

It would be interesting to look at other novel programming models that enabled creation of more efficient applications. For example, approaches to design applications given that things are going to break (design for failures or resiliency) and creating a programming paradigm for the same would be interesting to look at. New programming languages may evolve out of that.

There are many blogs [31] and articles [32] written on open research items in Cloud Computing that the reader can refer to. Also, the different cloud technologies and case studies described in all the chapters of this book will be very handy to get started in trying to solve any of these research problems.

SUMMARY

In this chapter, various research directions in cloud technology have been described. The first two sections deal with efforts to reduce lock in to a cloud vendor in different ways. The first section deals with cloud standards, which help to reduce vendor lock-in by standardizing cloud APIs and models, so that migration from one cloud provider to another or back to a private cloud would be simpler. The second section deals with benchmarks, which allow customers to assess which cloud vendor is better suited for their application. In the *Emerging Standards* section, it can be seen that different standards organizations are trying to standardize different aspects of cloud services. Some of the important efforts are the SNIA CDMI standard, which is an effort to standardize storage services and applications, the DMTF's Cloud Incubator Standards on standardizing cloud management, the IEEE's draft standards on interoperability between different clouds, as well as the Open Grid Forum's cloud standards. It can be seen that though these standards efforts deal with different aspects of cloud technology, there is still some overlap. As of this writing, it is difficult to state which effort is likely to get greater acceptance.

Benchmarks can be used for comparing various cloud systems, tuning and configuring cloud systems, as well as for capacity planning. The benchmarks described in this chapter can be used for all three purposes. Similarly to the standards, it can be seen that they cover different aspects of cloud computing. The Cloudburst benchmark attempts to estimate the cost of running an application on the cloud by running a standard cloud application and taking detailed measurements which can be used to estimate the cost per transaction of the application. The disadvantage of this approach is that the Cloudburst application supplied may not be similar to the application the cloud customer is interested in. This can make extrapolation of the results obtained problematic. The Yahoo Cloud Storage Benchmark attempts to measure various aspects of the storage infrastructure in the cloud. It is tunable and can be used to simulate the storage requirements of any application. Finally, the CloudCmp benchmark makes standard measurements of a cloud infrastructure and attempts to project the performance of any application running on the infrastructure using a simple model of the application. The disadvantage of this approach is that the accuracy of the model is difficult to estimate.

The next section on end-user programming focused on technologies for enabling non-programming users to write programs that can combine information from various parts of the web to synthesize new uses. An example is that of a travel reservation, where it is necessary to book the room at a hotel as well as a flight.

The importance of such technologies arises from the fact that, without them, while cloud computing will lead to optimization of data centers, users will not be able to use the cloud to its full potential by synthesizing the information on the Web. In this section, a description of such technologies, particularly programming by example was presented. TaskLets, a framework whose objectives are to facilitate building of mobile widgets for performing complex operations on the Web, were described in detail. Finally, Open Cirrus, a research cloud at HP, was described, together with a description of some of the important research projects in progress. The chapter concluded with a list of research challenges that are yet to be addressed before Cloud Computing becomes the global mainstream computing methodology.

References

[1] Cloud computing scenarios: 2010 and beyond, By Diptarup Chakraborti, Gartner. http://informationweek.in/Cloud_Computing/10-06-28/Cloud_computing_scenarios_2010_and_beyond.aspx?page=2; 2010 [accessed July 2011].

[2] CDMI tutorial. http://www.snia.org/education/tutorials/2010/fall/video/carlson_interoperable_video; [accessed July 2011].

[3] SNIA, Cloud Data Management Interface, Version 1.0, SNIA Technical Position, April 12, 2010.

[4] http://snia.cloudfour.com/sites/default/files/CDMI_SNIA_Architecture_v1.0.pdf; [accessed July 2011].

[5] Architecture for Managing Clouds: A White Paper from the Open Cloud Standards Incubator, DMTF. http://www.dmtf.org/sites/default/files/standards/documents/DSP-IS0102_1.0.0.pdf; [accessed July 2011].

[6] Draft Guide for Cloud Portability and Interoperability Profiles. http://standards.ieee.org/develop/wg/CPWG-2301_WG.html; [accessed July 2011].

[7] Draft Standard for Intercloud Interoperability and Federation. http://standards.ieee.org/develop/wg/ICWG-2302_WG.html; [accessed July 2011].

[8] Welcome to the httperf Homepage. http://www.hpl.hp.com/research/linux/httperf; 2009 [accessed July 2011].

[9] SPECweb2005. http://www.spec.org/web2005/; 2005 [accessed July 2011].

[10] Sucharitakul A, et al. Cloudstone: Multi-Platform, Multi-Language Benchmark and Measurement Tools for Web 2.0 by Will Sobel, Shanti Subramanyam. http://radlab.cs.berkeley.edu/w/upload/2/25/Cloudstone-Jul09.pdf; 2009 [accessed July 2011].

[11] Baldi P, Frasconi P, Smyth P. Modeling the internet and the web: probabilistic methods and algorithms Wiley; 2003. 978-0470849064; [accessed July 2011].

[12] Nginx Primer 2: From Apache to Nginx, Martin Fjordvald. http://blog.martinfjordvald.com/2011/02/nginx-primer-2-from-apache-to-nginx/; 2011 [accessed July 2011].

[13] Cooper BF. Yahoo! cloud serving benchmark. http://www.brianfrankcooper.net/pubs/ycsb-v4.pdf; 2011 [accessed July 2011].

[14] IOzone Filesystem Benchmark. http://www.iozone.org/; 2006 [accessed July 2011].

[15] Zipf, Power Laws, and Pareto – a Ranking Tutorial. http://www.hpl.hp.com/research/idl/papers/ranking/ranking.html; 2002 [accessed July 2011].

[16] Cooper BF, Silberstein A, Tam E, Ramakrishnan R, Sears R. Benchmarking cloud serving systems with YCSB. Indianapolis: ACM Symposium on Cloud Computing; http://research.yahoo.com/node/3202; 2010 [accessed July 2011].

[17] CloudCmp: Pitting Cloud against Cloud. http://www.cloudcmp.net/; 2010 [accessed July 2011].

[18] Li A, Yang X, Kandula S, Zhang M. CloudCmp: Shopping for a Cloud Made Easy. 2nd USENIX Workshop on Hot Topics in Cloud Computing (HotCloud), http://wwwcs.duke.edu/~angl/papers/hotcloud10-cloudcmp.pdf; 2010 [accessed July 2011].

[19] Li A, Yang X, Kandula S, Zhang M. CloudCmp: Shopping for a Cloud Made Easy (Slideset), 2nd USENIX Workshop on Hot Topics in Cloud Computing (HotCloud). http://www.usenix.org/events/hotcloud10/tech/slides/li.pdf; 2010. [accessed July 2011].

[20] Li A, Yang X, Kandula S, Zhang M. CloudCmp: Comparing Public Cloud Providers, Internet Measurement Conference. http://www.cs.duke.edu/~angl/papers/imc10-cloudcmp.pdf; 2010 [accessed July 2011].

[21] Blythe J, Kapoor D, Knoblock CA, Lerman K, Minton S. Information Integration for the Masses, JUCS2007.` Also http://www.isi.edu/~blythe/papers/pdf/iiworkshop07.pdf; 2007 [accessed 08.10.11].

[22] Lieberman H, Paterno F, Klann M, Wulf V. End-user development: an emerging paradigm. In: End user development. Springer-Verlag; 2006.

[23] Manjunath G, Thara S, Hitesh B, Guntupalli S, et al. Creating personal mobile widgets without programming. Developer track. In: 18th intl conference on world wide web, Spain: Madrid; 2009.

[24] Manjunath G, Murty MN, Sitaram D. End User Programming of Task-based Mobile Widgets. HPL Tech Report, 2011.

[25] Leshed G, Haber E, Lau T, Cypher A. CoScripter: Sharing 'How-to' Knowledge in the Enterprise. GROUP'07, November 4–7, 2007.

[26] Little G, Lau TA, Cypher A, Lin J, Haber EM, Kandogan E. Koala: capture, share, automate, person-alize business processes on the web. CHI'07. 2007.

[27] Avetisyan A, et al. Open cirrus a global cloud computing testbed. IEEE Comput 2010;43 (4):42-50.

[28] Wang C, et. al. Online detection of utility cloud anomalies using metric distributions. In: Proceedings of the 12th IEEE/IFIP network operations and management symposium (NOMS); 2010 [accessed July 2011].

[29] Linux Virtual Containers with LXC. http://www.techrepublic.com/blog/opensource/introducing-linux-virtual-containers-with-lxc/1289; [accessed July 2011].

[30] Hellerstein JM, Berkeley UC. Datalog Redux: Experience and Conjecture. Key Note address; [accessed July 2011].

[31] Llorente IM. Research Challenges in Cloud Computing, Cloud Computing Journal. http://cloudcomputing.sys-con.com/node/1662026; 2011 [accessed July 2011].

[32] Cloud Computing Roundtable. Hosted by qatar computing research institute (QCRI). http://www.qcri.qa/wp-content/uploads/2011/06/session9-summaryAll.pdf; [accessed 08.10.11].

Index

Page numbers in *italics* indicate figures and tables